THE

INVESTMENT
TRUSTS
HANDBOOK

2021

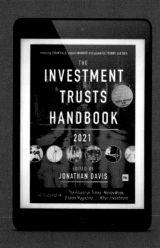

THE
INVESTMENT
TRUSTS
HANDBOOK

2021

*Investing essentials, expert insights and
powerful trends and data*

EDITED BY
JONATHAN DAVIS

www.ITHB.co.uk

HARRIMAN HOUSE LTD
3 Viceroy Court
Bedford Road
Petersfield
Hampshire
GU32 3LJ
GREAT BRITAIN
Tel: +44 (0)1730 233870

Email: enquiries@harriman-house.com
Website: harriman.house

First published in 2020.

Paperback ISBN: 978-0-85719-894-5
eBook ISBN: 978-0-85719-895-2

British Library Cataloguing in Publication Data
A CIP catalogue record for this book can be obtained from the British Library.

www.ITHB.co.uk

CONTENTS

INTRODUCTION

A strange and eventful year

IT IS HARD to think of a year when a single topic has dominated conversation as much as the Covid-19 pandemic has dominated 2020. It even makes Brexit pale a little in comparison. Unsurprisingly therefore the viral pandemic and its aftermath features prominently in this year's annual edition of *The Investment Trusts Handbook*, the fourth since we launched it in 2017.

There is an expanded review of the year section in which our regular contributors look back on how the investment trust sector has responded to this global health hazard. We explain, in words and numbers, how the global bias and diversified nature of the investment trust family has enabled it, in aggregate, to come through the crisis in remarkably good shape.

Although a number of individual trusts have prospered and/or suffered disproportionately, the sector overall has performed well and protected diversified investors against the worst effects. Indeed the Equity Investment Instruments Index, which is one measure of the overall performance of investment trusts, has at the time of writing (end October) recovered to be around five per cent up on the year, while the FTSE All-Share index languishes almost 20 per cent below its level in February.

A central purpose of the *Handbook* is to share with readers the insights and perspective that only those who have lived through and survived a series of earlier market cycles can offer. Charles Ellis, author of the classic text on investing, *Winning the Loser's Game*, reminds us that there is no substitute for integrity and experience in an investment manager. I am happy that we have contributions this year from several of the most respected and experienced players in the investment trust world.

They include:

- **Peter Spiller**, the longest serving investment trust manager in the UK, who offers us some of his thoughts in a new feature, a multi-participant forum on the future of the sector.

- **Hamish Buchan** and **Robin Angus**, for many years the top-rated investment trust analysts in the City, who are retiring this year after many years as directors of Personal Assets, the pioneering trust for private investors.

- **John Baron**, one-time fund specialist at Hendersons and Rothschild Asset Management, who writes regularly for the *Investors Chronicle* and manages a series of real-life investment trust portfolios for his own online subscription service.

We also have contributions from three of the top-ranked investment trust analysts, **Simon Elliott** (Winterflood Securities), **Ewan Lovett-Turner** (Numis) and **Alan Brierley** (Investec), who have succeeded Buchan and Angus as pace setters in the stockbroking research community. **Alex Davies**, founder of *The Wealth Club*, explains why VCTs, tax-advantaged funds that support new and early stage businesses, may also be particularly popular this year.

Looking in more depth at the behaviour of the stock market, there has rarely been a more polarised market than the one we have witnessed this year. Our interviewees include a number of well-known investment trust managers who find themselves at the centre of the big thematic debates of the day: value or growth as a style of investment? A UK or global focus? Large or small cap bias? Technology or banks; which sectors offer the best potential as an investment?

This year's edition also includes sections that address important practical questions, such as:

- How to read an investment trust annual report – Tim Cockerill of wealth management firm Rowan Dartington offers his expert perspective.

- Which investment trust directors and managers have the largest personal shareholding in the trusts they are responsible for?

- What should investors be looking for when researching ways to adopt the highest environmental, social and governance standards?

- Are trusts right to pay dividends by using revenue reserves or even drawing on capital to preserve their income credentials?

- Which trusts have the longest serving managers and the best track records over the past 10, 20 and 30 years?

- Which trusts performed best in the six months running up to and the six months following the Covid-inspired market crash in March 2020?

All these questions are answered in a completely revised and updated series of articles and data pages running in all to some 300 pages. There are also links to useful online sources of information and my own personal observations, in the Editor's Notes, on the year just gone and the ones that lie ahead.

I have also updated the section on analysing investment trusts and added some new data tables. Overall, more than 90% of the content in this year's *Handbook* is either entirely new or has been comprehensively revised. Together with the archive of past articles you can find at www.money-makers.co, it aims to live up to its status as what one specialist financial magazine gratifyingly described as "truly the definitive guide to the sector right now".

I hope that you will find this year's edition a useful record of this strange and eventful year, and a valuable companion as we head into a new year of great uncertainty and further profound challenges. If you find the *Handbook* useful, why not also sign up on the *Money Makers* website (www.money-makers.co) to hear the free weekly investment trust podcast I have been recording every week with Simon Elliott since April this year. You will also find there plans for a new *Money Makers* subscription newsletter.

JONATHAN DAVIS *MA, MSC, MCSI is one of the UK's leading stock market authors and commentators. A qualified professional investor and member of the Chartered Institute for Securities and Investment, he is a senior external adviser at Saunderson House. His books include* Money Makers, Investing with Anthony Bolton *and* Templeton's Way with Money. *After writing columns for* The Independent *and* Financial Times *for many years, he now writes a private circulation newsletter. His website is: www.independent-investor.com.*

Cut through with conviction

FIDELITY INVESTMENT TRUSTS

Truly global and award-winning, the range is supported by expert portfolio managers, regional research teams and on-the-ground professionals with local connections.

With 370 investment professionals across the globe, we believe this gives us stronger insights across the markets in which we invest. This is key in helping each trust identify local trends and invest with the conviction needed to generate long-term outperformance.

Fidelity's range of investment trusts:

- Fidelity Asian Values PLC
- Fidelity China Special Situations PLC
- Fidelity European Trust PLC
- Fidelity Japan Trust PLC
- Fidelity Special Values PLC

Past performance is not a reliable indicator of future returns. The value of investments can go down as well as up and you may not get back the amount you invested. Overseas investments are subject to currency fluctuations. The shares in the investment trusts are listed on the London Stock Exchange and their price is affected by supply and demand.

The investment trusts can gain additional exposure to the market, known as gearing, potentially increasing volatility. Some of the trusts invest more heavily than others in smaller companies, which can carry a higher risk because their share prices may be more volatile than those of larger companies and their securities are often less liquid.

To find out more, go to fidelity.co.uk/its or speak to your adviser.

ACKNOWLEDGEMENTS

Compiling *The Investment Trusts Handbook 2021* has once again been an intensive and collective effort. Thanks to all of those who have helped to bring it to fruition, whether as contributors or handmaidens to the production process.

At Harriman House: Stephen Eckett, Myles Hunt, Sally Tickner, Emma Tinker, Christopher Parker and Tracy Bundey. Thank you also to Chris Wild.

Contributors (past and present): Robin Angus, John Baron, Rachel Beagles, Hamish Buchan, James Burns, Charles Cade, James Carthew, Geoffrey Challinor, Tim Cockerill, Sandy Cross, Susie Cummings, Richard Curling, Piers Currie, Mark Dampier, Alex Davies, Alex Denny, Clare Dobie, Simon Elliott, Nick Greenwood, David Johnson, George Kershaw, Max King, John Newlands, Ian Sayers, William Sobczak, Peter Spiller, Bruce Stout, Tony Yousefian.

Research: Charles Cade, Ewan Lovett-Turner (Numis), Simon Elliott, Kieran Drake, Emma Bird (Winterfloods), Christopher Brown (J.P.Morgan Cazenove), Alan Brierley (Investec), Annabel Brodie-Smith (the AIC), Ross Leckie (Artemis), Richard Pavry (Devon Equity Management), William Heathcoat Amory (Kepler Intelligence), Ed Marten (Marten & Co/Quoted Data), David Elliott.

Statistics: big thanks this year to David Michael and Sophie Driscoll at the AIC for all their help in creating the pandemic performance statistics and a lot of other data.

At the publishing partners: Louise Bouverat, Piers Currie (Aberdeen Standard), Claire Dwyer (Fidelity), Lisa Ferris (J.P. Morgan), Vik Heerah, Gary Corcoran, John Regnier-Wilson (Polar Capital), Simon King (Bellevue), Oliver Lago (Allianz Global), Vicky Toshney (Baillie Gifford), Pauline Vadot (Axiom Alternative Investments).

Actual investors think in decades.

Not quarters.

SEARCH FOR ACTUAL INVESTORS

 Investment managers

INVESTMENT TRUST BASICS

*For first-time investors in trusts, here is an overview of investment trusts –
what they are and how they invest – from editor* JONATHAN DAVIS.

What is an investment trust?

INVESTMENT TRUSTS, ALSO known as investment companies, are a type of
collective investment fund. All types of fund pool the money of a large number
of different investors and delegate the investment of their pooled assets, typically
to a professional fund manager. The idea is that this enables shareholders in the
trust to spread their risks and benefit from the professional skills and economies of
scale available to an investment management firm. Funds are able to buy and sell
investments without paying tax on realised gains.

Collective funds have been a simple and popular way for individual investors to
invest their savings for many years, and investment trusts have shared in that success.
Today more than £200bn of savers' assets are invested in investment trusts. The first
investment trust was launched as long ago as 1868, so they have a long history. Sales
of open-ended funds (unit trusts, OEICs and UCITs funds) have grown faster, but
investment trust performance has generally been superior.

How do investment trusts differ from unit trusts and open-ended funds?

There are several differences. The most important ones are that shares in investment
companies are traded on a stock exchange and are overseen by an independent
board of directors, like any other listed company. Shareholders have the right to
vote at annual general meetings (AGMs) on a range of things, including the election
of directors, changes in investment policy and share issuance. Trusts can also, unlike
most open-ended funds, borrow money in order to enhance returns. Whereas the
number of units in a unit trust rises and falls from day to day in response to supply
and demand, an investment trust is able to deploy permanent capital.

What are discounts?

Because shares in investment trusts are traded on a stock exchange, the share price
will fluctuate from day to day in response to supply and demand. Sometimes the
shares will change hands for less than the net asset value (NAV) per share of the

company. At other times they will change hands for more than the NAV per share. The difference between the share price and the NAV per share is calculated as a percentage of the NAV and is called a discount if the share price is below the equivalent NAV and a premium if it is above the NAV.

What is gearing?

In investment, gearing refers to the ability of an investor to borrow money in an attempt to enhance the returns that flow from his or her investment decisions. If investments rise more rapidly than the cost of the borrowing, this has the effect of producing higher returns. The reverse is also true, meaning that gains and losses are magnified. Investment trusts typically borrow around 5–10% of their assets, although this figure varies widely from one trust to another.

What are the main advantages of investing in an investment trust?

Because the capital is largely fixed, the managers of an investment trust can buy and sell the trust's investments whenever they need, rather than having to buy and sell simply because money is flowing in or out of the fund, as unit trust managers are required to do. The ability to gear, or use borrowed money, can also potentially produce better returns. The fact that the board of an investment trust is directly accountable to the shareholders is important. So too is the ability of boards to smooth the payment of dividend income by putting aside surplus revenue as reserves.

Because their capital base is permanent, investment companies are free to invest in a much wider range of investments than other types of fund. In fact, they can invest in almost anything. Although many of the largest trusts invest in listed stocks and bonds, more specialist sectors, such as renewable energy, debt securities, aircraft leasing and infrastructure, have also become popular in recent years. Investment trusts offer fund investors a broader choice and greater scope for diversification, in other words.

And what are the disadvantages?

The two main disadvantages are share price volatility and potential loss of liquidity. Because investment trusts can trade at a discount to the value of their assets, an investor who sells at the wrong moment may not receive the full asset value for their shares at that point. The day-to-day value of the investment can also fluctuate more than an equivalent open-ended fund. In the case of more specialist trusts, it may not always be possible to buy or sell shares in a trust at a good price because of a lack of liquidity in the market. Investors need to make sure they understand these features before investing.

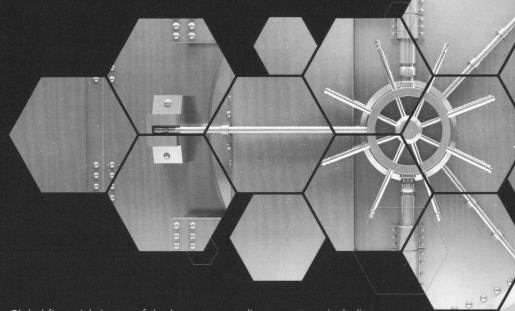

How many trusts are there?

According to the industry trade body, the Association of Investment Companies, there were just under 400 investment trusts with more than £200bn in assets (as at the end of September 2020). They are split between a number of different sectors, reflecting the regions or type of investments in which they invest. The largest trust has approximately £14bn in assets.

What are alternative assets?

While investment trusts have traditionally invested primarily in publicly listed stocks and shares, whose values are known every day, the last decade has seen significant growth in so-called alternative assets. These are trusts which invest in longer term assets which are mostly not traded daily and therefore can be valued only at less frequent intervals. Examples include commercial property, renewable energy, infrastructure and private equity. Many of these alternative trusts are popular because of their ability to pay higher levels of income.

How are they regulated?

All investment companies are regulated by the Financial Conduct Authority. So too are the managers the board appoints to manage the trust's investments. Investment trusts are also subject to the Listing Rules of the stock exchange on which they are listed. The board of directors is accountable to shareholders and regulators for the performance of the trust and the appointment of the manager and are legally bound by the requirements of successive Companies Acts.

How do I invest in an investment trust?

There are a number of different ways. You can buy them directly through a stockbroker, or via an online platform. Some larger investment trusts also have monthly savings schemes where you can transfer a fixed sum every month to the company, which then invests it into its shares on your behalf. If you have a financial adviser, or a portfolio manager, they can arrange the investment for you.

What do investment trusts cost?

As with any share, investors in investment trusts will need to pay brokerage commission when buying or selling shares in an investment trust, and also stamp duty on purchases. The managers appointed by the trust's directors to make its investments charge an annual management fee which is paid automatically, together with dealing and administration costs, out of the trust's assets. These management fees typically range from as little as 0.3% to 2.0% or more of the trust's assets.

What are tax wrappers?

Tax wrappers are schemes which allow individual investors, if they comply with the rules set by the government, to avoid tax on part or all of their investments. The two most important tax wrappers are the Individual Savings Account (or ISA) and the Self-Invested Personal Pension (SIPP). The majority of investment trusts can be held in an ISA or SIPP. There are annual limits on the amounts that can be invested each year (currently £20,000 for an ISA). Venture Capital Trusts (VCTs) are a specialist type of investment trust which also have a number of tax advantages, reflecting their higher risk. VCTs invest in start up and early stage businesses.

Who owns investment trusts?

Twenty-five years ago life insurance companies were the biggest investors in investment trusts, which they used to manage their client funds and pensions. These days such institutional investors mostly manage their own investments directly. Other than some specialist types of trust, the largest investors in trusts today are wealth management firms (formerly stockbroking firms), other types of intermediary and, increasingly, private investors. The growing number of individual investors reflects the growing influence of online platforms, which give individual investors the ability to choose their own investments for ISAs, SIPPs and taxable share/fund accounts.

Are they as difficult to understand as some people say?

Investment trusts are a little more complex than a simple open-ended fund, but no more difficult to understand than most types of listed company. It is important to understand the concept of discounts and premiums before you start to invest, but buying, selling and following the fortunes of your investment could not be easier. If you like the idea of making the connoisseur's choice when investing, you will find the effort of understanding investment trusts worthwhile.

Key terms explained

Investment trusts (aka investment companies) pool the money of individual and professional investors and invest it for them in order to generate capital gains, dividend income, or both. These are the most important factors that determine how good an investment they are:

SHARE PRICE

The price (typically in pence) you will be asked to pay to buy or sell shares in any investment company. You want it to go up, not down.

SPREAD

The difference between the price per share you will need to pay if you want to buy and that you will be offered if you wish to sell – can be anything from 0% (good) to 5% or more (bad).

MARKET CAPITALISATION

The aggregate current value of all the shares a trust has issued – in essence, therefore, what the market in its wisdom thinks the investment company is worth today. (The market is not always wise and would be a duller and less interesting place if it were.)

NET ASSET VALUE (NAV)

The value of the company's investments less running costs at the most recent valuation point – typically (and ideally) that will be yesterday's quoted market price, but for some types of investment trust, whose assets are not traded on a daily basis, it might be one or more months ago.

NET ASSET VALUE PER SHARE

This is calculated, not surprisingly, by dividing the NAV (see above) by the number of shares in issue. You can compare it directly with the share price to find the discount or premium.

DISCOUNT/PREMIUM

When the share price is below the investment company's net asset value per share it is said to be trading 'at a discount'; if it trades above the NAV per share, then the trust is selling 'at a premium'.

DIVIDEND YIELD

How much a trust pays out as income each year to its shareholders, expressed as a percentage of its share price. The usual figure quoted is based on the dividends a company has paid in the previous 12 months.

THE FUND MANAGER

The person (or team) responsible for choosing and managing the investment trust's capital. Will typically be professionally qualified and highly paid. How much value he or she really adds is a lively source of debate.

THE BOARD

Investment companies are listed companies, so they must comply with stock exchange rules and appoint a board of independent directors who are legally responsible for overseeing the company and protecting the interests of its shareholders, which ultimately means replacing the manager or closing down the trust if results are not good.

We strive to explore further.

Aberdeen Standard Investment Trusts ISA and Share Plan

We believe there's no substitute for getting to know your investments first hand. That's why we look to analyse and speak to companies intensively before we invest in their shares and while we hold them.

Focusing on first-hand company research requires a lot of time and resources. But it's just one of the ways we aim to seek out the best investment opportunities on your behalf.

Please remember, the value of shares and the income from them can go down as well as up and you may get back less than the amount invested. No recommendation is made, positive or otherwise, regarding the ISA and Share Plan.

The value of tax benefits depends on individual circumstances and the favourable tax treatment for ISAs may not be maintained. We recommend you seek financial advice prior to making an investment decision.

Request a brochure: **0808 500 4000**
invtrusts.co.uk

Aberdeen **Standard**
Investments

GEARING

A fancy word for borrowing money in order to try and boost the performance of a company's shares – a case of more risk for potentially more reward. A number of different types of borrowing (e.g. with fixed or variable interest rates) can be used.

FEES AND CHARGES

What it costs to own shares in an investment trust – a figure that (confusingly) can be calculated in several different ways. More important than it sounds on first hearing.

OCR

Short for Ongoing Charge Ratio, one of the most commonly used formulas used to measure the annual cost of owning a trust. Expressed as a percentage of the NAV.

SECTORS

Investment trusts come in many shapes and sizes, so for convenience are categorised into one of a number of different sectors, based on the kind of things that they invest in.

PERFORMANCE

A popular and over-used term which tells you how much money an investment trust has made for its shareholders over any given period of time – by definition, a backward-looking measurement. Does not guarantee future performance will be as good.

BENCHMARK

The outcome against which a trust and its shareholders have agreed to measure its performance. This is typically a stock market index relevant to the area or style in which the portfolio is being invested (e.g. the FTSE All-Share index for trusts investing in UK equity markets).

TOTAL RETURN

A way of combining the income a trust pays with the capital gains it also generates (you hope) over time, so as to allow fair comparisons with other trusts and funds. Shown either as a simple percentage gain over the period or as an annualised gain, the compound rate of return per annum.

RISK AND RETURN

Riskier investments tend to produce higher returns over time, typically at the cost of doing less well when market conditions are unfavourable and better when they are more helpful. Risk comes in many (dis)guises, however – some more visible than others.

BETA

This is a term used in financial economics to measure the extent to which the shares of a company rise or fall relative to the stock market as a whole. The stock market has a beta of 1.0, so if the market rises 10 per cent, then a trust with a beta of 1.2 is expected to rise by 12 per cent ($=10 \times 1.2$). If it falls by 10 per cent, the shares should fall by 12 per cent.

ALPHA

A statistical measure of the additional returns that a trust has made after adjusting for the relative risk of its portfolio. It is often used (not entirely accurately) as shorthand for fund manager skill.

ACTIVE MANAGEMENT

What is going on when the investment manager of a trust makes a conscious decision not to include in its portfolio all the stocks or shares that make up its benchmark index. The latter can be easily and much more cheaply replicated by a computer – what is known as passive management. All investment trusts are actively managed.

INVESTMENT STYLE

An attempt to characterise the way in which the manager of a trust chooses to invest. One common distinction is between value and growth. The former style aims to find companies whose shares are cheap relative to their competitors or historic price. The latter concentrates on finding companies with above average sales and profit growth prospects.

IS THERE ANY DIFFERENCE BETWEEN AN INVESTMENT COMPANY AND INVESTMENT TRUST?

Basically no. Strictly speaking, investment trusts are investment companies but not all investment companies are investment trusts. Feel free to use either term interchangeably, without fear of embarrassment.

CLOSED-END FUNDS

Investment trusts are an example of what is called a 'closed-end fund', meaning that its capital base is intended to be fixed and permanent (unlike unit trusts, OEICs and horribly named UCITs 3 funds, which take in and return money to investors on a daily basis and are therefore called open-ended). The distinction is no longer quite as important as it was, as it has become somewhat easier for successful investment companies to raise new money through regular share issues.

USEFUL SOURCES OF INFORMATION

Industry information

The Association of Investment Companies | www.theaic.co.uk

Data, news and research

The Investment Trusts Handbook official website | www.ithb.co.uk

Morningstar | www.morningstar.co.uk

Trustnet | www.trustnet.co.uk

Citywire | www.citywire.co.uk

DigitalLook | www.digitallook.com

Platforms

Interactive Investor | www.iii.co.uk

Hargreaves Lansdown | www.hl.co.uk

A.J.Bell | www.ajbell.co.uk

Fidelity International | www.fidelity.co.uk

Alliance Trust Savings | www.alliancetrustsavings.co.uk

Research

Edison | www.edisoninvestmentresearch.com

QuotedData | www.quoteddata.com

Trust Intelligence (Kepler Partners) | www.trustintelligence.co.uk

Specialist publications

Investment Trusts Newsletter (McHattie Group) | www.tipsheets.co.uk

Investment Trust Insider (Citywire) | www.citywire.co.uk

Publications that regularly feature investment trusts

Financial Times | www.ft.com

Investors Chronicle | www.investorschronicle.co.uk

Money Makers newsletter | www.money-makers.co

MoneyWeek | www.moneyweek.com

The Telegraph | www.telegraph.co.uk

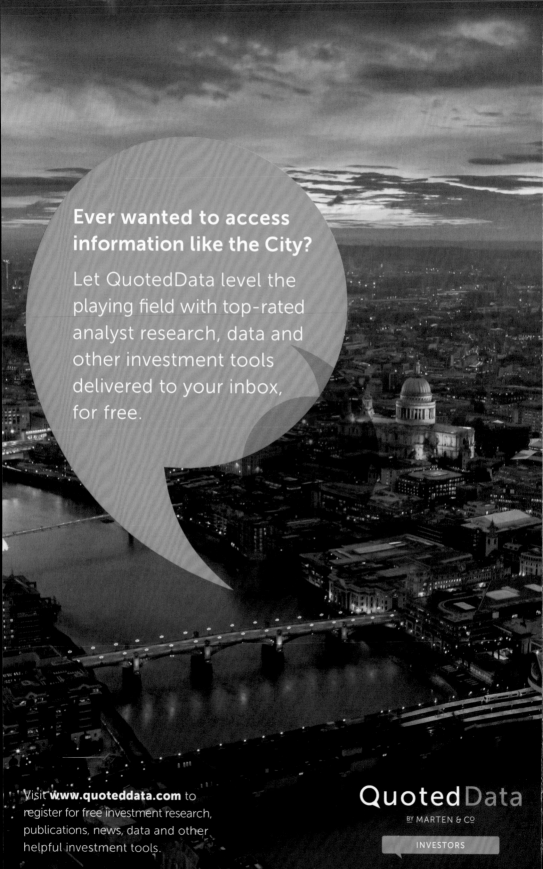

EDITOR'S NOTES

JONATHAN DAVIS *reviews the year just gone.*

I T HAS BEEN such a remarkable year for the investment trust sector, as for the UK and global economies, that it is difficult to know what *not* to write about. In the interests of space, however, I shall confine myself to a number of short but I hope salient observations. There is plenty of meat in the contributions from the expert contributors whose thoughts you can read elsewhere in the *Handbook*.

The lessons of the pandemic

The detailed data on the performance of investment trusts during the pandemic (see page 72) holds some important and timeless lessons for investors. Lesson one: the unexpected happens, and it is best to be prepared for whatever that proves to be. Lesson two: the best way to guard against 'unknown unknowns' is through broad diversification, ideally by geography, style and type of asset. Lesson three: the label on the tin can be misleading – I dare say the founders of Secure Income REIT, highly experienced property investors though they are, did not expect to have their chosen name confounded so soon by events! Lesson four: if you are going to panic during a market meltdown like the one we saw in March, it is best to panic early. Lesson five: far better still however is to acknowledge that if you wake up in a cold sweat during a market panic, the chances are that either your portfolio is not right for you (it has more risk than you realise) or you are not the long-term investor that you thought you were. It is fine to make some positive thematic bets where you have high conviction, but the diversified long-term investor can afford to be patient and wait for the market to come back from reverses, as it has done impressively this year.

Superior performance

It is impossible to prove at a level of statistical certainty that satisfies academic students of finance, but everything that has happened so far in 2020 reinforces the belief that investment trusts do indeed deserve to be described as the connoisseur's choice when it comes to picking investment funds for a globally diversified portfolio. While far from immune in the short term, the breadth of the sector's investment mandates and their global bias has been critical in enabling the sector to display such overall resilience in a tough year for the global economy and the UK in particular.

While the FTSE All-Share index remains nearly 20 per cent below its level at the start of the year, the Equity Investment Instruments Index, which measures the performance of listed investment trusts, has produced a small but creditable positive return at the time of writing.*

A highly successful decade too...

The investment trust sector has flourished in the last 10 years, thanks mainly to the popularity of a new generation of alternative-asset trusts which are typically capable of paying dividend yields in the 4–7 per cent range and have some scope to add modest capital gains on top. IPOs in total have brought £24bn of new money into the sector in the last 11 years, and secondary issuance has contributed £45bn more over the same period, helping to boost the size of the sector to some 390 companies and £200bn in assets. The sector's resilience during the pandemic, you would think, can only add to its attractions as a home for discerning investor capital.

...but consolidation is coming

Past growth notwithstanding, a report from the influential broking firm Numis in July made a strong case for believing that we will – or at least, should – soon be seeing a wave of consolidation in the investment trust sector.† The logic is compelling and certainly in keeping with the 'adapt or die' imperative that is one of the sector's historic strengths. To prosper these days investment trusts need to demonstrate that they are large enough, or growing fast enough, to attract continued support from both private investors and the larger wealth management firms. The key to that is not just good performance, but making sure that the trust's mandate offers something that is distinctive and ideally makes good use of the advantages of the investment trust structure (permanent capital, superior corporate governance, gearing and so on).

A fair few do not pass this demanding test, being either sub-scale (about 20 per cent have less than £100m in assets) or indifferent performers with a 'me too' strategy that can be more profitably accessed through different funds. To the extent however that the drive for scale is being driven by consolidation in the wealth management industry and by increased regulation, it is possible to regret those trends. Neither trend seems to me to be wholly positive for the individual, as opposed to institutional, investor. Patient private investors do not have the same liquidity concerns as their professional counterparts, who need to be able to deal in size, so can more

---

*   28 October 2020

†   You can obtain a summary of this report from the *Money Makers* website.

OUR INVESTMENT TRUSTS BRIDGE COUNTRIES, STYLES AND MARKETS. OUR EXPERIENCE SPANS CENTURIES.

Investment trust expertise since 1889

Allianz Global Investors and its predecessors have been managing investment trusts since 1889. Our trusts span investor needs – from income, to growth, to the specialist sector of technology – and offer a path to investment opportunities around the world. Whatever your investment goals, we believe that Allianz Global Investors' broad experience makes our investment trusts worth a closer look.

Please note: Investment trusts are listed companies, traded on the London Stock Exchange. Their share prices are determined by factors including demand, so shares may trade at a discount or premium to the net asset value. Past performance is not a reliable indicator of future performance. Some trusts seek to enhance returns through gearing (borrowing money to invest). This can boost a trust's returns when investments perform well, though losses can be magnified when investments lose value.

0800 389 4696   uk.allianzgi.com/investment-trusts

Allianz (ll)
Global Investors

readily tolerate a smaller investment trust, provided that performance is adequate. Nevertheless, the tide is clearly moving in the opposite direction.

Turkeys do (sometimes) vote for Christmas

Ewan Lovett-Turner of Numis makes the point that boards of investment trusts are reluctant to vote themselves out of existence, whether through liquidation or merger with other trusts, and while there is truth in that observation, there have been some notable exceptions in the past year, including one very rare merger, between Perpetual Income and Growth (PLI) and Murray Income (MUT). The trust whose board I am on, Jupiter UK Growth (JUKG), is another example, as it happens. The investment manager whom the board appointed from within the Jupiter stable four years ago proved, despite coming with a strong reputation, to be a big disappointment. After considering various alternatives, we have reluctantly concluded that the best option, given the sub-scale size of the trust, is to liquidate the trust while offering shareholders with embedded capital gains a rollover into another recommended fund. (I am saving my account of the protracted and, I think, impressively conscientious internal board deliberations that led to this decision for another day.)

High turnover in the UK equity income sector

Of more than half a dozen trusts whose boards have voted to sack their investment manager this year, three – Temple Bar (TMPL), Perpetual Income and Growth (PLI) and Edinburgh (EDIN) – are in the UK equity income sector and a fourth, Securities Trust of Scotland, in the global equity income sector. With equity income being such a popular sector in an era of very low interest rates, boards of underperforming trusts are clearly under greater pressure to act than those in less visible sectors. Management of the three UK trusts is moving to RWC, Aberdeen Standard and Majedie respectively. All three trusts have suffered from poor performance under their previous managers, attributable in good part to the adoption of a traditional 'value' strategy, buying stocks that look cheap on yield or price/earnings ratio grounds, a style which has performed badly for many years. Only one, Temple Bar, has opted to maintain the value approach, a brave contrarian call which deserves some credit. Don't be at all surprised however if at some point in the next five years (but please don't ask me when) Temple Bar starts to outperform the peer group.

Fund managers the trust world needs

Although consolidation is inevitable, it is a shame, as far as I am concerned, that it has become harder for conventional equity investment trusts managed by talented fund managers with good track records in open-ended funds to gain a foothold in the trust sector. I can think of half a dozen whose presence would add quality to the sector. While managers with a high personal profile, such as Terry Smith and (sorry to remind you) Neil Woodford, have been able to attract hundreds of millions for an IPO, many promising younger managers do not have the same opportunity to sample the superior qualities of an investment trust structure. It is particularly difficult for firms without experience in the trust sector either to launch new IPOs or to win mandates from existing trusts (the succession at Temple Bar being a notable exception). At least two IPOs launched this autumn attracted insufficient demand to get off the ground. If the inability to refresh and regenerate the sector persists, it will be to the longer-term detriment of the sector.

A small Brexit bonus

Whatever happens following the end of the transition agreement with the EU at the end of 2020, something still unknown at the time of writing, there should at least be one small benefit for shareholders in investment trusts. The introduction of EU-wide rules designed to make it easier for investors to understand the nature of the funds they are investing in was responsible for the absurdity known as the Key Information Document (KID), which all trusts are these days required to publish. KIDs are patently unfit for purpose, as both the risk ratings and future performance scenarios which are mandatory inclusions are nonsensical and misleading – a classic example of how well-intended regulation often produces a diametrically opposed outcome to the one intended. The Financial Conduct Authority has already said it is prepared to review KIDs when we finally leave the EU and Ian Sayers, the director of the AIC, tells me he is confident that at least one of the two problematic faults in the KID methodology will be resolved "by the end of 2021". That sadly is the pace at which industry regulators tend to move.

Why not become an investment trust director?

While talking about the work of the AIC, it is encouraging to see it launch a campaign to help recruit new investment trust directors from outside the traditional universe of 'male, pale and stale' City veterans. Rachel Beagles, the chairman of the AIC, explains more about its 'pathway' campaign on the AIC website and it is worth taking a look. She notes that the number of women directors of trusts in the

FTSE 350 index has reached 37 per cent, a higher total than in the other companies in the index, and three of the past five directors of the AIC have also been female. The track record attracting a representative number of directors from different ethnic backgrounds remains much less impressive and will take time to improve.

While there may be some generalised evidence that greater diversity on boards produces better decision-making, it will be some time before we can be sure that the change in composition of investment trust boardrooms is in fact producing more effective corporate governance. As with those closed-ended open-ended comparative performance statistics, it is one thing to believe it and another to prove it. Is there a case for expanding the size of trust boards in order to accommodate the gradual integration of directors with more diverse backgrounds and skills? Rachel says it is an interesting idea, but it would of course come with a price tag in the shape of higher costs and potentially less effective boards. Charles Plowden's comments about teamwork in his interview are pertinent to this debate.

The next big challenge for boards

While we can all agree that good corporate governance is essential for the future prosperity of the sector, one thing that I would like to see is more boards making active steps to establish better direct communications with their shareholders. Turnout in shareholder votes and at general meetings remains poor, which speaks volumes about shareholder indifference, but there are some notable examples of trusts which have successfully embraced the need to invest in easier to navigate websites with more frequent and informative content. Building brand loyalty is an important challenge for all investment trusts these days, and anyone who looks across to the success that Terry Smith has had in building a loyal following for his open-ended Fundsmith fund could usefully take some of the lessons on board.

In that context, given the growing domination of share registers by private investors who hold shares through a platform, it may well make sense for trust boards to add some professional expertise in digital marketing and communications to help them develop a deeper relationship with their shareholders, as some trusts have done. The days when trusts could leave it to corporate brokers to keep a magic circle of institutional shareholders happy and informed are going. If investment management firms were doing that job properly themselves, however, it would not be so necessary to add those skills in the boardroom. I suspect that incentives and who picks up the cost are hindering progress on this score.

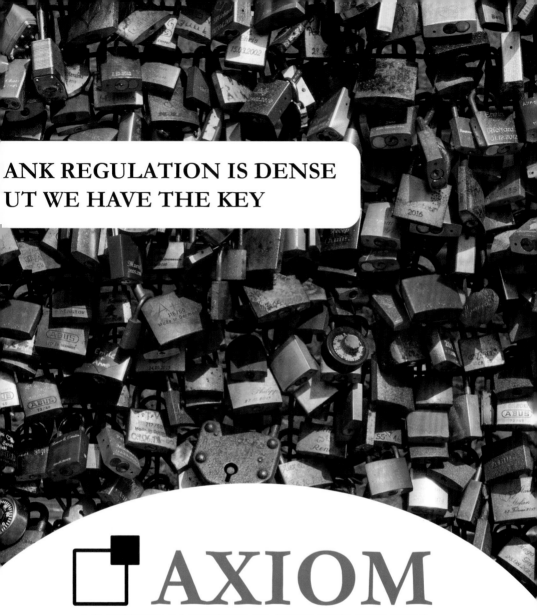

**ANK REGULATION IS DENSE
UT WE HAVE THE KEY**

r further information on Axiom AI, please visit our website www.axiom-ai.com

AXIOM
ALTERNATIVE INVESTMENTS
A specialist in Financial Institutions

Axiom Alternative Investments is an indepedent asset management company specialized in the financial sector. Created in 2009, the company manages USD 1.9bn[1] through a range of UCITS IV funds, closed-ended funds, dedicated funds and mandates. Axiom AI markets its funds to institutional clients, private banks, familly offices and independant financial advisors accross Europe.

[1]October 30st, 2020

A high conviction investment trust invested in listed or quoted global healthcare equities

A compelling and differentiated approach for investing in the rapidly evolving healthcare paradigm. Managed by Bellevue - Healthcare expert since 1993.

B|B **Healthcare Trust**

Bellevue Investments

The year of Baillie Gifford

Even after 40 years tracking the behaviour of the stock market, it is hard for me to recall a time in which a single firm has dominated the performance statistics to the extent that Baillie Gifford has done in the past two years. No fewer than three of the best performing trusts in the year to 30 September 2020 are managed by Baillie Gifford and the Edinburgh-based firm has in the last two years also successfully launched two new trusts and taken over the management of three others. It would be a shoo-in for an *Investment Trusts Handbook* award as trust of the year if we had such a thing, which I am reasonably certain we won't, given that most fund awards are marketing exercises motivated primarily by commercial considerations and of limited value to anyone else. While it is clear that the success of Baillie Gifford owes much to its growth style, which is going through a golden patch, there is a lot more to it than that. A partnership is an ideal structure for an investment management firm, and it is clear that Baillie Gifford have analysed and understood the competitive dynamics of the post-financial crisis world – such as the scale advantages offered by digital technology and the secular growth potential of capital-light businesses in a low interest rate world – far more effectively than most.

Most entertaining new trust

In our weekly investment trust podcast, launched in April this year, Simon Elliott, head of investment trust research at Winterflood Securities, and I review all the week's news and latest trust announcements. We have been (royally?) entertained by the seemingly unlimited number of updates that the fast-growing music royalties trust Hipgnosis (SONG), a recent newcomer to the investment trust sector, is able to put out, each one announcing the signing to the catalogue of some new singer, songwriter or musician. Is Barry Manilow's back catalogue a better prospect as an income generator than, say, that of Whitney Houston or the heavy metal band Mötley Crüe? It is a small but telling example of how the flood of new alternative-asset trusts is demanding new skills from investment trust analysts.

Handbook portfolio update

Each year I provide a progress report on the model investment trust portfolio which I started for the first edition of the *Handbook* when it came out three years ago. The portfolio has 13 components, all of which I either own or have owned myself at some stage, and has what I would call a medium risk profile. Most are run by long-standing managers with a significant personal stake in their trusts, a good track record over many years and, most importantly of all for me, a reputation for personal integrity. At the time of writing, the last week of October, the value of the portfolio stands at just under £160,000, including reinvested dividends, a gain of 59 per cent over four years. This compares with £148,000 a year ago and £100,000 at launch. The gain equates to a compound annualised rate of return of 12.2 per cent since launch. The portfolio has served its purpose well so far. The performance is far ahead of the FTSE All-Share index, which has barely produced a positive total return since the start of 2017, and around 10 per cent better than the FTSE All-World ex UK index. More details and updates on the *Money Makers* website.

Where next in 2021?

It seems evident that the coronavirus will continue to dominate market sentiment for the course of this winter and well into next year, with all eyes on the prospect of finding one or more successful vaccines. (It seems unlikely, incidentally, that all the companies whose share prices have soared in anticipation of producing a successful vaccine can be winners at the same time.) By the time the *Handbook* appears, the US election should be over and the deal/no-deal Brexit outcome close to being known. The one thing that we can be pretty sure about is that next year will produce plenty of new challenges for investors to absorb. The first year of the four-year presidential cycle tends historically not to be one of the best. Discounts on investment trusts, which started the year averaging around one per cent, fell briefly to a low of 20 per cent in March and have currently recovered to around five per cent, will again be a useful barometer of the state of investor confidence.

YEAR IN REVIEW

MONTH BY MONTH IN 2020

W E SUMMARISE HERE some of the main events of the year to date in the investment trust world.

OCTOBER 2019

Sector performance

The UK market fell in October, with the FTSE All Share Index down 1.4%. Investment trusts outperformed the UK market for the fourth time in the last six months, with the FTSE Equity Investment Instruments Index down just 0.5%. In the first 10 months of the year the sector was ahead of the FTSE All Share Index, with a rise of 13.0% compared with 12.8%.

Corporate activity

European Investment Trust announced the appointment of Baillie Gifford as its investment manager, replacing Edinburgh Partners. JZ Capital Partners' interim results were delayed over issues concerning the value of its US property portfolio. Sanditon Investment Trust announced plans to liquidate after "certain significant shareholders" indicated they would not support a continuation vote. Woodford Patient Capital appointed Schroders as its portfolio manager, which is expected to be effective by the end of the year.

Share issuance

October was the strongest month of the year so far for issuance, with £1,424m raised across the sector. Demand for infrastructure funds was strong in October, with £785m raised. This included The Renewables Infrastructure Group (£228m), 3i Infrastructure (£223m), International Public Partnerships (£117m) and Foresight Solar Fund (£65m). October also saw SDCL Energy Efficiency Income (£100m), Gresham House (£42m) and Gore Street Energy Storage (£11m) raise capital. RTW Venture Fund (£119m) was launched, while the largest fundraising was for Hipgnosis Songs' C share issue (£231m). Supermarket Income REIT (£100m) and Real Estate Credit Investments (£17m) also raised money.

31

NOVEMBER 2019

Sector performance

The UK market rose in November, with the FTSE All Share Index up 2.2%. Investment trusts outperformed the UK market for the fourth time in six months, with the FTSE Equity Investment Instruments Index up 3.3%. In the first 11 months of the year the sector was ahead of the FTSE All Share Index, with a rise of 16.8% compared with 15.3%.

Corporate activity

The board of Hadrian's Wall Secured Investments announced that the fund would not continue in its current form following a provision for a material loss. JPM Chinese announced proposals to adopt an enhanced dividend policy equivalent to 4% of net assets. The chairman of Perpetual Income & Growth noted that the fund's board was closely monitoring its progress after an extended period of poor performance.

Share issuance

November was a quiet month for issuance, with £267m raised across the sector. Infrastructure remained the asset class of choice. Over the month there have been placings for HICL Infrastructure (£100m) and International Public Partnerships (£76m), while Octopus Renewables Infrastructure Trust raised £350m through an oversubscribed IPO. Other fundraising included Impact Healthcare REIT (£35m), AVI Japan Opportunity (£14m) and RM Secured Direct Lending (£10m), while Fidelity Asian Values raised £12m through the final exercise of its subscription shares. £173m was raised through regular secondary issuance in November including Finsbury Growth & Income (£20m), Smithson IT (£20m), City of London IT (£16m) and Personal Assets (£8m).

DECEMBER 2019

2019 in review

The uncertainty that bedevilled markets at the start of 2019 largely dissipated in 2020, with US economic recessionary fears subsiding, hard Brexit concerns postponed (for now) and the 'phase one' deal between the US and China providing at least a hiatus in the trade war. Markets have responded positively, rising to historical highs, certainly in the US, and even the UK being not as unloved as once was the case.

With central banks apparently keen to prolong the period of low interest rates and steady global economic growth, most commentators are predicting another year of plenty. Against this backdrop, it is tempting to borrow a phrase from a previous Conservative prime minister and suggest that the investment trust sector has never had it so good.

Net capital inflows into the sector rose last year from £2.5bn in 2018 to £5.1bn and the average discount is at eye-watering levels (currently 2.4%), with around 37% of the universe trading on a premium or around NAV at present. There is downside risk to ratings, particularly in the event of deteriorating market conditions. However, Winterflood concludes, "we would be surprised to see a significant de-rating of the sector in the short-term as a result of the dividend certainty that the investment trust structure can provide".

Corporate activity

In corporate activity, December saw 3i Infrastructure announcing that it had agreed to sell both its UK projects portfolio and its stake in Wireless Infrastructure Group for £581m in aggregate. Edinburgh Investment Trust announced the appointment of Majedie Asset Management to replace Invesco following a period of underperformance.

Share issuance

December was a strong month for issuance, with £989m raised across the sector. This included the IPO of Octopus Renewables Infrastructure (£350m) and placings for GCP Student Living (£77m), International Public Partnerships (£76m), Greencoat Renewables (€125m), SDCL Energy Efficiency Income (£54m) and Impact Healthcare REIT (£35m). £253m was raised through smaller, secondary issuance in December, which included Smithson IT (£37m), City of London IT (£25m), Finsbury Growth & Income (£22m) and BlackRock Throgmorton Trust (£17m).

JANUARY 2020

Sector performance

The UK market fell in January, with the FTSE All Share Index down 3.2%. Investment trusts outperformed the UK market for the fifth time in six months, with the FTSE Equity Investment Instruments Index down just 1.8%. Over 12 months the sector is ahead of the FTSE All Share Index, with a rise of 13.9% compared with 10.7% for the index.

Corporate activity

The board of Henderson Alternative Strategies announced proposals for a managed wind-down after a review and meetings with shareholders. Invesco Income Growth will hold a continuation vote at its AGM in September as a result of its persistently wide discount. SQN Asset Finance Income announced that it expects to record an impairment of between 5% and 14% of its NAV and a strategic review is underway.

Share issuance

January was a quiet month for issuance, with just £321m raised across the sector, down 68% from December 2019, but up 15% on the same month last year. 2020 is yet to see the first IPO of the year, although several potential launches are being marketed, including Global Sustainable Farmland Income and Cabot Square Alternatives. Fundraising in January was confined to placings and regular tap issuance. This included HICL Infrastructure (£17m) and RTW Venture Fund (£9m). £265m was raised through smaller, secondary issuance for funds including Impax Environmental Markets (£39m), Smithson IT (£31m), JPM Global Core Real Assets (£30m), Bankers (£22m), City of London IT (£21m), Personal Assets (£17m) and BlackRock Throgmorton Trust (£14m).

FEBRUARY 2020

Sector performance

The UK market fell dramatically in February, with the FTSE All Share Index down 8.9%, as fears of the impact of the coronavirus sent financial markets into a tailspin. Investment trusts outperformed the UK market for the ninth time in the last 12 months, with the FTSE Equity Investment Instruments Index down 7.1%. In the first two months of 2020 the sector declined 8.8%, compared with a fall of 11.9% for the index.

Corporate activity

The board of Jupiter UK Growth announced the appointment of Richard Buxton following the proposed acquisition of Merian Global Investors by Jupiter. The board of Pollen Street Secured Lending revealed that the fund had received a possible offer of 900p per share, but then proceeded to fall out with Pollen Street Capital, the incumbent investment manager, who responded by reporting the board to the FCA.

Share issuance

Despite the market turmoil, February was a reasonable month for issuance, with £624m raised across the sector. February saw the first IPO of 2020 with the launch of Nippon Active Value Fund, which raised £103m. Other potential IPOs, including

DRI Healthcare and Cabot Square Alternatives, have seen their timetables pushed back. The largest fundraising in February was for Sequoia Economic Infrastructure Income (£300m). The Renewable Energy Infrastructure subsector saw fundraisings for JLEN Environmental Assets Group (£57m) and Gresham House Energy Storage (£31m), while Urban Logistics REIT (£136m) and AEW UK REIT (£7m) raised money in the Property sector. Real Estate Credit Investments raised £34m through an oversubscribed placing.

MARCH 2020

Sector performance

Amidst a dramatic and precipitous further decline in stock markets, prompted by fears of an economic depression, March saw investment trusts outperform the UK market for the tenth time in 12 months. The FTSE Equity Investment Instruments Index was down 11.3% in March, compared with a fall of 15.1% for the FTSE All Share Index. In the first quarter of 2020 the sector saw a decline of 19.1% compared with a fall of 25.1% for the index. The market rout only halted in the final week of the month when central banks and governments announced a series of measures to stabilise their economies.

Corporate activity

Aberdeen Japan announced that its discount level to the end of March had triggered a continuation vote. The board of Perpetual Income & Growth served notice on Invesco, following an extended period of underperformance. The search for a new manager is underway. Gresham House was appointed manager of Strategic Equity Capital, with the existing management team moving across with the fund.

Share issuance

Unsurprisingly, issuance levels were subdued in March, with £406m raised across the sector compared with £624m in February and £1,229m in the same month last year. The amount raised in the first quarter of the year was down 50% from the £2.68bn raised in the same period in 2019. Thirty-six investment companies raised new capital in March and the largest fundraising in March was for Urban Logistics REIT (£136m), followed by JLEN Environmental Assets Group (£57m), Aquila European Renewables (£35m) and Gresham House Energy Storage (£31m). In addition, £133m was raised through smaller, secondary issuance in March including Finsbury Growth & Income (£23m), City of London IT (£22m), Capital Gearing (£19m), Impax Environmental Markets (£17m), Monks (£6m), Merchants (£6m), BB Healthcare (£5m) and Personal Assets (£4m).

APRIL 2020

Sector performance

After its dramatic fall in March, the UK market saw a partial recovery in April, with the FTSE All Share Index up 4.9%. Investment trusts outperformed the UK market for the seventh consecutive month, with the FTSE Equity Investment Instruments Index up 9.1% in April. In the first four months of 2020 the sector was down 11.7% compared with a fall of 21.4% for the index.

Corporate activity

SQN Asset Finance Income announced the appointment of KKV as manager following a strategic review. This is a newly formed firm led by senior personnel from SQN Capital. The fund faced a continuation vote in June. The board of Temple Bar served notice on Ninety One after Alastair Mundy, the fund's manager, was given an extended leave of absence for health reasons.

Share issuance

Issuance levels remained relatively subdued in April, with £429m raised across the sector compared with £406m in March and £703m in the same month last year. The largest issuer was Supermarket Income REIT (£140m). An estimated £289m was raised through regular secondary issuance in April compared with £133m in March. This included Worldwide Healthcare (£32m), Allianz Technology Trust (£29m), Finsbury Growth & Income (£29m), Smithson IT (£24m), City of London IT (£18m), BlackRock Throgmorton (£14m), Polar Capital Technology (£13m), Merchants Trust (£13m), TwentyFour Select Monthly Income (£12m), Baillie Gifford US Growth (£10m) and Impax Environmental Markets (£8m).

MAY 2020

Sector performance

May saw the UK market continue its recovery after the precipitous sell-off in March, with the FTSE All Share Index up 3.4%. Investment trusts outperformed the UK market for the eighth consecutive month, with the FTSE Equity Investment Instruments Index up 4.9%. In the first five months of 2020 the sector was ahead of the FTSE All Share Index, with a decline of 7.4% compared with a fall of 18.8% for the index.

FTSE index changes

The results of the annual FTSE UK Index Review were announced on June 3, with changes to take effect after the market close on Friday 19 June. Six investment companies are due to be promoted to the FTSE All Share/FTSE Small Cap: JPM Global Core Real Assets, M&G Credit Income, Augmentum Fintech, AVI Japan Opportunity, Aurora and Gabelli Value Plus+. Highbridge Tactical Credit and Macau Property Opportunities were demoted.

Share issuance

Issuance levels picked up a little in May, with £483m raised across the sector compared with £429m in April and £1,153m in the same month last year. The largest issuer was The Renewables Infrastructure Group (£120m), while M&G Credit Income raised £14m at the start of June. £363m was raised through smaller, secondary issuance in May including Scottish Mortgage (£95m), Worldwide Healthcare (£70m), Allianz Technology Trust (£35m), Polar Capital Technology (£24m), Edinburgh Worldwide (£20m), Personal Assets (£18m), Impax Environmental Markets (£15m), Smithson IT (£14m) and BB Healthcare Trust (£11m).

JUNE 2020

Sector performance

The UK market saw a third consecutive month of positive returns in June, with the FTSE All Share Index up 1.5%. Investment trusts outperformed for the ninth consecutive month, with the FTSE Equity Investment Instruments Index up 4.2%. In the first six months of 2020 the sector was ahead of the FTSE All Share Index, with a decline of 3.5% compared with a fall of 17.5% for the index.

Corporate activity

European Opportunities saw its NAV hit by the scandal engulfing Wirecard. This had been its largest holding, but the entire position was sold the same day as the announcement of possible fraud and the manager publicly apologised. A number of investment companies face key continuation votes in the near future, including Gabelli Value Plus+ and SQN Asset Finance Income, while others are looking to wind-up, such as Aberdeen Frontier Markets, SQN Secured Income and Henderson Alternative Strategies.

Share issuance

Issuance declined 6% month-on-month in June, with £454m raised across the sector. In the first six months of the year £2,717m was raised, down 46% from the £5,050m raised in the same period in 2019. The largest issue in June was for SDCL Energy Efficiency Income (£110m), while June also saw fundraising from M&G Credit Income (£14m) and EJF Investments, which issued 6m 2025 ZDPs with a gross redemption yield of 7.0%. In addition, Gore Street Energy Storage Fund raised £24m early in July to invest in energy storage projects. £324m was raised through smaller, secondary issuance in June including Scottish Mortgage (£48m), Smithson IT (£29m), Edinburgh Worldwide (£28m), Impax Environmental Markets (£22m), Allianz Technology Trust (£22m), Worldwide Healthcare (£20m), Personal Assets (£20m), Polar Capital Technology (£19m) and BB Healthcare Trust (£17m).

JULY 2020

Sector performance

After three consecutive months of positive returns, the UK market stumbled in July, with the FTSE All Share Index down 3.6%. Investment trusts outperformed for the tenth consecutive month, with the FTSE Equity Investment Instruments Index up 0.3%. In the first seven months of 2020 the sector was ahead of the FTSE All Share Index, with a decline of 3.2% compared with a fall of 20.5% for the index.

Corporate activity

Honeycomb Investment Trust announced proposals for a merger with Pollen Street Secured Lending. HWSI Realisation Fund announced a recommended cash offer of 55.5p per share. KKV Secured Loan Fund's continuation vote saw its ordinary share class pass, while its C share class failed. After a search for a new manager, Perpetual Income & Growth announced proposals to merge with Murray Income. M&G announced that it had approached UK Mortgages with a view to making a recommended cash offer. Witan Pacific announced proposals to appoint Baillie Gifford as its investment manager and adopt a China growth strategy.

Share issuance

July was the strongest month of the year so far in terms of issuance, with £792m raised across the sector. The largest fundraisings were for Hipgnosis Songs Fund (£233m), Warehouse REIT (£153m), HICL Infrastructure (£120m), Gore Street Energy Storage (£24m) and Manchester & London Investment Trust (£15m). £244m was raised through smaller, secondary issuance in July including Scottish

Mortgage (£30m), Worldwide Healthcare (£28m), Edinburgh Worldwide (£27m), Personal Assets (£26m), Smithson IT (£25m), Allianz Technology (£24m), Pacific Horizon (£12m), Polar Capital Technology (£11m), BB Healthcare (£10m) and Capital Gearing Trust (£9m).

AUGUST 2020

Sector performance

The UK market delivered a positive return in August, with the FTSE All Share Index up 2.4%. Investment trusts outperformed the UK market for the eleventh consecutive month, with the FTSE Equity Investment Instruments Index up 4.6%. In the first eight months of 2020 the sector was ahead of the FTSE All Share Index, with a rise of 1.3% compared with a fall of 18.5% for the index.

Corporate activity

Invesco Asia revealed proposals for a conditional tender offer and enhanced dividend policy in an attempt to broaden its appeal and narrow its discount. Honeycomb Investment Trust confirmed that it would not make an offer for Pollen Street Secured Lending, which entered into an advisory agreement with Waterfall AM. Matthew Dobbs, the manager of Schroder AsiaPacific and Schroder Oriental Income, will retire in 2021, after a 40-year career with Schroders. Richard Sennitt will assume responsibility for both funds. M&G's increased cash offer for UK Mortgages was rejected by its board, who are focused on a strategic review to improve the fund's liquidity and wide discount.

Share issuance

August was the quietest month of the year so far in terms of issuance, with just £186m raised across the sector. This represented a decrease of 77% on the £792m raised in July. £186m was raised through smaller, secondary issuance in August including Smithson IT (£35m), Worldwide Healthcare (£25m), Personal Assets (£18m), Allianz Technology Trust (£18m), Edinburgh Worldwide (£16m), Scottish Mortgage (£14m), BB Healthcare Trust (£10m), Pacific Horizon (£10m) and Capital Gearing Trust (£9m).

SEPTEMBER 2020

Sector performance

Investment trusts outperformed the wider UK market for the twelfth consecutive month in September, with the FTSE Equity Investment Instruments Index up 0.1% compared with a fall of 1.7% for the FTSE All Share Index. In the first nine months of 2020 the sector was ahead of the FTSE All Share Index, with a rise of 1.4% compared with a fall of 19.9% for the index.

Corporate activity

In recent corporate activity the tussle between the Board of Gabelli Value Plus+ and its largest shareholder, Associated Capital Group, which is linked to its investment manager, continued after the fund failed its continuation vote. Securities Trust of Scotland appointed Troy Asset Management as its manager, replacing Martin Currie, while Temple Bar appointed RWC to replace Ninety One as its manager. Both funds 'rebased' their dividends, while other cuts came from Genesis Emerging Markets and Henderson EuroTrust. However, dividend increases or reinstatements came in September from CVC Credit Partners European Opportunities, Amedeo Air Four Plus, LXI REIT and Schroder European Real Estate.

Share issuance

September saw an increase in issuance activity, with £343m raised across the sector, up 84% from the £186m raised in August. In the first nine months of the year £4,036m was raised, down 35% from the £6,256m raised in the same period in 2019. The largest fundraising last month was for Hipgnosis Songs Fund (£190m), while this month has seen Greencoat UK Wind raise £400m and Supermarket Income REIT and Urban Logistics REIT raise £200m and £89m respectively. In addition, Merian Chrysalis raised £95m through an oversubscribed placing.

These month by month summaries are extracted from the excellent monthly investment trust reports prepared by the Winterflood investment trusts research team and are reproduced here with their permission.

KEEP UP TO DATE

Join Jonathan Davis and Simon Elliott for the free *Money Makers* weekly investment trust podcast, reviewing all the week's news, results and market movements in the investment trust sector. Every Saturday from *Money Makers* (www.money-makers.co).

FIRST QUARTER 2020

Figure 1: Best performing funds in price terms over Q1 *	(%)
Adamas Finance Asia	24.8
BH Macro GBP	23.1
Schiehallion	17.5
Marble Point Loan Financing	15.7
BH Global GBP	13
RDL Realisation	11.7
Civitas Social Housing	11
Life Settlement Assets A	7.7
Allianz Technology	3.1
Greencoat Renewables	3.1

Source: Morningstar, * excluding funds with market cap. below £15m

Figure 2: Best performing funds in NAV terms over Q1*	(%)
BH Macro GBP	23
BH Global GBP	15.5
Pershing Square	10.3
Riverstone Credit Opportunities Income	9.6
Fair Oaks Income 2017	9.6
DP Aircraft I	9.2
BioPharma Credit	8.5
Tufton Oceanic Assets	8.1
Globalworth Real Estate	7.9
US Solar	7.4

Source: Morningstar, * excluding funds with market cap. below £15m

Figure 3: Worst performing funds in price terms over Q1*	(%)
Infrastructure India	-78.5
Riverstone Energy	-64.7
DP Aircraft I	-64.6
JZ Capital Partners	-57.5
Riverstone Credit Opportunities Income	-55.5
Carador Income Fund USD	-54.6
SQN Asset Finance Income	-54.5
Chelverton UK Dividend	-54.3
Aberforth Split Level Income	-53.7
Crystal Amber	-53.4

Source: Morningstar, * excluding funds with market cap. below £15m

Figure 4: Worst performing funds in NAV terms over Q1*	(%)
Chelverton UK Dividend	-55.3
Aberforth Split Level Income	-55.2
Temple Bar	-46.6
BlackRock Latin American	-45.4
JPMorgan Brazil	-44.4
Blue Planet	-43.8
Aberforth Smaller Companies	-43.2
Acorn Income	-40.6
JPMorgan Mid Cap	-39.4
Jupiter UK Growth	-39.3

Source: Morningstar, * excluding funds with market cap. below £15m

Figure 5: Money entering the sector over Q1	£m
Sequoia Economic Infrastructure	300
Nippon Active Value	103
Impax Environmental Markets*	65
JLEN Environmental Assets Group*	55
Smithson*	46
City of London*	42
Bankers*	36
Blackstone/GSO Loan Financing*	34
Aquila European Renewables Income*	32
JPMorgan Global Core Real Assets	28

Source: Morningstar, * approximate value of additional capital at 31/03/2020, proceeds raised from the initial public offering

Figure 6: Money leaving the sector over Q1	£m
Pershing Square*	-85
CVC Credit Partners Euro Opps. GBP*	-58
Baillie Gifford European Growth*	-32
Scottish Mortgage*	-31
NB Global Floating Rate Income GBP*	-26
Biotech Growth*	-24
Fidelity China Special*	-22
Honeycomb*	-17
Alcentra European Floating Rate Income*	-13
Africa Opportunity*	-13

Source: Morningstar, * approximate value of shares bought back at 31/03/2020

SECOND QUARTER 2020

Figure 1: Best performing funds in price terms over Q2*

	(%)
Riverstone Energy	155.1
Golden Prospect Precious Metals	88.4
Riverstone Credit Opportunities Income	84.3
Miton UK Microcap	67
Pacific Horizon	66.3
Augmentum Fintech	60.6
Biotech Growth	55.9
Baillie Gifford US Growth	55.3
India Capital Growth	52.2
Edinburgh Worldwide	51.7

Source: Morningstar, *excluding funds with market cap. below £15m, as at 31 March

Figure 2: Best performing funds in NAV terms over Q2*

	(%)
Golden Prospect Precious Metals	109.7
Augmentum Fintech	60.6
Baillie Gifford US Growth	49.9
Pacific Horizon	49.9
CQS Natural Resources Growth & Income	48
Edinburgh Worldwide	47.1
Weiss Korea Opportunity	46
Scottish Mortgage	44.7
BlackRock World Mining	43.2
TR European Growth	41.1

Source: Morningstar, *excluding funds with market cap. below £15m, as at 31 March

Figure 3: Worst performing funds in price terms over Q2*

	(%)
Marble Point Loan Financing	-42
DP Aircraft 1	-41.7
JZ Capital Partners	-35
Drum Income Plus REIT	-28.1
EJF	-25.7
Standard Life Investment Property Income	-23.6
NB Distressed Debt Investment Extended Life	-23.2
NB Distressed Debt New Global	-17.1
BMO Real Estate	-16.7
UK Commercial Property REIT	-15.3

Source: Morningstar, *excluding funds with market cap. below £15m, as at 31 March

Figure 4: Worst performing funds in NAV terms over Q2*

	(%)
Riverstone Energy	-41.6
Fair Oaks Income 2017	-38.2
Symphony International	-38.1
Crystal Amber	-31.5
Marble Point Loan Financing	-30.3
Electra Private Equity	-28
LMS Capital	-15.4
Chenavari Toro Income	-14.7
Dunedin Enterprise	-13.5
Schroder UK Public Private	-12.1

Source: Morningstar, *excluding funds with market cap. below £15m, as at 31 March

Figure 5: Money entering the sector over Q2*

	£m
Scottish Mortgage*	151
Supermarket Income REIT	140
Worldwide Healthcare*	128
Renewables Infrastructure Group	120
SDCL Energy Efficiency Income	110
Allianz Technology*	74
Smithson*	72
Polar Capital Technology*	61
Edinburgh Worldwide*	55
Finsbury Growth & Income*	48

Source: Morningstar, *Note: based on approximate value of shares at 30/06/20

Figure 6: Money leaving the sector over Q2*

	£m
Pershing Square Holdings*	-108
Polar Capital Global Financials*	-86
Fidelity China Special*	-57
Riverstone Energy*	-41
Witan*	-33
JPEL Private Equity*	-20
Templeton Emerging Markets*	-19
Alliance*	-18
Diverse Income*	-17
CVC Credit Partners Eur. Opps. GBP*	-13

Source: Morningstar, *Note: based on approximate value of shares at 30/06/20

THIRD QUARTER 2020

Figure 1: Best performing funds in price terms over Q3	
	%
FastForward Innovations	110.0
Infrastructure India	83.3
Merian Chrysalis	30.9
UK Mortgages	26.4
JPMorgan China Growth & Income	25.2
Baillie Gifford US Growth	24.6
India Capital Growth	24.3
EPE Special Opportunities	22.9
Baillie Gifford Shin Nippon	22.8
Scottish Mortgage	22.3

Source: Morningstar, *excluding funds with market cap. below £15m, as at 30 September

Figure 2: Best performing funds in NAV terms over Q3	
	%
Crystal Amber	29.3
EPE Special Opportunities	28.7
Merian Chrysalis	26.3
Scottish Mortgage	24.6
Baillie Gifford US Growth	23.9
India Capital Growth	23.4
HgCapital	19.4
Pacific Horizon	18.7
Marble Point Loan Financing	16.3
Apax Global Alpha	16.2

Source: Morningstar, *excluding funds with market cap. below £15m, as at 30 September %

Figure 3: Worst performing funds in price terms over Q3	
	%
KKV Secured Loan	(46.0)
Standard Life Investments Property Income	(24.3)
Riverstone Energy	(20.1)
Symphony International	(18.7)
Adamas Finance Asia	(15.8)
Temple Bar	(15.1)
BMO Private Equity	(15.0)
Life Settlement Assets A	(14.8)
Crystal Amber	(13.2)
Henderson High Income	(12.9)

Source: Morningstar, *excluding funds with market cap. below £15m, as at 30 September

Figure 4: Worst performing funds in NAV terms over Q3	
	%
Aberdeen New Thai	(14.3)
Aseana Properties	(13.7)
Ceiba	(13.3)
KKV Secured Loan	(11.8)
Temple Bar	(10.9)
Secure Income REIT	(10.1)
Baring Emerging Europe	(9.8)
Livermore	(9.7)
Regional REIT	(9.7)
Merchants	(8.8)

Source: Morningstar, *excluding funds with market cap. below £15m, as at 30 September %

Figure 5: Money entering the sector over Q3	
	£m
Greencoat UK Wind	400
Hipgnosis Songs*	212
HICL Infrastructure*	120
Aquila European Renewables Income*	115
Smithson*	103
Worldwide Healthcare*	72
Personal Assets*	63
Edinburgh Worldwide*	54
Allianz Technology*	47
Pacific Horizon*	40

Source: Morningstar, Marten & Co. *Note: based on the approximate value of shares at 30/09/20

Figure 6: Money leaving the sector over Q3	
	£m
Scottish Mortgage*	(118)
NB Global Monthly Income GBP*	(113)
Amedeo Air Four Plus*	(70)
Pershing Square*	(57)
Witan*	(52)
Alliance Trust*	(38)
Templeton Emerging Markets*	(27)
F&C*	(25)
UK Mortgages*	(25)
JPMorgan American*	(25)

Source: Morningstar, Marten & Co. *Note: based on the approximate value of shares at 30/09/20 £m

These charts are drawn from the invaluable monthly and quarterly round-ups of investment trust news produced by the research firm QuotedData. In addition to these regular charts, the round-ups also provide news and commentary on recent trends in the investment trust sector and are free for private investors who sign up at www.quoteddata.com.

A BREAKTHROUGH YEAR FOR INVESTMENT TRUSTS

Investment trust expert MAX KING *reviews the performance of equity investment trusts in 2020.*

2020 HAS BEEN a year of shocks and surprises and more may be in store for the final quarter. This makes jumping to conclusions about equity markets for the year as a whole as dangerous as ever. What is surely not in doubt, though, is that this year has been the making of the investment trust sector, for two reasons. Firstly, the sector has generated exceptionally strong performance relative to the broad market and secondly, direct investors have moved into pole position as owners of trusts and look set to stay there.

Anyone who predicted the market crash of the first quarter in which the FTSE All-share index fell 35% in five weeks, would also have predicted that investment trusts would underperform, owing to widening discounts to net asset value and the debt employed to enhance returns in rising markets. Those were certainly negative factors on the way down, when the average discount of the sector widened from 2% to 22% before narrowing to 11% on 3 April. By then, with the All-share index still down 29% year to date, the investment companies sector was already 7% ahead and that lead continued to grow. At the end of September, the total return of the All-share index was still −19.9% but the investment companies sector was up 1.4%, 21% ahead, helped by the sector average discount falling to 6.2%.

Against the MSCI World index, up 2.5% in the first nine months, performance looks less impressive, but this ignores the heavy geographic bias of the sector, which has a higher exposure to the UK markets (4% of the MSCI All Countries index) than to the US (58%). When each sub-sector is compared against its respective index, investment companies outperformed across most areas, often by significant margins, though the disparity with rivals was often huge. For example, Scottish Mortgage, the sector's £14.5bn giant, returned 76% while Witan lost 14%. Few UK specialists did well, not helped by the underperformance of smaller and mid cap companies 'in the first half,' but technology and healthcare specialists had an outstanding nine months.

Alternative income funds accounted for 39% of the sector at the start of the year and would have been defensive on the way down, notwithstanding widening discounts, but they didn't hold the sector back on the way up. Meanwhile, open-ended funds continued, on average, to underperform their benchmarks, encouraging the relentless shift of investors from active to passive funds. The strong performance of investment trusts together with the growth of platforms and hence the ease of low-cost dealing also encouraged a continuing shift of private investors into direct ownership of investment trusts.

The veteran sector guru Piers Currie produced a report on behalf of Richard Davies Investor Relations that estimated that 35% of investment trust shares were held directly by investors (£38bn out of £110bn) at the start of the year, compared with 29% held by investment institutions, 28% by national wealth managers and 6% by regional wealth managers. Moreover, direct investors were the single largest buyer, accounting for 35% of the net cash-flow of £19bn into the sector in 2019, while the wealth managers were modest net sellers. Admittedly, the research only covered 70% of investment trusts by market value but the data for the rest is unlikely to change the picture much.

This has important implications for investment trusts. Direct investors are concerned about costs, discounts to net asset value and corporate governance largely because of their effect on performance. What they are not concerned about is size, except to the extent that small size precludes economies of scale and thereby raises costs. The self-serving pressure from wealth managers for trusts to grow to a minimum capitalisation of £200m, or else merge or liquidate, must surely abate. Investment trusts will need to do more to communicate to direct investors, making podcasts, presentations and information accessible to investors once disparaged by one head of investment trusts as "hobbyists". Of course, wealth managers and institutions will continue to be important; trusts in the alternatives sector are a significant asset class for multi-asset funds, charities and private clients but brokers and trusts, when issuing new stock, all too often make no provision for direct investors.

Despite the good overall performance of trusts, individual performance has varied widely. At the start of the year, many believed that growth stocks were over-extended and that value was due a revival. The pandemic and the associated economic slump, however, knocked traditional businesses for six and boosted technology or tech-enabled businesses massively. According to Satya Nadella, chief executive of Microsoft, "we've seen two years of digital transformation in two months" but that now looks like an underestimate. While growth-orientated trusts, particularly those managed by Baillie Gifford, benefited massively, value managers were in trouble.

With the All Share index down 22% in the first nine months, the UK saw the most casualties. Temple Bar, with assets well over £1bn at the start of the year but now little more than £620m, saw its net asset value (NAV) fall 48%, its veteran manager retire and its directors put the management contract out to tender. The 34% drop at Perpetual Income & Growth (£630m of assets), previously managed by Mark

Barnett at Invesco, opted for a merger with Murray Income (£535m of assets), down just 17%. Its sister trust, Edinburgh (£980m of assets), down 26%, moved to Majedie but the directors of Law Debenture and Lowland, down 32% and 30%, are sticking with Janus Henderson on the basis of long-term performance.

The performance of mid and small cap funds was even worse in the first half, with the Numis small cap index down 25%, though the 4.7% bounce in the third quarter represented strong outperformance. With managers struggling and discounts widening – a dramatic reversal of fortunes after the extraordinary outperformance and discount-narrowing of 2019 – the average share price was down 28% in the first nine months while Aberforth, the sole value trust in the sector, saw its share price fall 46%. Other weak spots were Latin America, Eastern Europe and frontier markets but trusts in other regions and most global trusts rode out the turbulence well. As always, market turbulence has exposed weak investment strategies at the same time as it has proved the resilience of strong ones

Most global trusts were helped by heavy weightings to the US in general and the giant technology growth stocks in particular, but the 14% drop in NAV at Witan (£1.9bn of assets) led it to shake up its list of managers. At the other end of the performance table are Baillie Gifford's trusts; Scottish Mortgage (+76%) and Edinburgh Worldwide (+45%). Ahead of both was their US Growth fund, launched in 2019, which returned 83%. In contrast, the £120m Gabelli Plus, focused on the US market, has struggled since launch and an 18% fall in NAV led to its shareholders voting against continuation.

Regional funds managed by Baillie Gifford also did well, with Pacific Horizon returning 75% and Baillie Gifford European 29%, both ahead of all their competitors. In Japan, though, Baillie Gifford have faltered and JP Morgan lead the performance pack, ahead of Fidelity. The funds of JP Morgan and Fidelity focused on China were also among the best performing funds in the whole market, but now have a new competitor to contend with as Witan Pacific has become Baillie Gifford China.

There were a couple of casualties among the sector specialists, but the technology and healthcare sectors produced some startling performances, with Biotech Growth, Polar Technology and Allianz Technology returning 34%, 52% and 39% respectively. The commodity sector, as in 2019, produced the best and the worst: Golden Prospect, helped by a rising gold price, returned 73% after 54% in 2019 and Riverstone Energy, which lost 24% in 2019, lost another 60%, supporting the old investment rule about the wisdom of running winners and cutting losers.

There was only one new equity issue in the first half (£103m by Nippon Active Value in February), but three more were announced in September: Schroders British Opportunity, Telworth British Recovery & Growth and Buffetology Smaller Companies. The latter two issues were pulled and the first is struggling, which contrarians will regard as a bullish indicator for the UK. Issuance by existing trusts in the first half was solid at £3bn, though down 43% year on year, while the £1.5bn of capital returned, including £800m of buy-backs, represented an increase of 22%. Under the circumstances, the net issuance of shares is remarkable. What is even more remarkable is that equity issuance, at £1.44bn, accounted for half the total and was actually up 23% on 2019, with nearly all of the money going into growth-orientated trusts, especially those managed by Baillie Gifford.

The normally quiet third quarter brought another £1.35bn of secondary issuance (about half equity and half alternatives) and £910m of capital returned (again, half and half). Smithson raised £100m and Worldwide Healthcare £70m but the tide seemed to turn against Scottish Mortgage; though it issued £45m of new shares, it redeemed £150m as investors grew sceptical about the continued success of its high growth strategy, pushing the shares to a discount to net asset value. The switch to Baillie Gifford's management of Witan Pacific brought £68m of redemptions in a tender offer though Edinburgh Worldwide and Pacific Horizon issued £88m of new shares between them.

The average discount to net asset value of equity funds is down to 7.4% and will surely fall further as markets settle down while net issuance will accelerate. There were widespread dividend cuts in the first half across the world, especially in the UK, but investment companies have protected investors from them by digging into their revenue reserves or paying out of capital, reinforcing the sector's long-term reputation for dividend resilience.

The strong overall performance in 2020 can only increase the confidence of investors in investment companies. Performance was excellent in the stable market conditions of last year, was even better in relative terms in the volatility of 2020, and looks set to continue strongly as economies and markets return to normal. Investment companies sector has been through a baptism of fire and emerged stronger than ever.

MAX KING *was an investment manager and strategist at Finsbury Asset Management, J O Hambro and Investec Asset Management. He is now an independent writer, with a regular column in* MoneyWeek, *and an adviser with a special interest in investment companies. He is a non-executive director of two trusts.*

ALTERNATIVES WEATHER THE STORM

MAX KING *continues his review of the year with a look at the alternative asset sector.*

A YEAR AGO, THE 'alternatives' segment of the investment trust sector had expanded to account for 39% of the £180bn universe. This was mainly driven by secondary issuance of already listed funds, but new funds had also continued to be launched. Cracks, however, had started to appear in the sector with a number of funds proving to be far higher risk than originally thought. Tread carefully, I advised. Established funds whose management has a strong record of adding value would continue to do well, but investors should be more sceptical about share issuance, they needed to scrutinise business models more deeply and embark on a bit of a clear-out of their portfolios.

As warned, 2020 has shown a marked difference in the performance of funds. All funds dropped dramatically in the pandemic sell-off, but performance then diverged sharply. At one end of the scale, the shares of two survivors of the steady decline of the hedge fund sub-sector, Pershing Square and BH Macro, had returned 43% and 40% respectively by the end of September while, at the other end, four aircraft leasing companies, already weak last year, plunged between 54% and 88%. Despite falling bond yields, there were plenty of losers among the debt funds and property funds, supposedly delivering safe income from long-term rentals. Infrastructure and renewable energy funds did well overall but gave their investors a nasty fright along the way. The theory that a high yield was the anchor for low risk and low volatility returns was shot to pieces.

With investors stuck at home in the lockdown, spending much more time than usual staring at computer screens, not panicking required almost superhuman self-control. If the shock of the crash numbed investors into inaction, it was to their benefit as most but certainly not all share prices soon started to recover. Investors began to differentiate between funds that were unaffected by the pandemic and consequent lockdown, those that were adversely affected and those that actually benefited. The collapse of air traffic was a heavy blow to the aircraft leasing funds; they were highly geared, their customers couldn't pay and the planes had little value. Funds providing student accommodation suffered from the closure of universities and those owning retail or leisure properties from the suspension of consumer activity.

As the lockdown was eased, confidence in the outlook for these funds improved but the realisation that the pandemic has accelerated some long-term trends has kept some areas under a cloud.

As much more shopping has moved online, the prospect for logistics warehouses seems secure but many retailers are in serious trouble and so able to force rent reductions on their landlords for the sites they are retaining. Food retailers are the exception, hence the positive return of Supermarket Income REIT. Enforced working from home has been so successful and popular that most office workers and their employers intend to continue it for at least some days each week for the foreseeable future. This casts a heavy cloud over office property and the consumer services that depend on office workers. There are other notable exceptions to the gloom enveloping many of the property funds, such as healthcare (funds owning care homes and doctors' surgeries) and social housing but the sector looks likely to remain in the doldrums until growth in demand fills the empty space or vacant properties are converted to other uses.

For most countries, 2020 will mark the most serious recession in living memory. As it has been the result of governmental action, it should prove sharp but short. Well-financed businesses will ride out the storm but those with high borrowings may sink, hence the initial but misplaced concern about private equity, whose investments are often highly leveraged. Though many funds have investments that are currently problematic, such as Audley Travel for 3i (but not its European retailer, Action), these are more than counterbalanced by technology-related businesses that continue to do well. HGT and Merian Chrysalis, floated only last year, have thrived, Neuberger Berman, JPEL and Electra have performed poorly but other listed funds have had only temporary setbacks. The long-suffering shareholders of Schroder UK Public-Private, the £540m residue of what was once Neil Woodford's Patient Capital, can at last see a glimmer of recovery. The assumption that recessions are always a disaster for private equity has been proved wrong.

The recession has caused problems for a number of the debt funds, particularly those lending on property, but the principal problem continues to be that the returns they offer investors plus their own management costs requires either a demanding return on capital or for that return to be enhanced with plenty of debt. This means that the funds investing in debt (and many others as well) are often much riskier than investors realise. Some funds, however, stand out for their solid performance, including the two TwentyFour Asset Management funds, Henderson Diversified, M&G Credit, City Merchants High Yield and Biopharma Credit. The managers of these funds don't hide from the risks they are taking but manage them shrewdly.

Though the infrastructure funds are back on an even keel, there have been a few wobbles along the way. Investors were gung-ho about the prospects for renewable energy, thereby encouraging relentless expansion, but the increasing dependence on sales at market as opposed to guaranteed prices threatens to undermine revenues. Fortunately, the downward trend of electricity prices has reversed in recent months. An exceptionally sunny spring helped revenues for the solar energy generators but the weather since then has been less favourable. Falling interest rates reduce discount rates and raise valuations, but higher corporation tax is a negative.

The same applies to the general infrastructure funds. A tough regulatory outcome in the water industry undermined the value of HICL's investment in Affinity, while the economic slump impacted the growing proportion of investments which have some economic sensitivity. Dividends have continued to be increased and the shares again trade at large premiums to asset value but managers have, hopefully, learned to be a bit more cautious about acquisitions.

Across the whole sector, most funds have survived but, unlike in the conventional trust sector, few have thrived. Share issuance in the first half was £1.45bn; still substantial but down 64% year on year and there were no new issues. Much of the secondary issuance, including £300m raised by Sequoia Economic Infrastructure, was raised before Covid-19 hit the markets. Other significant issuers were Assura (healthcare property, £185m), Supermarket Income (£140m) and Urban Logistics Reit (£140m). These and three other issues over £100m accounted for over 75% of the secondary issuance in the half year.

Many of 2019's new issues have performed well, though the blizzard of acquisitions by Hipgnosis (music rights), with another £446m raised in the third quarter, should worry investors more than it appears to. Still, the absence of new issues in 2020 proved temporary when Home REIT announced its wish to raise £250m in September and Triple Point Energy Efficiency sought £200m. Secondary issuance continued in the third quarter, with £153m raised by Warehouse REIT and £120m by HICL. A flurry of announcements in September, including £400m from Greencoat UK Wind, £150m from Supermarket income and €150m from Aquila European Renewables, suggests that while overall issuance for 2020 will still be down on 2019, it will be healthy

Return of capital of £1.5bn in the first half through share buy-backs, fund wind-ups and partial redemptions were outpaced by share issuance by two to one across all trusts, but by much less for alternatives. Paradoxically, the largest return of capital came from one of the best performers; Pershing Square bought back £173m of stock as its discount to net asset value remained stubbornly high. Most of the other returns of capital came from the debt funds due to poor performance causing unacceptably high discounts; in the third quarter, Hadrian's Wall returned £89m and Alcentra £77m. The return of capital by poorly performing trusts has streamlined the sector and allowed capital to be recycled into better propositions.

The level of issuance shows that there is continuing investment demand for alternatives, even in the most challenging times, if they are well-managed funds delivering consistent returns that are not or only weakly correlated to equity markets. Returns on government and safe, high quality corporate bonds have collapsed and many UK equity income funds have tripped up, but the demand for securities with a high and steadily rising yield has not gone away. In time, though, investors will need to be wary of excess demand for such shares outstripping the supply of new investments that can generate the required return. This could lead to a worsening balance of risk and reward and a corresponding fall in quality across funds.

We can be sure that there will be more shocks and surprises to markets in future years, but most funds in the alternatives sector continue to deliver on expectations.

MAX KING was an investment manager and strategist at Finsbury Asset Management, J O Hambro and Investec Asset Management. He is now an independent writer, with a regular column in MoneyWeek, and an adviser with a special interest in investment companies. He is a non-executive director of two trusts.

VCTS ARE ON A ROLL

ALEX DAVIES explains why Venture Capital Trusts are likely to reman a popular choice for wealthier investors

COVID-19 HAS SPURRED a global economic tsunami. The International Monetary Fund (IMF) predicts the world economy will take a $12trn (£9.6trn) hit, with the UK economy on course to shrink by 10.2% in 2020. The UK stock market has been putting investors' nerves through a painful and prolonged stress test: the FTSE 100 is down 19.8% (as at 30 September 2020) and appears to be trading like an emerging-market stock exchange – underperforming just about every major European exchange and major U.S. index.

As a result, investors have been taking note and shunning UK equity funds; the period of June to August 2020 was the worst three months of outflows on record. So one might wonder: if the UK's largest companies (on the FTSE 100) are struggling – what hope is there for the younger, smaller companies which Venture Capital Trusts (VCTs) target? Why would anybody in their right mind invest in VCTs in the current climate?

There are at least three reasons why VCTs still look attractive – and *especially* so in the current climate. The first reason is to do with tax. The other two relate to the type of investments VCTs tend to make.

Generous tax breaks as wealthier investors brace for tax hikes

There seems to be little doubt tax hikes are on the horizon – it's just a matter of time. Indeed an Institute for Fiscal Studies (IFS) thinktank warns we may be looking at years of punishing tax rises to cover the massive cost of the Covid pandemic. Suggestions include raising taxes by 10p in the pound for the wealthy and limiting further pension tax relief.

That would be in keeping with the trend we've seen in the last few years. Wealthy investors have been directly in the taxman's line of sight for some time: the amount of tax they pay has gone up year after year. At the same time, many of the traditional ways to mitigate tax have been heavily restricted.

Against this backdrop of increasing tax and restrictions, and with more punitive measures potentially on the cards, VCTs stand out as one of the last bastions of tax efficiency (along with ISAs, which still bear an annual limit of £20,000).

These are the main tax benefits for those who choose to invest in VCTs:

1. You get up to 30% income tax relief when you invest.

2. All dividends are tax free. So, if a VCT pays a dividend of 5%, this is what you actually get in hand. By comparison, to get the same income from a unit trust, a top-rate taxpayer would have to receive a gross dividend of more than 8% (a figure increasingly unlikely in the current climate).

3. You don't need to declare VCTs – or any dividends thereof – on your tax return.

4. The allowance is generous and, importantly, simple: £200,000 a year for anyone.

Increasing tax pressure has probably been one of the key drivers of record-high levels of VCT investment in recent years. Latest HMRC figures show that VCT investors claimed Income Tax relief on £670m in the tax year 2017/18 – a 33% increase on the previous year. The number of VCT investors also swelled (by 24%). When published, figures for 2018/19 are likely to be higher still, as VCTs raised more again than the previous year.

Meanwhile, in 2019/20 VCTs raised £619m – the third-highest amount since 2006 (when VCT income tax relief was set at 40%). This is particularly impressive considering the political uncertainty at the end of 2019 and how the escalating Covid-19 crisis slowed fundraising in March, the very time it would normally speed up.

Historic VCT fundraising

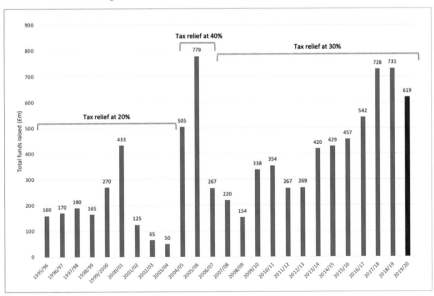

Looking beyond the tax relief, there are two more reasons VCTs could be appealing today.

Hard-to-match exposure to the biggest growth story of the decade

Thirty-two of the world's 100 fastest-growing companies are in the technology sector. Even Covid-19 has not slowed this trend. Technology companies dominate the list of those managing to prosper in the pandemic, according to the *Financial Times*. Although behind the United States, as all countries are, the UK is well and truly part of the tech growth story. The UK ranks #1 in Europe for both past and potential future unicorns (unlisted companies with a valuation of $1bn or more). Despite the challenging macro conditions, the UK tech sector is still outperforming all European neighbours in 2020.

Yet surprisingly, this growth (and resilience) story is most likely passing the average UK investor by. If you look at the FTSE All Share index, for instance, you'll find the tech sector woefully under-represented. It accounts for just 1.10% of the index. Put another way, for every £100 invested in a FTSE All Share tracker, only £1.10 would be invested in tech. The bulk of the money would be going into "old economy stocks" – mining, oil and gas, banks and so on.

By contrast, the largest VCT, Octopus Titan VCT, is invested only in technology stocks. At a conservative estimate, the five largest generalist VCTs (Octopus Titan, Albion, Baronsmead, ProVen VCTs and Northern) and the five largest AIM VCTs (Unicorn, Amati, Octopus and Hargreave Hale) have on average 39% exposure to the technology sector. Since most tech sectors have dodged the Covid bullet, this exposure to the technology sector is probably one of the reasons VCTs appear to be more resilient than the main stock market.

The numbers illustrate this. Take a look at the chart below and you'll see the best-performing VCT in the cohort, Amati AIM VCT, has delivered 12.3% in 2020, while the worst-performing Northern 3 VCT at −12% is still significantly better than the FTSE All Share (−19.9%).

2020 performance: five largest VCTs (generalist and AIM) vs FTSE

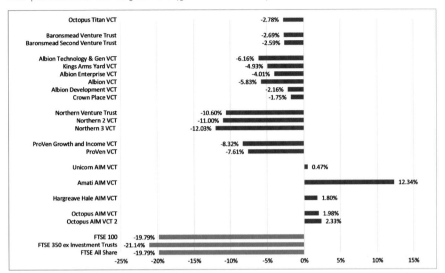

Source: Morningstar. The chart shows NAV Total Return for the period 31/12/2019 to 30/09/2020

Looking over a 10-year period to September 2020, VCT performance is even more impressive. Since 2010, the best-performing VCT within this cohort, Amati AIM VCT, has delivered 156.4% – that's more than twice what the FTSE All Share achieved in the same period (63.9%). It is notable that the best performance has come from AIM VCTs and generalist VCTs which have a long-standing focus on growth-capital investing (the only style of VCT investment permitted since new rules were introduced from 2015).

This brings us to the third reason why VCTs are still attractive today.

10-year performance: five largest VCTs (generalists and AIM) VS FTSE

VCT	Return
Octopus Titan VCT	121.45%
Baronsmead Venture Trust	84.76%
Baronsmead Second Venture Trust	94.15%
Albion Technology & Gen VCT	46.76%
Kings Arms Yard VCT	79.09%
Albion Enterprise VCT	97.68%
Albion VCT	68.01%
Albion Development VCT	91.72%
Crown Place VCT	95.09%
Northern Venture Trust	92.06%
Northern 2 VCT	84.52%
Northern 3 VCT	82.87%
ProVen Growth and Income VCT	58.04%
ProVen VCT	78.55%
Unicorn AIM VCT	154.42%
Amati AIM VCT	156.42%
Hargreave Hale AIM VCT	98.12%
Octopus AIM VCT	108.03%
Octopus AIM VCT 2	103.40%
FTSE 100	55.31%
FTSE 350 ex Investment Trusts	59.47%
FTSE All Share	63.90%

Source: Morningstar. The chart shows NAV Total Return for the period 30/09/2010 to 30/09/2020

An avenue into growth investing in the UK

If you want to get exposure to companies with serious growth potential, irrespective of their sector, you're unlikely to find them on the main stock market. Companies are staying private for longer or are being snatched up by the likes of Microsoft, Amazon or SoftBank.

If you look at the FTSE 350 index, only 21 (6%) of its constituents grew their revenue by more than 25% in 2019 – and that was before the Covid tsunami hit. By comparison, out of the 80+ companies in the Octopus Titan VCT portfolio, 25 more than doubled their revenues in 2020 and 43 had revenue growth of more than 25%, again despite the Covid crisis.

An example is used-car marketplace Cazoo, which launched in December 2019. In its first three months, it generated revenue of £20m. By June 2020, it reported revenues of £40m and achieved a $1bn unicorn valuation, thereby becoming the fastest ever British 'unicorn'. In October 2020, the valuation rose to $2.5bn. Perhaps this comes as little surprise, considering Cazoo founder Alex Chesterman previously founded property website Zoopla, the first VCT-backed British unicorn, as well as online DVD rental service LoveFilm, eventually acquired by Amazon in 2011 for close to £200m ($317m). The investment team behind Octopus Titan VCT has backed Alex Chesterman in all three ventures.

Another example is Moteefe – a platform that sells unique and personalised merchandisable products – now the fourth fastest-growing technology company in the UK, according to the Deloitte Fast 50. Moteefe's revenues grew 117.81% in the three years to December 2019. The onset of Covid accelerated this growth: revenues grew 150% in the first half of 2020. The Baronsmead VCTs are the largest shareholder.

In a completely different area, FinTech company Quantexa helps banks and other financial institutions detect suspicious activities in their systems and fight financial crime. Started in 2016, it reported revenues of just over £5m in 2018 which more than doubled to £10.2m in 2019. It will reportedly break £20m in revenue this year. Five of the six Albion VCTs have invested in Quantexa and together hold a 12.44% stake in the company.

Of course, as impressive as these companies and their growth are, they are all very young and still have to prove themselves. Moreover, these are the standout examples. For every Cazoo, Moteefe and Quantexa in a VCT portfolio, there will be many more companies that fail or languish. Risk capital is called risk capital for good reason. The few that do succeed, however, can deliver impressive returns.

Zoopla, for instance, was Octopus Titan VCT's best performing investment. The VCT invested a total of £3m over several rounds. Zoopla listed on the London Stock Exchange in 2014 and the holding was completely exited in February 2017. The sale price of the last remaining shares represented a multiple of more than 33 times the price paid originally.

Watchfinder, one of the first online platforms for watch enthusiasts to sell, buy and service pre-owned luxury watches, is one of the ProVen VCTs' standout performers. Beringea, the manager of the ProVen VCTs, invested in 2014. By 2018, turnover had trebled. Richemont, the Swiss luxury goods group, which owns brands such as Cartier, Van Cleef & Arpels, Jaeger-LeCoultre and Vacheron Constantin, bought the company in early 2018, generating a return of 8.89 times for the VCTs.

Grapeshot is another example. The company has created a marketing analytics platform that helps companies more effectively customise their marketing and target relevant audiences. The Albion VCTs originally backed the company in 2014 and proceeded to invest a total of £2.9m. In the following four years, Grapeshot saw a 15 times increase in revenue, from £2m in 2014 to £30m in March 2018. Grapeshot was acquired by Oracle in April 2018 for an undisclosed amount. The sale generated a return of around 10 times the original investment for the Albion VCTs.

Overall, in the past 10 years VCTs have generated average investor returns of 75.2% before tax relief (compared to 63.9% for the FTSE All Share).

So who invests in VCTs?

Contrary to popular belief, there is no such a thing as a typical VCT investor. The average age of our clients who invest in VCTs is 57. The youngest is 19, the eldest 101. 85.7% are male, only 14.2% female. In the last tax year, they invested £34,069 on average across a number of VCTs. The average amount invested in each VCT was £15,203. We don't record occupation, but those we speak to who invest are typically professionals such as doctors, lawyers, higher earners in the City, business owners, but also head teachers and civil servants. They all have investments elsewhere (e.g. ISAs, pensions, property) to which VCTs add diversification, and they tend to have been affected by tax rises and pension restrictions.

For someone who doesn't have sufficient assets or earnings, and doesn't clearly understand the risks, VCTs are unlikely to be a suitable investment. Young, small companies are more likely to fail than older and larger ones. If something goes badly wrong for a small company, it is much harder for it to recover than it is for a large and well-established company. They are also a lot more illiquid, as are the VCTs themselves, meaning it may be difficult to buy and sell the shares.

However, if you have sufficient assets elsewhere, you have already used your pension and ISA allowances, and you have a certain level of financial sophistication, then VCTs may well be a worthwhile option for you to consider. As a general rule of thumb, VCTs should be no more than 10% of your total portfolio. Typically, your money will be spread over 30 to 60 companies, which provides an important degree of underlying diversification.

Secondly, just as professional venture capital investors find it difficult to know in advance which start-up businesses are going to become their biggest successes, so investors in VCTs should consider spreading their capital across more than one trust. We always suggest you spread your annual investment over a number of VCTs, preferably with different investment strategies, to further diversify your risk. Don't forget you also have a 30% cushion in the form of tax relief should things go wrong.

One final thought

VCT season started early this year and so far investor demand appears buoyant. For instance, the Baronsmead VCTs opened their fundraising offer on 16 September. Within the first three days, over £2.15m was invested through the Wealth Club platform alone. This is a sign of the continued popularity of established VCTs, but also a reminder to investors that if they spot a VCT they like, they should act quickly whilst there is still capacity.

ALEX DAVIES is the founder and CEO of Wealth Club, the largest broker of VCTs and tax-efficient investments for experienced investors.

THE TRIUMPH OF GROWTH

JAMES CARTHEW *investigates why value investing is so out of favour.*

THERE USED TO be a fairly healthy debate over the best way to manage money, which could be summed up as 'value' versus 'growth'. Either you bought well-established companies trading at unusually low valuation multiples relative to the market and to history – in the expectation that these would be re-rated in time – or you bought companies that were often more highly valued than the market average, but you thought had exceptional long-term growth potential. Markets seemed to cycle between periods when one worked better than the other, but it looked as though value investing worked best over the long term.

Today, it feels as though very few people believe that value investing works. Long-standing value managers are often pilloried in the press and in the comments sections of investing websites. Growth managers are heroes and their funds are ballooning in size – what happened?

Let us start by looking at the following charts. The first shows the performance of value and growth styles relative to market averages over the past 34 years and uses data for the MSCI World Index (translated back into sterling). The second chart just looks at the UK market, but because there is more data available goes back a bit further – to January 1975.

When compiling these indices, MSCI has assigned stocks to value or growth portfolios based on three measures: price to book, price/earnings and dividend yield. These portfolios are then rebalanced every six months, so that stocks may move from one category to the other.

Figure 1: MSCI World value and growth relative   Figure 2: MSCI UK value and growth relative

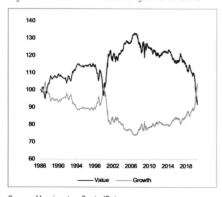
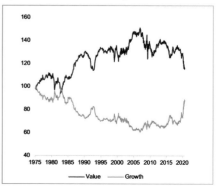

Source: Morningstar, QuotedData

Value investing used to work well

The ideas behind value investing were set out by Benjamin Graham in the 1930s and '40s. He reasoned that there was a margin of safety in buying assets for less than their intrinsic value. Investors should be contrarian and exploit volatility – sell when others are optimistic and buy when other investors are panicking. Academic work carried out in the late '80s demonstrated the power of value investing. A 1988 study by Michael Lenhoff of CapelCure Myers Capital Management analysed returns on UK stocks from January 1955 to December 1988 and found that the highest yielding stocks gave you the best returns. Refining this to avoid the stocks with the very highest yields, the ones most likely to be in distress, gave even better results.

However, looking at the charts in figures 1 and 2, there are clear periods when growth is doing better than value. They coincide with things like the recession in the early 1980s, the early '90s recession in the UK and the tech boom in 2000 (which is far more pronounced in the global index than in the UK). Growth has also done exceptionally well over the period since the global financial crisis in 2008 and this is particularly true over the past 18 months.

Winning ways of growth investors

Figure 3: 10 year returns to close of business on 31 October 2020

STOCK	NAV RETURN (% PER YEAR)	SHARE PRICE RETURN (% PER YEAR)
The Biotech Growth Trust	23.2	23.6
Baillie Gifford Shin Nippon	22.6	25.5
Scottish Mortgage	22.4	23.8
Allianz Technology	22.3	23.4
Polar Capital Technology	20.8	20.4

Source: Morningstar, QuotedData

The trust that best illustrates the recent success of the growth style is Scottish Mortgage. Its net asset value per share has compounded at almost 24% a year over the past 10 years and its performance has been particularly strong in 2020, leaving competing funds trailing in its wake. Investors have flocked to it in droves and the company is a multiple of its size in 2008.

Scottish Mortgage's managers are growth stock investors. They believe that over the long term, stock market indices are driven by a handful of successful stocks. The thinking is that, if you can identify these stocks early in their life and then hang onto them, you can make supernormal returns.

The managers cite a study, that they helped to fund, by Hendrik Bessembinder, Te-Feng Chen, Goeun Choi and K.C. John Wei. Their research paper, published on 5 July 2019, asks: do global stocks outperform US Treasury Bills? They looked at the returns on 62,000 global stocks between 1990 and 2018 and concluded that just 1.3% of these stocks created all the gains in global markets over that period. Most stocks did not beat US Treasury Bills.

The study is interesting in that it suggests that relatively few companies create lasting value for investors, but to my mind it is flawed in that it assumes a buy and hold strategy. The reality is that the fortunes of most companies wax and wane. Very few have characteristics that allow them to flourish for decades. The vast majority of active investors will seek to hold those companies while they are doing well and sell them before they go into decline. As an aside, this is also a strong argument for favouring active investing over passive investing.

Ben Rogoff, manager of Polar Capital Technology, believes the best stocks to hold are those undergoing explosive growth. He points out that technologies go through cycles, like any other product. New entrants tend to displace yesterday's winners. Sometimes these big companies can reinvent themselves, but usually not. By the time that technologies become mainstream, the buyer's focus is shifting to the next exciting product and greater emphasis is being placed on the price of the product or service. Sales and profit growth stalls and market valuations of these companies begin to fall.

Ben suggests that the best returns can be made as a product or service moves from the early adoption phase to the mass adoption phase. Growth rates can look exponential as a product or service shifts from around 5% to around 30% penetration. Many analysts find it hard to model this sort of growth, particularly in the early stages as companies invest to support this growth and rack up losses. The implication is that growth stocks may look expensive, but this might be misleading.

Value traps

One of the trusts that falls just outside the table (with annual returns of 13.9% a year for 10 years) is BlackRock Throgmorton. Its manager, Dan Whitestone, is a growth investor but he also has the ability to short stocks. A core part of his investment approach is identifying industries undergoing disruptive change and then buying the winners and selling the losers. He highlights a number of sectors and companies that are value traps. These companies may appear to be attractively valued but declining revenues and falling margins can quickly translate into losses and stretched balance sheets. One of Dan's bugbears is companies that fall into this category but are paying dividends in preference to investing in transforming their fortunes.

One theory as to why value investing is struggling is that the pace of disruption is accelerating. New technologies can render long-established companies obsolete. Dan cautions that whole industries could disappear.

The impact of Covid-19

At the beginning of 2020, there was a feeling in some quarters that the bull market in equities was running out of steam. Given this uncertainty and harking back to the experience of previous recessions, many investors were casting around for stocks that they felt were capable of delivering growth even if the economy weakened. Many technology and healthcare stocks fitted that bill. By contrast, it was already evident that industries such as high street retail were struggling.

Measures taken to tackle Covid-19 seem to have accelerated some of these trends. The use of online shopping has soared, hitting high street retail; restaurants were shuttered and, even after the temporary respite supplied by 'eat out to help out' many will not survive the Deliveroo/Just Eat trend. The same is true of pubs.

Other important value sectors have been impacted too. The price of oil collapsed early on, encouraged by a price war instigated by Russia and Saudi Arabia. Riverstone Energy, which is focused largely on North American shale and the Gulf of Mexico, has been an obvious casualty. The energy sector is one experiencing a sharp increase in defaulted debt. This is contributing to the perceived problems faced by the banking sector, another key component of value indices.

Lower for longer

The banking sector is also out of favour because interest rates are at historically low levels. Investors reason that banks cannot earn acceptable margins while this is the case. However, managers specialising in investing in this area, such as those behind Polar Capital Global Financials, argue that banks can still make reasonable returns from their lending activities (consider interest rates on credit cards, for example).

Figure 4: UK base rates

Figure 5: Yield on US 10-year treasuries

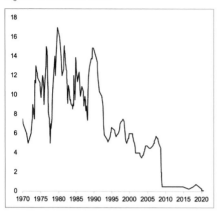

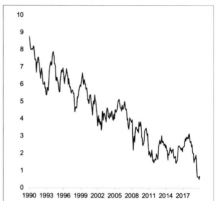

Source: Bloomberg, QuotedData

When the financial system looked to be in meltdown in 2008, the global policy response was to cut interest rates and pump liquidity into the system through quantitative easing. Business models valued by discounting their future cash flows suddenly looked more attractive. This provides support to equity markets generally, but flattered growth stocks in particular.

Growth stocks are often perceived as long duration assets – their valuations are usually based on a discounted cash flow analysis, which gives higher outcomes when discount rates are low. By contrast, value stocks tend to be perceived as short-duration assets – valued on multiples of last year's or next year's earnings or cash flow.

Low interest rates have also aided the survival of so-called zombie companies, whose debt burdens would not be sustainable if interest rates normalised. This prevents much-needed rationalisation of some industries and depresses margins.

At the same time, inflation has been low. Technological advances have driven down the cost of many consumer goods. Globalisation allowed the production of goods to shift to countries with cheaper labour. The internet is facilitating something similar in services. Companies that do not have pricing power are struggling in this environment.

Boards are pulling the plug on value managers

Investment trust boards face a difficult choice in this environment. One of the great attractions of investment trusts over open-ended funds is an independent board with the ability to hire and fire the investment manager. Boards recognise the importance of taking a long-term view, however. Switching managers and/or investment styles after a period of underperformance could end up with a much worse result if the market changes tack shortly afterwards.

The tale of what is now Baillie Gifford European Growth Trust is a cautionary one. The company was launched as F&C Eurotrust and managed by Peter Jarvis with a growth style. However, after a period of poor performance, the board awarded the management contract to Edinburgh Partners in February 2010. Their choice was based on the performance of the open-ended EP European Opportunities Fund, managed by Dale Robertson with a value style. From its launch in April 2004, it had generated 5% per annum outperformance of its benchmark. However, from about 2015, as value stocks struggled, the trust started to lag its benchmark. An internal switch of managers within Edinburgh Partners – from Dale to Craig Amour – did not resolve the situation. Eventually, the board decided to jump ship to Baillie Gifford, who now run the trust with a growth style once again. Fortunately, it has got off to a good start.

Two high profile UK equity income trusts have also made a switch in the past year. Both were managed by Mark Barnett of Invesco Perpetual. Edinburgh Investment Trust moved first, ending up at Majedie, where it is now being managed by James de Uphaugh. Perpetual Income & Growth waited to see if December 2019's election would signal a recovery in its fortunes, and then opted to merge with Murray Income Trust, managed by Charles Luke at Aberdeen Standard Investments.

In both cases this does not represent a wholesale shift away from value investing. James de Uphaugh uses a pragmatic approach that has both value and growth elements. Charles Luke looks for high quality stocks with sustainable earnings. Both should therefore be focused on avoiding value traps. Murray Income has been faring better than Edinburgh since the Covid-19 outbreak.

One of the worst performing UK trusts this year has been Temple Bar, which until recently was managed by Alastair Mundy using a strict value approach. Again, the board has decided that it needed to find a new manager, but it will stick with a value style. The board reasoned that a switch to growth now might see it selling its portfolio at the lowest point of the value versus growth cycle. The new managers are Nick Purves and Ian Lance at RWC Partners. They say that value stocks have never looked more unloved in the 30-odd years that they have been managing money.

Part of the RWC team's argument is that investors have a natural tendency to become over-exuberant about some stocks and overly pessimistic about others. These investors then extrapolate from short-term setbacks and apply very low valuation multiples to trough earnings.

Winners and losers if value returns to favour

Temple Bar is one of very few trusts managed with an out-and-out value style. Another good example is Aberforth Smaller Companies Trust. At the end of June 2020, the average stock in its portfolio was trading at a price/earnings ratio of 6.1 times and a yield of 3.7%. Global investors are shunning the UK, largely on Brexit uncertainty and our dire Covid-19 track record. Even within the UK, smaller companies are out of favour. In addition, the trust trades at a discount of 13%. If you are convinced that the market is about to make a decisive switch in favour of value stocks, it may be a bargain. For the brave, there is even a highly geared split capital version in the form of Aberforth Split Level Income Trust.

If value comes back into vogue, the corollary is that growth will be suffering. I should also point out that between September 2000 and September 2001, Scottish Mortgage's NAV fell by over 40% as the tech bubble burst.

But how likely is a value renaissance?

It is unlikely that value investing is dead and the Covid-19-related leg down in valuations of value stocks may have brought us a lot closer to the bottom of the value versus growth cycle. However, the conditions needed to trigger a shift away from growth stocks are probably some way off.

Interest rates may need to rise, but policymakers are terrified of this given the sheer volume of debt we have been running up while rates have been depressed. Inflation is very low/negative and resurgent inflation could also see rising rates. This is some way off given soaring unemployment and the Covid-19 hit to the global economy. However, governments have become more profligate and the money supply is increasing.

The dangers of value traps created by technological advancements will not go away. Neither will the proliferation of exciting new investments created by advances in medicine, for example. My guess is that some air will be let out of overinflated valuations in some areas but we could be waiting for years for a decisive shift in style.

JAMES CARTHEW *is a director at Marten & Co, which provides research and corporate advice for the investment trust sector and manages the QuotedData website (www.quoteddata.com).*

INCOME FROM WHERE?

SANDY CROSS *discusses whether paying income out of revenue or capital reserves is good or bad for investment trust shareholders.*

COVID-ERA HEADLINES ABOUT dividend cuts make for distressing reading for investors seeking income. Global dividends fell by $108bn in the second quarter of 2020 to $382bn according to the Janus Henderson Global Dividend Index report. Second quarter UK dividends were down over 40% versus 2019 (excluding special dividends). HSBC, Lloyds and Royal Dutch Shell were among the once reliable market stalwarts that cut or completely eliminated payments. The misery of this has been added to by the awful yields on government bonds – generally either so low you could easily mistake them for a rounding error (the UK 10-year gilt yields 0.2% to redemption at the time of writing) or actually negative.

If you want to have a hope of getting anything like an attractive running income from bonds, you need to take levels of credit or sovereign risk that will quite rightly leave you feeling a little queasy. There is also no sanctuary to be found in bank accounts: none will pay you an interest rate greater than the rate of inflation. The risk of Covid-related fiscal and monetary stimulus measures eventually generating proper inflation (2% plus) only makes things look worse. It may be that in time the effects of the pandemic will pass and dividends will soar again, but this is far from a given. It may also be that company managements use this crisis as an opportunity to shift dividend payouts down over the longer term.

There's a problem here for investment trusts. They have always been an important income vehicle for the UK. Everyone remembers how Mr Darcy in Jane Austen's *Pride and Prejudice* was known more for the £10,000 a year he took as income from his assets than for his sparkling conversation and stately home. Income was what really counted in the 1800s and the same was very much true of the investment trusts which emerged later in the century – this was a low inflation age and a regular income was considered by the rentier class to be the sum and total purpose of investing.

The earliest UK investment trust, Foreign and Colonial Investment Trust played to this need – it was originally invested in a diversified range of foreign government bonds with a view to achieving a safe yield a little higher than that on offer from UK government securities. A glance at the portfolios of the other early trusts also shows a preponderance of fixed income securities and preference shares, many in higher risk activities (notably railway development) or countries, but always with a strong bias to fixed coupons.

Not all these investments will have worked out – the Baring Crisis of 1890 would have hurt the Latin American bonds in an 1888 portfolio of which I have a copy – but enthusiastic diversification would have helped, with over 200 securities held in the trust. Over time, as investment became increasingly professionalised and equity markets matured, a greater focus on capital gains as a component of return began to emerge. Investment trusts were quick to jump on that opportunity (this is not a sleepy sector), but they did not leave the old one behind. This has proved to be fortunate given the way in which pension freedoms have created a whole new world of keen income investors in the UK.

In 2020 income trusts are still a very important part of the market: the UK income trust sector alone contains 20 trusts managing in excess of £10bn. But what is an income trust to do when income is hard to find? Part of the answer is to look for new sources and new structures. These range from conventional equity trusts investing outside the UK with an income strategy (such as Schroder Oriental Income Fund) to alternative assets class funds such as infrastructure funds which are designed to produce a high income (The Renewables Infrastructure Fund being one example). The low interest rate environment since 2008 has encouraged all manner of new income trusts to be created in the UK, investing all over the world. Some of the alternative asset classes now being promoted have been increasingly esoteric, with yields often enhanced with cheap gearing – something which always adds risk. Some of these strategies have proved more successful than others.

The other part of the answer as to how to deal with a low income environment has been to begin to convert capital to income on behalf of investors. Investment trusts have a few things going for them over OEICs in this kind of environment. The first is that trusts are able to accumulate income reserves from which they can pay dividends (they can hold back 15% of the income they receive every year if that's what their directors decide). This means they can smooth payments over time: if the dividends they get in one year fall, they dip into reserves and keep the payout to their investors constant (or as the AIC's dividend heroes have, rising). OEICs can't do this. They have to pay out all the income they get in every year. If it falls, it falls.

The second is that investment trusts have the ability – if approved by their shareholders via a change in company articles – to pay dividends out of the trust's capital. Neither of these things will sound as good as paying income out of actual income. The first method is as much an accounting trick as anything else. Trusts do mostly have reserves – some very large (there are some eight years worth of dividends in Caledonia Investments for example), others negligible or even negative (if the trust's expenses have been greater than its income for example). In the high dividend paying UK Equity Income sector, the average number was 1.2 years of reserves at the most recent pre-Covid era year end (source JPM Cazenove).

However these reserves don't represent an actual pile of cash. In paying them out the company is effectively drawing on past success in accumulating income to sub a current dividend payment. It is a good discipline … but you are still paying yourself your own money rather than accessing a secret cave full of treasure. The second method boils down to nothing more than the trust facilitating you in the consumption of your own capital – possibly by selling assets at depressed prices. And as Mr Micawber said to David Copperfield: "Annual income twenty pounds, annual expenditure nineteen and six, result happiness. Annual income twenty pounds, annual expenditure twenty pounds ought and six, result misery."

That said there may be good reason for doing it anyway: the need for income, for example among pensioners, does not fall simply because the income available falls. The essential question then is this: if you need to draw a relatively high level of income in percentage terms in comparison to market income levels, are you better achieving this through investing in higher yielding stocks or taking the return from a mix of dividend and capital returns (better known as total return)? Everyone in the industry has an opinion on this.

The key matter to my mind is this – in the end will there be more cake to eat overall if you follow the high dividend portfolio approach or the total return approach? Countless studies have shown the importance of dividend reinvestment in generating long-term stock returns. These studies mostly ignore the tax position of dividend recipients (if you are paying 40% in tax, you have a lot less dividend to reinvest) and also the fact that for many investors the lesson is useful, but the dividend represents their income and they cannot afford to reinvest it.

A slightly different and more important dimension to this in my view is – do companies which pay above average dividends tend to produce a different level of total return and capital to the average? If we perform a simplistic analysis and compare the 10 year total return of the FTSE 350 Index (which comprises the 350 largest UK companies by market capitalisation) with that of the FTSE 350 Higher Yield Index (the companies in the FTSE 350 paying above average yields), the returns over the last 10 years provide some supporting evidence for the notion that an excessive focus on high yield can damage total return. The figures are 69% for the index versus 44% for the high yielders.

In broad terms, I believe that the market values the ability to grow dividends more highly than it does a high absolute level income. High income is often associated with businesses with limited growth prospects and this has tended to be reflected in dull share price performance. High income equities may have periods of strong share price performance, but long term compounding of business value and the ability to generate cash/pay growing dividends will tend to be a better formula for generating returns.

What does this mean for investment trusts income policy? It appears to suggest that paying dividends from a trust's total return (combining both income and capital) and of course from reserves does indeed make sense. The 'Spartans' of the investment trust world will kick back against this by insisting that the actual income a trust earns should alone be the bedrock of dividends. I suspect however they will find that fewer and fewer people are listening. Not many investors requiring income want to get stuck with an obvious bias to high yielding shares in sunset industries such as oil and tobacco.

It is also perfectly reasonable to note that in the days before pension freedom was introduced many of the investors in income funds would have bought annuities instead. Ask any of them what kind of product they want today and they may tell you that it is still an annuity-type vehicle (that is, one which promises a regular income partly paid out of capital), yet also allows them control over the remaining capital. An income investment trust which pays dividends out of capital could not fit the bill better.

This may be one reason why so many boards and managers have been flirting with prioritising income for some time. Another is the apparent evidence that trusts which do smooth their income and/or adopt a total return approach are being rewarded with a narrowing of the discount at which their shares trade. In the case of alternative sources of income, the same phenomenon is reflected in the premiums bestowed on many trusts with mandates of that kind. If demand for income generates higher ratings, you can be sure that it will stimulate more supply, in the form of IPOs and secondary issuance.

It is important to note that the use of gearing, covered calls and the allocation of fees to capital are all techniques which can be – and are already being – used to 'pimp' income at the expense of capital gains. There is risk involved in such manoeuvres of course: paying out too much capital too fast doesn't help anyone in the end, nor does setting income expectations too high in volatile times. There are also tax implications. Capital gains tax is paid at 20% by higher or additional rate tax payers, but income tax rates are twice or more this level. In theory higher income investors might be better off selling shares than receiving their capital as dividends. This does not matter if your investments are "wrapped" in SIPPs or ISAs, but it is a consideration for direct investors. That said, tax rates and the differential between CGT and income tax are under review by the Treasury in the wake of the pandemic, so the position may soon change.

The key point here for investors is that trusts have something many other investment vehicles do not have – structural flexibility. It is often right for boards and managers to use reserves over short time periods if they anticipate conditions may improve. It can make good sense to distribute capital returns as income for a certain investor base such as pensioners and ISA investors. Predictability of income is valued by many of them. Total return investing has a number of investment advantages. All these approaches are reasonable approaches. It's just a matter of using them in the right way and at the right time. The most important thing for shareholders is simply to be aware where their income ultimately originates.

SANDY CROSS *is a partner at Rossie House Investment Management in Edinburgh.*

PANDEMIC PERFORMANCE

JONATHAN DAVIS *analyses the way that different trusts navigated the Covid-19 crisis.*

T HE COVID-19 PANDEMIC has been responsible for an extraordinary switchback ride for the UK equity market and the investment trust sector during the course of 2020. In the first weeks of the year, few investors had any inkling of the drama which was to follow. It was only in the third week of February that the financial markets began to factor in the seriousness of the virus, the speed with which it was spreading and the scale of its potential impact on the global economy.

Once those factors became widely apparent, the market reaction was remarkable for the speed and severity of the decline it produced, leading to something not easily distinguishable from panic. In the 33 days between 19 February and 23 March, the FTSE All-Share index fell by 33 per cent, or one per cent a day. The MSCI World index declined by 34 per cent. The yield on a 10-year Treasury bond, normally regarded as a bellwether of sentiment in the fixed income market, also fell from 1.5% to 0.5%.

If you accept the familiar definition of a bear market as being marked by a decline of more than 20 per cent in share values, this was the most precipitous bear market in recorded history. Even in the 1930s depression bear market, share prices did not fall this far in such a short time. For as long as the severity of the pandemic, the scale of the economic disaster and its likely duration remained seemingly impossible to measure, share prices continued to fall in a more or less straight line.

But then, unlike the virus itself, the market panic suddenly subsided. Investors reacted with relief to the massive monetary and fiscal measures hurriedly announced by governments and central banks and to hopes that the depth and longevity of the pandemic would in fact be contained once the initial wave peaked. By coincidence, although not a surprise to anyone familiar with how contrarian markets can be, the day the markets turned was the exact day that the World Health Organisation officially designated the coronavirus a 'global pandemic'. It was also the day that the UK government announced it was putting the UK economy into an economically crippling national lockdown.

From 23 March onwards, stock markets around the world started to rise and have continued to do so almost continuously ever since, a testament to the ability of financial markets to try and price the future, not the present. By the middle of

October, despite an unprecedented setback to global economic growth, the MSCI World index was at a higher level than it was when the panic started in late February. True, not every country's index has shared fully in this remarkable recovery. The FTSE All-Share index, notably, was still trading some 20 per cent below the high point it had reached in early 2020. A particularly strong performance was meanwhile seen in China, where the pandemic started, and several other Asian markets.

How did investment trusts fare during this remarkable rollercoaster of a ride? The answer is shown in the tables on pandemic performance that follow. To illustrate the contrasting fortunes of different sectors, we broke down the performance of more than 340 investment companies into four distinct periods; (1) the six months leading up to the start of the market sell-off; (2) the five-week market sell-off leading up to the market low on 23 March; (3) the six-and-a-bit months following the market low, taking us to 30 September 2020; and (4) the whole 13-month period from 20 August 2019 to 30 September 2020.

While this will not capture the precise experience of every individual trust over the course of the year, the data illustrates some interesting trends and provides a useful pointer to how different trusts and sectors might behave should we see another damaging market sell-off in the near future (for example, if a second wave of Covid-19 infections were to prompt a new set of more restrictive lockdowns, as it is doing in Europe at the time of writing).

Note that these tables show the share price total return over each period, not the movements in net asset value per share. In other words, they take account of movements in discounts. The change in discount between each period, which was a significant factor in some sectors, is also shown separately. The universe excludes venture capital trusts and those not listed in London or the Channel Islands, making a total of 343 companies.

The first set of charts summarises the behaviour of the largest investment company sectors over each of the four periods. Note first how in the six months leading up to the market panic, almost every sector was performing well, with positive share price performance and narrowing discounts. UK trusts rallied strongly in the wake of the Brexit deal and the Tory election victory. In February 2020 the average discount across the whole investment trust universe had narrowed to little more than two per cent, the tightest in living memory.

Moving on to the market sell-off the charts show which sectors suffered the best and worst share price losses during the sell-off, and the extent to which discount movements contributed to that. It is evident that no sector proved immune to the crisis, although some fared considerably better than others. Almost every sector produced a temporary share price loss of more than 20 per cent and suffered some degree of rerating. Only eight trusts managed a positive return.

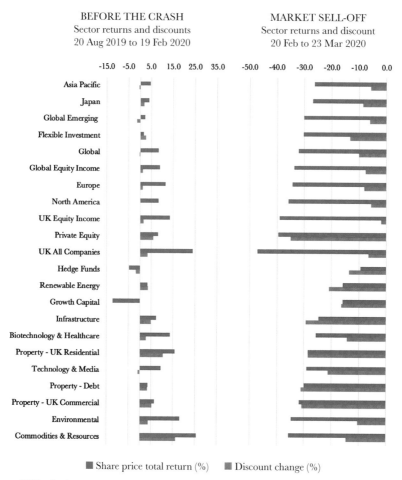

BEFORE THE CRASH
Sector returns and discounts
20 Aug 2019 to 19 Feb 2020

MARKET SELL-OFF
Sector returns and discount
20 Feb to 23 Mar 2020

■ Share price total return (%)   ■ Discount change (%)

Source: AIC/Morningstar

Note in particular how poorly equity trusts with predominantly UK exposure performed during the sell-off, while the Asian region showed more defensive qualities. Private equity trusts on average did just as poorly as the UK equity sectors, though this was primarily due to the widening of discounts (which in turn reflects the fact that private equity trusts issue NAV updates less regularly and trade in less liquid assets, so the accuracy of their published NAVs is more open to question).

Smaller company sectors almost everywhere in the world (although not shown in the chart) performed about 10% worse on average than equivalent mainstream equity trusts, reflecting their higher risk and illiquidity. The best performing sectors during the crisis were those with more secure long-term contracted cash flows, such as infrastructure and renewable energy, and property companies whose rents were either paid for by the State, such as health centres and social housing trusts, or by tenants operating warehouses and logistics centres, beneficiaries of the boom

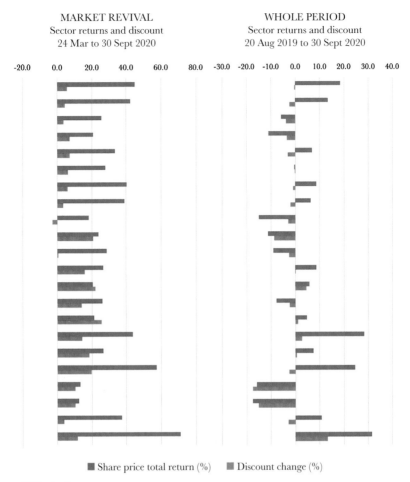

MARKET REVIVAL
Sector returns and discount
24 Mar to 30 Sept 2020

WHOLE PERIOD
Sector returns and discount
20 Aug 2019 to 30 Sept 2020

■ Share price total return (%)   ■ Discount change (%)

Source: AIC/Morningstar

in online shopping and the trend towards working at home. Even here however discounts widened and the average discount across all sectors briefly touched 20 per cent, with conventional commercial property trusts suffering the worst derating.

The third set of charts shows how the picture completely reversed over the next six months. It is notable however that the sectors which suffered most during the sell-off were not in general the same ones that did best in the recovery phase, so this was not a uniform V-shaped recovery. The outperformance seen in Asian and overseas markets compared to the relatively less impressive recovery of UK trusts is marked, as is the poor performance of commercial property companies. While most trusts saw their discounts narrow again in the market recovery, as you would expect, the extent to which they narrowed during the recovery was less marked than the derating they suffered in the earlier decline.

The final panel of charts illustrate the enduring effects of the pandemic on sector performance. They show how share price returns and discounts performed over the whole period from August 2019 to the end of September 2020. It presents a very mixed picture, with non-UK markets generally performing well, helped by weaker sterling, while UK trusts, private equity and commercial property are all well down over the period. The two secular growth stories, technology and biotech/healthcare, lead the field along with the highly cyclical commodities sector. Note that over the whole period discounts have generally declined, with the average discount ranging for most of the period between five and eight per cent.

Best and worst individual trust performance

Market decline (20 Feb to 23 Mar 2020)

BEST SHARE PRICE PERFOMERS	TICKER	SECTOR	SPTR (%)	CHANGE IN DISCOUNT (%)
Schiehallion Fund Ord	MNTN	Growth Capital	15.4	8.4
Life Settlement Assets A Ord	LSAA	Insurance & Reinsurance Strategies	15.3	-3.8
Marble Point Loan Financing Ord	MPLF	Debt - Structured Finance	12.7	21.3
CATCo Reinsurance Opps C	CATC	Insurance & Reinsurance Strategies	7.8	-12.0
BH Macro GBP Ord	BHMG	Hedge Funds	6.1	-25.0
US Solar Fund Ord	USF	Renewable Energy Infrastructure	1.5	-8.6
BH Global GBP Ord	BHGG	Hedge Funds	1.5	-17.3
BH Macro USD Ord	BHMU	Hedge Funds	-0.9	-35.1
BioPharma Credit Ord	BPCR	Debt - Direct Lending	-1.1	-13.5
JPEL Private Equity Ord	JPEL	Private Equity	-1.2	-0.3
EJF Investments Ord	EJFI	Financials	-1.5	16.1
Ruffer Investment Company Ord	RICA	Flexible Investment	-2.6	-4.1
Greencoat Renewables	GRP	Renewable Energy Infrastructure	-4.9	-19.3
JPMorgan China Growth & Income plc	JCGI	Country Specialist: Asia Pacific ex Japan	-5.5	-5.6

Source: AIC/Morningstar

The tables highlight the best and worst performing individual trusts over the period of the market's decline, the six-month period that followed, and the whole period from 24 August 2019 (six months before the sell-off) to 30 September 2020. These tables exclude investment companies with total assets of less than £50m. If you want to look in detail at how every trust performed over these periods, including any that you own, a spreadsheet containing the data for all 343 trusts in the survey over all periods can be downloaded from the handbook page on the *Money Makers* website (www.money-makers.co).

The effects of the pandemic have been felt not just in share price and discount movement, but also in dividend-paying capacity. The table on pages 50 to 55 summarises all the key announcements made by trusts about dividends since March 2020, whether axed, cut or suspended.

Market decline (20 Feb to 23 Mar 2020)

WORST SHARE PRICE PERFORMERS	TICKER	SECTOR	SPTR (%)	CHANGE IN DISCOUNT (%)
KKV Secured Loan Fund Ord	KKVL	Leasing	-64.6	-2.6
Riverstone Energy Ord	RSE	Commodities & Natural Resources	-63.7	-47.9
Amedeo Air Four Plus	AA4	Leasing	-60.8	-7.0
DP Aircraft I Ord	DPA	Leasing	-59.2	13.9
BMO Commercial Property Trust	BCPT	Property - UK Commercial	-58.7	-21.1
Doric Nimrod Air Two Ord	DNA2	Leasing	-58.5	-21.2
JPMorgan Smaller Companies Ord	JMI	UK Smaller Companies	-56.0	-9.8
Temple Bar Ord	TMPL	UK Equity Income	-55.4	2.0
NB Private Equity Partners Ord	NBPE	Private Equity	-54.8	-32.1
Aberforth Smaller Companies Ord	ASL	UK Smaller Companies	-54.3	-2.5
JPMorgan Mid Cap Ord	JMF	UK All Companies	-53.5	7.1
Henderson Smaller Companies Ord	HSL	UK Smaller Companies	-53.4	-3.0
Regional REIT Ord	RGL	Property - UK Commercial	-52.8	-15.6
Schroder UK Mid Cap Ord	SCP	UK All Companies	-52.8	0.6

Source: AIC/Morningstar

Market recovery (24 Mar to 30 Sep 2020)

BEST SHARE PRICE PERFOMERS	TICKER	AIC SECTOR	SP TR (%)	CHANGE IN DISCOUNT
Pacific Horizon Ord	PHI	Asia Pacific	125.8	19.6
Riverstone Energy Ord	RSE	Commodities & Natural Resources	95.2	47.9
Augmentum Fintech Ord	AUGM	Technology & Media	93.2	51.0
Scottish Mortgage Ord	SMT	Global	91.2	15.7
Baillie Gifford US Growth Ord	USA	North America	87.9	8.3
Baillie Gifford Shin Nippon Ord	BGS	Japanese Smaller Companies	87.4	12.6
Miton UK Microcap	MINI	UK Smaller Companies	84.5	17.3
Alternative Credit Investments plc	ACI	Debt - Direct Lending	81.8	41.9
Edinburgh Worldwide Ord	EWI	Global Smaller Companies	81.4	15.3
CQS Natural Resources G&I Ord	CYN	Commodities & Natural Resources	80.9	6.0
Pershing Square Holdings Ord	PSH	Hedge Funds	80.3	17.0
Baillie Gifford European Growth Trust	BGEU	Europe	78.4	9.3
Biotech Growth Ord	BIOG	Biotechnology & Healthcare	76.6	18.9
India Capital Growth Ord	IGC	Country Specialist: Asia Pacific ex Japan	76.2	16.4
Allianz Technology Trust Ord	ATT	Technology & Media	75.5	19.4

Source: AIC/Morningstar

Whole period (20 Aug 2019 to 30 Sep 2020)

BEST SHARE PRICE PERFOMERS	TICKER	AIC SECTOR	SP TR (%)	CHANGE IN DISCOUNT
CATCo Reinsurance Opps C	CATC	Insurance & Reinsurance Strategies	105.6	42.4
JPMorgan China Growth & Income plc	JCGI	Country Specialist: Asia Pacific ex Japan	90.3	10.6
Scottish Mortgage Ord	SMT	Global	88.0	-0.9
Baillie Gifford US Growth Ord	USA	North America	81.4	3.9
Pacific Horizon Ord	PHI	Asia Pacific	80.9	11.9
Biotech Growth Ord	BIOG	Biotechnology & Healthcare	69.5	6.5
Baillie Gifford European Growth Trust	BGEU	Europe	60.1	10.9
Fidelity China Special Ord	FCSS	Country Specialist: Asia Pacific ex Japan	54.8	4.0
Edinburgh Worldwide Ord	EWI	Global Smaller Companies	49.9	0.4
Pershing Square Holdings Ord	PSH	Hedge Funds	47.9	-1.8
Allianz Technology Trust Ord	ATT	Technology & Media	46.2	-1.8
Polar Capital Technology Ord	PCT	Technology & Media	46.0	2.2
HgCapital Trust Ord	HGT	Private Equity	41.7	17.5
JPMorgan Japanese Ord	JFJ	Japan	39.0	1.7
BB Healthcare Ord	BBH	Biotechnology & Healthcare	35.0	-1.4

Source: AIC/Morningstar

Market recovery (24 Mar to 30 Sep 2020)

WORST SHARE PRICE PERFORMERS	TICKER	AIC SECTOR	SP TR (%)	CHANGE IN DISCOUNT
DP Aircraft I Ord	DPA	Leasing	-71.9	-13.9
JZ Capital Partners Ord	JZCP	Flexible Investment	-40.6	-11.9
Marble Point Loan Financing Ord	MPLF	Debt - Structured Finance	-38.2	-21.3
EJF Investments Ord	EJFI	Financials	-24.7	-16.1
Symphony International Holding Ord	SIHL	Private Equity	-24.3	14.9
Electra Private Equity Ord	ELTA	Private Equity	-21.0	13.1
Standard Life Inv. Prop. Inc. Ord	SLI	Property - UK Commercial	-19.9	-9.9
JPEL Private Equity Ord	JPEL	Private Equity	-18.8	0.3
Life Settlement Assets A Ord	LSAA	Insurance & Reinsurance Strategies	-12.3	3.8
Schroder Real Estate Invest Ord	SREI	Property - UK Commercial	-11.1	-1.5
Tufton Oceanic Assets	SHIP	Leasing	-10.8	2.2
Schiehallion Fund Ord	MNTN	Growth Capital	-6.3	-8.4
Fair Oaks Income 2017 Ord	FAIR	Debt - Structured Finance	-5.8	28.6
KKV Secured Loan Fund C	KKVX	Leasing	-5.6	-1.1
KKV Secured Loan Fund Ord	KKVL	Leasing	-5.2	2.6

Source: AIC/Morningstar

Whole period (20 Aug 2019 to 30 Sep 2020)

WORST SHARE PRICE PERFOMERS	TICKER	AIC SECTOR	SP TR (%)	CHANGE IN DISCOUNT
DP Aircraft I Ord	DPA	Leasing	-90.3	-74.4
JZ Capital Partners Ord	JZCP	Flexible Investment	-79.7	-39.3
KKV Secured Loan Fund Ord	KKVL	Leasing	-77.6	-58.1
Amedeo Air Four Plus	AA4	Leasing	-60.9	-49.9
Crystal Amber Ord	CRS	UK Smaller Companies	-58.2	-9.4
Doric Nimrod Air Two Ord	DNA2	Leasing	-57.5	-49.7
Symphony International Holding Ord	SIHL	Private Equity	-57.0	-9.8
Doric Nimrod Air Three Ord	DNA3	Leasing	-57.0	-43.4
KKV Secured Loan Fund C	KKVX	Leasing	-52.7	-46.2
Riverstone Energy Ord	RSE	Commodities & Natural Resources	-52.3	6.2
Macau Property Opportunities Ord	MPO	Property - Rest of World	-50.2	-22.1
Standard Life Inv. Prop. Inc. Ord	SLI	Property - UK Commercial	-43.0	-35.8
Electra Private Equity Ord	ELTA	Private Equity	-42.9	-18.7
Aberforth Split Level Income Ord	ASIT	UK Smaller Companies	-41.6	-10.0
Temple Bar Ord	TMPL	UK Equity Income	-41.1	-8.5

Source: AIC/Morningstar

Dividend Announcements since 1 March 2020

Dividend changes announced by trusts since the pandemic sell-off.

FUND NAME	DATE OF ANNOUNCEMENT	HISTORICAL YIELD AS AT 28 FEBRUARY 2020
PROPERTY		
Alternative Income REIT	6 May / 6 August	7.8%
BMO Commercial Property Trust*	16 April / 4 August	6.2%
BMO Real Estate Investments	3 June	6.5%
CEIBA Investments	3 April	7.0%
Custodian REIT	9 April / 30 July	6.2%
Drum Income Plus REIT	17 April	7.7%
Ediston Property Investment Company	6 May	7.3%
Empiric Student Property	31 March	5.4%
LXi REIT	18 May / 17 September / 5 October	4.4%
Picton Property Income	28 April	3.6%
PRS REIT	31 March / 18 June	6.0%
Regional REIT	21 May / 26 August	7.3%
Schroder European Real Estate	15 April / 24 June / 15 September	6.3%
Schroder Real Estate	6 April / 20 July	5.6%
Standard Life Investments Property Income*	3 August	5.4%
Tritax Big Box REIT	8 April	5.2%
UK Commercial Property REIT	27 April	4.6%

NOTES

Quarterly dividend cut by 40% from 1.375p to 0.825p and then increased to 1.425p for quarter to 30 June 2020 reflecting strong rent collection

Dividends suspended on 16 April but reintroduced in August at 50% of previous level

Quarterly dividend cut by 50% from 1.25p to 0.625p

No year-end dividend declared in respect of FY2019

Quarterly dividends for H1 of FY ending 31 March 2021 will be broadly linked to net rental receipts, with support from reserves if required, but no less than aggregate of 1.5p vs previous quarterly rate of 1.6625p. On 30 July 2020 fund announced quarterly dividend of 0.95p after 92% of rent was collected in Q2 2020

Dividends suspended for next 2 quarters. Position will be reviewed again for the September 2020 quarter, which is also the fund's year-end

Monthly dividend reduced by 30% to 0.3333p

Future dividend distributions suspended until market conditions stabilise

Quarterly dividend cut from 1.4375p to 1.3p, followed by increase in guidance to 1.35p in respect of Q3 2020 and then additional increase to 1.44p in respect of Q4 2020

Quarterly dividend cut from 0.875p to 0.625p

Q3 dividend deferred for review in Q4 then declared at 1.0p per share. Target total dividend for FY ending 30 June 2020 reduced from 5p to 4p

Dividend of 1.90p declared for Q1 2020, in line with Q1 2019 but down from 2.55p paid for Q4 2019. Dividend of 1.50p declared for Q2 2020 with the aim of maintaining this level for the remainder of FY to 31 December 2020.

Future dividend payments announced as under review with anticipation of postponement or reduction, followed by announcement of 2nd quarterly dividend for FY to 30 September 2020 of 0.925 Euro cents, equating to 50% of target dividend level, followed by 50% increase to 1.39 Euro cents, equating to 75% of pre-Covid target level

Dividend payment for quarter to 31 March postponed, to be reviewed as clarity improved and with intention of paying it in part or whole at a later stage. Dividend reinstated at 50% rate of 0.38575p for quarter to 30 June

Quarterly dividend reduced to a rate of 60% of last year's level, equating to 0.714p

Dividend of 1.5625p declared for Q1 2020, down 9% from previous rate, and FY2020 dividend target of 7p withdrawn

Quarterly dividend reduced by 50% to 0.46p

FUND NAME	DATE OF ANNOUNCEMENT	HISTORICAL YIELD AS AT 28 FEBRUARY 2020
DEBT		
Blackstone/GSO Loan Financing*	23 April	12.5%
Chenavari Toro Income	30 April / 8 June	10.2%
CVC Credit Partners European Opportunities*	24 April / 25 September	5.5%
Fair Oaks Income	30 March / 20 July	12.1%
Marble Point Loan Financing	8 April / 23 July	10.9%
Starwood European Real Estate Finance	24 July	6.5%
TOC Property Backed Lending	31 March / 22 April / 3 August	5.8%
UK Mortgages	8 April / 22 July	7.1%
Volta Finance	2 April / 11 May	10.0%
LEASING		
Amedeo Air Four Plus	6 April / 24 July / 23 September	10.9%
DP Aircraft I	3 April	13.0%
KKV Secured Loan Fund*	18 March	15.0%
FLEXIBLE INVESTMENT		
Tetragon Financial Group	30 April	6.3%
PRIVATE EQUITY		
Princess Private Equity	1 May	5.8%

NOTES

Dividend target moved from €0.10 to between €0.06 and €0.07; quarterly dividend of €0.015 declared

25% reduction in quarterly dividend from €0.02 to €0.015, followed by announcement of enhanced dividend policy targeting dividend of 2.5% of NAV per quarter

Dividend target reduced from 5.5p / 5.5 Euro cents to 4p / 4 Euro cents but 8% medium-term TR target unchanged, followed by increase to 4.5p / 4.5 Euro cents for next 12 months

Declaration of dividends suspended in light of uncertainty then reinstated at variable rate on quarterly rather than monthly basis. First quarterly dividend of 1.5 cents announced at end of July

Dividends suspended as revenues expected to decline, then reinstated in July with declaration of quarterly rate of US$0.02, down from rate of US$0.025 for quarter to 31 December 2019 but in line with rate prior to this

Annual dividend target reduced from 6.5p to 5.5p from 2021 onwards in light of lower interest rate environment

Dividend of 1.5p due for payment on 3 April deferred until 1 June. Second and third quarterly dividends for current FY will not be declared, with a final balancing payment to be made at end of FY to at least fulfil investment trust requirements

Quarterly dividend reduced from 1.125p to 0.375p due to uncertain revenue outlook then increased to target of 4.5p p.a.

Dividend due to be paid on 28 April cancelled due to uncertainty. Reinstated at €0.10 versus previous rate of €0.155

Dividends suspended as discussions continued with Thai Airways and lending banks. Board stated it was hopeful that dividends could be reinstated in late October, followed by announcement of intention to declare an interim dividend of 1.15p in October. Board will re-assess whether continuous quarterly dividends can be resumed and at what rate once there is greater clarity on financial position of Emirates and Thai Airways

Dividends suspended until further notice

Dividends on ordinary and C shares suspended until further notice in light of ongoing uncertainty and in order to conserve liquidity. Dividends payable on 27 March were paid

Q1 2020 dividend of US$0.10 declared vs US$0.1825 for Q1 2019. Shareholder return policy modified in light of market conditions to include share repurchases

50% reduction in dividend guidance for FY2020, with total dividend not less than €0.29 (FY2019: €0.58)

FUND NAME	DATE OF ANNOUNCEMENT	HISTORICAL YIELD AS AT 28 FEBRUARY 2020
INFRASTRUCTURE		
GCP Infrastructure	29 May	6.5%
HICL Infrastructure	20 May	4.7%
UK		
Aberforth Split Level Income	30 July	6.1%
British & American	7 April	26.8%
Crystal Amber*	21 September	5.1%
Invesco Perpetual UK Smaller Companies	17 April / 23 July	3.6%
Temple Bar	23 September	4.5%
Troy Income & Growth	11 May	3.6%
GLOBAL		
Securities Trust of Scotland	17 September	3.3%
EUROPE		
Henderson EuroTrust	2 October	2.7%
ASIA & EMERGING MARKETS		
Genesis Emerging Markets	6 October	2.1%
Invesco Asia Trust	28 August	2.4%
Jupiter Emerging & Frontier Income	26 August	4.9%
SPECIALIST EQUITY		
Polar Capital Global Healthcare	22 July	1.0%

Source: Winterflood Securities, The Funds, Bloomberg as at 7 October 2020
*Denotes a corporate broking client of Winterflood Securities

NOTES

FY2021 dividend target reduced from 7.6p to 7.0p

FY2021 dividend target reduced from 8.45p to 8.25p. Dividend target of 8.65p for FY2022 removed with guidance to be revisited once economic recovery becomes clearer

4.22p dividend for FY to 30 June 2020 represents increase of 1.4% but supported by 0.75p of revenue reserves. Dividend expected to be cut in FY2021

Board will not recommend payment of final dividend for FY2019 and will review 2020 dividends as the year progresses

In FY2020 results it was announced that no interim dividend was declared in July 2020 in light of Covid-19

4% of share price target yield reduced to no less than 2% of share price as at 31 January 2021, paid from available revenue and capital. Board then stated in July that it was targeting dividend of at least 15p for current FY, with aim of increasing this annually

Dividend reduced by 25% to target of 38.5p per annum following appointment of RWC to replace Ninety One as investment manager

Dividend will be reduced to a more sustainable level with effect from FY starting 1 October 2020

Dividend reduced by 14% to 5.5p for current FY following appointment of Troy Asset Management to replace Martin Currie as investment manager

Dividend policy changed from progressive payments to paying out revenue received. FY2020 dividend reduced by 19% vs FY2019 to 25p

FY2020 dividend reduced by 10.5% to 17 cents from 19 cents in FY2019 following fall in income caused by reduction in dividends at holdings affected by Covid-19 as well as long-term shift in Emerging Markets towards lower income technology and internet companies

Enhanced dividend policy proposed to address discount, involving payment of six-monthly dividends equivalent to 2% of NAV on last business day of September and February

Board expects FY2020 dividends to total 4.4p, down 4.3% from 4.6p in FY2019. Total dividend for FY2021 expected to be at least 4.0p

Board intends to continue paying dividends in line with current policy but at reduced rate to reflect reduced level of income now being received from portfolio following repositioning, utilising revenue reserves where necessary to smooth payments

PROFESSIONAL PERSPECTIVES

WHERE AND WHAT NEXT?

SIMON ELLIOTT, *head of investment trust research at Winterflood Securities, looks back on 2020 and ahead to 2021.*

How well has the trust sector coped with the pandemic?

O VERALL, THE INVESTMENT trust sector has coped with the pandemic well. At the start of 2020 the sector found itself in rude good health: the sector average discount was sitting at just 1%, a historically narrow level, while new launches and additional capital raisings were buoyant. However, by mid-March the sector average discount had widened out to 22%, a level not seen since the Global Financial Crisis in 2008, while a number of specialist investment companies were forced to cut or suspend their dividend levels. Since then there has been a rapid recovery in ratings against a backdrop of rebounding markets and, while discounts remain wider than at the start of the year, they are comparable to the average levels over the last five years. In addition, the sector has continued to see fundraisings, while a number of specialist investment companies have seen fit to reinstate their dividend payments.

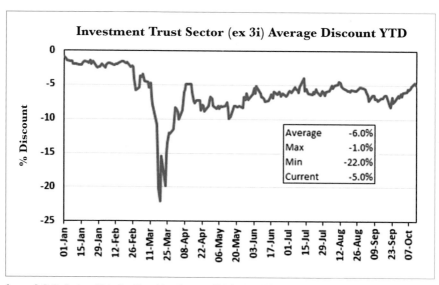

Source: Refinitiv Reuters, Winterflood Securities, data as at 13th October 2020

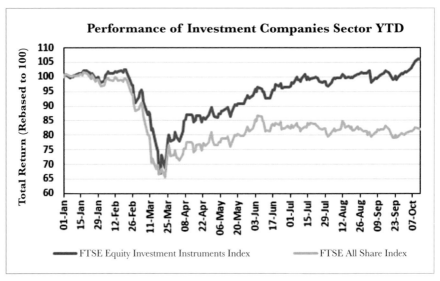

Source: Refinitiv Reuters, Winterflood Securities, data as at 13th October 2020

Discounts have been up and down this year – what is the outlook from here?

The trend over the last 10 years has been for discounts to narrow across the sector and we would expect this to continue over time. One of the key drivers for this trend is rising demand from often well-informed retail investors who are using platforms to access investment trusts, particularly the larger ones with strong performance records. In addition, trusts that can demonstrate an ability to maintain and grow their dividends are likely to remain in demand in a low interest rate environment.

Alternatively, those that constantly trade on wide discounts as a function of weak demand stemming from poor performance or out-of-favour asset classes are increasingly likely to see corporate activity. This may involve a change of manager or mandate, or even a return of capital including the ultimate sanction of liquidation. This could be driven by activist shareholders or in some cases long-term shareholders, who are increasingly focused on governance issues. In addition, the boards of independent directors have to demonstrate their fiduciary duty to all their shareholders and have become more proactive as the years have gone by.

Some subsectors, such as infrastructure and renewable energy infrastructure, continue to trade on significant premium ratings, reflecting their attractive yields and strong, long-term performance records. Others, such as commercial property and private equity, continue to languish on wide discounts, arguably as a function of the uncertainty over the valuations. I subscribe to the view that investment trusts always offer value opportunities to the informed investor and that is certainly true at present. While there are certain trusts that absolutely justify their wide ratings, there are others which lend themselves to a contrarian investment approach.

IPOs have been few and far between – do you think confidence will return next year?

Since the start of 2013 there have been over 100 IPOs across the sector, an unprecedented period of new launches. However, launching a new investment trust remains a difficult business, requiring substantial support from a dwindling pool of institutional investors, including the larger wealth managers, who have sufficient resources and the inclination to ensure critical mass on day one. The IPO market in 2021 will depend on market conditions. Asset managers and brokers are clearly incentivised to launch new products and there are a number of asset classes that remain in demand. However, 'me-too' products are increasingly given short shrift, with the preference being to provide additional capital to existing investment companies. If you are looking to raise new funds, you really do not want to be in the third or fourth cab off the rank…

Where would you like to see more launches and will they be mainly alternatives or equity trusts?

The IPO market over the last 10 years has been dominated by investment companies providing exposure to specialist illiquid asset classes, invariably with an attractive yield. This shows no signs of changing, and indeed is a good reason to use the closed-ended fund structure. One area that remains strongly in demand is renewable energy infrastructure, where the combination of attractive yields and socially responsible investing continues to prove attractive.

Equity investment trusts have been generally harder to launch over the last 10 years, as there is already a significant number, many of which trade on discounts. The unsuccessful IPO of Tellworth British Recovery & Growth Trust late in 2020 is perhaps reflective of the fact that there are many existing investment trusts exposed to UK small-caps that, at the time, were trading on widening discounts.

Is it right for wealth managers to say that you need to be large to do a successful IPO?

There was a time when £100m was the minimum market cap size that a wealth manager would consider before backing either an IPO or investing through the secondary market. However, as the largest wealth managers have grown even larger through both acquisitions and organic growth, the level has risen. £200m is now the minimum size for many, with some signalling a preference for even bigger launches. This reflects both the largest wealth managers' ability to write substantial tickets of tens of millions and their wariness of holding too large a position in an individual trust. Many will have internal limits of between 10% and 15%, with anything over 20% regarded as a potential issue, given liquidity considerations.

What has been the trend in secondary issuance and how might that develop?

While there was huge volatility in investment trust ratings in the market sell-off in March, most saw a rapid rebound and at present around 80 are trading either on premium ratings or around NAV. This compares with around 110 at the start of the year and represents around 25% of the sector. Despite this fall in premium rated trusts, regular secondary issuance has actually, perhaps surprisingly, been stronger in the first nine months of 2020 than it was in the same period a year earlier.

This reflects the fact that certain trusts have been able to issue significant amounts of new shares at a premium rating to their NAVs. This includes popular names such as Smithson Investment trust (SSON), Worldwide Healthcare Trust (WWH)*, Scottish Mortgage (SMT), Impax Environmental Markets (IEM) and Allianz Technology (ATT)*. Healthcare, technology and growth mandates have certainly captured investors' interest, but there has also been demand for defensive multi-asset trusts such as Personal Assets (PNL) and Capital Gearing Trust (CGT).

Market conditions will play a large part in the ratings of investment trusts over the next year and will in turn determine whether issuance at a premium is possible. However, in general, my expectation is for the larger, more successful trusts to continue to see strong demand.

Which sectors have been the biggest disappointment over the last 12 months?

In my opinion, the UK equity sectors have been the biggest disappointment in 2020 and the UK is on course for its worst calendar year return since 2008. Its underperformance has become a familiar story in recent years, partly reflecting its composition, with a large exposure to oil and gas and banks and a modest weighting to technology, but also the considerable political uncertainty that has bedevilled the UK over the last five years, including the Brexit vote and its many ramifications.

With Boris Johnson's general election victory in late 2019, it felt as if a corner had been turned and the UK market enjoyed a decent rally in the final months of 2019. However, the double whammy of the coronavirus and a slump in the oil price has left the UK market in the doldrums once again. In addition, the coronavirus has had a large impact on dividend payments this year, which has long been one of the key attractions of the UK market.

"INVESTMENT TRUSTS ALWAYS OFFER VALUE OPPORTUNITIES TO THE INFORMED INVESTOR."

Were you surprised by the number of changes in managers we have seen this year?

While every year can expect to see some management changes, 2020 has been particularly busy. This is partially a reflection of the disparity in the performance records of investment trusts, particularly when those with a value style are compared with those with a growth style. The outperformance of the latter is so large, it is not a surprise to see a number of investment trusts opt for a growth-orientated manager. Perhaps the biggest surprise of the year therefore was the decision by the Board of Temple Bar to maintain its value approach, by appointing RWC to replace Ninety One Asset Management. The team at RWC has a good long-term record but, in common with other value investors, have found the last few years difficult. To look through this and elect for the road less travelled is to the credit of that particular board, in my opinion.

Do you think it is premature to expect a revival in value as an investment style?

The valuation gap between growth and value styles has never been so great, not even in the tech boom of the late 1990s. There is an argument that this is unsustainable and that when there is greater economic certainty in the developed world value will have its day. However, to counteract this thesis is the evidence of the period after the global financial crisis in 2009. This led to huge monetary stimulus from central banks and unprecedented low interest rates. This was a boon for asset prices and growth investors in particular. My expectation is that what was true then will be true again and that growth managers will enjoy a significant tailwind for some time. That said, I believe that there are attractive returns to be made from deploying a value style, as long as the obvious value traps can be avoided. In addition, economic conditions will probably have to be in their favour, i.e. the worst of the pandemic will have to be behind us.

Are we going to lose some more dividend heroes in the next couple of years?

So far, we have seen three dividend heroes fall in 2020: British & American, Perpetual Income & Growth* (which is to merge with Murray Income) and Temple Bar. That leaves 18, all with records of 20-years consecutive dividend growth or more. The highest yielding hero at present is The Merchants Trust, which has a record of 38 consecutive years of dividend growth. While it has undoubtedly been hit hard by dividend cuts and suspensions from its portfolio holdings, its manager, Simon Gergel, is confident about the prospects for dividend resumptions and points out the trust's considerable revenue reserves. This is a familiar story across all of the remaining heroes and, assuming that we do see dividends being resumed across markets sooner rather than later, I would be surprised to see any more heroes fall. Certainly the managers and boards connected to these heroes are rightly proud of their records and appear to be willing to go the extra mile to preserve them.

Have boards generally made sensible use of revenue reserves to preserve their dividend capacity?

I believe that Boards have been sensible in their use of revenue reserves to date. For those investment trusts with an income element to their return profile, there is an implicit promise that revenue reserves will be used in the event of a rainy day and it is one of the oft-cited advantages of the trust structure. While perhaps it was difficult to envisage the extent of the storm of 2020, I still believe that shareholders expect revenue reserves to be used to provide greater dividend sustainability. These reserves also buy trusts more time to determine what the underlying dividend picture will be like as we go through 2021 and look to 2022. If the restoration of dividends is slower than is currently projected, there may be a reassessment as to whether it makes sense to continue funding income from reserves.

Have any trusts paid dividends out of capital as well – do you approve of that?

A number of investment trusts have adopted enhanced dividend policies over recent years in an attempt to attract new investors and narrow their discount levels. While this conversion of capital into income is controversial in some quarters, I believe that this is a legitimate use of the listed closed-ended fund structure as long as shareholders are aware of how their income is being created. Certainly JPMorgan Asset Management has enjoyed success with a number of their investment trusts in pursuing this policy, including JPMorgan Global Growth & Income* and JPMorgan Asia Growth & Income, both of which have moved from discounts to premium ratings.

Has there been any change in the trend towards lower fees – what is the future direction of travel?

There is no sign that the trend of recent years to lower investment management fees is fading. My view is that while it is right for independent boards to insist on highly competitive fee arrangements, particularly with an eye to the fee levels on any open-ended equivalent funds or immediate peers, we believe that the general abandonment of performance fees is a lost opportunity. To my mind, it is legitimate to incentivise the manager or investment team to generate outperformance, subject to appropriate benchmarks, measurement periods, high watermarks, and so on. In addition, in years of underperformance, the fee base would be reduced, thereby cushioning the impact on shareholders. That aside, one of the features that is being increasingly seen is the tiering of management fees, i.e. lower percentages being applied to higher asset levels. This is a positive development, in my opinion, and helps share economies of scale with shareholders.

Which sectors do you think might produce the best returns over the next three to five years?

Always a tricky question! I suspect that the consensus reply to this question is Asia, and in particular China, as well as healthcare and technology, i.e. all the things that have done so well in 2020. However, while the future growth prospects of companies in these sectors are indeed impressive, much of this is in the price. Consequently, I have a soft spot for slightly out-of-favour sectors such as UK mid- and small-cap sectors, where discounts have widened this year, and private equity, where some decent trusts find themselves on discount levels wider than 20%. Europe appeals to my contrarian nature too, despite a wave of negativity from UK-based investors. I think the trick is to ignore the continent's political machinations and consider the strength of the companies based there and their valuations relative to their US counterparts.

Anything else you would like to say about the year ahead?

As 2019 came to a close, UK-based investors were understandably focused on the outcome of the imminent general election and the country's relationship with the EU. While the ramifications of Brexit still linger, 2020 will of course be remembered for the impact of the coronavirus, something that for obvious reasons no mainstream commentator was forecasting as a realistic threat 12 months earlier. Investment is something akin to future gazing, despite repeated instances of events derailing even the wisest of sages. For me it shows the importance of diversification and, while hoping for the best, being prepared occasionally for the worst. The investment trust sector's illustrious 152-year history encapsulates feast, famine and war, and for me, the key lesson is the importance of adapting to changing circumstances. The sector's continuing evolution provides a window into both the world of investment management and the needs of a society prepared to part with its capital in exchange for the hope of attractive returns. Let's hope for a better year in 2021!

SIMON ELLIOTT has covered the investment trust sector since 2002 when he joined Winterflood Securities and has been head of investment trust research since 2008.

---

*   Denotes a corporate client of Winterflood Securities

ZOOMING WITH
THE ODD COUPLE

Editor JONATHAN DAVIS *caught up with* HAMISH BUCHAN *and* ROBIN ANGUS *to talk about the past, present and future of the investment trust business.*

A s soon as I heard the news last year that Hamish Buchan and Robin Angus were planning to retire from the board of Personal Assets this autumn, I immediately booked them for an interview in this year's *Investment Trusts Handbook*. For a period in the 1980s and 1990s these two very different characters – both unmistakeably Scottish in voice and manner – were the heads and public faces of an analyst team that regularly scooped up awards for the most penetrating and authoritative analysis of the investment trust sector.

Their annual reviews of the industry were must-read documents, the release of which used to attract a ballroom-size crowd of City folk, anxious to hear their ineffably un-rose-tinted assessment of the highs and lows, winners and losers of the year just gone. One of their favourite tools to dissect individual fund performance was so-called inertia analysis, which calculated how a trust would have performed if the managers had left the portfolio's geographical disposition unchanged for a year and merely performed in line with the geographical indices. The results were then compared to the result that the managers did in fact achieve with all the things they bought and sold during the year.

This was well before index tracking funds had become such a dominant feature of the investment landscape – the first index funds only appeared in the UK in the late 1990s – and the results of the inertia analysis invariably exposed how few fund managers were in fact adding much by the way of value through active management. In this respect, as in many ways, the Buchan-Angus team were well ahead of the game. A few years later they were prominent in warning of the dangers that the looming split-capital investment trust scandal could do to the sector that has been the focus of their professional lives for more than 40 years, during virtually all of which they have worked in tandem.

It is many years since these two disparate characters – sometimes known as the Odd Couple after the Walter Matthau-Jack Lemmon film of that name – stepped back from their analyst duties to focus on more hands-on careers in the trust world. While

Angus has concentrated on his duties as an executive director and public voice of Personal Assets (ticker PNL), Buchan has done multiple tours of duty as chairman and director of a string of investment trusts, of which Personal Assets, where he has been chairman since 2009, is among the largest and probably the best known, certainly amongst private investors.

Both men have played a huge part in the extraordinary success of a trust which can proudly claim to have both pioneered the effective use of zero discount and premium control mechanisms and demonstrated that it is possible to pursue a genuine absolute return investment strategy, designed to preserve shareholders' capital through all the ups and downs of the stock market cycle – a feat which nearly all hedge funds have expensively failed to achieve. It is 30 years this year since the late Ian Rushbrook, with Angus alongside, took over the management of a tiny failing investment trust with the aim of making it a distinctive self-managed trust that offered private investors something new and different from what the investment trust world had seen before.

Since 1990, the trust has grown from a minuscule £6m to its present leadership position in the flexible investment sector, with over 5,000 shareholders and some £1.3bn in assets. Although Rushbrook sadly died in 2008, just as the sub-prime market crash he had forecast so presciently was reaching its nadir, the trust has gone on from strength to strength, accelerating even, with Buchan as chairman, Angus as executive director and principal employee and Troy Asset Management as its investment adviser.

Much of this growth has come from the regular issuance of shares to new investors, made possible by the success of that pioneering zero discount control policy. Until 1999, and a change in the regulations (which marks what Angus dubs "discount freedom day"), investment trusts were unable to buy back shares and hold them in Treasury for subsequent reissuance at a small premium, which is the essence of how an effective discount and premium control mechanism can be made to work.

Buchan and Angus are not giving up on the investment trust sector, though. After giving up their roles as directors of Personal Assets in September this year, they are in the throes of setting up a charity, the PAT Foundation, to help promote knowledge and understanding of the investment trust sector, beginning with Scotland and building on the more informal work which they have been doing through their professional careers (and in Buchan's case through another charity that brings financial education to sixth forms at Scottish schools). The plans are still being finalised, but will include funding prizes and potential internships for undergraduates from disadvantaged backgrounds, initially at a number of Scottish universities.

"The investment trust industry has been very good to us" says Angus "and we want to give something back and try to pass on some of our enthusiasm to another generation". Is there anything you can do to help the benighted English, I ask, tongue in cheek? Well, replies Buchan in terms, it is not impossible. There is no point in competing with other charities trying to do the same thing, and who knows how far the good work might spread in time, but "I don't think we will still be around if and when it reaches every single university in the UK".

Surely the notoriously financially canny Scots don't need help – or is that myth, I say? "I am afraid" says Angus "that 2007–08 demonstrated the answer to that, with the Royal Bank of Scotland and the Bank of Scotland. Mind you, it shows what a bad prophet I am because when the Bank of Scotland and the Royal Bank went bust, I said that Scottish nationalism was dead for a generation. It wasn't even dead for a month!"

Going back to the seeds of their long and productive partnership, Buchan hired Angus in 1981 after the latter had spent four years at Baillie Gifford and started his lifelong fascination with investment trusts. Buchan himself started out as an actuarial student at an insurance company in 1963 and on joining the broking firm of Wood Mackenzie in 1969 became an investment trust analyst. He remained there until 2000 through its many corporate successors (the firm changed ownership five times after Big Bang). Buchan has always been a people and numbers guy, while Angus is the one who brings both analytical nous and an extravagant verbal facility that draws heavily on references from classical literature.

The most striking aspect of their careers – and one they are keen to emphasise when we eventually sit down to talk (remotely, via Zoom, naturally) – is how rapidly and how fast the business they work in has changed over the years. The 1970s, when Buchan was starting out, was a terrible time for investment trusts, encompassing as it did a severe bear market, capital controls, unprecedentedly high levels of taxation (capital gains tax having been introduced in 1965) and the first evidence that insurance companies, the backbone of most trust share registers, were ready to start developing their own investment expertise, rather than contracting it out to investment trusts.

"The trust sector had really had its day" Buchan says now. "It had a fantastic run through the late Forties, Fifties and Sixties because of the leverage trusts could use and because they were offering a product which institutions wanted. By the Seventies, however, the institutions were beginning to do their own thing. They didn't need the trust sector any more". At one point so weak was sterling as the UK morphed into "the sick man of Europe" that the dollar premium, effectively the extra amount investors had to pay in order to invest their money overseas, amounted to a quarter of the value of the whole investment trust sector. The average investment trust discount for years was around 20 per cent and widened to more than 40 per cent at its worst.

Nevertheless, though it is hard to believe now, in the early 1970s the investment trust sector was still three times the size of the unit trust business. Now it is the other way round; open-ended funds are five times as popular as investment trusts, and both are riding high on the back of many years of falling interest rates and strong stock market performance. That is not all to do with performance; as Buchan says, over his five decades in the funds business, he is happy to bet that the aggregate alpha* across the whole collective fund management business has been negative, as inertia analysis used to suggest. Yet investment trusts, though their shares are more volatile, have generally had the better of any statistical comparisons of performance.

Will that continue? The industry cannot afford to be complacent, he says. One of the reasons for the relative outperformance of investment trusts has been that their open-ended competitors for many years had to shoulder the cost of absorbing higher fees and trail commission to intermediaries – a powerful incentive for driving new business in their direction (which is why unit trusts outsold investment trusts for years), but at the same time a barrier to delivering superior returns. Since the Retail Distribution Review in 2013, and faced with the relentless rise of passively managed funds, investment trusts no longer have the guarantee of lower costs to help them perform better.

The important point though is that trusts have always had the advantage of better corporate governance, semi-permanent capital, gearing and – not least – the need to adapt to survive. "The sector has this self-cleansing process, if you like. You cannot get rid of tiny unit trusts. The only time you seem to be able to get rid of unit trusts is when two fund managers merge and, say, they have got two Japanese Smaller companies funds. They will put them together, and keep the track record of the better one to publicise the fund". But there is "no divine right to exist as investment trusts". The history of the trust sector is one of continuous comings and goings as trusts that fail to perform disappear and new ones are launched.

Mind you, Angus chips in, he and Buchan retired as analysts before the arrival of most of the alternative asset trusts – property, infrastructure, reinsurance, debt funds and so on – which now account for almost half the value of the investment trust sector. "I have a lot of admiration" says Buchan "for the three or four brokers who still send out their daily notes on all this. It is amazing how much knowledge they have had to acquire to understand these companies. It is not like dealing with listed securities. They are very different".

The trust structure is of course well suited to these kind of investments. The regulator, he goes on, should put an end to the problem of open-ended property funds, which three times in the last 12 years have had to be "gated" because of illiquidity issues (during the financial crisis, after the Brexit vote and again this year in the wake of the pandemic). Why not, he says, instead of investment trusts being unitised, do it the other way round and insist that the open-ended property funds become investments trusts instead? The main reason that so many property trusts are currently trading

---

* Alpha = in financial theory, the excess returns a fund manager can achieve through successful stock selection relative to the return of a benchmark index.

at a discount during crises is because there is a time lag between the market turning down and valuations being published, so prices quickly adjust.

"Don't get them started on the shortcomings of regulators", I recall somebody telling me before we do this Zoom interview, and sure enough, Angus and Buchan are united in decrying the absurdity of the KIDs (key investor documents) which have been foisted on the investment trust industry by over-zealous European regulators who know nothing about how investment trusts work. The projections of what might happen in a market crash, which in KIDs are based on extrapolating past performance, predictably turned out to be "absolute rubbish" when the market plunged in March this year.

Another contentious issue is the threat to investment trusts from the rise of passive funds. Angus is not a fan of indexing; "managing an index fund must be like driving a car with no brakes and no steering wheel. When the slippage starts, nobody is in control. The index just drives you lower and lower". Buchan says he can see why some people find them useful for part of their portfolio, but reserves his greater fears for exchange-traded funds that use derivatives, rather than physical ownership, to replicate the strategy they are pursuing. That is a potential disaster in the making, just as many years ago the split-capital scandal could be seen coming well in advance.

Fears of the underlying security of ETFs was one reason why Personal Assets has switched its chunky holdings of gold out of ETFs and into physical bars, now safely stored in the vaults of JPMorgan in London. The fees, says Angus, are also much lower, six basis points instead of 40 basis points for the ETF. The difference more than pays for the fees of the directors of the trust each year.

Ah yes, fees, a hot topic in the trust world these days. Buchan approves of fees coming down, but says the good news is that trust boards are waking up to the fact that what matters is not so much the level of fee but whether they are tiered as the size of a trust rises. Neil Woodford in his heyday while at Invesco, he points out, was earning £200m a year in management fees when he was running £20bn of investors' money. Yet he would have had exactly the same portfolio if he had a tenth as much money to look after. "The fact is funds that size are just a cash cow when they are holding the same stocks for so many clients".

The problem, he says, is that too many fund managers "come to think that it is their money". For years there was nobody on the board of the Investment Association, the open-ended fund trade body, representing the people whose money it actually was. They all seemed to be current or retired chief executives of the big fund management houses. Boards of investment trusts "should always be looking to see how they can save a bit of money – it all belongs to the shareholder at the end of the day. Too many people have been ripped off over the years".

Which brings us back to the issue of corporate governance. Buchan thinks that the board of Woodford Patient Capital should never have included so many people from the companies that Woodford was subsequently to invest in. He mentions another example of a blatant conflict of interest at a well-known trust where he was on the board and it turned out that without telling the board the investment manager had become a director of a company in which the trust also held a large position. "We told him straightaway that either he stepped down immediately, or we would sell the entire position in the company". He goes on to recount a number of other examples of blatant poor behaviour by directors, managers and auditors that he has come across in his years of board experience.

"Woodford's real problem," Buchan says, "was that he just thought he walked on water. People wouldn't say no to him and therefore he got away with pushing and pushing the rules. It was a disaster and it shouldn't have been allowed to happen. For the investment trust sector, fortunately, it is just the one vehicle that was affected".* He thinks that the FCA should devote particular attention to monitoring new management firms in their first few years to make sure that they are not bending the rules.

Mostly however, he says, the FCA seems content to leave boards of trusts to do the heavy lifting that the regulator has to shoulder elsewhere, and that is no bad thing. Standards of governance are much improved and assuming boards do their job there is no danger of our returning to the bad old days of the 1970s and a 40 per cent average discount. Angus notes with a chuckle how people keep coming up to him and saying how much he must be fed up and depressed with the way the market has been performing in the wake of the virus. "One of them asked me that on the very day when the share price of my two biggest holdings, Personal Assets and Scottish Mortgage, reached all-time highs!"

The story of the year has been that, on average, thanks to diversification and its global focus, the trust sector has done its job of protecting investors from the worst of the pandemic's effects. Shareholders' memories remain short however, says Buchan, and it may be worth remembering that the worst stock market crises tend to come round at 10-yearly intervals. P. G. Wodehouse once observed that it is never difficult to distinguish between a Scotsman with a grievance and a ray of sunshine, but the Odd Couple rightly seem more than happy with what they have wrought over the years.

---

* Woodford Patient Capital, now renamed Schroder Public and Private (ticker SUPP) and with a new investment manager.

SECRETS OF A TECH INVESTOR

WALTER PRICE, *manager of the Allianz Technology Trust, explains what has been driving the remarkable surge in technology stocks.*

How did you get to become an investor in tech stocks?

I went to study at MIT, but to be an engineer, not an investor. In my junior year I was working as a design engineer for a company called Teradyne that makes test instrumentation. During that summer, I worked for an extraordinary engineer and found that unlike him I wasn't extraordinary. His ability to visualise circuit design, which was what I was involved in, was just much better than mine. So I decided to go on to Sloan [MIT's management school] because he said there are other ways to be involved in a company than just engineering.

I really liked those classes and did well in them. I did a project at Sloan on mutual funds and I found that some of the mutual funds that we examined using SEC data outperformed over a period of time. That was the time of modern portfolio theory and the random walk and everybody saying you couldn't outperform as a fund manager. I thought "well, some of these guys are doing it, so maybe I should look seriously at this industry". So, when I was offered a job, I jumped at it. I worked in Boston for a couple of years and then moved to what was then Rosenberg Capital on the West Coast. And I've been there ever since.

How did that develop your style of investing?

Rosenberg Capital was started by a guy named Claude Rosenberg who was a growth investor. He had written a book about growth investing and that philosophy appealed to me. They hired me as a chemical analyst, not as a technology analyst, because technology was less than 10 per cent of the S&P at that point, whereas chemicals and materials were 20 per cent. It was a hot sector in the Seventies. I took over technology because nobody was covering it and I said "I know something about this area". I started following it, started building credibility with some of my stock picks, and then after about 10 years we hired another chemical analyst and I focused on technology. That's the story.

I don't suppose you spend a lot of time thinking about modern portfolio theory in the day job now?

I don't think much about modern portfolio theory. My philosophy is if you find good companies at good valuations and they grow at 20 or 30 per cent for a reasonable period of time, the valuation takes care of itself and the company grows into its valuation – particularly if you pick a company that's developing a new area or a much lower cost way of doing things. Initially they may look expensive, but if you pick the right company they'll grow into their valuation and keep growing after that. There may be periods of time when the valuation corrects, but those companies will grow through it if you pick the right company and the right sector. Technology has got all these sub-sectors that have very long periods of high growth. That's the reason why I'm attracted to that area.

Is your engineering and chemical knowledge relevant to what you're doing now?

The technologies that I learned in school are totally irrelevant. I think having a critical mind is the most important thing in investing, not just accepting what the companies are telling you, but trying to understand what's driving the growth, why it's going to continue, what the benefit is that you're bringing to users. You can obviously do that without a technical background, because we have to learn new technologies all the time.

Whenever I go into a new area, I have to study it for months, I have to meet with competitors and different participants in the sector to try to understand what's driving it. There's not a lot of help from Wall Street, because it's usually a small sector and so they're not spending a lot of time on it. With my partners, I have to learn these new areas. We're doing that all the time.

I think it helps to know that we've done it in the past. It is easier to find the new high growth areas, because in the area that we're in, in San Francisco, there's a lot of venture capital, there are a lot of friends going to new companies that are still private and they're talking about what the hot company is and what the hot trend is. It is a little bit easier to focus on the things that people are excited about and learn about them. Some of those things aren't good investments and some of them are. Constantly having a curious and sceptical mind is essential.

Are there common features in the way the technology sector performs?

One common feature is that when a sector is recognised, initially there's the discovery process and people jump into the sector, get enthusiastic about it, and the stock prices very often overshoot. I would use Tesla as an example of that. Initially when we bought the stock the common view was: no car company had been successful in 50 years and so everybody said it was going to go bankrupt, like every other car company. There was very high short interest *[Editor: a lot of investors betting that the share price would fall]*.

I had bought one of the cars and my co-manager, Huachen Chen, bought one of the cars and we both said "this is a really good car". We really enjoyed driving it. Our view was: they're not going to go bankrupt because more people are going to buy these cars as they realise they're good cars. The stock went from $20 dollars to $250 dollars in a couple of years. Then our question was: we know they make a good car, but how many people are going to buy a $100,000 car? Can they make money being a car company?

The stock had overshot our objectives, so we sold the stock. It promptly went into what I would call a period of proving itself for about two or three years where the stock sat around that level. Then the company started making money and started bringing out cheaper cars. The Model 3 was a huge hit. The Model Y we think is an even bigger hit. They got a new CFO who focused on profitability, they raised some more money, and we realised "this company is going to make money".

So we bought the stock back when we started doing the math on their incremental profitability. We saw that the company could easily earn $5 a quarter in the fourth quarter. That was a year ago. That's a $20 dollar annualised rate at a $300 price. That's only 15 times earnings. That's a pretty reasonable evaluation for a company that's growing 50 per cent a year. So we said it's time to buy the stock back and we did, although it was super controversial and there continued to be high short interest. We saw that the company is now going into another phase where earnings are going to power the stock.

To make the case for the stock at today's valuation you have to believe that the company is going to continue to grow their revenues at 40 or 50 per cent a year and the company is going to have to be quite profitable, not just a little profitable – not just the 10 per cent operating margins we were assuming when we bought the stock back then! Actually I think that's possible because they're moving into lower cost manufacturing. Fremont is the worst place to make a car in the world; it has the highest costs and the lowest efficiency. Texas, China, and Germany, those are places that know how to make cars much better than in Fremont. I think there's a reasonable possibility that the company could have 20 per cent margins because of the software capability of the company.

We've cut back the stock a couple of times as it's gone up, but that's the process that very often these tech stocks will go through. I think Salesforce.com went through that same process and then they got religion about profitability after the financial crisis in 2008/2009 and started focusing on making money, as well as growing revenues, the stock got rerated and the category got rerated. We see that process all the time.

What is the most important trend in the technology at the moment?

What we've seen is the consumer adopt new technologies and new ways of doing things associated with the internet. I can't live without Google. Facebook is an interesting way to spend time. Those companies weren't around 10 or 15 years ago. So, they've made my life much easier. Amazon's made my life much easier. Those companies have been growing rapidly, but they've also sucked away the oxygen from newspapers and now TV. It's much more efficient. Even old school advertisers have to respond to return on investment and what their competitors are doing. The ROI on a targeted ad is so much higher than blasting something out where 95 per cent of the people watching it couldn't care less.

On the consumer side, you could say the same thing, that e-commerce was growing rapidly but the pandemic poured gasoline on that trend. That is why you have these huge stores of value now in the case of Apple, Amazon, to a great extent Microsoft, Facebook, Google – huge, trillion-dollar companies. I think the same thing is now going to happen, or is in the process of happening, on the enterprise side. They're redoing the infrastructure of the world, it's going to be based around cloud computing, artificial intelligence and software as a service. You're taking 10 or 20 or 30 years of embedded technology and you're transitioning it over a period of 10 years. The pandemic has shown that these new businesses are much more resistant to economic cycles. If you are a subscription-based business, growth rates will slow down, but they keep growing.

This new infrastructure of the world is being built around these new technology companies – cloud computing companies, like Amazon, Microsoft, Alibaba in China, and the SaaS (software as a service) companies. There are 10 or 15 different SaaS companies that we own in different parts of the enterprise value chain. I think they are all going to continue to grow rapidly and create value for investors. It's an exciting time. Then you have Tesla that is transforming the auto industry, electric cars, connected cars, like Apple transformed the phone industry. Your car is going to be a different item from the previous hundred years of internal combustion cars, just like your smartphone is a different item than it was.

We see this happening in other industries too. Factories are being remade digitally with digital twins. They're taking information from sensors in your factory and putting them into a model in the cloud and monitoring what your best operators do and what your best practices are, and you're tuning your processes, reducing the waste of your factory, and increasing the efficiency. The transformation is going to take a while, but it's going to be great for the guys who are participating in that transformation and many of them are technology companies.

Is it sensible to think about technology as a standalone sector, given that it is now pervading all aspects of industry?

The way we think about the technology sector is that it includes the companies that do technology well and are primarily driven by technology. I think you're right that every company has to become a technology company. The last one to change is probably the food industry. But every company is being impacted by technology, whether it is AI or analysing how you can do things better. Everybody needs productivity, the world needs productivity.

Even if you're an air conditioning manufacturer, if you don't do technology well, then some variant of Tesla with their filtering technology and more efficient electrical motor technology has the possibility of running you over.

So you'd better do technology well. You'd better focus on it, you'd better assimilate it, you'd better hire software people or have software consultants and workers that can transform your company. In that sense, every company has to have a technology capability or know how to access technology to be able to survive in this world that we're embarking on.

A few years ago people were saying General Motors is a technology company. They're investing in Cruise and electrical vehicles – and for a period of time General Motors was a really good stock because people were looking at sum of the parts valuations – you had the auto company valued at X and the autonomous electrical vehicle business valued at Y. They'd use the analogy of Tesla and say that GM is worth 50 per cent more than they're selling for because of its technology component. But the fact is that the technology component of GM is simply not competitive with Tesla. We're finding out that they've cut back the funding of Cruise because they can't compete, and they don't have an economically viable model. The theory goes away if you're not really good at technology.

So our view is that the best technology companies are built from the ground up to be technology companies. We own the company Twilio and their engineers are on call 24/7. If a customer has a problem, they get out of bed at one in the morning on a Sunday and they respond to the problem. That isn't going to happen at General Motors! The importance of companies that are built from the ground up in technology, the pure players as we call them, was one of the early lessons that I learned. It is very difficult for incumbents to keep up with the pure companies.

What about banking? Is it possible for a large bank to re-engineer their technology to become a tech company in any sense?

I would say again, it's really hard. The large banks of the world have very good technology departments; they spend a lot of money on technology. The large banks spend 15 per cent of their revenues on technology. That's as high as any company around except for pure technology companies. Do I think that banks can transition? Yes. Do I think that a pure fintech company is a better investment? I think yes. Would I rather own Square or PayPal than Chase, which has Chase Paymentech, the largest payment processor in the world? Yes. I'm not going to bet on Chase leading the world in fintech, as powerful as they are. I'm not putting J.P. Morgan in the portfolio instead of these other stocks.

In such a fast-moving sector how do you look to manage the portfolio?

I think there are two things we do. One is, as the British call it, we top slice our portfolio. We take some money off the table in stocks that are doing really well so they don't become super large positions in the portfolio. The other thing we do is we're constantly watching how management is executing. If management is struggling, then we'll reduce or sell the position. It's really hard to manage a company growing at 50 per cent a year.

The companies that do that well over a long period of time, meaning more than five years, are very few. We try to own them if they're executing well and they can be wonderful investments, but there are a lot of companies that try and fail. They just can't hire the people, they can't handle the new product and the old product asset allocation. I think having an active manager is a good idea in technology investing.

If we look at the great investments in technology, they always have great management. I would say maybe Alphabet [=Google] is an exception to that. That's been a great investment and I think that the management is solid, it's the best business in the world, but they've kind of lost that founder zeal for focusing on shareholders. They are shareholders, but they're not big shareholders. In most cases we like managements that we would want to work for, because in a technology company, your employees are your fuel and you need your employees to love to work there and want to work really hard.

Your trust has produced a total return of more than 700 per cent over 10 years. Do you still have regrets at things you have missed?

If you look at the technology index – one of my partners, Huachen Chen, has done this analysis – most of the appreciation over the last several years has come from just six companies. So, our biggest mistake has been not having 10 per cent of the portfolio, the most we can own of an individual stock, in those six companies. That would have been so much easier than trying to find the Teslas or Zooms that can outperform those six companies, because most companies don't in technology.

We didn't own enough Apple last year. That was one of the reasons that we didn't perform as well as the indices. Apple had an 80 per cent increase in valuation on flat earnings! We saw it coming, but we thought it was going to come this year, not last year. So we didn't have enough Apple. You could say we didn't have enough of any of those six companies because they've been such extraordinary investments. We keep thinking it's harder to double when you're a $1 trillion company than if you're a $20 billion one. Yet, some of these companies have acted as if there's no problem doubling from a trillion dollars.

Don't you worry that the market has become so concentrated at the top end?

Well, those stocks are not extremely expensive. In the case of Apple, its valuation has gone from 10 times earnings to 30 times earnings. It's been revalued as more of a software and services company than a hardware company. But 30 times earnings for a company about to embark on a hardware cycle and with an increasing percentage of software and services in the mix, you could argue that's what it should have been selling for all along.

Facebook is another example. Yes, it's done extraordinarily well, but it's still only in the low twenties in terms of multiple of earnings. These stocks are not super expensive. Can they keep going? We own all those stocks, so we obviously think they can. Do we think that some of these other companies that are growing faster and have higher valuations will grow into their valuations and keep going? Yes, we do. That's why our portfolio has other stocks instead of just six.

Can you give examples of companies that could grow into their valuations?

Twilio is a company that we're very enthusiastic about, as is the whole communications area, whether it's Twilio, Zoom, or RingCentral. We think there's a lot of reasons for communications to change from being just a phone attached to a piece of hardware in your office or home to a communications service that involves messaging, video, and voice. That industry is being transformed and it's still early in its transformation. All of those companies are continuing to grow rapidly and the pandemic has reinforced that trend. The idea that people can be in different places and still communicate and work efficiently means that industry is changing dramatically.

A second area is the whole software area that I talked about, where Salesforce.com is the leader in the transformation of software-as-a-service. Some of these companies are expensive, like Veeva, a vertical healthcare software company that is basically developing the infrastructure and software for the healthcare industry. Rather than each company building its own software stack for sales, product development, product management, compliance, safety and so forth, why not have one company build it for the whole industry? It's so much more efficient.

You're not going to distinguish yourself with your sales software system versus your competitor. You are going to distinguish yourself with your product and how you tell the story. The idea of infrastructure software as something that one company manages and runs for an industry is going to become more popular. Those are examples where the world is transitioning to a new model and they're in the middle of it.

Did you expect that the pandemic would lead to such a strong performance this year?

What we weren't expecting was for the monetary authorities to reduce interest rates to basically zero and come to the rescue of a lot of industries: the airline industry, the travel industry, different aspects of the infrastructure industry, like real estate. They've come in and kept them alive because they don't want a depression. The result of that is you've had a reduction in the discount rate that you use on equities. Offsetting that, you've obviously had really bad earnings results from a lot of companies. You may have a higher multiple on earnings, but if the earnings are a lot lower, then the net effect is still a lower stock price. For a lot of companies that haven't had resilient earnings, the higher multiple has netted out to be about a zero factor.

But for technology, we had this view that the new models were much more resilient and that earnings wouldn't decline. We saw that in 2008/2009, when the new models held up well. The growth rates of the earnings went down, but the earnings did not decline, they just grew at a lower rate. We felt that would happen again. That's why we owned a lot of those companies and when we restructured the portfolio, we held on to those companies. What we didn't expect, as we emerged out of this pandemic and life went back to the new normal, was that companies would say we've got to go faster on digital transformation because it is the key to getting customers back and getting revenue growth back.

The double impact of the growth rate being pretty stable and in some cases accelerating, and the discount rate that you pay for that growth going down – that's why technology has done well, I think.

Do you think that this favourable backcloth will continue?

I think the outlook for the next year is continued good growth in earnings and improvements in profitability. The pandemic has shown a lot of these companies they can be more efficient. We own a payroll processing company. They got really hurt because their customers laid off employees, but they also got really helped by the fact that their salesmen, instead of doing two meetings a week, because they had to travel to the customer, and assemble all the people at the target company that they needed to discuss why their payroll system was better than somebody else's, now they can just do five meetings a day on Zoom.

Their sales are at record levels because they have such a compelling story. They can tell the HR department "you can pay for our system in six months, which is an extraordinary payback". The growth in new business has accelerated, even though the existing business has declined. I think you see that story in a lot of technology companies. Having just a few key decision makers, with all the supporting people on the Zoom call, is a much more efficient process; it's a more efficient meeting and the customer can make the decision faster and get to value faster. If the solution gives you productivity, higher sales and more efficiency, then it helps these companies to make those decisions faster. And that's what they want right now.

Why aren't we seeing all this show up in terms of rising productivity?

Technology is still a small part of spending for companies. It's five or 10 per cent spending of their revenues. It's going to take a while. Just as in the early Nineties, when we had a revolution in PCs, there was a big argument as to whether it was efficient or not. Then once we started getting the investment made in the mid-Nineties, we saw a burst of productivity for the next five or 10 years. If you look at the percentage of operations that are running in the cloud for the typical company, it's less than five per cent. So yes, development and R&D has been transformed, but development and R&D are not very important to a company's productivity. What's important to their productivity is getting the new things running in their operations. Less than five per cent of manufacturing has a digital twin involved. We're at the beginning of this productivity improvement but I'm confident it will show up.

What is your main pitch to potential investors in your trust?

The message that we give to financial advisors and individual investors is that technology is a complex area. We're working really hard to figure it out and create capital appreciation for their portfolios. If the trust goes to a discount, if technology has a period of being less popular, average down. Over time, we think they're going to be happy with the investment. For someone with a five-year horizon, you can be comfortable that the long-term growth of the sector will come through. I think that message works well for shareholders who look at us as part of their growth portfolio, to build their wealth over time.

There are always different ways to invest. When I first started the business there was the Nifty Fifty concept. You'd just own 50 stocks and you'd never have to worry about valuation or anything – one decision stocks, they were called. Then they all went down. As I look at the big technology giants, the biggest threat to them is not their business and their ability to grow, it's what kinds of constraints our governments and society are going to put on these companies because they've gotten so big and so powerful there are going to be some constraints for sure. The EU has already extracted billions of dollars from these companies and they're not going to stop. The US government is saying we need to think about that too. There are going to be more taxes. Amazon pays sales taxes now. There'll be a constant sharing of success, I guess.

WALTER PRICE is the lead manager of the £1 billion Allianz Technology Trust and has 40 years of experience in investing in technology. Allianz manages $4 billion of technology assets.

DISCIPLINE IS THE KEY

JOHN BARON *explains how he came to specialise in the selection and management of investment trust portfolios.*

What was the first investment trust you ever bought for yourself and why? Do you still own it?

It was Scottish Mortgage Trust (SMT) in 1987 during a brief period of R&R at home when serving in the Army. This was long before Baillie Gifford adopted its more 'growth' orientated approach, so the performance was not quite as stellar as it has been in recent years! I seem to remember its global remit and solid track record appealed. I no longer own the company, but still recommend it.

Did you know anything about investment trusts before you joined the City?

A little bit – some basic research made clear even then that investment trusts in general performed well relative to other types of fund, were able to gear a portfolio and possessed an independent board to help oversee progress on behalf of shareholders. Their 150-year history was also of interest. However, it was not until the City that I came to fully appreciate their worth.

How has your earlier experience in the Army helped your investment career?

It probably helped develop a sense of independence and discipline. Although during my gap year I had driven cars from London to their owners in Iran just prior to the revolution, it was not until the Army did these qualities become truly honed. The importance of properly weighing up competing factors (risk analysis) before making decisions and then seeing them through are important attributes – particularly when it comes to investment and making contrarian calls. Risk thereafter was always seen in perspective.

What were the most important things you learned during your time in the City at Hendersons and Rothschild Asset Management?

In some ways, they were very different organisations. Henderson Private Clients did not operate a centralised list of portfolio holdings for most clients and this allowed fund managers greater latitude. This became apparent to me when I was approached by Rothschild to run their private client core list. The distinction is important because the former encouraged individual flair and the latter team discipline – each had their advantages and disadvantages.

Why did you start writing your Investors Chronicle column?

There was no shortage of good commentary on individual stocks and markets but little attempt to weld this together into a portfolio. All investors make mistakes but the real challenge is to outperform the benchmarks. So, having approached a number of people, Jonathan Eley at the Investors Chronicle was brave enough in 2009 to allow me to start writing a monthly column which to this day reports on the progress of two real investment trust portfolios. While I am never complacent, both have performed well. I enjoy writing the column and donate the fee to charities.

Has the Retail Distribution Review been more or less helpful for investment trusts than you hoped?

The investment landscape has been tilted in unit trusts' favour for so long that any improvement was always going to be gradual. RDR was a welcome development, essentially because it no longer allowed open-ended funds to reward IFAs for recommending them to clients. In part because of their structure, investment trusts do not do this. But while recognising that they are growing in popularity, there is still a long way to go.

For example, research from the AIC last year found that, despite the RDR rules being introduced in 2013, around just 5% of the money invested on advisor platforms was accounted for by investment trusts. Something is wrong when the best fund is coming a poor second. The latest edition of my book (*The Financial Times Guide to Investment Trusts*) explores this in more detail.

What is the biggest mistake investors in investment trusts make?

Impatience or trying to take advantage of short-term mispricing is probably one of them. By their very nature, investment trusts are more volatile than their open-ended cousins because the share price is influenced by a range of factors other than just their Net Asset Value per share. Discounts can vary accordingly. This can create opportunities and pitfalls.

Having the humility to stick with good quality trusts over time usually results in better long-term performance than constantly dealing. It can also save on dealing costs. This is certainly the approach we adopt when reporting in real-time to members on the progress of the nine investment trust portfolios on our website www.johnbaronportfolios.co.uk.

Are the nine portfolios you describe in your website real portfolios?

Yes – all nine are real (i.e. they exist in fact). Five portfolios represent a risk-adjusted investment journey which, over time, increasingly diversifies away from equities into other assets (mostly bonds, infrastructure, renewable energy, 'capital preservation', commodities, gold, etc) to help protect past gains while generating a higher income. The four remaining portfolios pursue distinct objectives including high income and environmental protection.

How would you describe the process you use to manage the portfolios?

The portfolios pursue a range of investment strategies and income objectives. However, their common remit is to invest in entrepreneurial 'growth' companies which have the potential to grow and create wealth in excess of the market over time. Little attention is paid to short-term market 'noise'. The focus remains on the long-term when assessing sentiment and fundamentals, and volatility is seen as an opportunity.

We also believe investment is best kept simple to succeed – complexity adds cost, risks confusion and usually hinders performance. We consider time spent in the market is more rewarding than market timing. Such an approach also allows the full harvesting of dividends which become an increasingly important contributor to total returns over time. In remaining invested, we recognise the importance of rebalancing and diversification to ensure portfolios remain in sync with the desired remits.

What have been your biggest successes?

The commitment to entrepreneurial 'growth' companies mentioned previously. For example, the portfolios have long been overweight technology, healthcare and smaller companies. A common factor regarding other successes is where we have backed unpopular sectors and companies, and sentiment has then caught up with the fundamentals – narrowing discounts and rising markets can be a powerful combination.

And any failures that taught you valuable lessons?

A number. But perhaps the one that stands out is when we have top-sliced weightings prematurely, particularly when backing sectors or companies against the consensus. Having made good gains, we have sometimes succumbed to the temptation of reducing weightings when we should have retained our positions. However, we continue to occasionally top-slice our 'growth' holdings, while remaining overweight, in part to help ensure portfolio balance.

What government or regulatory changes would most help promote investment trusts?

Chief among them must be reform of Key Information Documents (KIDs). EU regulations have stipulated these documents were to be produced from 2018 for every investment trust so investors better understood what they are buying. Whatever the intention, the execution has been poor and perhaps even dangerous. The central problem is that KIDs can be very misleading for investors regarding the assessment of risk, the projection of returns and the comparison with open-ended 'sister' funds which the documents are obliged to convey.

Little wonder the Association of Investment Companies (AIC), the sector's respected trade body, has advised investors to "burn before reading"! After a call for input consultation, the FCA (Financial Conduct Authority) agreed and said the regulation could cause consumer harm. It set about pressing the EU to think again but without success. However, when the EU Transition Period finishes on 31 December, discussions with Government suggest that this will soon be addressed with the help of the FCA, AIC and other interested parties. Something to watch in the coming months.

Where do you see the sector in 10 years' time?

It will continue to be evolving to meet investor requirements, just as it has always done. Most recently it has helped investors access alternative sources of income, music rights and fintech among others. The next 10 years could see the sector venture more into precious metals, environmental technology and smaller companies overseas offering income.

Furthermore, as the search for yield continues, more investment trusts will pay dividends out of capital. They will benefit because their investment remit is less restricted, while investors will benefit from income hitherto not available and better performance over the long-term.

JOHN BARON *is a leading authority on investment trusts who writes a popular monthly column in the* Investors Chronicle *magazine. A new edition of his book,* The Financial Times Guide to Investment Trusts, *was published this year. The track record of the nine real portfolios he mentions is shown on the performance page of the website www.johnbaronportfolios.co.uk. Since leaving the City, he has also helped charities monitor their fund managers and regularly speaks at investment seminars.*

LEADER OF THE PACK

CHARLES PLOWDEN, *joint senior partner of Baillie Gifford, and lead manager of the Monks investment trust, discusses the reasons for his firm's recent remarkable run of success. He joined Baillie Gifford as a graduate trainee in 1983.*

Baillie Gifford has been associated with investment trusts, all the way back to its origins. How has the business changed since you started?

The shareholder register is very different now. The insurance companies and other institutions were the dominant shareholders back then. Now individual investors and wealth managers and intermediaries, where the ultimate owner is an individual, account for around 80 per cent. Probably it was the other way around thirty years ago. The Institutional shareholder base wanted reasonably cheap access to the index, plus a bit. They were looking for the beta of the market, not really the alpha. They will now be investing mainly in index trackers rather than active managers. Our client base has been moving towards intermediaries and private individuals more or less everywhere, in part because defined benefit pensions are declining almost everywhere.

As the ownership has changed, to people who just want their investment to appreciate and perform as they expect, I think we've all sharpened our pencils in terms of performance aspiration. There's a lot more focus on being ambitious. We are more performance seeking than risk avoiding. Monks (MNKS), for example, is explicitly all about capital gains. When my team took it over, five-and-a-half years ago, almost the first thing we did was cut the dividend and say that the dividend will be whatever the dividend is. The policy of Monks at the moment is to pay out the minimum dividend consistent with maintaining investment trust status. The board and we reckon that the best use of our money is to reinvest in future capital growth. We are very explicit about that.

How has the growth of the firm changed the way you manage it?

As a business, when we had eight or nine partners, most decisions were made with all eight or nine in a room. That isn't the case now, when we have 46. Autonomy for individual teams and business units is an acknowledgement that decisions aren't made centrally, they're made locally. About 25 years ago we moved from all partners being involved to having smaller decision-making groups. Small teams are much more enjoyable to work in, they make much better decisions and are much less political. We'd much rather have a larger number of smaller teams than one huge bureaucracy.

The way all the investment trusts were managed when I joined was quite different from how it is now. The manager was more of an asset allocator or strategist than a stock picker. Max Ward [head of the UK investment team and manager of Scottish Mortgage, and now manager of the Independent Investment Trust] would sit there and say, "I think we need more in America" and he'd give a bit of money to the American team to pick the stocks. Now the managers are responsible for picking the stocks and building the portfolios as a whole. It's become much more hands-on. They have complete discretion to do what they want, with no one looking over shoulders and telling them what not to do. Every team is free to make its own judgements and decisions.

Did you change a lot of things when you became senior partner?

What we did change was to put more emphasis on ambition and culture. Everything became more delegated. The teams were given much more freedom. Before it had been centralised. In many cases, that meant more concentrated portfolios. There was greater focus on 'active share', making sure we were different from the index in conscious ways, rather than just trying to track the index.

That required a change in the type of research that we were producing. At that point we stopped what we call maintenance research. The whole object of research should be to try to develop insights. Our research became much less about regular quarterly updates and much more deep-dive thoughtful, trying to develop an edge through an understanding of business models, or getting closer to management teams, understanding culture and so on.

How would you describe the culture at Baillie Gifford?

Communication, encouraging collaboration, a total ban on office politics and a focus on long-termism. It is also about being open to people who say, 'I've got a better way of doing this. Let's improve'. The constant drive for self-improvement is particularly relevant for Baillie Gifford at the moment because things have been going so well. The obvious risk is that we'll get complacent, lazy and whatever, so we have to guard against it.

So we're really banging the table saying every individual, across the whole firm, should have a personal programme for how they're going to get better. Very often the answer to that isn't 'I'm going to work twenty minutes longer every day'. It's 'I'm going to take myself off to university', or 'I'm going to go and build up a relationship with an industry expert'. It's about broadening your perspective and refining your insights rather than just saying I'm going to work harder and take fewer holidays.

Will Baillie Gifford get too big to be manageable or to retain the culture?

We have worried about getting too big and diluting the culture for thirty years! It's always question number one. I think the important thing is that we're not driven by scale. We're not trying to get bigger; we don't have any growth targets. Growth is an outcome, not an objective. What motivates all of us across the firm is the quality of what we do for clients, to have happy clients. The point is that we will live or die by our investment performance and the level of service.

The danger is that if you get too big or grow too fast, both your service levels and investment performance can suffer. However we've never had an accelerator. All we've had is a brake. On a regular basis since the early Nineties, if any area of the firm looks as though it's growing too fast or for too long, we will close it voluntarily just to let the clients settle in and to let the team maybe grow up a bit, mature around the challenge. In the global team I'm in, for example, we've been closed to new mandates for five years, although we have recently re-opened.

That is because there is a natural attrition now at Baillie Gifford, because about 60 per cent of our business is still Direct Benefit pension funds. As you know, they are slowly closing, becoming more risk averse, putting more money into bonds, or winding up altogether. They obviously have no cash flows because they're almost all closed, apart from the local authority schemes. From an investment perspective, they're moving more and more money away from so-called risky and volatile equities and switching into what they perceive as safe things like index-linked bonds.

So in that sense we're up against a headwind. The real question for us for a while hasn't been how big you can get, it's what we can do to offset shrinkage. The firm's flows have been negative for seven of the last eight years, although modestly so. We've managed to replace lost business, but most of the growth is from our outperformance. Volumes are unchanged, it's just the value that has gone up. That is why we have recently restated our group strategy which is to have more long-term clients, to retain our clients for as long as we possibly can.

You have had a great run in attracting new investment trust mandates – how important are investment trusts to the business?

At the end of June, we had just over £20 billion in investment trusts, which is an enormous number. But the firm's total was £260 billion. So, it's less than 10 percent of the total. For years, we watched investment trusts becoming a smaller proportion of the whole. But now, because of the move towards intermediaries and private investors, we see the investment trust area as fertile ground, instead of being the bit of the business that was shrinking and without any growth prospect.

Even the long-established trusts are issuing and growing, after years and years of shrinkage. Monks returned almost half of its share capital between 1999 and 2015. Every year there was another three or four per cent share buyback. It was quite depressing. Over the last five years, we've stopped that and now it's very gently started having positive issuance. There's more demand than there is supply, which is great.

Launching a new investment trust was difficult for a long time. We launched Baillie Gifford Shin Nippon (BGS) in 1985 and we didn't do another launch until 2018. It wasn't because we didn't try. But why would anyone pay a hundred for something that is going to start trading at eighty-five or eighty the next day? All trusts were trading at discounts. So the only real way you could grow your investment trust business was by taking on mandates from others. You have to be opportunistic and have the right teams and the right offering. We've obviously been quite successful with that.

So although it's a small part of our business, it's a growing part. I strongly believe investment trusts are the best investment vehicle available to most of us, certainly in the UK. It's permanent capital. Trusts can gear. They have external oversight through boards, they tend to be cheaper than other pooled alternatives, from a tax perspective you can buy them now and sell them in 40 years' time, and there's not a tax payment to pay in the meantime. They also are the vehicles that have the widest opportunity set because they can invest in less liquid and private investments. They've got all these levers that our other poor old clients aren't able to take advantage of.

You say your fund managers are encouraged to do their own thing, but are you happy to be associated with growth as an investment style?

The whole firm is behind the growth investment style and I think there are probably two main reasons for that. One is, there are lots of ways of investing, but we think that it's growth that creates value. A company that isn't growing isn't creating value. It may be paying out a dividend, but it's not creating future value. It is fundamental growth that creates wealth and leads to higher levels of investment, innovation and so on. So if you're going to own equities, then make sure you're not in the half of the market that is ex-growth, because they won't give you equity-like returns. If you want a nominal or fixed nominal return, buy a bond or a property. That's the way to get that certainty.

The other more pragmatic reason for sticking with growth is that it's what we're good at. Part of the cultural shift is to focus on our strengths, not our weaknesses. We think we understand growth analysis and growth investment and just as we've never done long-short funds because we don't understand shorting, we don't think we'd be very good value investors. We will do what we're best at and hopefully we can carry on being very good at it.

Clearly growth indices have outperformed value indices, but part of that is that a lot of value stocks have been shown to be value traps. The energy sector and the banking sector look cheap today, but next year their profits could be 20 per cent lower and they won't be quite so cheap, so the share prices will have to go down again. In both cases, their business is going to be chipped away by newer technologies, newer entrants, companies without the legacy costs of once enormous workforces on generous pensions and so on. I think focusing on growth means you're investing in the future, not the past. There's a danger with value that you get sucked into what were once big, great, successful companies.

How does your analytical method for growth stocks differ from other people?

We don't really use many spreadsheets. We say we'd rather be roughly right than precisely wrong, and spreadsheets lead you to spurious precision. The mistake most people make is looking too close to home, looking at last year and this year, and trying to work out whether a stock is cheap or expensive. The key is you need to look forward five years, or even longer, and work out whether the company will be growing in five or 10 years' time.

If you think it will be, why will it be growing? How much of the market will it have and what will the margin structure typically be? Where in its life cycle as a company will it be? If it's still expanding then you can assume it will be on a relatively high valuation; the share price is just a function of what the profits will be in five or 10 years' time and what valuation it will be on in five or 10 years' time. All that comes with huge uncertainty and a wide range of possibilities. So, we don't come up with precise models and spot valuations. It's the time horizon rather than the precision of the numbers that gives you your advantage.

It's not unique. I think anyone can do this. I would say our approach to valuation and analysis is rather more imaginative and optimistic than others. What we're looking to see is can this stock be an enormous success? Then we can try to put a probability on that. Is it a five per cent probability or a 30 per cent probability? If it's a 30 per cent probability, you want to have it on your portfolio. There's no such thing as a sure thing, but if you can have a portfolio full of companies that have that latent potential, then enough of them will succeed to drag up your whole portfolio return.

I think a lot of other investors are either too worried about the downsides, or too worried about the near-term valuation, that they miss out on the long-term. The big winners, whether over fifteen years or one year, the Amazons of this world, or even Microsoft going back to the 1980s and 1990s were always overvalued for a value investor, because they were on high multiples. But such has been the growth, and the duration of the growth, that by the time the five years has passed, they've got another big market opportunity to address and they're building a second business.

One of the things I most love about broker research – and we don't really spend very much of our time reading investment bank research – is that they all have to put in these price targets. If you track Amazon or Microsoft, or the most fun one Tesla, you have these people who have Tesla as a sell with a price target 40 per cent below the share price and then every six months they upgrade their forecast. It's still a sell, but they've just doubled their share price target and they still say the company is overvalued! I think it's a failure of imagination.

But surely you do come across companies where you're enthused about their growth potential and indeed their ambition, but you baulk at the price.

Absolutely. But you don't have to buy them today, do you? You can follow them, and you'll get an opportunity to buy them at a more appealing price, or maybe at a higher price, but at some point in the future when many of the risks and competitive threats have reduced. That's one of the other lessons. Every manager will have a shortlist of a dozen stocks that they really wished they owned, but they're not prepared to pay today's price. Those are the ones that you monitor for opportunities.

Can you give an example of that?

One company that Monks has recently bought is Estée Lauder, the cosmetics business. It's halfway between regular consumer goods and luxury products. It has the strength and solidity of a consumer staple, but some of the economic sensitivity and the travel-related sensitivity of some of the luxury brands. The question is not whether L'Oréal or Estée Lauder are good companies, but are we prepared to pay today's share price? While the prices didn't crater as a result of travel bans, they were relatively soft, so we stepped in and bought a holding.

S&P Global, the global ratings business, was very much the same. We've owned its rival Moody's in size for fifteen years, and it's been a great winner. We thought we've got one ratings agency, but if they're really special businesses, why not have more than one? So in the early summer we took advantage of a bit of share price softness there. We're looking at some of the luxury goods companies at the moment. Both profits and valuations are pretty high for my tastes. We are crossing our fingers and hoping that they come back a bit.

Do you think this is a golden age for your style of investing?

I think it probably is, and almost entirely because of technological change. One of my colleagues has just written a piece saying, "why do we still talk about internet businesses? Any business that isn't using machine learning is unlikely to be there in twenty years' time". She said, "it'll be as quaint as talking about electrical powered businesses". The information and data are available. Every industry either chooses to use it or not. That's as true of energy and mining as it is of banking, drug research and so on.

So, I think this is a period of accelerating change. From a growth perspective, that is creating new opportunities at a rapid rate, and because of the ability to scale in a digital world, it's not like Ford Motor going global and taking thirty years to do it, because it's got to build a factory and hire a workforce. These companies can distribute many of their products globally without infrastructure. So, they can grow surprisingly rapidly, not just without infrastructure, but without massive amounts of capital as well.

That's great if you're looking for those sorts of growth businesses. It's also increasing the risks to the slower beasts, the companies that aren't adapting. They can go from hero to zero very, very quickly, much faster than their contingency plans and their budgeting will suggest. The risk of being on the right or the wrong side of history has become more and more serious. You need to focus your research less on who's going to lose than on who's coming to threaten you and who's going to win.

A lot of the traditional obstacles to growth and success have gone. Even in consumer goods, it used to be that the consumer brand that won was the one that could control the final aisle in the supermarket for the display of its products. But on the internet, there's infinite shelf space so, it's no longer about scale. Being big does not confer the same brand advantages that it once did. Which is why we're getting all these craft gins, craft beers, craft cosmetics, craft everything. They can scale incredibly quickly. That's great if you're one of these challenges, or if you're a Shopify or someone who's powering these challenges. It's a lot less great if you're Unilever or Nestlé or Kraft Foods.

Do you worry about political risk and the threat of deglobalisation?

It's not anything that we're particularly focused on, and that's partly because it's not an area where we can add any value. It's quite hard to develop insight. When it depends, for instance, on the lottery of the US election system. We don't spend a lot of time thinking about 'what if' and 'what might'. But it also reflects the fact that our portfolios are not very exposed to globally traded goods. Our portfolios are more about IP and technology and knowledge than they are about a network of ships, factories, warehouses, and things that could be disrupted. We're quite wary of stranded assets. It can be great investing in capital intensive businesses, but it can be very bad if your customers leave you, if you've got a shopping mall or a chain of supermarkets, and everyone starts buying online. Those things go from being an asset to a liability.

Investing in unlisted companies is obviously something that's been associated with the Baillie Gifford approach. Is that because the listed market is getting smaller, or is it because you think there are inherently superior things to own?

It's the second. It wasn't that we were running out of public companies. It's because of the changing technology. Companies don't need to come to stock markets for external capital. They can self-finance. Typically these companies have one, two, three fund raises early in their career and then they can grow because it doesn't take a lot of capital to grow. They don't need stock markets. The function of a stock market now is a place for trading second-hand shares, not a place for raising primary capital to help the economy to develop. We think that more attractive companies, if they come to the market at all, will do so later, after a lot of the value has been created. Why wouldn't you try to be involved at the time of maximum value creation?

CHARLES PLOWDEN *was appointed senior partner of Baillie Gifford in 2006 and has been head of the Global Alpha equity team since its inception in 2005. He will be succeeded as joint senior partner by Malcolm MacColl in May 2021.*

MEET THE MATRIX MAN

Veteran small cap fund manager HARRY NIMMO *talks to* JONATHAN DAVIS.

W
HAT MAKES HARRY Nimmo an interesting guy to talk to is that his background is somewhat different to many of his peer group. Having gained degrees in geography and surveying, he spent the first few years of his working life doing jobs for Aramco in the oil fields of Saudi Arabia, saving a chunk of cash and starting an equity portfolio. That was in the early 1980s, when the oil price was still riding high and income tax remained punitive in the UK.

By his mid-20s however Nimmo had decided that there were better opportunities to be had in asset management than in the notoriously cyclical oil business. He signed up for an MBA at Edinburgh University with an eye on acquiring a useful qualification and then landed a job as a securities analyst with Standard Life. After eight years covering US and then large UK stocks, he was made head of the smaller companies team in 1993, initially for the life company's internal funds.

Then in 1997 the company launched its open-ended smaller companies fund, which has since grown to become the largest in its sector and boasts a long term track record that, according to Trustnet, few of his peers come close to matching. The investment trust he manages, Standard Life UK Smaller Companies Trust (ticker: SLS), followed in 2003 when Standard Life took on the mandate from a trust managed by Edinburgh Fund Managers.

As Nimmo recalls, that win turned out to be the start of a five-year struggle to secure its future. It took some time to untangle and reshape the portfolio, which had overloaded on tech stocks during the TMT bubble and was lumbered with an expensive high coupon 25-year debenture that needed to be refinanced at significant cost (at a cost equivalent to 8 per cent of NAV). The discount, though down from a worst case 40 per cent, remained stubbornly wide at around 20 per cent. A well-known activist investor built up a big stake in the trust and with a number of others campaigned to have it liquidated.

The board was eventually forced to make a tender offer to shareholders, which resulted in 49 per cent of the shareholders (by value) opting to take cash. Had just one per cent more of the votes opted for the cash, the trust would have had to be liquidated. The market capitalisation of the trust fell to just £28 million at one stage. With the market deep in the throes of the global financial crisis, and debt for gearing hard to find, the future of the trust was hanging by a thread.

Move forward another 12 years however and you would be hard pressed to know any of that. A combination of consistent good performance and a timely merger with Gartmore Smaller Companies in 2009 helped to bulk up assets and the discount started to come in. When Standard Life and Aberdeen merged their asset management businesses in 2018, the trust agreed to merge with Dunedin Smaller Companies, which was one of Aberdeen's small cap trusts. Today the trust has a market value in excess of £500 million, making it one of the big boys in what most of us regard as one of the most impressive and competitive of all investment trust sectors.

Surprisingly perhaps for an investment trust, or so those of us who are fans of the sector would like to think, the trust has struggled to quite match the performance of Nimmo's open-ended fund, although the difference is marginal. Since 2003, the trust has produced a near sevenfold total return. He puts that down primarily to its early struggles and the hit to NAV from two expensive debt refinancings.

There is around an 85 per cent overlap between the portfolios of the two funds and the investment process is the same. Over the last 10 years, however, the trust is comfortably ahead, albeit with higher volatility. As you would expect, it performs better when the market is rising and worse than its sister fund in down markets. The continuing popularity of the trust is underpinned not just by Nimmo's long-term track record, but also by its being the only smaller companies trust to have adopted a semi-hard discount control mechanism.

The board aims to protect a discount of around eight per cent with share buybacks. From time to time more recently its shares have traded around par or even at a small premium, enabling some secondary issuance. The majority of trusts in the sector meanwhile continue to trade at double digit discounts, reflecting investors' enduring disenchantment with the UK market. The trust is well supported by both wealth managers and all the main retail investor platforms, so liquidity has never been a problem, even during the pandemic-inspired market meltdown in March.

Experience during the market collapse in March was painful, with the NAV down 50 per cent and the discount falling from zero to a 20 per cent discount at one point, before stabilising. However relative performance was good. "The experience showed", Nimmo says, "that we can be resilient in difficult market conditions. March was a good month for us on a relative basis. We did what is said on the tin in that respect". His biggest regret was not making more use of gearing when the market collapse started to throw up bargains. "I have not always been terribly clever in timing being fully invested and I should have been fully invested in March".

The Aberdeen Standard Investments smaller companies team adopts a distinctive approach to managing its portfolios. At the heart of it is an in-house quantitative screening process, known rather grandiloquently as The Matrix, which ranks companies in the smaller company universe on a wide range of statistical measures, looking primarily for what professional investors like to call 'quality growth' companies. That of course is not unusual in equity investment management, but what is different – and Nimmo believes is the key to its success – is that he adds momentum to quality and growth, and valuations in the shape of price/earnings ratios and dividend yields are not the starting point, merely a final factor to be considered when and if a potential investment has passed all the other screening tests.

The inputs, always forward looking by choice, include forecast earnings growth rates and trends in analysts' earnings forecasts, as well as measures of balance sheet strength, such as Piotroski scores, and – equally important – earnings revisions momentum. Every stock is given a stock rating, on a scale from minus 40 (bad) to plus 40 (good), with zero being the average. To be considered as a buy a stock needs to score plus 10 or above. Minus 10 or below is a sell signal. The higher the average score in the portfolio the more encouraging it is.

The screening system was not devised by Nimmo himself – he attributes its intellectual rigour to a former fund manager colleague, Jeff Saunders, and the number-crunching expertise it embodies to his long-standing quant colleague Simon McCallum – but although he relinquished the role of head of the team in March, he remains what he calls "the guardian of the process" for the firm as a whole, making sure that his fund management colleagues stay true to the discipline that The Matrix provides. If they are buying stocks that score badly in the system, they know that "I will be on their tail, asking the question why".

Why does this approach work better than conventional stock screening processes which have dividend yields and p/e ratios at their heart? One purely practical advantage, says Nimmo, is that it is so cost-effective. "How are we able to run global, UK and European portfolios with a team of just half a dozen people? It is because we have a screening process. It really cuts down on the legwork. You don't have to be experts on every single company – just buy what makes the short list, and only then start on the fundamental research".

"It also means we need to employ a third or a quarter of the number of analysts. That's good for the client. It's good for Aberdeen Standard Investments because there are fewer expensive fund managers to employ. It's good for the client because we're very consistent in our investment process. We have not changed it, in essence, in more than twenty years. And we've been through four economic and market cycles in that time".

There is also the fact, he does not need to say, that the results show that it works, at least most of the time. The big exception, Nimmo says, is when the stock market is coming out of a slump and into a so-called "dash for trash" phase, when any number of beaten up cyclical companies which have somehow survived the previous downturn suddenly roar ahead. One such period might be coming in the wake of the virus, he suspects, but the good news for him is that these episodes tend to be relatively short-lived.

Philosophically the reason why The Matrix has served his team well has a lot to do with how many professional investors are trained these days. The MBA he earned from Edinburgh University, Nimmo reckons, was useful, giving him a grounding in the language of business and a smattering of accountancy, business finance, marketing, and organisational behaviour. It has helped him to converse with senior management in an intelligent way and form judgements about which businesses are going well and which are not.

But the standard investment theory which you find being taught in all business schools, including the Capital Asset Pricing Model, the Efficient Markets Hypothesis and so on, he says, was hopeless for his career as a fund manager. "I found that a lot of that is just tosh. If I'd stuck with that, I'd be struggling. It wasn't until the mid-Nineties that I was really able to figure it out. When we launched our smaller companies fund, I needed to find an investment process that stacked up. It needed to be concise and consistent and understandable to potential investors".

A lot of backtesting went into The Matrix before the model and its components were fully worked out. The emphasis on quality growth criteria and price momentum works, in his view, because it reflects much more accurately how businesses operate. "I suppose I always have had a fundamental belief that what we are looking for are situations where things are getting better. The basis for that is that the business environment and the market environment are not static. It's dynamic. It's changing all the time. Either things are getting better or they're getting worse".

At the heart of the Efficient Markets Hypothesis and mainstream finance theory, in contrast, is the idea "that things are static and that there is always a correct value for a business. You need to have a price point. You analyse a company and find a value for it and that's the value – if the share price is below that you buy. If it's above that you sell. And once it gets to the price point, you get out".

"We don't do that. Because the market is dynamic, we want to find the companies that are changing for the better and sell the companies where things are changing for the worse. The internet, the arrival of cloud computing and all that, has meant that change has accelerated. That plays into the hands of those of us who are focused on the dynamic of change and finding improving situations". This also helps to explain why share price momentum – the idea that good investments will tend to have rising share prices already – is another critical input into the screening process and one of the most important of all the variables it tracks, anathema though it is to ivory tower academics.

If a system like The Matrix can work so well, why don't more managers of actively managed funds go down the same route? "It is surprising, but there's a couple of things going on, I would say" he replies. "One is that many people, when they go to university and do economics and investments, or when they do their professional exams or CFAs, are trained in the Efficient Markets Hypothesis approach. Once you start on that, it's incredibly difficult to drag yourself away from it. It's perpetuated and built into the way many investment companies behave".

"The other reason that others don't do what we do is on the sell side, where the standard approach is completely built into the way they think. The idea of mean reversion and fade rates is fundamental to the way sell side analysts figure out their spreadsheets and forecasts. The assumption is that no company can grow faster than about eight per cent per annum for more than a couple of years, since competitors will rush in and compete away that advantage. Even with the fastest growing companies, there's this huge fade rate in forecasts".

"Our belief though is that competitive advantage can often be maintained in these improving companies for many years. We try to get on board with that. There are companies that as a result consistently see earnings upgrades from the sell side analysts as they beat forecasts year after year after year.[*] They may look optically expensive using the sell side's current forecasts, but they are not expensive because they consistently beat expectations. In many companies, finance directors often are also very assiduous at controlling the sell side analysts, making sure they don't put out forecasts that are much too challenging and hard to beat".

That is why earnings revisions – the direction of travel suggested by company guidance and in analyst forecasts – is more important than the earnings forecasts themselves. But what happens when the market breaks down suddenly in the face of a big unknown, as it did in March with the pandemic panic? How did The Matrix cope? Well, says Nimmo, "there was a lot of confusion and earnings revision momentum wasn't telling us anything about the future. There was no earnings guidance. But the good news is that the factor that really worked well at that point was quality. It was the only thing that counted in March. It is what helps our funds to provide resilience when markets collapse".

As it happened Nimmo was away on business and then a family holiday during the worst of the market sell-off, only returning a day before the market started to rally. "I did put on a few sell orders on things that looked most at risk before I went on holiday, but it all happened very quickly. In all honesty, I should have twigged back in January that this could be bad, but I didn't. In any case, we've got a lot of assets invested. We can't just slew the portfolio around and invest in a whole lot of different

---

[*]   Charles Plowden of Baillie Gifford makes a similar point – see page 122.

things. Market timing is phenomenally difficult, and you can see for yourself, by the time we would have sold all of our bad things, the market would have turned".

Standard Life UK Smaller Companies changed its benchmark a couple of years ago to combine an AIM index with a Smaller Companies index for the first time. Nimmo has been been struck by how well the AIM market, much reviled in the past, has performed during the pandemic crisis. "It's come of age. It took a hell of a long time – I'd say fifteen or twenty years. But I noticed in the last five years it's become a lot better. The basis for that is several things. One is far more of them are profitable. I'm looking at the top hundred AIM stocks, those with market caps of a couple of hundred-million and upwards. I'd say about three quarters of them are profitable. Seventy per cent of them pay dividends".

"You've obviously still got to be careful, but you definitely don't want to avoid AIM. It has come of age in the last few years. The days when AIM was dominated by oil and mining stocks and dodgy real estate companies seems to be a thing of the past". The quality of the new issues coming through on AIM is also much higher than it used to be, he says, and AIM stocks now account for 31 per cent of the portfolio (as of 30 September 2020).

To be an equity investor it helps to be an optimist and Nimmo is no exception in becoming much more positive about the outlook than he was. Experience counts for a lot in years like 2020. "I've seen a few downturns. There's always something new coming along. I've never seen as many dividend cuts, for example, as we have this year. Even during the banking crisis, we had only one or two of our holdings cut their dividends. Around half of our holdings that pay dividends suspended them this time".

Most of those have since reinstated their dividends, however, and many of the companies in his portfolio when we last spoke were coming through with earnings ahead of expectations and trading strongly, both big positives in The Matrix process. Nimmo says that despite having promised the board of Standard Life UK Smaller Companies that he would be carrying on until 2022, he might now stay even longer. "I've stepped down from being head of the team and I'm doing what I really love doing, which is running money, so I'm thinking, do I really want to go when I'm sixty-five? The money's good and it's still working well. I'm really enjoying it. So, I don't know, I might stay a bit longer!".

HARRY NIMMO *has been managing UK equities for more than 25 years and the Standard Life UK Smaller Companies trust since 2003.*

MORE INCOME, PLEASE

SIMON CRINAGE, *head of investment trusts at J.P. Morgan Asset Management, looks back on a 36-year career in the investment trust business and explains how enhanced income has helped keep the firm competitive.*

How did you start in investment trusts?

I started my career in investment trusts with Robert Fleming in August 1984. At the time, I wanted to be an accountant and Flemings gave me an opportunity to do so in the investment trust business. After learning all about general ledgers, I quickly became passionate about investment trusts and 36 years later, that's still the case!

Flemings was a big player in investment trusts back then.

Absolutely. When I joined, we had eight investment trusts and I think about £640 million in assets, which was a lot in those days. Roll things forward to today and, while obviously the market has been up and down this year because of the pandemic, we've now over £11 billion in 22 investment trust companies. For an industry that people have written off many times before, it's been a great business for us and a fantastic product for shareholders.

When did the tie-up with J.P. Morgan happen?

Flemings was sold to Chase Manhattan Bank in 2000, and then Chase merged with J.P. Morgan later that same year. So, essentially within nine months, we'd gone from being Robert Fleming to being Chase to being J.P. Morgan. Fortunately for us, J.P. Morgan had no presence in UK retail at the time. It had no investment trust business, and it didn't have a UK mutual fund or open-ended fund business. So it was a highly complementary merger, one that worked. You can see that from the way the business has grown since then.

Has the way you manage the business changed?

The model is no different in the sense that there's always been a head of investment trusts and a dedicated team of people that look after our investment trust boards and the shareholders of the investment trusts. Investment management has always been delegated or outsourced to our investment management colleagues across the globe. So at Flemings, for example, our Asia and Japan funds were run by Jardine

Fleming; now they're run by our Tokyo, Hong Kong and Singapore colleagues. It's the same model, just a much bigger and more powerful organisation.

What is the biggest challenge you face as a business?

The big challenge is to attract the attention of investors. People say now that investment trusts need to be of a minimum size to make them work, particularly for the wealth management market. Some people say £350 million. Pick a number! It is certainly going to be bigger than £100 million. It's probably more realistically £200 million to £300 million. In that sense our trusts need to be big enough to gain interest from the shareholders.

We also need to make sure that we have a business that is competitive in terms of our fund management capacity – how much money the fund managers can run for each strategy, how many mandates they can run, and so on. In that sense we have to demonstrate that we can get a trust off the ground and that the trust is going to be a suitable size and scale to justify doing it. What we hear from wealth managers is that we need to demonstrate the ability to grow these companies.

The ability to issue shares to meet demand is an important factor in that?

Yes. Share issuance has come round again, let's put it that way. In the late Eighties, and early Nineties, we were launching new trusts and we had trusts trading at a premium. JPMorgan Claverhouse, for example, was trading at a premium to its NAV. Then the discount drifted off. More recently Claverhouse has been issuing shares again. These things do go in cycles to a certain degree. Generally there's been a lot more corporate activity in terms of issuance and share buybacks, which only came in back in 1999.

There is also a lot more attention being given to the investment structure. If you roll the clock back before my time, investment trusts were very much in conventional long-only equity and the mainstream asset classes. Flemings had a continental European fund, a UK fund, a Far Eastern fund – Asia including Japan – and a Japan fund. They were all very much outsourced.

In those days, the registers were dominated by insurance companies, names such as Guardian Royal Exchange and Sunlife. These investors owned the shares because they were effectively subcontracting the investment management capability to Robert Fleming. That's all gone and the industry has had to become a lot more specialist as well to meet the demands of today, particularly as a source for income or even providing access to alternative sources of income, from illiquid assets in infrastructure and things like that.

The shareholder registers now have a much bigger private investor element too.

Yes, there has been a renaissance in retail. There was a big wave of retail interest in the late Eighties and early Nineties. That too tailed away. However, retail investors are a growing presence on the share registers of pretty much all investment companies these days. Ownership is much more fragmented, compared to the days of the big pension funds. The big wealth managers are still very important to us, but what I would call independent wealth management firms and retail demand through the platforms are where the growth is.

Platforms have become dominant. Twenty-five years ago, if you wanted to buy a share in an investment trust, you either had to have an account with a stockbroker or you dealt through one of the managed savings schemes. They were all paper-based. You paid for your shares by cheque or with a regular standing order. Now, it's about four clicks on a platform. The industry has definitely benefited from the ease with which a direct investor can now buy trust shares. There is no point in us providing a savings scheme any more because so many clients have an arrangement with a platform.

Do you now place more emphasis on advertising, marketing and branding than you did?

We did a fair amount of that back in the late Eighties and early Nineties, but not on the scale we're doing it now, for sure. The relationship has changed, because all the shares are effectively held through platforms. The challenge now is to be heard. We have had to learn to communicate with investors effectively, which these days means mainly through electronic communications, principally the website. That was particularly important this year because of the pandemic, where we have made a big effort to keep shareholders up to date with the views of our managers and sector/economic analysts as the crisis unfolded.

You have launched a number of investment trusts recently. Are you responding to perceived demand or trying to create new demand?

That's a good question. I'd say we've found it easier to meet new sources of investor demand than to come up with an innovative investment idea to take to the market. We've come up with ideas that we think would be a cracking investment proposition but ultimately turned out to be too sophisticated or just not of sufficient interest to the buying community, professional or retail. Obviously, you have to test demand for these things before you go live with them. At the moment certain asset classes, particularly in the alternative income space, are trading at premiums to NAV. That tells you there is still demand there. Clearly it is important to have the capability to come up with new ideas, but it is what investors want that is the key. It's definitely that way around.

"FOR AN INDUSTRY THAT PEOPLE HAVE WRITTEN OFF MANY TIMES BEFORE, INVESTMENT TRUSTS HAVE BEEN A GREAT BUSINESS AND A FANTASTIC PRODUCT FOR SHAREHOLDERS."

With so many trusts, is it fair to say that there isn't a distinctive J.P.Morgan management style, in terms of growth, value and so on?

The style will vary from trust to trust, but I would say that we're looking more for consistent outperformance than for high outperformance. We have quality growth strategies, we have some value strategies, growth and value, income – all sorts of different strategies. It all comes back to what we were saying about the size of J.P. Morgan. We can move from one strategy to the other if we think that would be a good idea and the board agrees.

The big gap for us at the moment, which we have only just started to fill, is in the alternatives space. We launched the Global Core Real Assets Trust (JARA) in September 2019. That trust has grown pretty well since we launched. When people think of J.P. Morgan, in addition to equities and fixed income, many know us for our expertise in alternatives. We have over £100 billion in real assets today, for example. Being able to bring that capability to the marketplace in a liquid structure, which investment trusts have, makes perfect sense.

The demand for income has grown dramatically since the global financial crisis, with interest rates going down so far. When did you first become aware of that?

Demand for income has been there for ages. JPMorgan Claverhouse (JCH) was launched back in 1963 as a UK growth and income trust, for example. In 1989 we launched Fleming High Income in response to demand. The trend has clearly accelerated since the global financial crisis, however. The need for income was behind the launch of JPMorgan Global Emerging Market Income (JEMI), which is what I would call a genuine income fund, one which is not manufacturing but earning the income it pays out.

The idea was essentially to leverage the capabilities in our emerging market franchise – where we are strong and have a very big footprint – and to provide people with a diversified source of income at a time when they didn't have that opportunity. At launch I think JEMI raised just over £100 million. That trust today is around £400 million in size, having delivered an income to investors of around four per cent per annum. People hadn't thought about emerging markets as being a source of income much before that. A number of the quality stocks in Asia in particular are paying very good dividends.

When did you start to market the idea of a growth and income trust, which is a proposition with which J.P. Morgan is closely associated in investment trusts?

You are right that growth and income has been the sweet spot for us more recently. That trend also started after the global financial crisis. The first trust in our stable that moved was JPMorgan Overseas, which we renamed JPMorgan Global Growth and Income (JGGI). JPMorgan Overseas was, as the name implies, a trust that invested principally outside the United Kingdom, a global generalist. It was buying back shares all the time, sat alongside a large number of other trusts in the global growth sector and frankly struggled for airtime.

We worked with the board on what we might do to stem the level of buybacks, make the company more appealing to investors and try to reset the trust for the future. We came up with the idea of using enhanced distributions. Essentially what this means is that the trust earns a level of income from dividends in its underlying investments, but supplements that with some realised capital profits, which it can then also pay out to investors as dividends.

What that trust says is "we will pay at least four per cent of our Net Asset Value on the last day of the financial year to our investors in equal instalments over the next four quarters". Once we had done that, we found that the trust moved pretty rapidly to rerate from what was a double digit discount to trade towards a premium. Obviously, there was movement on the register, with some people exiting and others, particularly retail investors, buying. Since then it has traded pretty consistently at a premium for the last three years. It even issued shares in March 2020, when the markets dived as the pandemic hit. JGGI has issued shares every month this year despite what's happened in the world.

That is remarkable, given that shareholders could effectively do the same thing themselves if they wanted to [by selling shares to fund income].

I think the attraction for a lot of people is that they can effectively plan ahead. They know with certainty that the next four quarters' dividends will be the same. They know at 30 June each year that at least four per cent of the NAV will be distributed as dividend. Each year since the trust adopted this policy, the dividend per share has in fact been higher, including in 2020 – which you might not have expected.

Despite going through one of the most challenging market environments in March this year, the trust rode that storm and has ended up eking out just under a one percent dividend rise year on year. On the other side of the equation there are no revenue reserves anymore. The trust is paying out a hundred per cent of its revenue and it's supplementing that with its capital reserves, or realised capital profits.

Is there not a tax disadvantage to shareholders in this?

Well, there is a risk and that's why the caveat is in there. The question to ask is what happens if there is a persistent bear market for a number of years, or maybe even a decade. The trust could devour itself, so to speak, because effectively it's paying out four per cent every year and if that persists for too long, it could theoretically shrink to nothing. However, the board did not take this decision lightly, I can assure you. We did a lot of modelling, Monte Carlo simulations and so on, to assess the risk of that happening. There is a chance it could happen, you can never say never, but in practice if you had a persistent bear market for multiple years, even trusts which have capital reserves would soon be running into problems, let alone the ones that are calling on revenue reserves

You obviously chose a very good year end, apart from anything else!

Yes, you're right. To be frank, if it had been the 31 March for example, just after the big market sell-off, it could have been a different situation. Nevertheless the board still had the discussion that they didn't have to have. They could have asked themselves: should we pay out more than four per cent as a dividend? We say "at least four per cent" is our policy. We could have paid out five per cent. The flexibility of the structure allows them at least to have the opportunity to discuss and debate the situation, were it to arise.

How many of your other trusts have cloned that policy?

We now have four trusts in the stable that are doing something of this kind, but the others are doing it slightly differently. Three of them now have growth and income in their title. Apart from the one we've been talking about, Global Growth and Income, there's JPMorgan Asia Growth and Income and JPMorgan China Growth and Income. Another of our trusts, JPMorgan Japan Smaller Companies Trust, also has an enhanced dividend policy.

The difference with the last three is that they pay one percent of their NAV at each quarter end, not setting it at four per cent of the NAV at 30 June for the whole year ahead. So, if the NAV is a pound at one quarter end, the trust would pay 1p. If at the next quarter end, it's two pounds, it would pay 2p. There's more volatility in this formula, but on the other side there is an argument that it effectively smooths the dividend from year to year. Time will show how that plays out.

In the meantime we have seen the Asia Growth and Income discount come in from double digits to trade close to asset value, we have seen China Growth and Income come in from a double digit discount to about a six per cent discount today. The discount that is still looking relatively wide is Japan Smaller Companies, which is still in double digits. At the moment, however, the name doesn't necessarily imply what it does in terms of income, so that is something which I think the board will consider. Enhanced distributions have definitely garnered an interest amongst the retail investing community, and we've seen the retail ownership of all four of those trusts increase significantly.

Has it changed the way that the fund managers manage the fund?

Absolutely not. This is one of the great things about our approach. The fund managers can manage the fund to maximise total return because the board has taken control of the dividend policy. Whether Global Growth and Income earns one per cent in dividends from its underlying investments, or three per cent, it doesn't affect the level of dividend that's being paid to shareholders. So the fund manager can just focus on maximising total return. If anything it's given the fund managers more flexibility than before.

And this is something which you couldn't do in the open-ended space effectively?

Absolutely not. You can't even have revenue reserves in open-ended funds. The enhanced distribution system can't be utilised either. There is another way of looking at it too. When an investment trust buys back its shares for discount management purposes, it's using its realised capital profits to do so. Now, a share buyback effectively involves buying shares in the market from individual sellers. You're going into the market and sweeping up surplus stock. With the enhanced dividend process you're not doing that. I hesitate to use these words, but it's for the many, not the few, in the sense that you're paying some of your capital profits to all the investors, not just to those who are benefiting from the buyback.

Why aren't more trusts going down the enhanced income route if it works so well?

It's still early days. This is a long-term industry. I think you're likely to see more trusts do it as we go forward, particularly given how many trusts may have to dip into revenue reserves this year. Ultimately, of course, even if revenue reserves are depleted, all trusts have the ability to return to utilising capital profits. I suspect people just want to see this continuing to work before they think about adopting it. I wouldn't wish to see the entire range of JPMorgan investment trusts taking the same approach. Ultimately, it needs to fit with what shareholders want. There will be some shareholders that don't want income, for example.

SIMON CRINAGE *has been head of investment trusts at J.P. Morgan since 2013.*

GROW THOSE DIVIDENDS

Fund manager SAM MORSE *is happy to be anything but flashy in his investment approach, he tells* JONATHAN DAVIS.

IDELITY EUROPEAN IS the heavyweight investment trust specialising in European equities, with assets of more than £1,300 million, making it more than twice the size of all but one of its eight competitors. Next year it will be celebrating its 30th anniversary. Sam Morse is the fourth manager the fund has had since it was launched as a new vehicle for Fidelity's famed contrarian stockpicker Anthony Bolton. So, given that the trust has recently decided to drop the word 'values' from its name, it seems fair to kick off our conversation by asking whether it is still being run in the same style.

The answer is no, Morse says, although he dissents from the view that Bolton was an out and out value investor, as many people say. "I worked with Anthony for many years and I would say that there were many more strings to his bow than being an out and out value investor. Some of his most successful stocks you could actually describe as growth stocks. Quite often they started off as a hidden jewel – Nokia springs to mind, where he noticed that there was this small mobile phone business tucked away in a large Finnish conglomerate making anything from wellies to whatever. He hung on and hung on and ultimately it did become much more of a growth stock than a value stock".

In its first 10 years, from 1991 to 2001, the trust outperformed its index by a remarkable six per cent an annum, which is the stuff of dreams these days, when the market for European stocks is many times more researched than it was when Bolton was starting out. Back then shareholder returns were a long way from being the primary focus of most large European companies' managements. I remember Bolton telling me, for example, how it was still possible back in the 1980s to visit a large European company and discover that you were the only UK investor to have visited.[*]

"Yes" says Morse. "It is much better covered now and better researched. The whole attitude towards stock ownership has also changed dramatically in Europe. Most of the European CEOs now have been educated at business school. It is a very different environment. Of course the size of the trust is completely different as well. Then it was quite small. You could take quite aggressive positions in smaller and medium sized companies. It's a much larger beast today. It is a slightly different proposition".

---

[*] As described in my book *Investing with Anthony Bolton*.

That is fair comment and Morse freely admits that the way he approaches the trust is different to that of all his predecessors. The main thing that all four have had in common is that they have the benefit of being able to draw on the huge and well-resourced research team that Fidelity has always had at the centre of its investment process. More than 300 of its analysts, he calculates, will have helped the manager of the trust over the past 30 years. It is rare for its fund managers not to have spent several years working as an analyst before taking the helm of a fund and competition to run the best funds is intense. Once in place, however, there is no one pre-determined style they must follow.

Morse started his career as a stockbroker, and his career has taken a slightly different path to many of his colleagues, not least because he is one of the very few fund managers to have left Fidelity voluntarily and then later been invited to return to the fold. It happened in 1997 when Morse was running equity income funds at Fidelity and, by his own admission, puzzling over the reasons that M&G, the market leader, continued to attract and keep 20 times as much business as Fidelity was doing, despite producing less impressive returns.

When he had a call from a headhunter asking if he was interested in running the M&G UK Growth fund, he was intrigued enough to go along for an interview, hoping, he says now, to find out how they were able to steal such a march. Instead of the UK Growth fund job, he found himself being asked to run the whole 20-man UK equity operation for M&G, an offer that he found difficult to refuse. (Roll on a few years and the man who offered him the job, Vivian Bazalgette, the CIO of M&G at the time, is now the chairman of the Fidelity European trust). It was a "massive step up for me at the time" Morse recalls "and they said I could run the fund as well, a bit like being the player-manager of Chelsea. I guess I was a young man and I had aspirations to manage people as well as money. I thought I would really enjoy the opportunity to run a whole department".

And so it proved initially, until two years later M&G was bought by the mighty Prudential, an insurance company keen to expand and grow its investment management business. Instead of running a team of 20 people, he suddenly found himself running a department of 40 people, of whom "about 20 hated me because they thought they would be taking us over", when in practice it was the M&G people who came out on top (a common enough experience, and one reason why deals between fund management companies often run into difficulties).

The bottom line, Morse says, was that he had to give up managing money in order to manage people and found it both more complicated and difficult than he expected. He probably "hung around too long" and ended up being unceremoniously fired in 2003, told in classic City style to be out of his desk by 9.30 that morning. Fortunately it turned out that Fidelity was prepared to take him back as head of the UK institutional team, despite the initial reaction being that "of course" he would not be managing funds, since "nobody leaves and comes back to that".

In the event, by the time he rejoined in 2004, he was allowed to run some pension fund accounts, thereby achieving another 'player-manager' role like the one he had at M&G before. "I've been made to sit on the naughty step many times since coming back" Morse laughs. "Every time we have one of those ceremonies that celebrates your five year or 10 year anniversary, they always make a point of reminding me that if I hadn't left, I would have done thirty years by now and would have got that wonderful golden clock or whatever it is". For the past decade or so Morse has been running both the Fidelity European trust (since 2011) and the larger sister open-ended Fidelity European fund (since 2009).

Both trust and fund have continued to prosper. Despite there being about a 98 per cent overlap between the two funds, the investment trust has the better performance, which Morse attributes mainly to its ability to use gearing. £10,000 invested in the trust at launch would now be worth almost £400,000, assuming reinvestment of dividends. The total return to shareholders works out at just under 14 per cent compounded over 30 years. Over the past 10 years the comparable figure is 12 per cent per annum, second by a small margin only to Henderson Euro Trust in its AIC sector.

People always talk about Europe being "a rather sad place to invest", Morse says, and it is true that European trusts remain relatively unloved, with most trading on double digit discounts. "People read the headlines and say, 'why on earth do you want to invest in Europe?' Certainly in recent years Europe has underperformed the US market, but over that whole 30-year period, on a total return basis the European stock market has marginally outperformed the MSCI World Index". The return since 2010 has been 210 per cent, helped by a fall in the discount (the NAV return is around 175 per cent).

So how does the style of the current manager differ from that of Anthony Bolton? Whereas the latter was an aggressive contrarian stockpicker whose portfolios took no notice of what was in its benchmark, the approach that Morse has taken is more of an institutional one, reflecting his background and temperament and the fact that the trust is a much larger vehicle that the trust has become. He is happy to say that he manages it in a "benchmark-aware" manner, aiming to outperform the FTSE Europe (ex UK) index by an average of one to two per cent per annum after fees over a period of years. The board of the trust says that its objective is to be "the cornerstone long term investment of choice for those seeking European exposure across market cycles".

When a few years ago he and his colleagues dug out the first annual report of the trust, there was only one name that is still in the portfolio today and that is Nestlé. ("You wouldn't really associate that as a typical Anthony Bolton stock either",

Morse says. "Although Nestlé is considered rather a dull company, people don't always appreciate that fact that it has outperformed. That may be partly because it's quoted in Swiss francs, and the Swiss franc has appreciated so much.")

"My style really comes out of my background. When I first started running funds at Fidelity, I was running growth and income funds. We launched a fund called UK Dividend Growth on Valentine's Day in 1994, which very much represented what I was trying to do in terms of my investment approach, in which the focus is not just on dividend yield but on growing that distribution over time. I also actively take a lot of interest in the risk profile of the fund and try and diversify such that it is the stockpicking that really drives the performance of the fund, rather than taking aggressive sector positions or following particular themes".

"Typically I'm looking for companies that I think will grow their dividends consistently on a three to five year view. As a result the turnover in the portfolio tends to be fairly low. Obviously having a low turnover means that the transaction costs in the fund are quite low, which on a compounded basis over time is not a bad thing for performance. I'm also quite a cautious chap. I spend quite a lot of time focusing on managing downside risks. The beta of the portfolio is quite low, typically about 0.9.[*] As a result I tend to do poorly in relative terms when markets are exuberant, and vice-versa, so my best periods tend to be when everyone is rather gloomy and risk averse and the market is falling".

There is plenty of evidence, he says, that if you're successful in identifying companies that can grow their dividends consistently, you will outperform. "That's really what I spend all my time doing. Compared to previous managers of the fund and to the market generally, we have a pretty good hit rate. Around 75 per cent of our companies consistently grow their dividends over a three to five-year investment horizon. Obviously we're not successful 100 per cent of the time. But if we can come anywhere near close, we will be able to deliver decent performance".

"It is worth saying however that this is not dividend growth at any price. If you were to describe it in one line it is dividend growth at a reasonable or attractive price. The strength of the balance sheet is an important factor. In theory, you should be able to use a lot of leverage to enhance the returns to equity holders. But I don't want to own any companies where I think the financial leverage could jeopardise their ability to grow the dividend if times get tough. Ultimately it's a judgement".

What are the prospects for European funds now? "Europe tends to be a high beta play on global growth, and I would say if you think that we are now beginning a new cycle, and are in economic recovery mode, that's probably good for Europe

---

[*]   Beta = in financial theory the sensitivity of a portfolio to movements in the overall stock market. A beta of 0.9 suggests that the portfolio will only fall 9 per cent if the market is down 10 per cent.

relative to other regions in the world. The strength of the euro is obviously very important. I know some people talk about that as a negative, in the sense that there are a lot of exporters in Europe and they would be harmed by euro strength, but I take a different view". What about Brexit? "I am sorry but for most companies in Europe it is really a bit of sideshow".

The European market now is very global like all other markets. Only about 50 per cent of the sales of European companies comes from Europe. "That's still a pretty big amount and the exposure of European companies to the euro is probably higher than other regions. Nevertheless I think a strong euro is quite important for the relative performance of European stock markets. In the long run, as you say, there are some big global multinational players in Europe. I don't think they're necessarily any cheaper than similar companies in other parts of the world, but if you can find the good companies and add some value through stockpicking, you won't get a shabby return".

Although the trust is run in a benchmark-aware way, the one thing that Morse says he will never do is put a stock in the portfolio if he doesn't like it, just to avoid being too different from the weightings of the benchmark. "So Nestlé is a big part of the benchmark and because I like it, it's a large position in the fund and a top 10 holding. Roche is another case in point. On the other hand, Novartis is a big stock in the benchmark – about three or four per cent – but I don't own any. I won't hedge my bets in that respect. If I don't like a stock, I won't own it. But if I do like it, I will make sure that I own more than the benchmark weight such that if it performs well, I'm adding value".

"I am quite mainstream. You can call it institutional. It is a benchmark aware approach and clearly institutions like the approach. I don't think that's anything to be ashamed of, but it's not loaded up with lots of illiquid, mid-cap, small-cap stocks, and very high gearing, which some investment trusts have done very successfully over the years. The reason I keep saying to the management and to the board 'are you happy with me running it in this way?' is because, to be frank, I've been doing this for the last 25 years. I'm unlikely to change my behaviour. But they keep on coming back and saying, 'no, we like the way you do it. We're happy with it and a lot of the customers seem to like it as well'".

What did he learn from his experience at M&G, I ask? "The one thing that I really learnt was that if you invest in companies that pay you a high dividend yield, but they aren't growing their dividend, watch out. These are the sorts of companies that you can lose a lot of money in. That was the M&G problem. M&G in the 1980s was very much about dividend growth, but at some stage – and I don't quite know how – it had turned into a dividend yield shop. It was buying things on a very high yield, but it was basically buying dud stocks".

"They had lost sight of the fact that investing is a combination of price and quality. That's what value is. If you just focus on price, you'll end up with shoddy goods. If you just focus on quality, you'll spend far more money than you should ("maybe that's a warning for today" he adds, in reference to the currently high valuations on many popular stocks). So it is always a combination of the two". The Fidelity European trust has a yield of 2.5 per cent, just covered by earnings, but dividend growth has been above 15 per cent per annum for the past five years.

Isn't his approach a little bit dull, some might say? Morse is unrepentant. "My whole goal is to try to get the investors to buy the fund, stick with it over a long period of time, and then wake up after five or 10 years and say, 'Wow, actually it's done all right relative to the benchmark and it's also done all right relative to peers. Not the top performing fund – Sam hasn't shot the lights out; he's not Anthony Bolton – but it's done fine'. That's really what I would love for my investors to look back and say at the end of my period". That may not sound particularly heroic, but what we know from the fund performance statistics is that a consistently extra one or two per cent of performance after costs is guaranteed to beat the great majority of competing funds, so nor would that be a small achievement.

SAM MORSE *has decades of investment experience and has managed*
Fidelity European Trust PLC since 2011.

INVESTOR FORUM

We asked some of the most experienced investment trust investors we know to give their answers to some topical questions.

Who's Who

Peter Spiller is the longest serving manager of any investment trust. He has been the manager of Capital Gearing Trust plc since 1982.

Alan Brierley is the director of investment company research at Investec and has covered the sector since the early 1990s.

Nick Greenwood has been the manager of Miton Global Opportunities (MGO), a specialist trust that invests only in other investment trusts, since its launch in 2004.

Richard Curling is an investment director at Jupiter Fund Management with wide experience of the investment trust sector, including managing the Jupiter Fund of Investment Trusts.

Ewan Lovett-Turner is head of investment companies research at Numis Securities and has more than 15 years experience in the sector.

What has been the main lesson of the virus as far as you are concerned?

Peter Spiller: In investing the risks that are easiest to overlook are low-probability high-impact events. That is why it is wise to be prepared for a storm even when the sun is shining.

Alan Brierley: "Don't fight the Fed."

Nick Greenwood: That face-to-face meetings are far more productive than video calls, especially when exploring a new investment idea or discussing our investment trust with a potential new investor.

Richard Curling: Extremely unlikely events do happen! Whole industries have been shut down (e.g. airlines) and previously rare events, like companies not paying due rent, have become commonplace.

Ewan Lovett-Turner: There are always surprises around the corner, short-term forecasts are invariably wrong, and we are perpetually living in uncertain times. Despite this, we need to keep investing with a long-term view.

Which trust(s) has/have most pleased you this year with its/their performance?

Peter Spiller: Capital Gearing Trust materially increased its exposure to Pershing Square Holdings on very wide discounts in March 2020 and it performed stunningly over the next six months. The market poorly understood Bill Ackman's $27m position in credit default swaps which generated a $2.6bn profit.

Alan Brierley: Pershing Square. After a highly impressive 2019, the company has again delivered stunning absolute and relative returns; to early October, the NAV is up 47%, vs a 4% increase in the S&P. This includes the greatest trade the UK closed-end industry has ever witnessed in Q1, when the manager purchased credit default swaps for $27m, sold them for $2.6bn a few weeks later, and re-invested proceeds into equities at deeply discounted levels.

BH Macro and its sister fund BH Global. We have highlighted their defensive qualities, particularly inverse correlation characteristics in a risk-off environment. Shareholder total returns YTD of 39% and 23% compare favourably with the FTSE All Share total return of –18%

Nick Greenwood: Merian Chrysalis. We backed it at launch for the longer term, but it has found itself on the right side of the online divide.

Richard Curling: Scottish Mortgage (SMT) has to be the standout performer amongst the generalists – not least because of its size and high profile and their successful use of the closed-end structure to invest in unquoted companies.

Ewan Lovett-Turner: The performance of Scottish Mortgage (SMT), has been incredibly impressive. The managers, James Anderson and Tom Slater at Baillie Gifford, take a long-term approach and have been advocates on the trends of digitisation and healthcare innovation for some time. The trust has benefited from the swift acceleration of these trends in the Covid-19 environment.

Which have most disappointed you?

Peter Spiller: KKV Secured Lending plc, a direct loan fund, which Capital Gearing Trust also acquired in March 2020. With hindsight the 40%+ discount to NAV was not as attractive an opportunity as it appeared at the time!

Alan Brierley: Many companies in the specialist debt sector. The investor experience in KKV Secured has been catastrophic. Having given shareholders comfort on the

NAV a few days before a continuation vote and then expressed concerns over a significant portion of the portfolio a few days after is more than awkward.

A close runner-up is JZ Capital. The decision to employ two relatively inexperienced real estate investors to build a $1bn+ portfolio has unravelled and proved to be not the smartest decision ever.

Nick Greenwood: India Capital Growth. It was caught wrong footed by the non bank crisis and then allowed its discount to blow out to 42%.

Richard Curling: Secure Income REIT, which turned out to be not so secure after all. Riverstone Energy, which shows that bad corporate governance is still around. More generally there are still too many small undifferentiated trusts that really should be closed.

Ewan Lovett-Turner: Value investing has been firmly out of favour and the performance records of many trusts with this style have been destroyed as cyclicals have fallen further out of favour. Perhaps the most disappointing has been the saga at Gabelli Value Plus (GVP). The vast majority of shareholders and the board are seeking to wind down the fund, but this is being frustrated by the largest shareholder, which is closely linked with the manager.

Do you expect to see significant style rotation (including value/ growth) any time soon?

Peter Spiller: Every dog has its day; value will surely outperform at some point, but it is very difficult to say when.

Alan Brierley: No. I expect investors to be prepared to pay excess multiples for companies that can deliver sustainable growth in an uncertain world. That said, I am mindful that value is so bombed out and valuation of growth stocks are elevated. Should the yield curve start to steepen, this could be a catalyst for a reversal, and this could be quite dramatic.

Nick Greenwood: The policy response to Covid-19 will usher in a new phase which will have a different set of winners and losers than the one we are leaving.

Richard Curling: Whilst growth vs value style performance and valuations are currently at all time extremes, I do not expect this to reverse significantly whilst interest rates remain very low.

Ewan Lovett-Turner: Changes in behaviour that have been triggered by the lockdown environment are likely to provide a long-term tailwind to many technology companies. These have accelerated business plans of many "growth" companies and it is difficult to see these trends reversing in the near term.

If so, will it be temporary or persist through a longer cycle?

Peter Spiller: Growth equities have enjoyed a decade long outperformance, but over the last century value equities have prevailed. The value reversal could be short and sharp, slow and long lasting or maybe both.

Alan Brierley: Not got a clue. I don't think we are there yet.

Nick Greenwood: We are moving into a new cycle.

Richard Curling: There may possibly be a temporary correction due to the extremely extended valuation difference, but I would not expect this to last more than a quarter or so.

Ewan Lovett-Turner: When pressures from Covid-19 abate, I can see scope for a recovery in a sub-set of "value" stocks that have been cyclically challenged, rather than suffering from structural decline.

Will interest rates and/or inflation be higher in two years time?

Peter Spiller: We can be almost certain that short interest rates will not rise in a meaningful way over the next two years. Inflation is a different matter; as the economy recovers from this huge recession it is likely to strengthen.

Alan Brierley: I doubt it. That said, given the amount of debt in the system – government, corporate and personal – inflation is the only way out. I have no idea when it happens.

Nick Greenwood: Both will be higher.

Richard Curling: I expect interest rates to continue to be very low, but I would expect that we might be seeing some signs of inflation picking up by then.

Ewan Lovett-Turner: The adage "Don't fight the Fed" seems appropriate at the moment. The Federal Reserve has indicated that interest rates are likely to stay near zero for a number of years. A rise in inflation has become more likely given the scale of monetary and fiscal stimulus, against a backdrop of high household cash balance and supply chain disruptions.

Do you expect average discounts to widen or narrow from today's levels over the same time frame?

Peter Spiller: Both! The discounts on today's fashionable sectors will tend to widen and the unfashionable sectors will tend to narrow. It was ever thus.

Alan Brierley: The weighted average sector discount is still relatively narrow and it is difficult to see a further contraction, until we have Covid-19 under control. That said, there are pockets of value beginning to emerge.

Nick Greenwood: It will be a barbell result. The big trusts will continue to have narrow discounts whist small ones will stay wide.

Richard Curling: I would expect to see overall average discount levels to remain broadly similar to today, but I also expect we will continue to see a big divergence of discount rates between several trusts that will trade on quite high (apparent) premiums with several small undifferentiated trusts with little obvious attraction that will continue to trade at wide discounts.

Ewan Lovett-Turner: The breadth of investment strategies in the sector mean that overall averages can hide the true picture. Equity trust discounts currently average around six per cent, which has narrowed from double-digits in March, but wider than the 3% or so we saw at the start of the year. Further narrowing will depend on growth-oriented trusts remaining popular. Baillie Gifford funds on their own narrow the sector average by more than 2%!

In addition, the ability to deliver a consistent yield is likely to support ratings for equity income trusts. On average, alternative asset trusts are trading on a small premium. Those that promise income, such as infrastructure and renewable energy, should remain in strong demand given the low interest rate environment and hits to equity market dividends. I also see scope for discounts to narrow in private equity, given high-quality portfolios, as well as some areas of specialist debt if the economic outlook becomes clearer.

In which sectors would you most like to see new IPOs?

Peter Spiller: We would like to see more conventional investment trusts launched with firm commitment to zero discount polices. Japan looks a particularly interesting opportunity at the moment.

Alan Brierley: I expect IPOs to be focused on alternative investments. There has been a sharp reduction in IPOs in the past couple of years, and we expect fund-raisings to be dominated by secondary issues.

Nick Greenwood: New closed-end launches tend to be sectors that are hot so we tend to stay away. So many new UK launches recently are eye catching, as the UK as a sector is definitely cold.

Richard Curling: IPOs are most likely to be seen in areas that have seen most investor demand – so alternatives (such as infrastructure and renewable energy especially those generating income) and where the investment company structure (permanent capital) is being used effectively to invest in illiquid assets.

Ewan Lovett-Turner: Low interest rates mean that alternative income trusts are likely to remain the focus of IPOs. The sweet spot for new issuance remains a yield of 5% or more, with a target total return of 6–9% per annum, ideally from an asset class that offers security of income, particularly through some form of government backing, and preferably a degree of inflation protection. Further IPOs around ESG and social impact themes are likely. Increasing scrutiny of liquidity in open-ended funds may also drive continued interest from managers of less liquid equity strategies, such as small cap stocks, to look at launching investment companies.

Most impressive newcomer trust?

Peter Spiller: Whilst we have not been big backers of the growth style, all of the Baillie Gifford new launches have been extremely impressive. We worry the next 10 years may not be as supportive as the last 10 years.

Alan Brierley: Smithson Investment Trust stands out. It was the largest investment trust IPO ever. It raised £823m in October 2018, and following strong performance and ongoing investor demand, its market cap is now £2.1bn.

Nick Greenwood: Slight cheat as Merian Chrysalis was launched at the very end of 2018.

Richard Curling: I would nominate Hipgnosis Songs Fund and Merian Crysalis. Both trusts have performed well and have offered investors an exposure to new, interesting and exciting areas that cannot be had in the open-ended world.

Ewan Lovett-Turner: In a relatively barren period for IPOs since the start of 2019, even quieter than during the global financial crisis, the strongest performing IPOs in share price terms have been Schiehallion and RTW Venture, both up c.50% in sterling terms (helped by sterling weakness against the dollar). Schiehallion is an interesting addition to the sector, although it launched with little fanfare and has a non-traditional shareholder register. It is managed by Baillie Gifford using their growth approach and targets investments in private companies that it would own for the long term once they became public. Unlike most private equity funds the management fees are low at 0.9%, with no performance fee. It is issuing more shares and I expect the shareholder register to diversify over time.

Most sorry to see leave the field of play this year?

Peter Spiller: Witan Pacific, a well-managed value fund investing in the Asia Pacific. It is now Baillie Gifford China Growth Fund. The move of portfolios from value managers to growth managers is understandable (see above) but we are sorry to see the change.

Alan Brierley: Matthew Dobbs at Schroders has announced he will retire next year. He leaves big shoes to fill. I am also sorry to see Sir Michael Bunbury, chairman of HarbourVest Private Equity, hang up his boots. He has set very high corporate governance standards. The best trusts don't really leave the field of play. They get wound up because they haven't delivered and don't deserve to survive.

"TIPS FOR LONG-TERM OUTPERFORMANCE? BUY HIGH QUALITY INVESTMENT COMPANIES, DON'T OBSESS OVER DISCOUNTS, IGNORE ANY SHORT-TERM NOISE, HOLD THEM FOREVER AND LET THE POWER OF COMPOUNDING DO THE REST."

Nick Greenwood: Alistair Munday of Temple Bar. I suppose his departure rings the bell for value.

Richard Curling: I am sorry to see the departure of both Alastair Mundy and Mathew Dobbs, both great managers and the investment trust world will certainly be duller without them.

Ewan Lovett-Turner: Matthew Dobbs is retiring in early 2020. He is a highly experienced manager who has built a strong track record investing in Asia over the long term. He has managed both Schroder Asia Pacific and Schroder Oriental Income since their launches in 1995 and 2005 respectively. He leaves the funds in good hands with Richard Sennitt – they have worked together for 13 years.

Most interesting piece of research (or book/article) you have read this year?

Peter Spiller: *Radical Uncertainty* by John Kay and Mervyn King. Analytical and intellectual models can never fully incorporate the complexities of the real-world processes they seek to explain. You need to apply judgement, humility and common sense as well as mathematical models when thinking about risk.

Alan Brierley: *He's One of Our Own: The Story of Chris Wilder's Blades Revolution* by Danny Hall (Editor: a book about the manager of Sheffield United).

Ewan Lovett-Turner: I'm currently reading *Good Economics For Hard Times* by Abhijit V. Banerjee and Esther Duflo, which is appealing for their more rigorous use of evidence, rather than assumptions, to assess big economic problems.

The most striking statistic you have come across?

Peter Spiller: That the market capitalisation of Apple surpassed the market capitalisation of the entire FTSE 100 in 2020. It is reminiscent of the late 1980s when Japanese asset prices were extraordinarily high. For a brief period the grounds of the imperial palace in Tokyo was worth more than all the real estate in California. Thirty years later, the Japanese stock market is 40% lower than it was in 1989.

Alan Brierley: The market value of Amazon is now equivalent to 87% of the value of the entire FTSE 100. Ten years ago, I asked James Anderson of Scottish Mortgage if he was comfortable paying a P/E multiple of over 800× for Amazon. His answer ensured I never needed to ask the question again!

Nick Greenwood: That Apple is bigger than nearly all stock markets.

Richard Curling: That Apple is bigger than the entire UK market. That Scottish Mortgage is now the 39th largest company in the FT All Share index.

Ewan Lovett-Turner: Of the 326 Investment Companies launched in the decade prior to the global financial crisis, only about 15 per cent survive in their original form. Many of the funds that have disappeared were AIM or Euronext-traded funds in esoteric asset classes, often with poor corporate governance, high fees and over-leveraged balance sheets. It serves to highlight that the investment company sector is constantly reinventing itself. Strategies that don't work out fall by the wayside, while the trusts that have survived, e.g. infrastructure, have flourished.

Is Numis right to expect a wave of further consolidation in the sector?

Peter Spiller: Yes, at least 300 trusts appear to lack relevance for investors and need restructuring in one way or another. That said it will not happen in a hurry, as board members seem reluctant to face the inevitable.

Alan Brierley: Yes, the sector needs further consolidation. There are too many zombie companies that lack critical mass and have poor liquidity, where an extended bull market has hidden a distinct lack of alpha. The practice of boards, of giving the incumbent manager another chance in return for a reduction in fees is not constructive; we would welcome greater creativity.

Nick Greenwood: Yes.

Richard Curling: I hope so – there are still too many small undifferentiated trusts.

Ewan Lovett-Turner: Yes! It appears to have started and indeed accelerated since we wrote our note in July this year.

What is the most important improvement you would like to see in the investment trust sector?

Peter Spiller: Widespread adoption of zero discount policies by conventional investment trusts with liquid underlying portfolios.

Alan Brierley: Strong corporate governance has always been a core, differentiating feature of the closed-end industry. However, there have been a handful of cases in the past couple of years where the experience has fallen short of high standards.

Nick Greenwood: Directors should be more focused on managing discounts.

Richard Curling: I would like to see closer alignment of interests between the manager and the investor in externally managed funds where unfortunately we have sometimes seen asset gathering trump investor returns. We also need to see more scaling of fees as funds grow.

Ewan Lovett-Turner: I would like to see more engaged shareholders and more active boards. Steps are being made in the right direction, but more work needs to be done to tackle some of the smaller, underperforming funds that do not have widespread appeal or are not delivering a differentiated proposition to investors.

And what is the biggest challenge investment trusts face?

Peter Spiller: Lack of liquidity and volatile discounts. That is why zero discount policies should be widely adopted by conventional investment trusts.

Alan Brierley: Convincing wealth managers and retail investors that they are a superior investment vehicle with structural competitive advantages.

Nick Greenwood: Liquidity is getting difficult and not helped by institutions and wealth managers consolidating into bigger businesses. This means that many former buyers of trusts can no longer buy enough shares to move the needle.

Richard Curling: Being relevant and competitive in today's investment world and making sure they use the advantages of a closed-end structure.

Ewan Lovett-Turner: Costs are understandably an increasing focus of investors, but reporting under the KIDs regime puts ICs at a disadvantage versus open-ended funds. About half the sector is now focused on alternative assets, which are generally more intensive and more expensive to run than managing a traditional equity fund. Relatively high KIDs costs are leading investors to ration exposure to investment companies.

Top tips for long-term outperformance (own funds excluded)?

Peter Spiller: North Atlantic Smaller Companies plc. A study a few years ago by JP Morgan entitled "Back to the Future" revealed that North Atlantic Smaller Companies had delivered the second-best long-term returns in the investment trust sector, second only to Capital Gearing Trust.

Alan Brierley: Buy high quality investment companies, don't obsess over discounts, ignore any short-term noise, hold them forever and let the power of compounding do the rest.

Nick Greenwood: Baker Steel Resources and Atlantis Japan. For those with a higher risk tolerance, Macau Property Opportunities.

Richard Curling: Focus on growth sectors such as healthcare and technology and extend beyond just the quoted equities pool.

Ewan Lovett-Turner: Back managers with conviction and a differentiated approach. Understand how the funds are expected to perform in various market conditions and measure them against these expectations, rather than just a generic benchmark.

THE CASE FOR HEALTHCARE

Fund manager PAUL MAJOR *says that healthcare is tailor-made for an investment trust strategy.*

First obvious question: why set up an investment trust dedicated to healthcare?

Healthcare is an esoteric and technologically complex sector with the intersection of many different disciplines. You'll know this yourself. If you go and see a GP and there's something wrong with you, the first thing that happens is they refer you on to a specialist in a particular discipline. Then if you think about the many different ways that you are touched, physically and from a data point of view when you go in for any kind of procedure, there's a hugely complex ecosystem. It's like the technology sector in that regard. A lot of it is wrapped in complexities and jargon and other things.

It's also a very high risk sector in the sense that if you look at product development, it's long, it's expensive, it has high failure rates. Not because things don't necessarily work, but you can spend hundreds of millions of dollars developing something and if it's not actually meaningfully better than what's already out there, you don't have a viable business proposition. So our view is that technology and healthcare are sectors that lend themselves uniquely to both an active and a specialist approach. I think our results as a firm – Bellevue Asset Management has a long-standing history as a healthcare fund manager – bear that out.

Within that, most healthcare funds tend to be focused on geographical or subsectors of healthcare. You might get a pharma fund, a biotech fund, a med-tech fund, Asian healthcare, American healthcare or whatever. We take a different view. Our view is that we want to look at this globally because, in the end, the issues that everybody struggles with from a healthcare perspective are global in nature. As countries industrialise, they tend to inherit the healthcare problems of the Western world. We're all rowing in the same overall direction and therefore a global approach makes a lot of sense.

Why is an investment trust a good vehicle for that?

From our perspective, it gives you the most freedom to maximise the potential for returns. There are few constraints, as there are with UCITS 3 funds, around the concentration of the portfolio. As long as you are clear in your investment mandate with your investors as to what you're going to do, you have a great deal of freedom.

You also have the ability to deploy leverage when it's opportune to do so, to further compound your returns.

Another thing is that, as in the crisis in March and the similar market wobble that we had at the end of 2018, having permanent capital gives you tremendous opportunities. What you tend to find is that when markets panic, people bail out at the point of maximum opportunity. In reality, that's generally the best moment to go bargain hunting. Having that permanent capital structure means you can take advantage of mispricing in the market.

The final thing I'd say is that we are long-term focused. We have a low turnover portfolio and the trust structure obviates the need to provide daily liquidity within the fund, so we can run our positions. If you have a redemption request in an open-ended fund, then obviously you're forced to crystallise losses at what might be the wrong time. With a permanent capital structure, the share price takes care of that for you. The market provides the liquidity and we can just focus on running the portfolio.

How do you make the case that there are good returns to be made from this sector?

I would start by saying that the provision of healthcare is the secular growth story of our age. Why? Well, we know for certain there are ever more people; we know for certain that irrespective of the direction of economic growth, those people will get sick and they will require healthcare. We also know that the population is ageing and there is a very strong correlation between age and morbidity, particularly in the over sixty-fives. Evolution never optimised us to last as long as we do. By the time they're sixty-five, the vast majority of people have chronic medical conditions which cannot be cured and which need to be managed, regardless of what the economy does.

On top of that, there is a very strong correlation between economic growth and the proportion of GDP spent on healthcare, which is obvious if you think about it. Once you have food in your belly and a roof over your head, you have the opportunity to worry about staying fit and well. Whenever you see developing economies reaching middle income and advanced economy status, then you see this significant increase in healthcare expenditure and particularly preventive healthcare expenditure.

So – and this is something that is very much unchanged, despite Covid-19 – healthcare will be one of the fantastic growth stories of the next thirty years. On top of that, if we take a step back and think scientifically, the panoply of human disease is ever better understood. Everything that you can be diagnosed with is given something called an ICD code. There are about thirteen-thousand ICD9 coded diseases out there for all sorts of obscure ailments of varying types, and only a fraction of those are defined as curable.

If we think about it in those terms, there are literally thousands and thousands of diseases that we've barely tackled yet and as our scientific understanding of the body, genetics, and medicine improves, so more and more things will fall into that group of ailments that are treatable. So R&D will lead to ever more opportunities to improve and enhance the human condition. I can't really think of any other industry where you could argue that there are so many positive factors at the same time.

Where are the opportunities for profit within this?

Everything I've just told you is absolutely fantastic, wonderful and brilliant, and there's a classical bottom-left to top-right graph of demand. There's only one small fly in the ointment and that is that society can't afford any of this! The society that we live in was not designed to support people retiring at sixty-five and then inconveniently living another twenty years and dying in hospital at great expense. We can't afford end of life care, we can't afford lengthy retirements. Every time we crack the code of another disease and make something else manageable from a mortality perspective, we improve quantity of life. But this doesn't necessarily do very much for improving quality of life; people will still need ongoing care. That means we have this inexorable pressure on the total amount that's likely to be spent.

If you look at the healthcare industry as an abstract concept, for reasons that are totally unclear to anybody, no one in a central planning function of any Western country saw any of this coming. The demographic trends are long-standing, and medical innovation has been accelerating since the 1990s, but nobody really foresaw this. We're now in a situation where healthcare systems are buckling under the strain from a capacity point of view and are struggling to afford to provide the care that people reasonably want and expect. Once society knows and understands that something is treatable, the next question is: why can't I get treated for it? Which is a perfectly reasonable question.

So, we need to reshape and reform the healthcare system to make it fit for purpose. Now, if you look at it as an abstract business, it's not very well organised and horribly inefficient. One in four NHS appointments are not medically necessary; around a third of frontline care staff time is spent on administration; we have a chronic shortage of highly trained physician and nursing personnel which is almost impossible to bridge because the deficit is so enormous. It's a problem all around the world. We're fighting for an unscalable human resource.

What we need to do is to invest and invest quickly into tools that enhance healthcare productivity whilst simultaneously allowing improvement in care quality. All of the analysis that we've done – and the NHS has done some very similar analysis itself – says that those tools now fairly readily exist. What's required is the political will to embrace them and fundamentally change the way that we deliver care, which is what the NHS laid out in its 10-year plan, published in January 2019.

So the biggest problem is what we used to call time and motion studies, getting the right things into the right place at the right time with the minimum of unnecessary interventions. Is that right?

Yes, to a large extent, but also we need to acknowledge that human beings are fallible. There are all sorts of amazing statistics out there about how, if you are given drugs for asymptomatic disease reduction, you'll be horribly uncompliant with your therapy. For things like statins, blood pressure lowering drugs, those sorts of things, people don't remember to take them. As a consequence, their effectiveness in the real world versus their effectiveness in a clinical trial is dramatically different. If we could, for example, help people to manage their own conditions better, then we would save huge amounts of money and greatly improve life quality.

One of the biggest problems is the correlation between obesity and type two diabetes. It's an absolutely perfect correlation. It's almost impossible to get type two diabetes if you're not obese and sedentary. But at the same time, everybody knows that being obese and being sedentary is bad for you. Yet still we have an emerging epidemic of type two diabetes. Can we adopt behavioural and treatment strategies that enable people to manage these conditions better? We need to try different strategies in order to nudge people into better behaviours.

Some of the things that go on in hospitals are faintly ridiculous, like the idea of nurses doing ward rounds in the middle of the night. They're walking around the ward in the hope that if someone's going to have a heart attack it will be just as they pass their bed. It's not a particularly productive or efficient way to use somebody's time. With the availability of all that cheap technology to connect things together, such as cheap sensors and big data algorithms, you can very easily imagine a world where fairly simple tools can be aggregated together to enable people to operate much more efficiently.

That's where we spend our time, trying to find and identify what works and what could be genuinely revolutionary for the provision of care. We spend a lot of time investing in things like surgical and patient management software, diagnostics, health management strategies. We live in an age where everybody is walking around with a device in their pocket that's connected to the cloud and therefore connected all the time to almost supercomputing levels of analytical power, enabling us to deploy things that we never imagined even five or 10 years ago.

Is the fact that our healthcare system is mainly done by the state sector an issue?

It's a fair question, but a UK centric view of the world. The reality is that with the possible exception of the UK, every other country in the world has what we call a mixed system of private and public care. Even in the US, the government pays roughly half of all medical expenses. It's a mixed system in France, Germany, Italy and so on. So we're unique. We are very centralised and very bureaucratic and particularly inefficient, but the NHS is much beloved by the population, which makes it politically challenging to reform. However if you ask me, if system change is inevitable, where is it going to change first? You certainly wouldn't put the UK at the front of that queue.

We used to think about healthcare as drug companies and medical supplies, but this is now a much wider canvas?

Yes. I think that's why we have what we call an unconstrained mandate. What we are trying to invest in are the agents of change that will enable this revolution in healthcare technology. A lot of it is unsexy stuff: admin, planning, identifying how to intervene and manage patients better. It's not some clever medical device or cool new drug that treats a previously untreatable medical condition. If you look at drugs and devices, they're a tiny percentage of total medical expenditure. Once you start thinking about healthcare as a societal, financial, and structural problem that needs to be fixed, then you see it differently. That is the prism through which we view the world.

At various points in time you're going to want to be in different areas of healthcare because of political risk, global events, valuations and so on. The pandemic has been interesting in the sense that it has caused a narrow subset of healthcare companies to be valued in an irrational way. If you happen to be exposed to the beneficiaries of that, it's fantastic for you in the short term. In the longer term though, you don't want to be left holding companies which you literally cannot explain why they are valued as they are. I am thinking in particular of the companies involved in vaccine manufacturing and to a lesser extent some of the diagnostics companies.

The unconstrained nature of our mandate is very different to most healthcare funds which tend to have some benchmark constraints around how they operate. The most commonly used benchmark is the MSCI World Health Care Index. If you want to invest in a benchmark, then go and buy an ETF and save yourself a huge amount of money on fees. You don't need an active manager like us to do that for you. Bear in mind though that all benchmarks suffer the same problem which is they are a historical representation of success, in the sense that they are all market cap weighted and therefore they inevitably include the biggest companies in the world.

But just because you are the biggest company in the world today, it doesn't mean that you are going to be the fastest growing company and will be generating the best incremental returns for investors moving forward.

If you're talking about healthcare, roughly 40 per cent of the benchmark is in mega cap pharmaceuticals – Pfizer, Johnson & Johnson, Novartis. We don't normally own those sorts of companies because the kinds of innovations we're looking at are outside that area. Drugs and medical devices are less than 20 per cent of total healthcare expenditure. We have a more holistic view. We like to own focused smaller companies you've probably never heard of that are specialists in particular areas of healthcare.

As a result our portfolio looks nothing like the benchmark. Since our inception in December 2016, the MSCI World Health Care has delivered a total return of 67 per cent in dollars. We have delivered a total return of over 85 per cent. These numbers compare to the MSCI World Index's 50 per cent (data as at 1st October 2020). Our active share has averaged over 85 per cent since inception. Something like 40 per cent of our fund isn't even in the benchmark. Either they are not considered to be healthcare stocks, or they're too small to get into the benchmark because the benchmark is, roughly speaking, the 150 largest quoted healthcare companies.

And that means that your performance will tend to be more volatile than the market?

Yes, that's fair. We have a higher beta than the index, not surprisingly. When the market dives, as it did in March this year, and again in Q4 2018, you inevitably get a flight to liquidity. Funds that are more benchmark-constrained than we are tend to hide in stocks they're confident that they can sell quickly if they need to. We are also very different to the other six funds in the healthcare investment trust sector, as well as BB Biotech, the other Investment Trust managed by Bellevue. If you were to try to correlate the performance, you won't see any great correlation.

How do you go about building your portfolio?

Notionally there are about 3,000 quoted healthcare companies we could theoretically invest in. We have various liquidity parameters for our fund which reduce that to about 800 companies. We have identified 21 key healthcare transformation themes that we want to invest in, which leaves us with a realistic universe of a couple of hundred companies. By design our core portfolio can only hold a maximum of thirty-five of them.

We also have a watch list, which are things that we would be prepared to own under certain circumstances – be it news flow, data being released or valuations changing slightly. Right now it includes thirteen companies. They could go into the portfolio tomorrow under the right circumstances. But we have this cap of thirty-five stocks. So, once we get to thirty-five, it's a one in, one out scenario.

We are cognisant of potential concentration and downside risk. We look to have a balance in the exposure to the themes and different subsectors. The market has recovered quite strongly, and valuations are, in a historical context, not cheap. The economy is not exactly looking great, is it? So a key factor in our recent cap flow allocation decisions has been revenue defensibility. We've concentrated a bit more on reasonably valued essential medicines and shied a little away from more expensive stuff that's linked to hospital footfall, how many people are willing to go to hospital.

Let's discuss the virus. You seem to be saying that you think both the public and investors have got this wrong.

I wouldn't go that far. There is always a danger in over-extrapolating early signals in medicine in general. Failure rates are high and that's as true, if not more true, for vaccines as it is for any other area of development. So be careful not to get overexcited by the early data. We have data that shows that giving people vaccines has some effect and they seem to generate antibodies and they seem to generate T-cells. That's great in as far as it goes. But the next question is, what is the persistence of the effect? What is the benefit it gives?

The thing about Covid is that it's not very dangerous to the vast majority of people. It's dangerous to a narrow subset of people who are elderly and immuno-compromised. The reason it is dangerous to them is that when you're elderly or by definition immunocompromised, your immune system doesn't work the same way. With that being the case, you need to demonstrate that any vaccine will work sufficiently well in those people who are elderly and immunocompromised. The data in the public domain on efficacy in these high risk populations is still very limited; literally a handful of patients.

I'm not saying this isn't going to happen. What I am saying is that when you see Moderna publishing its Phase 1 vaccine results from 45 young and healthy people in July and the whole US stock market goes up by one per cent, which in value terms is hundreds of billions of dollars, that's bonkers.

Bearing in mind that there are seven billion people in the world and many of them live in less developed nations with unfavourable climates, in order to make this go away, you need to have probably two-thirds of the world's population immunised to prevent there being reservoirs of potential infectivity. For many of those people, it's not going to be practical to distribute a vaccine that requires what we call cold chain storage – essentially, kept freezing cold during transport. There are vaccines in development that don't require cold chain, but they're further behind. Then we've got to manufacture and distribute this stuff to everybody. I think we're going to be living with Covid for a long time.

And possibly some other viruses in due course?

Well, yes. That's ever the case. The last time we were in this situation was a hundred years ago, broadly speaking, where we were on the back foot. We were on the front foot with swine flu back in 2009. That didn't really present much of a problem. We got lucky there, I think. It wasn't that we were better prepared, it was that the virus was overestimated in terms of its lethality. It didn't live up to people's expectations. But we had SARS in '03, MERS in '09, another coronavirus in 2019 – yes, this will happen again. Who knows when? But hopefully lessons will be learnt from this debacle that will inform the next one a bit better.

So do you think that Covid-19 has significantly changed the opportunities in healthcare?

I don't think it is much of a game changer. Coming back to those demographic drivers of healthcare demand, the virus changes very little. In a global context, many of those who have tragically died in this pandemic were very elderly and going to fall off the healthcare utilisation curve in the short-to-medium term. What it has done, as all crises inevitably do, is it has accelerated some natural trends that we were forecasting and expecting, like more use of electronic diagnostics, telemedicine, point of care diagnostics, treatment of people in lower acuity settings, more separation of care between emergency and ambulatory care. In that respect, the pandemic has probably had a favourable impact on the rate of change in the evolution of the healthcare system.

The other thing it's done is it's highlighted – as if it didn't need highlighting anymore already – that governments around the world have underinvested in healthcare capacity and tools in recent decades and that needs to be reversed. What has changed is that probably that debate was more complicated six months ago because you would have had people saying, 'I don't want to pay more tax to fund better healthcare'. I think that debate has fallen away now. Most people would be very happy to pay more money in order to have a better healthcare system, and that is a healthy backdrop for what we are doing with the trust.

PAUL MAJOR, *a biochemist by training and a former top-rated healthcare analyst, has been the manager of the BB Healthcare Trust (ticker: BBH) since December 2016.*

WILL FINANCIALS REVIVE?

Specialist fund managers NICK BRIND AND GEORGE BARROW *of Polar Capital believe that the worst is finally over.*

I T IS HARD to remember now that banks were once the great growth sector in the stock market. In the years leading up to the global financial crisis, shares of almost every kind of bank roared ahead. The financial sector, which the big banks dominate, led the market upwards for several years. At its peak in 2007, financials accounted for a 22 per cent weighting of the S&P 500 index; since then its weighting has fallen by half.

It has been a spectacular reversal of fortune. Bank shares have been hit by a triple whammy of tighter regulation, falling interest rates and sluggish economic growth. Some, including Lloyds and RBS, had to be humiliatingly bailed out by the government. The share price of Lloyds tells the story. From a peak of 283p in 2007, the shares have fallen by 90%. It was only in 2015 that it was allowed to resume the payment of dividends and those too were stopped by government order when the Covid-19 pandemic broke out this year.

The financial sector is of course not just about the big banks, including as it does insurance companies, asset managers, stock exchanges and speciality lenders, as well as a number of technology (fintech) companies, all with growth potential. Neverthelesss, the decade-long slump in bank shares and the pandemic-inspired market crash in March makes it difficult to imagine a more unhelpful backcloth to the continuation vote which the board of Polar Capital's global financial trust put to its shareholders in April this year. The timing of the vote, which offered shareholders the chance to tender their shares back to the company at close to Net Asset Value, was determined by the seven-year initial life that the trust adopted when it launched in 2013.

Had it not been for the sudden, unexpected impact of the pandemic, the outcome would not have been in doubt. In the event, 60 per cent of the shareholders voted to keep the trust in existence, while 40 per cent tendered their shares. In the circumstances that was a more than creditable result, with a majority of shareholders acknowledging that there was still value in a specialist trust dedicated solely to the fortunes of the financial sector.

Nick Brind, co-manager of the trust with John Yakas since its launch in 2013, certainly believes that prospects were improving before the pandemic hit. The fact that the trust had promised shareholders at launch that there would be a continuation vote after seven years proved to be helpful in retaining investor loyalty. The trust has now promised to hold a regular tender vote every five years in future. "It means that we will be re-pitching the investment story again every five years and if we haven't performed, shareholders have the certainty of knowing that they can get their money back at that point if they want".

The ability to offer continuation votes, although far from universal, is one of the features that demonstrate the flexibility and accountability which can be built into the investment trust structure. The price that shareholders and trust managers pay is the potential loss of scale and liquidity if a lot of shares are tendered at the time of vote. After the tender in May the market capitalisation of the Polar Capital trust fell overnight to around £130m.* This is a little way below the minimum size of trust that some wealth managers say they need to see to be comfortable with in terms of market liquidity, but it is still a viable platform from which to look for future growth.

"I think the tenders reduce the concern there may be about the size of the trust. Shareholders would obviously prefer it to be larger and more liquid, but if you are taking a medium term view" says Brind "you have the certainty of an exit and there is the potential for the trust to grow when and if sentiment changes towards the sector". And that of course is the point: nobody can dispute that the financials sector is more unloved today than it has been for years. Valuations for banks, in particular, if measured on any conventional measure, such as earnings multiples and price-to-book ratios, have not been lower in living memory. The scars from the financial crisis, in which banks' massively imprudent lending practices brought the whole financial system to the brink of collapse, are deep and enduring.

An obvious question therefore is whether the virus pandemic has worsened the outlook for the bank sector – or would it have taken a beating anyway? The five-man Polar Capital financials team takes the view that even before the pandemic hit, the shares of banks were being marked down in anticipation of a slowing of the economy and possible recession. Banks have typically tended to underperform a year or two before the economy goes ex-growth.

"If Covid hadn't hit, the big question for us would have been how the banks would have performed going through the coming slowdown, given that we have had this huge increase in regulation, capital requirements and so on as a result of the global financial crisis. Talking to investors, that was what they were waiting to see". In other words, have all the measures taken to prevent another financial crisis made the banks more resilient to any future downturn?

---

* As at 30 September 2020.

The economic impact of the virus has only underlined the importance of that question. "If investors can see how the banks perform – and we will obviously find out over the coming months – and they don't lose large amounts of money from loans going bad and so on, and the underlying performance is good, investors are likely to see that things really have changed and that the banks now deserve a higher rating through the cycle". In that case a bank that is trading on a price earnings multiple of say eight today might be rerated to say 10 or 11 times for that reason alone. Add in the potential for economic recovery, and maybe higher interest rates, which are generally good for bank profitability and so-called value stocks, and the outlook for the sector could be transformed.

"We need to see what happens over the next six months and to what degree we see higher loan losses coming through" says Brind. "You can argue that last time [in the financial crisis] people were worried about the solvency of the sector, and that the banks were the core of the problem. Today, however, they are very much not the core of the problem. Balance sheets are materially stronger". The message that banks are not part of the problem, as they were during the financial crisis 12 years ago, was central to the case that the Polar team made to persuade shareholders to their side during the continuation vote. To the extent that lending will be the key to the economy's recovery, he suggests, you might even call them part of the solution, which would be a dramatic change.

To underline how different things are today from what they were in the financial crisis, Brind recalls going to meetings with the Chief Financial Officer of Northern Rock and asking him "Can you explain how you can lend 125 per cent of the value of a house to someone and say that you are prudently underwriting risk? He would say 'you just don't understand' – and he was right. We didn't! We came out looking at each other mystified". That was quite apart from the crazy phenomena of NINJA loans (giving mortgages to people with no income and no job), CDOs and synthetic CDOs and all the other cavalier lending practices of the pre-crisis period.

"Today it's so, so different. Some of that is obviously driven by regulation. Buy-to-let and mortgage market regulations have forced banks to underwrite at lower loan-to-values. Commercial property banks haven't been loaning at 70 per cent, they've been loaning at 50 per cent loan-to-values. So they've got much more of a cushion there. If loans go bad, they're going to lose less money".

Of course, he goes on, there will always be banks which have done "stupid lending", particularly in commercial property. "You still can't escape that businesses are going to fail, especially as a result of lockdown. You can't escape that you're going to see large losses. But I think we will find out that the riskiest lending has not been done by the banks this time round, but in the capital markets instead. The majority of the banks will probably turn out to be much more resilient than people thought coming into this".

As well as much stronger balance sheets, there are two other reasons for believing that there is value in the banking sector now that prices have come down so far. One is that changes to the accounting rules for banks effectively force them to make larger, earlier provisions against potential future losses. "That makes it interesting from a recovery perspective because if investors become confident that the banks have taken the P&L hit through provisioning at an earlier stage than in the past, once they then get visibility on the economic outlook, suddenly you could see a strong earnings recovery as provisioning falls".

The second reason, notes George Barrow, another member of the team, is simply that bank shares are now as cheap as they have ever been (as you would hope, given the many whose share prices have fallen by 90 per cent). Historically if you have bought shares in financials on these kinds of ratings, you have always done well, Polar's research demonstrates. Banks in particular are the "ultimate cyclical stock", and if there is recovery it would be normal for them to lead the way as the market recovers.

But can banks really do well if, as many observers still believe, interest rates will remain at rock-bottom levels and maybe even go negative, as they have done in some countries already? Historically bank profitability is closely linked to both the level and term structure of interest rates, as banks traditionally make money by borrowing short term (from depositors and money markets) and lending long, meaning the differential between short- and long-term rates is a critical factor. When both are low profit margins are poor.

Brind's response is that rising interest rates are not necessary for bank shares to start outperforming. Loan losses coming in below expectations will be a more important factor in the short term. Longer term, the massive increase in monetary stimulus and government-guaranteed loans since the virus broke could easily lead to higher inflation and fears of rising interest rates, and "that would be an extra positive for the sector", as well as for value stocks more generally.

The irony of course is that the same hopes of imminent recovery were what prompted the launch of the global financials trust back in 2013. It was launched in response to investors saying they were looking for a way to get back into what was already then the beaten up financial sector. The trust was deliberately pitched as a conservative way to play any such recovery. To minimise risk, it was designed to be a widely diversified global fund that would capture the expected improvement in the performance of banks and general insurance companies, while also having some exposure to growth in the form of emerging market banks, asset management companies and financial technology ("fintech").

Cumulative total return performance to end September 2020

	1 year (%)	3 years (%)	Since PCFT launch (%)
Polar Capital Global Financials Trust NAV	(18.5)	(11.3)	41.8
Polar Capital Global Financials Trust portfolio NAV	(18.5)	(11.3)	46.7
Polar Capital Global Financials Trust share price	(22.6)	(15.6)	29.6
Barclays	(56.1)	(48.8)	(57.3)
HSBC Holdings	(45.4)	(54.2)	(52.2)
Lloyds Banking Group	(28.5)	(47.1)	(42.8)
NatWest Group	(56.1)	(48.8)	(57.3)
Standard Chartered	(45.4)	(54.2)	(52.2)

Source: Bloomberg, Morningstar, Marten & Co

MSCI ACWI Financials and MSCI AC World Index, rebased to 100

MSCI ACWI Financials relative to MSCI AC World Index, rebased to 100

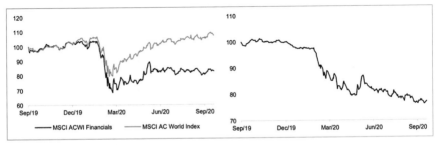

Source: Morningstar, Marten & Co

Weightings have remained closely correlated to the trust's benchmark, the MSCI World Financials index, and are designed to offer a balance between growth and income. Since launch the portfolio breakdown has moved a little, reflecting in part the growing maturity of the fintech sector, which now accounts for around 13 per cent of the portfolio, compared to just four per cent two years earlier. Payments companies such as Paypal and Mastercard have performed particularly well. There are also a few holdings of corporate bonds to bolster the yield.

The broad objective of the trust remains the same as it was. In terms of style and positioning, it sits between two open-ended funds that the team also manage, one of which prioritises growth and the other income. The broadly diversified nature of the trust and its global exposure helps to explain how the trust has managed to grow at all over the past seven years, even if the rate of growth has been lower in practice than shareholders were hoping for at the outset. As the table shows, despite the dreadful performance of the big UK banks, the trust's globally diversified portfolio has produced a total NAV return of 46 per cent over its seven-year life. With the shares slipping to a discount, the share price return currently lags that of its benchmark.

One unexpected consequence of the pandemic has been that the insurance company holdings have been badly hit by uncertainty about the validity of claims from holders of business interruption policies during lockdown and other restrictions. They are due to be tested in a court case. "Historically" says Barrow "non-life insurance has been a great place to hide during stormy periods, because it is counter-cyclical, defensive and normally driven by weather-related losses, winds, hurricanes, earthquakes and so on. We think that those concerns are overstated. We think this sector is offering a really interesting risk-reward ratio at the moment".

Nevertheless, despite the attractions of newer untried financial technology companies, it is the incumbent banks that will largely determine the performance of the sector over the next few years. If value and cyclical stocks are to make a comeback after so many years of dominance by growth investing, the banks will perforce be well to the forefront of that change. The investment trust structure gives the Polar Capital trust one great advantage over open-ended equivalents, by virtue of the board being able to call on revenue reserves to sustain the dividend. (It also can use gearing, but that remains at relatively modest levels.)

With some of the biggest UK banks being ordered to suspend dividends and extend more credit to struggling businesses in the wake of the national lockdown, the ability to smooth dividends has been an invaluable asset. Emerging market banks are still meanwhile paying good dividends and US banks can pay dividends if they can prove the health of their balance sheet. The board's policy is to aim to continue growing the dividend and has scope to use revenue reserves in support of that aim. The current yield has been ranging between four and five per cent, which is attractive on a comparative basis. The not unreasonable hope for shareholders is that any combination of style rotation, rising interest rates, improved loan loss experience and a narrowing discount will produce a geared and positive reaction well before the next five-yearly tender vote comes round for approval.

NICK BRIND *and* GEORGE BARROW *are fund managers
for the Polar Capital Financials Team.*

INSIDE THE BANK VORTEX

There are other ways to try and make money from the travails of the banking world since the global financial crisis. Specialist debt trusts are one, as DAVID BENAMOU *explains in this interview.*

BANK BALANCE SHEETS are notoriously difficult for the outside analyst to penetrate, so it helps to have some inside knowledge of how they are put together and what might really be hiding behind the apparently simple list of assets and liabilities you can observe in their Annual Report and Accounts. David Benamou is the head of one of a number of specialist investment management firms which are attempting to use their experience and expertise in this arcane area for the benefit of less privileged investors.

The investment trust world, it turns out, is as good a place as any to offer such a proposition. Since the global financial crisis, as regulators and governments have reined in the ability of the biggest banks to take on risk, the number of specialist debt funds has grown from almost nothing to comprise more than 40 trusts today. All these trusts are in different ways looking either to do the more specialist lending that banks are no longer able to do, or seeking to exploit anomalies in the pricing of the many varieties of tradable debt securities that banks and companies can issue.

M. Benamou's firm, Axiom Alternative Investments, is in the latter camp, and its Axiom European Financial Debt trust (ticker: AXI) is one of 14 trusts that make up the debt and bonds sub-sector of the wider debt category in the AIC classification. It aims to generate an attractive yield and additionally some capital gain by buying and trading the debt of banks and other financial institutions. They say that you will never eat a sausage once you have seen how it is made, and the temptation for ordinary mortals, when confronted with the complex and opaque world of bank debt securities, may well be tempted to adopt the same approach.

Nevertheless, the concept is exactly the kind of thing that investment trusts, with their permanent pool of capital and, ideally, a knowledgeable board to oversee the fund manager, are in principle well able to provide. Most of the trusts in the debt sector feature in the alternative asset category and are marketed on the strength of their ability to offer an above average yield, with additional potential for capital gain if market conditions and the manager's stockpicking skills are favourable.

In September 2020 the Axiom trust was offering a handsome yield of 7.5%, although in common with a number of other debt specialist funds its shares, having risen above its 100p issue price two years ago, have been trading below it for the past 18 months. With interest rates very low and possibly going negative, and the European economy facing a serious slowdown in economic activity in the aftermath of the pandemic, market conditions have been unhelpful recently.

Shareholders have nevertheless still obtained a better total return than the FTSE All-Share index has managed over the same period and Benamou says he is confident that conditions for the trust's strategy will become more favourable again in the future, now that the effects of the pandemic have been largely priced in by the debt market. He himself previously worked at Societe Generale, the big French bank, and many of his colleagues come from similar backgrounds.

Their idea in setting up Axiom AI in 2009 was to offer investors the services of a specialist investment management firm that could both analyse debt prospectuses professionally and assess the new regulatory constraints under which banks and insurers now have to operate. With so much of the new regulation being unprecedented and untested, it seemed likely that there were bargains to be had from investing or trading in securities and bonds which the wider market was as yet unable to fully understand or price correctly.

Since 2009 Axiom has expanded its range of funds to seven, each with a different risk-return profile. The investment trust, launched in 2015 at a price of 98p, is the one with the highest risk, but also the highest potential return, with a target return of 10 per cent per annum and targeted annualised volatility of around 5%. Since its launch the trust has generated an NAV total return of around 20%,[*] including a total of 27p in dividends. In company with most other debt funds, the shares have mostly traded at a discount since the last quarter of 2018, so the share price return has been more modest.

The investment trust, explains Benamou, "is the only product we have which is aiming for an over 10 per cent return. The secret sauce of the trust is quite simple. In this trust we try to add the best of what we do in the rest of the product range". It starts at one end with the most liquid, easiest to trade bonds, and ranges through less liquid instruments, special situation and recovery stories to issues by mid-cap financial institutions at the other end of the risk spectrum. All these types of debt issues require skilful and forensic analysis, based not just on intense scrutiny of the prospectus and the terms of the issue, but also modelling its likely performance in different market conditions.

One of the key regulatory changes that the trust has zeroed in on is the requirement that banks replace their old subordinated debt with what are called CoCos, short for contingent convertible securities. These are debt instruments issued by European

---

[*]   As at 30th September 2020

banks and other financial institutions whose key features are that they can be converted into equity when a financial institution falls below a specific trigger of capital (generally between 5.125% and 7% for banks).

The idea behind CoCos is to make sure that investors who lend to banks are no longer able to get off scot-free if the bank gets into trouble through excessive or foolish lending, as many were able to do during the global financial crisis. The risk of another systemic banking failure is reduced if some or all of the money a bank has borrowed from its debt-holders automatically becomes available to help bail it out should its losses exceed a certain pre-determined threshold in a time of crisis.

So the regulators now require that bonds issued by banks do so in the form of CoCos. There are crucial differences however between CoCos and older subordinated debt instruments in terms of coupon (interest payments), security and liquidity. Axiom were one of the first to specialise in analysing these new debt instruments and the firm boasts regular top quartile performance against other funds in this segment of the market.

To most of us this kind of work would be eye-swivellingly tedious, but to hear Benamou in full flow is to hear the authentic voice of an enthusiast. To give you a flavour, he purrs approvingly about "how complicated" the bonds in the special situations "bucket" in the trust's portfolio are. A good example is a bond which was formerly issued by Fortis Bank, but is now a BNP Paribas bond.

It is "very complicated to analyse in terms of capital, but the coupon is safer than the CoCos one for the same issuer because the language in the prospectus means it is payable nearly all the time. Today it has a Euribor +2% coupon of a cash price of 77%, which is basically quite nice considering the bank will have to clear up this legacy bond. And here, the funny part of it is that there is no redemption feature in the prospectus! So, if BNP wants to take it out, it has to buy in the market. If you hold it and want to keep the bond, it's up to them to pay more to buy it".

So how should potential shareholders expect the trust to perform, I ask? Well, says Benamou, the underlying yield of the trust's investments is around six per cent per annum before costs and to meet the target return the team need to add about five per cent or more through active management of the portfolio and/or favourable movement in the relevant markets.

Historically, he says, the trust has tended to outperform during bond bull markets while being reasonably defensive when bond prices are falling. The trust has to beat a hurdle rate of seven per cent per annum in order to qualify for a performance fee. "Although we haven't done so well this past year, in the past in general in bull years we have done much better than comparable open-ended funds (as an example the trust delivered +16.98% in 2019 versus an average +10% for the open-ended financial credit funds). In bear years, such as 2018, we've generally been in the middle of the pack".

"ALL THESE TRUSTS ARE IN DIFFERENT WAYS LOOKING EITHER TO DO THE MORE SPECIALIST LENDING THAT BANKS ARE NO LONGER ABLE TO DO, OR SEEKING TO EXPLOIT ANOMALIES IN THE PRICING OF THE MANY VARIETIES OF TRADABLE DEBT SECURITIES THAT BANKS AND COMPANIES CAN ISSUE."

What about interest rates going lower or even negative? Yes, of course, if it happens, that would be bad for bank profits over the longer term and increase the risk to the bondholders. Benamou makes the point however that bank balance sheets are immeasurably stronger than they were in the 2007–2009 financial crisis, so the risk of being "bailed in" by a bank in crisis, for example, is much more remote than it was then.

European banks have reduced their leverage by more than 60 per cent since 2017 and their average tier one equity capital ratio has risen from under four per cent to over 15 per cent in the same ratio. Recent stress tests have shown that bank fundamentals "have become so robust following the financial crisis that European banks have enough capital to absorb the shock of a magnitude equivalent to the 2008 crisis".

He also points to the experience of some of the Nordic banks which have shown how bank profitability can be improved, despite zero interest rates, by moving away from a branch business towards a lower cost online/digital business. As for the impact of the pandemic, it is self-evident that lockdowns and other restrictions that damage the economy also pose a threat to the future profitability of banks, and that is one reason why the price of CoCos and some other instruments fell quite sharply initially.

Both the Bank of England and the European Central Bank moved quickly to ease some of the capital requirements for the banks when the crisis hit, while the decision to force some banks to stop paying dividends for the moment – a controversial step for equity investors – has clearly not done the position of the debt holders any harm. No doubt for fear of scaring off investors in bank debt, the European Commission has been at pains to reassure holders of subordinated bank debt that they would not be asked to share the burden of losses even if the banks were to need state aid.[*]

Benamou says he is confident therefore that the price of bonds has now fully adjusted to the new post-Covid environment and the trust is well placed to benefit from any sustained economic rebound and improvement in confidence. The trust has promised shareholders a continuation vote in 2023, when the track record of its strategy will be reviewed. While he has been thinking of suggesting to the board that the trust broadens its remit to include some of the bigger US banks his team know well, that certainly won't happen before the continuation vote takes place.

In the meantime, although the returns are below target, the handsome yield of more than seven per cent continues to look attractive. Although family offices and wealth managers make up the bulk of the register, Benamou notes that private investors started to take an interest in the fund from June onwards when the discount of the trust's shares widened out to more than 15 per cent at one point, increasing the headline yield. Their buying since then has helped reduce the discount, at least for a while.

---

[*]   Editor's note: a cynic might be less sanguine. You never know what politicians may do if a new crisis materialises – if they have done it before they may do it again.

An article in the *Financial Times* "described well the fact that the trust is a good tool for people who want to diversify. Instead of buying one, two or three bonds, they can diversify their whole bond portfolio. Risk management is before anything else about diversification, as you know". Well said indeed, as the less you know or understand an asset class, the more important it becomes, and bank debt instruments are among the more complex of them all.

DAVID BENAMOU *founded Axiom Alternative Investments in 2009*
and was talking to JONATHAN DAVIS.

CAN NICE GUYS FINISH FIRST?

ESG has moved from hippy pipe-dream to corporate mainstream, but what is it really, asks DAVID JOHNSON *of Kepler Intelligence.*

ESG investing, Environmental, Social, and Governance respectively, is much in vogue and has ended up weaving its way into almost every manager's investment thesis, though with varying degrees of genuine integration. In this article we shine light on where ESG originated from, how *Kepler Trust Intelligence* goes about analysing ESG, and examples of trusts which demonstrate both good ESG credentials but also the nuances of assessing ESG.

The broader history of responsible investing, of which ESG investing is a part, can be traced back to the eighteenth century where religious groups such as Quakers and Methodists placed restrictions on the types of companies their followers could invest in. Fast-forward to the late twentieth century and to the rise of the collective investment scheme which suddenly concentrated a large amount of voting power to a number of professional managers. Where traditionally shareholders would have an opportunity to vote directly (if they chose) at an AGM, fund management houses have traditionally not seen it as their role to exercise this influence. However, changes in attitudes have seen responsible voting at EGMs become an important element of custodianship. Professional investors are now asked to pressure companies on key issues where deemed appropriate. As a precursor to this, we began to see dedicated 'responsible investors' appear, and the development of products to satisfy this new demand. The real watershed moment for ESG came in 2006, with the launch of the UN Principles for Responsible Investment (PRI), whose foundations had been laid over the prior two years. Signatories of the PRI, of which one can now count most major professional asset managers, are bound to follow six principles which demand the incorporation, disclosure and promotion of ESG issues.

Over the last decade or so the attention given to ESG has increased rapidly and not solely due to policy and initiatives within the financial sector, such as the PRI, but caused by a much broader societal understanding of the underlying issues. Climate change is the most pressing of these concerns; one would have to be living under a rock to not be aware of the global demonstrations against climate change, and the ensuing government policies towards reductions in CO_2 emissions and talk of 'green deals' for major economies – the list goes on. While social issues gain less coverage, there has been localised demand for improvements in employee safety, especially with the increasing labour intensity in emerging market economies, as well as calls for more diversification within corporate structures in developed economies.

Despite the momentum behind Environmental and Social, Governance remains the most established of the three factors; the spectre of Enron and the changes brought about by its collapse remaining relevant to this day. Years passed and it seems that the lessons have not been fully learned, as demonstrated by the collapse of Carillion in 2018. It is clear that there is still work to be done for something as seemingly obvious as analysis around the quality of company governance.

ESG: to what investment end?

As should be inferred by the governance aspect at least, ESG has the capacity to enhance the returns of an investment process, even if it were to only avoid the next major corporate catastrophe. The common motivation for ESG integration is risk management. Some of the largest corporate losses have been contributed to by governance failings and fraudulent behaviours. Environmental issues are also becoming an increasing headache; just ask BP. As a result, at a stock level ESG compliant companies are increasingly finding themselves with a lower cost of capital on a relative basis. This confers a real competitive advantage to companies.

From a governance perspective, companies which pay more than lip service to ESG can translate to superior policies surrounding independence of auditors, accounting transparency, and independence of the boards, allowing investors to more readily trust the stated accounts and their own valuations based on financial statements as a result. Environmentally friendly policies see companies less likely to incur regulatory fines, avoid being forced into larger volumes of carbon trading to offset emissions and face less risk from the increasingly tighter environmental regulation. It might also give the company an edge in terms of the attractiveness of their products to consumers.

Social factors often play a smaller role in improving return potential, most commonly rearing their head in the form of high profile workplace assaults or labour infractions. Yet we can expect the importance of social issues to quickly increase in the modern world of social media, the dominion of the few dominant names in the tech sector opening a Pandora's box of privacy and social anti-trust issues, brought about by their products which are designed to encompass many aspects of our daily lives, the consequences of which are only recently being felt.

Seeing the wood from the trees

It is important to note the distinction between an ethical, responsible or impact-driven investment process, and an ESG integrated process. Specific ethical, responsible or impact-driven processes will often define the objective of an investment trust (or fund), with the investment process built around the philosophical belief of the client or manager. Everything from the investment universe to the end portfolio is proactively designed around these beliefs. ESG investing, on the other hand, is far more flexible, and represents the integration of material ESG risk factors into a persisting investment process. There is nothing stopping metals and mining investment strategies integrating ESG analysis into their process, though the extent of the integration and its effectiveness in producing an ESG compliant portfolio will vary (see our example of the BlackRock Energy & Resources Income below).

When one assesses ESG at an investment strategy level, the process becomes somewhat opaque, as the underlying holdings can at times be withheld, or simply an analyst does not have the time to meticulously assess each underlying holding in a portfolio when they will likely cover multiple trusts concurrently, each with dozens of holdings. The process for assessing ESG must thus be adapted for collective investing, assessing both the manager's 'inputs' and 'outputs'.

The real crunch is being able to decipher if an investment manager is both sincere and effective in their integration of ESG into the investment process, and this is where much of Kepler's efforts will focus on. While the *Kepler Trust Intelligence* process continues to evolve, the core factors which we assess will remain the same:

- The first and most important step is to determine the extent to which the manager is sincere about ESG and how they go about integrating this into their process aka the 'input'. Questions may include:

  - Is ESG a formal part of the investment process, or is it done more holistically on a case by case basis?

  - Are the analysts and managers of a trust responsible for analysing ESG, or is it outsourced to another team or company?

  - Have the portfolio weightings been materially altered by integrating ESG into their investment process?

- It is also important to determine if the parent company is serious about ESG, as they will often lead their investment managers towards further adoption.

  - Is the company a signatory of the UN PRI?

  - Do they have an active voting policy?

- How does the company report on its ESG issues?

- The 'output' relates to how the final portfolio looks, and how it ranks versus its peers. This is an important step in determining whether the manager has 'green-washed' his process by implementing a trivial ESG analysis to comply with market demand.

- Does the portfolio reflect the amount of effort that has gone into ESG analysis?

Being led down the garden path?

While 'green-washing' is a major concern when assessing ESG, there are also many other issues and nuances at work. Certain sectors will naturally screen well for ESG, so even if the manager makes little effort to integrate ESG, the end portfolio may naturally look highly ESG compliant. The two biggest culprits for this are technology and European stocks. Technology stocks tend to have a small carbon footprint as well as young and more diverse workforces. Additionally, European companies are beholden to Europe's stricter standards around ESG issues, such as labour rights and emission regulations. They are also more likely to be in a position to report on ESG issues which may unjustly skew our beliefs, as reporting does not always mean action.

Another problem is that the definition of ESG investing is not yet entirely clear cut, with some potentially contentious issues which can lead one manager's understanding of ESG to differ wildly from another. This is often the case when managers differ on whether they consider certain industries ESG compliant from a moral view, accepting that there are no absolutes as to what constitutes morality, and can often depend on whose perspective one takes. Tobacco companies provide a case in point in this regard. While tobacco consumption can be understood as a social blight, the companies themselves can have strong ESG credentials, with British American Tobacco being named one of the best companies for diversity. Additionally, the tobacco crop is also an important source of income for many farmers in emerging markets; despite its high initial cost, it can remain profitable at low yields and is perceived to be resilient to adverse weather.

Direct ownership of alternative assets (such as real estate and private equity) can often bring additional complexity to traditional collectives analysis. Thankfully when looking at these funds from an ESG angle, in our view it is one of the few places it can actually simplify analysis. The theory is that if the manager has direct control over what he buys then the underlying assets should fully reflect his ESG beliefs. A manager should be able to implement a level of active ownership impossible for a manager that invests in publicly traded assets. A manager with a strong ESG integration should also be able to produce the respective filings to evidence this, instead of trusting the accounts a typical public company would submit.

Conclusion

With the host of factors and intricacies around ESG there are plenty of variations in its adoption and no shortage of examples of how trusts go about its implementation. We envisage adopting a scoring system on both the 'input' and 'output' of the managers, before comparing trusts with peers. The end result, we hope that in the near term we will be able to offer a categorisation of trusts which demonstrate the greatest exposure to ESG in all its forms.

In the immediate term, we offer these examples of trusts which in our opinion score highly on different aspects of ESG, while also offering examples of the complexities and nuances of ESG analysis. All of these trusts might suit ESG investors, but in different ways:

Necessity is the mother of innovation: not exactly ESG, but offers solutions…

BlackRock Energy & Resources Income (BERI) – BERI represents a complex but perhaps necessary evil within ESG (E in particular). While the broader energy and resources sector has a storied history, the extraction of natural resources still plays a vital part in the transition to clean energy, with large volumes of copper required to upgrade electric grids and more traditional power generation still needed to cover current shortages of renewable energy. Besides their holdings in conventional resource extractors, a key structural weight within BERI is now specifically to "energy transition" stocks which amounts to c. 30% of the portfolio, an obvious acknowledgment of environmental issues. Yet arguably more important is the manager's approach to active engagement with their non-renewable companies to ensure that management teams recognise the need to transition to a lower carbon economy. Few people would disagree that this is vital if fossil fuels are to fill the gap in our transition to clean energy. BERI offers a highly attractive (historic) dividend yield of 6.6%, and on a historically wide discount to NAV of 15.1%.* We believe that should ESG investors start to recognise the trust as an "ESG improver", there is considerable potential for the discount to narrow from here.

Above and beyond the standard expected…

NextEnergy Solar Fund (NESF) – NESF invests directly into primarily UK-based solar energy infrastructure assets (although it hopes to branch out geographically with future fund raises). The benefit solar energy provides in tackling climate change is clear. However, what some investors might not realise is the further commitments made to improving the environment in how those assets are managed.

---

*   All data in this article was correct at 15 October 2020.

NESF's manager, NextEnergy Capital Group, has a dedicated team devoted to biodiversity. These projects are designed to enhance the biodiversity of the local environment, via adherence to a Universal Biodiversity Management Plan for NESF sites. As of the end of March this year, NESF's sites housed 2.1 hectares of wildflower meadows with more development pending and a total of 4.8 hectares expected to be in place by this autumn. There are six bug hotels at these locations, and another four on the way as well as seven beehives and three more pending. Four hibernacula were also in development, although we note that the pandemic has slowed project completion. Early results are already visible: in the wildflower meadows seeded in 2017, the number of specialist plants has jumped from 20 to 37 and the number of bumblebee and butterfly observations has risen by 500% and 300% respectively. NESF trades on a 7% premium, below that of the two mature solar infrastructure funds.

Greencoat UK Wind (UKW) and **The Renewables Infrastructure Group (TRIG)** – Both have made great strides in expanding their ESG reporting and accountability. Of course, the nature of their investment propositions speaks to their green credentials, given their portfolios directly profit from the shift to a low carbon economy. However, both provide detailed guides on how they interpret ESG integration. For UKW, what is most promising is its clear disclosure of its ESG KPIs, something few strategies do regardless of sector. With these KPIs we can assess how effective they are over time. TRIG on the other hand reports its ESG policies and actions in unusually granular detail. It identifies which of the UN Sustainable Development Goals it fulfils, and outlines in great detail the various E, S and G initiatives it has undertaken over the year.

Output scores well, but what about input?

Henderson EuroTrust (HNE) – Investing in European domiciled equities, HNE has constantly ranked as one of the best trusts on Morningstar's sustainability rankings. As a result, one might expect HNE's manager to have ESG well-integrated in the investment process. As we note above, Europe naturally screens well for ESG, so without meeting the manager and analysing his process one could not infer whether the ESG credentials are coincidental or by design. The reality is that ESG is not specifically formalised within the investment process, and it is only when speaking with the manager (Jamie Ross) do you realise that typical ESG integration is not needed, as his investment process is so focused on governance and sustainability that it naturally aligns with ESG. HNE has performed extremely well through 2020 so far, thanks to stock picking alpha derived from Jamie's investment process which aims to provide an objective view of the best risk/reward opportunities. The trust trades on a discount of 9.9%, wider than the peer group average of 7.9%. We hope to publish updated research on HNE soon.

Input scores well, but what about output?

Jupiter Green (JGC) – JGC is a more typical sustainable investment strategy, investing in listed public equities on a global basis. As the trust's name suggests, the manager aims to generate attractive total returns by investing in companies which are developing and implementing solutions for the world's environmental challenges. The manager's approach to ESG is far more explicit than most others on this list, acknowledging the high amount of 'green washing' that occurs within the collective investment space. While the manager is acutely aware of the issues surrounding ESG, instead of focusing on merely 'good' ESG companies, he chooses to hone in on those that are offering genuine solutions to sustainability as opposed to simply not impacting it. JGC is a relatively small trust, but sister to a much larger open-ended fund. In early September 2020, the board and manager have agreed a shift of emphasis for the trust's portfolio, favouring smaller and more nimble "innovators" and "accelerators", over "established leaders". This means that whilst the portfolio will be still invested in companies providing solutions for the green economy, it will be exposed to higher growth opportunities, albeit with a likely higher volatility than JGC has exhibited historically. The portfolio transition has already begun, and so we look forward to seeing the trust embark on the next leg of its journey.

Impax Environmental Markets (IEM) – IEM has been a long-standing marquee fund in the investment trust universe for investors wanting a differentiated exposure to companies that will profit from the transition to a more sustainable economy. The core investment thesis of Impax Asset Management has long been that the global economy must transition from a depletive economic model to a sustainable one in which growth is achieved with improved social and environmental outcomes. Internationally, there are politicians calling to 'Build Back Better', labelling it a once-in-a-lifetime opportunity to embed low carbon energy systems and cleaner air in cities post-Covid. Many of the specialist companies that endeavour to achieve this can be found in IEM's diverse portfolio. Because of its mid- and small-cap focus, IEM offers exposures that are unlikely to be found in generalist global funds or trusts. With continued strong performance during 2020, IEM has remained on a persistent premium to NAV.

Fully integrated ESG process appears to pay off for performance...

Mid Wynd International (MWY) – While the previous trusts serve as examples of the nuances in ESG investing, MWY is far more straightforward with clear 'inputs' and 'outputs' to their ESG integration. It is an example of a typical but well integrated ESG screening process, which results in a portfolio which ranks amongst the top 10% for sustainability in the Morningstar global equity large cap sector. The managers clearly delineate ESG factors within their investment process, have an active and recorded voting practice, and even go so far as to operate an exclusionary screen for your typical sin stocks and major polluters. In our view, MWY employs a style of ESG investing which investors are increasingly reaching for. We believe that the strong performance the trust has delivered is good evidence for the effectiveness of a disciplined approach to ESG integration.

DAVID JOHNSON *is an investment trust analyst and joined Kepler in September 2020. Prior to this he ran multi-asset model portfolios as a discretionary fund manager, and has worked in both asset management and investment banking during his career. He holds a Masters in Finance from the University of Warwick and is a CFA charterholder.*

BEHIND THE NUMBERS

TIM COCKERILL *offers some advice to shareholders on how to read an investment trust Annual Report.*

I F YOU'RE AN investor you'll no doubt be familiar with the heavy thud of a report and accounts landing on your doormat. Indeed they might arrive quite frequently if you have a lot of holdings in investment companies. Fortunately, these days you can opt to have them arrive by email – much easier to deal with, I think (though not everyone agrees with me)! Despite their regular arrival I sense most investors rarely read them, or if they do only the summary. So why is it that this often hundred-page document is not given a great deal of attention, and why go to all the bother of writing them in the first instance?

The reason to write them is simple. It is a legal requirement that a public limited company produce an annual set of reports and accounts to enable its shareholders to scrutinise the accounts and company performance, to see what the company has been doing and how well it has been doing it, and to demonstrate that the board of directors and management have been fulfilling all the duties they are required to as stewards of the investor's capital. This is then signed off by an independent auditor who verifies the accuracy of the report and accounts (always look to see if there are any issues raised in the auditor's report that qualify their approval in some way).

The directors also have to make a statement that the accounts provide a true and fair and understandable picture of the performance of the company, an important source of protection for the shareholders and one that, since this requirement is laid down in law, directors are obliged to take very seriously. That's why the report and accounts are produced and it is clearly very important. A drawback though is that reading a set of accounts isn't something with which a lot of people are familiar, and a lot of the information in them is technical too (not to mention, thanks to the ever-increasing requirements of regulators, repetitive as well). To say the least, it can be daunting when confronted with a hundred pages of closely typed text and figures – something to read another time on a rainy day perhaps!

The good news is that a lot of report and accounts have become much more readable in recent years, very much encouraged and driven by the Association of Investment Companies (AIC). As someone who has been sitting on the judging panel of the AIC Communication Awards for a number of years, I can vouch for the fact that there is real improvement. Many investment companies now make an effort to make the report and accounts more interesting through innovative design and presentation, including articles that engage directly with readers.

This has been particularly true in the case of trusts in the 'alternative asset' classes, such as infrastructure. They can be excellent at providing portfolio information setting out where your money is invested and the nature of those underlying holdings – often accompanied by pictures that make a tangible connection between your investment and the real world. I like this in a report and accounts because the investment world can often seem rather abstract and remote, when in fact it is deeply rooted in the real world.

It's important to spend the time reading a report and accounts to understand in detail what you are investing in, preferably before you make your first investment in the company. Subsequent report and accounts can then be used to measure how successfully the company is delivering on its promises. Over time you will build a familiarity with the company that will make it easier for you to monitor its progress without the need to do your preliminary homework all over again.

After setting out on page one what the investment company's objective is, the report and accounts almost always start with a summary, or 'highlights' as they are often called. This sets out the key information at the date of report, including share price and net asset value, discount or premium, the yield, dividends paid, any increase in dividend and both recent and long-term performance. This is a simple way to see at a glance whether your investment company is living up to your expectations.

Of course, in a difficult year for markets you have to be careful to appreciate the market backdrop because not every year is going to be great. Most trusts have a benchmark, typically some form of relevant market index, such as The FTSE All-Share index, against which they expect their performance to be measured. (Look out again for companies that change their benchmark from one year to the next – it can be a red flag that something has been going wrong.)

Next comes the chairman's statement, which summarises the board's assessment of the year being reported on, including its performance, important developments, such as the appointment of new directors or a change in strategy, and a statement about the outlook for the company. The chairman's statement is meant to provide a compact overview of the most important things that shareholders need to know. If you have followed your investment company closely throughout the year, this is likely to provide a useful reminder, and if you don't it's a way to see the year and your investment in perspective.

Following this you typically find the investment manager's report, which will go into more detail about performance, the market backdrop and changes in the investment company's portfolio – the specific shares or other kinds of assets that it owns. These can vary somewhat in length, but should help you to understand how your investment company is being managed. No manager gets everything right and I like to see managers being honest and talking about the decisions that didn't go so well, as well as their success stories. Often there will be a page or two devoted to the people in the team that is managing your investment. It is always good to see the faces and experience of those responsible for the decision-making.

Although there are a series of reports that companies are required to include in their Annual Report, the format and order in which they present them can vary. Typically it is the detailed listing of the portfolio that comes next. All investment companies are required to give details of their top 10 holdings in their monthly factsheets, but the Annual Report is the only place where they are required to give you a complete listing of the portfolio at the most recent financial year end. This can then be compared to the previous year's listing, so you can track the changes in both the value and number of shares in the portfolio.

An increasing number of trusts now also include individual write-ups of their largest holdings. These can be really insightful, so I like to see a reasonable amount of detail here. It helps me to understand why a stock or asset is in the portfolio and how and where it sits within the manager's investment process. Unlike conventional equity trusts, whose holdings are publicly listed and therefore higher profile and much easier to research, private equity and infrastructure investment companies typically provide copious amounts of detail on the private companies or assets that they own.

This can be fascinating, particularly where small start-up companies are involved, because you can see the ambition behind the people running them and appreciate the business opportunities that they see. It is this area of the report and accounts that lends itself to the most innovation when it comes to presentation. One group that has been particularly innovative is Gravis Capital Management, who have really brought their investments to life through the way they are presented.

The heart of a set of reports and accounts is the accounts of course, which are usually found towards the back of the report and are better referred to as the Financial Statement. It is this critical section that has been independently audited and sets out in detail the financial performance of your investment. The numbers can run to many pages and will include notes on the accounts that also run to several pages. The 'balance sheet' report provides the detail most investors want, including the net asset value (NAV) per share. Comparing this year's NAV per share with last year's is one of the primary indications of how well your investment has performed, to which can be added the annual dividend per share, if any, that has been paid out as income.

Investment trusts are required to pay out at least 85% of the investment income that they themselves receive in order to retain their legal status as investment trusts (which in turn means that they can continue to buy and sell investments without paying capital gains taxes on any gains retained in the portfolio). Unlike other types of fund, investment trusts can also hold back up to 15% of their income as revenue (or rainy day) reserves. The figures in the notes, once you know where to look for them, will tell you the extent to which a trust is doing this and how much money cumulatively has been retained in this way, an important consideration when looking to judge the sustainability of a trust's dividend.

It is also important to 'see' how much debt the company has, which is typically referred to as gearing in the investment company world. Gearing is one of the advantages investment companies have compared with open-ended investment vehicles, as it allows them to 'gear up' to take advantage of opportunities they see (though it also reduces returns if an investment falls in value). Gearing can take different forms and some older types of debt, such as fixed rate debentures, are expensive which may act as a drag on performance. The notes to the accounts will give you that detail, along with a number of other important pieces of information.

Worth noting are the details of the investment management agreement that the trust has with the firm which is managing the portfolio (is there a performance fee as well as an annual fee?), the costs which the company has incurred during the year (which may be important if they change significantly from year to year) and, in the case of alternative asset trusts, the basis on which its investments are valued (again look out for any significant changes).

Governance has always been important and evermore so today, as the focus on doing the right thing is constantly in the public eye, so you'll find a section dedicated to this. This section will tell you who the directors are, which advisors the board is using, any conflicts of interest, how diverse the make-up of the board is, plus details of how much the directors are being paid and how many shares, if any, in the trust they own (generally speaking, the more the better, as it will mean the decisions they make will have an impact on their own pockets, not just yours). As the board's primary duty is to act in the interests of all the shareholders, it is critical that the directors are genuinely independent of the management company and that is well worth researching.

Investors today are increasingly looking for investment companies to integrate environmental, social governance (ESG) factors into the management of the funds they own. This is about understanding and reporting on the impact the investments held by the investment company have on the environment and society, and as mentioned above, how it is governed. It's pleasing to see that more details about a trust's ESG approach are now being included in report and accounts. It is an area which is bound to see much greater focus in future years. Although many trusts still confine themselves to bland and woolly statements of the obvious, the more enlightened trusts are using infographics to produce more interesting and dynamic reporting.

There was a time when most investors in investment trusts were professionals who knew where to look and what to look for in the report and accounts without much help, knowing for example that bad news often had a habit of appearing in small type... With more private investors now choosing to focus on investment trusts, and greater competition for investor attention, the challenge the production of report and accounts poses for companies is the need to present a massive amount of statutorily required information in a more readable and compelling way (and not, incidentally, to take too long about it – the longer the period between the end of the financial period and the appearance of the Annual Report, the less up to date the financial information will be).

Consequently we're seeing more and more 'design thought' go into their choice of layout. No one wants to be faced with just a wall of words and numbers, and I for one like infographics, photos and charts. If your investment company invests in renewable energy, it can be helpful to see pictures of the facilities and learn how much power has been produced and carbon dioxide emissions avoided.

You can argue that the relationship between an investment trust and its shareholders is in some ways more important than it is at other types of company, because a diversified investment trust is more likely to represent a larger proportion of the investor's overall savings and wealth than an individual company. As we enter the next decade, in which the world faces many new challenges, I believe it will enter a new phase. As the stewards of investors' capital, entrusted to them to generate a financial return, social and environmental responsibilities will become prominent and reporting how those responsibilities are met will be critically important. Covid-19 has changed many things, and the urgent need to address the climate crisis will govern and direct a lot of future investment. The report and accounts of investment companies will be their shop window on how they respond.

For me a good set of report and accounts is one that is engaging, educational, interesting, readable and which draws you in. Presenting the accounts themselves has to be done in a certain way which makes it harder to change the design, but clarity around what is being presented and clear explanatory notes are a big bonus. As a shareholder it's important that the report and accounts give you what you need to know, but it's an opportunity for the investment company to communicate a lot more than just the numbers and to build relationships with its investors. Articles about the latest technological developments from technology managers, insights into different asset classes, explanations about what businesses do, all help make investors feel more involved in the fate of their investments.

So, when the next set of report and accounts drops onto your doormat or into your inbox, the least you can do to repay some of the effort and expense that goes into preparing them is to take some time to study them. If you don't yet receive a copy (for example if you hold your shares through a platform), it is worth the trouble to track one down. On most platforms you can find an electronic version of the report and accounts through a link on the website and the more enlightened trusts will be happy to send you a copy by post or email if you contact them directly. Whether you are researching a new investment, or simply monitoring an existing one, the report and accounts should always be your first port of call.

TIM COCKERILL *has been Head of Research at the wealth management firm Rowan Dartington since 2011.*

———————————

ANALYSING INVESTMENT TRUSTS

by JONATHAN DAVIS

FINDING OUT MORE

By JONATHAN DAVIS

THERE WAS A time when getting hold of good data and information about investment trusts was quite difficult. Brokers' research was not widely available, as well as variable in quality, and investment platforms did not offer much coverage of closed-ended funds. Magazines and newspapers published weekly or monthly prices and some other bits of information, but often not much more.

Specialist data websites such as Trustnet (which originated many years ago as a broking firm's investment trust research centre), Morningstar and Digital Look continue to provide lots of data, but while all of them are very useful, and they do provide news and analysis these days as well as numbers, they have not always been the easiest sites to navigate. Citywire also carries data and has an excellent news and commentary service about investment trusts, but you need to subscribe to one of several services they offer in order to access it.

The good news is that the industry's trade body, the Association of Investment Companies, has taken it upon itself to maintain an excellent and comprehensive database of investment trust information, sourced from Morningstar and Financial Express (the owner of Trustnet). The AIC website (theaic.co.uk) is updated continuously with news and performance data, as well as providing a link to the relevant website of fund management groups and (where they have their own) the trust's own websites.

The AIC website also carries a news feed from Citywire and this year started a separate listing for podcasts which feature investment trusts, including – to declare an interest – the weekly *Money Makers* investment trust podcast that I put together each week with the help of Simon Elliott, head of investment trust research at Winterflood Securities, one of the main corporate broking firms that specialise in investment trusts.

Growing private investor demand

All of this reflects the fact that everyone in the fund business recognises that increasing numbers of private investors are becoming interested in investment trusts as an option for their savings and investments. Research shows that investment trust shareholders tend to have larger sums to invest and are also more sophisticated than the average investor in open-ended funds. They (or should I say you?) are not afraid to do their own homework.

More and more of these so-called self-directed investors use platforms such as Hargreaves Lansdown (the market leader), Interactive Investor and AJ Bell to hold their ISAs and SIPP money. Consolidation is underway in the platform business however, with Interactive Investor in particular taking the lead in acquiring the Alliance Trust's old platform and, in a further deal this year, that of the retail specialist firm The Share Centre as well.

The platforms in turn have responded by adding more information about investment trusts, including interactive charting tools, but for commercial or other reasons don't offer a huge amount of research. An exception can be made here for *Interactive Investor* which also recently purchased *Money Observer* magazine. It has subsequently decided to close down the printed versions of the monthly magazine, as well as its investment trust quarterly, while keeping on a number of their regular and better known contributors to write articles for its website.

How this will play out over time remains to be seen, but while consolidation generally reduces choice, for the moment it has certainly expanded the choice of weekly news and analysis of trusts that is available for free to investors. Among specialist financial magazines, *MoneyWeek*, the *Investors Chronicle*, *Shares* magazine and *Master Investor* all carry articles about investment trusts, while the long-running *Investment Trusts* newsletter is another subscription option.

Among national newspapers, *The Times* and the *Telegraph* stand out for the breadth of their coverage of funds. Highly recommended also is the subscription-based portfolio monitoring service run by John Baron, a former City professional now known to a wider audience through his regular columns in the *Investors Chronicle* and his contributions to this *Handbook* (see page 113).

Other types of research

If you are looking for some basic information about an investment trust, presented in a standardised form, it is worth looking at some of the newer web-based research firms that cover investment trusts. Of these the best known are Quoted Data, Trust Intelligence and Edison Research. Be aware however that all three firms have business models which rely on commercial relationships with fund management firms, including clients which sponsor research and use them for promotional events.

It is important to take note therefore whether the research on individual trusts you read there is sponsored or not, since if it is it can no longer be deemed to be independent and that inevitably raises a question about its value. These research firms, unlike broking firms, are not allowed by the regulator to publish specific buy and sell recommendations, but concentrate mainly instead on descriptive or thematic analysis* which will usually include at least some trusts run by clients of the firm.

Both Quoted Data and Kepler Intelligence have former City investment trusts analysts among their founders and in my experience that experience carries over into a well-presented professional level of research. Bear in mind that the only reason these firms exist is that broker research is now restricted to professional and wealthier clients, so they are filling a gap for basic analysis that private investors will struggle to find filled elsewhere, certainly if they are unwilling to pay for the privilege. My advice is to make full use of the research these sites provide for information and news, but do so with your eyes open. Don't make investment decisions about individual trusts without doing additional research.

When looking for a high level of detail about an individual investment trust, I also make regular use of the subscription share analysis service Stockopedia (www. stockopedia.com), which is based (as it happens) here in my home town of Oxford. Stockopedia does not yet offer a specific investment trust service, unfortunately, although I keep pressing them to do so and Ed Croft, the founder, tells me they are keen to do so and may be starting one next year.

For the moment the splendidly clear and well laid out company-by-company data pages are not adapted to show the specific data points that are of particular interest to investment trust shareholders. They only highlight share price performance, for example, and not the net asset value per share, which is of limited value in tracking discounts/premiums. However, once you find out how to get around the paywalled site, it is invaluable in quickly tracking dividend payments for example. I also use it, as well as Trustnet, to monitor the real and model portfolios which I run.

One of my complaints about most investment trust research sites is that they generally don't show historical performance over long enough periods. This is unhelpful because it is important to know how an individual fund manager has performed in past jobs, which may well have been at different firms, and during bull and bear markets. Trusts change their managers all the time and it is no use looking at the historical performance if some of it was during the tenure of another manager with a completely different style or success rate.

Fortunately sites such as Citywire and Trustnet do however rate individual fund managers, if you know where to look, and often provide a summary of their track record over the full course of their careers. If you are prepared to dig deeper into some of these details, it will help prevent you from being misled by the shorter term performance on which, unfortunately, so much buying and selling of funds seems to be based.

---

* An example is the article on ESG investing which is included in this year's *Handbook* (see page 175).

Using the AIC and other websites

In the 2020 edition of the *Handbook* I included several pages describing the initial steps that a potential investor in investment trusts might take to make best use of the information available on the AIC website. I don't propose to repeat that again this year, although you will be able to find an online version of those earlier pages on the *Handbook (Money Makers)* website. It has the most comprehensive database and range of information and a lot of thought has gone into how the material is presented.

A project of mine that is in hand when time allows is to record a number of short videos explaining the main features of the site – the tools that I find most useful and those where I look for supplementary information. In due course I may also add some more, looking at what other useful websites have to offer. The *Money Makers* website will have more information when these appear.

It may be helpful to suggest a possible 10-step process that a shareholder might want to follow when researching a particular individual trust. This covers many of the sources of information that I look at myself. Suppose for example that I have seen a media recommendation somewhere to invest in the Mid Wynd investment trust and want to investigate further.

Step 1

Go to the AIC website (www.theaic.co.uk), choose the 'find and compare investment companies' tab and then select the 'compare companies' option from the dropdown menu (it is the first item). Fill the first search box that appears with the name of the trust Mid Wynd. Several options beginning with the letter M will appear as you type, together with their stock market tickers. In this case it is MWY. If you know the ticker already you can use that as the search term instead.

Step 2

Choose 'Mid Wynd' and then have a quick initial look through the six tabs, which link to further details for each trust in the AIC statistics website. These are the 'overview', 'performance and charting', 'portfolio', 'charges and gearing', 'management' and 'capital structure'. This will give you some summary information about the trust, including who manages the trust (and the firm they work for), the names of the directors, its recent performance, the level of the discount and its annual cost (ongoing charge ratio). Note that the default chart shows both the share price and NAV over time but only compares that performance to other trusts in its sector, not to any benchmark, and it is possible to do better than that later.

Step 3

Next go back to the 'overview' section and find the sector in which the trust operates. In the case of Mid Wynd, this is the global sector. Click on the link to 'global' (which is coloured red to identify it as a link). This will then take you to a page where all the other trusts in the same sector are listed in alphabetical order. From this you can identify where the trust stands in relation to other trusts in the same sector on a range of metrics – past performance, dividend yield, the discount, level of gearing and ongoing charge ratio being the most important.

Company ▲	AIC sector ▲	Share type	Traded currency	Total assets (m) ▼	Price (last close)	NAV	Discount/premium (%) ▲ ▼	Gearing (%) ▲	Share price total return (%) 1yr ▼	5yr ▼	10yr ▼	AIC ongoing charge (%)	AIC ongoing charge plus perf fee (%) ▲	5yr dividend growth (%) p.a. ▲ ▼	Dividend yield (%) ▼
Sector average	-	-	-	-	-	-	-1.7	6	45.3	156.2	301.2	0.50	0.51	3.7	1.0
Lindsell Train	Global	Ordinary Share	GBP	222.1	1,155.00	1,110.64	4.0	2	-19.1	150.6	558.9	0.83	0.83	41.9	3.6
Monks	Global	Ordinary Share	GBX	2,808.5	1,200.00	1,165.58	3.0	5	36.7	210.3	283.7	0.48	0.48	-8.7	0.2
Mid Wynd International	Global	Ordinary Share	GBX	355.4	672.00	656.92	2.4	0	19.0	114.7	215.4	0.69	0.69	8.9	0.9
Martin Currie Global Portfolio	Global	Ordinary Share	GBX	286.7	356.00	350.71	1.5	1	28.9	123.8	280.0	0.63	1.53	0.5	1.2
Scottish Mortgage	Global	Ordinary Share	GBX	16,116.4	1,051.00	1,035.47	1.5	7	120.5	343.5	804.0	0.36	0.36	2.1	0.3
Bankers	Global	Ordinary Share	GBX	1,390.1	1,032.00	1,025.62	0.7	0	13.3	88.9	243.7	0.52	0.52	7.1	2.1
Manchester & London	Global	Ordinary Share	GBX	252.3	650.00	674.70	-3.7	0	26.4	215.5	149.6	0.78	1.04	13.4	2.3
JPMorgan Elect Managed Growth	Global	Ordinary Share	GBX	257.4	830.00	875.13	-5.2	0	1.7	52.2	147.4	0.58	0.58	19.9	1.9
Alliance Trust	Global	Ordinary Share	GBX	3,074.3	844.00	893.87	-5.6	4	10.8	91.4	201.5	0.65	0.65	7.3	1.7
Witan	Global	Ordinary Share	GBX	1,967.4	195.20	210.45	-7.2	13	-6.5	43.9	155.6	0.83	0.91	11.7	2.7
EP Global Opportunities	Global	Ordinary Share	GBX	112.8	262.00	287.31	-8.8	0	-11.2	28.7	81.0	0.98	0.98	12.7	2.3
F&C Investment Trust	Global	Ordinary Share	GBX	4,639.6	713.00	785.04	-9.2	9	4.5	82.4	197.5	0.54	0.54	4.5	1.6
Scottish Investment Trust	Global	Ordinary Share	GBX	683.8	709.00	783.61	-9.5	0	-10.2	39.9	100.0	0.58	0.58	13.7	3.3
AVI Global	Global	Ordinary Share	GBX	1,031.3	750.00	849.60	-11.7	11	6.2	79.4	96.1	0.85	0.85	9.5	2.2

Step 4

By clicking on the arrows at the top of each column you can then sort all the companies in this sector by any of the measures listed at the top of each column. You can do this in either ascending or descending order. In the example shown above I have sorted the data by discount/premium. A discount appears as a negative figure and a premium as a positive one. Mid Wynd ranks third best on this criterion, with its shares trading at a small premium of 2.4 per cent. You can repeat this exercise for the other headings as well to find out where the trust ranks in size, use of gearing, fees and share price performance (measured here as total return, a calculation which assumes dividends are reinvested immediately when paid out).

Step 5

Click on 'Mid Wynd' again in the first column and this will take you back to the pages you found with step 2. Now is the moment, I suggest, to download the Annual Report and two or three of the most recent monthly factsheets, which are saved in pdf format, all accessible from this page. If you see that there is an interim (half-yearly) report which is more recent than the Annual Report, save that also. You can download or bookmark these on your computer for studying now or later. It may also be worth having a quick look at recent announcements, to see if there is anything interesting there, but make sure you click 'view regulatory announcements' and exclude NAV announcements the first time you do so.

Step 6

Now is the time to go and look at some other websites for further information about the fund manager(s). A good first step could be to go to the Trustnet website (www.trustnet.com, registration required). Citywire and Morningstar are alternatives. In the fund universe search box, which is the first one you come to, enter 'investment trusts' and click 'close'. Then go to the second search box, 'management group', and enter Artemis and click close again. This will then show the results for the two investment trusts that Artemis currently manage, of which Mid Wynd is one.

Click on 'Mid Wynd' in the table and this will give you another batch of information, much of which you will have already seen on the AIC website. Scroll down to where you see the words 'fund manager' and if you look closely at that it will show you three names as co-managers of the trust, meaning that it is managed by a team. Click on their names to find out more about them. You will soon see that Simon Edelsten is the most senior of the three and is in fact the lead manager of the trust. By clicking on his name you will find that he is also the manager of four other funds (not investment trusts), all of which follow a similar strategy.

Step 7

Next step is go to the top of the page and click on the 'fund managers' tab, and from there to the 'A–Z manager factsheets'. This will now show you, to the extent possible, Mr Edelsten's track record as a fund manager going back all the way to the year 2000. This will cover not only the fund he manages now, but ones he managed before he joined Artemis. There is a useful graph showing you his long-term performance across all his funds and more details of his comparative performance against his peer group. This however will be based on Trustnet's own criteria, and will be different to the ones used in the graph on the AIC website, which come from Morningstar. You can also save a pdf version of all the information on this page.

With a little more effort – look for a link to 'interactive charting' – it is possible to create a bespoke chart of the trust's performance and compare that to its open-ended sister fund, as well as a range of other comparators. You can adjust the timescale of the chart and also the basis on which it is calculated. For the super-diligent, you can also find some standard statistical measures which attempt to describe the riskiness of the trust, such as the r-squared (degree of correlation to the performance of a comparable stock market index) and its beta (see the glossary for more and note that these are based on historic, not forward-looking data, and limited by that fact).

An example of this kind of output is given in the chart, although note – there are always caveats – that Trustnet only offers a FTSE World index for comparison in its charting function, not the MSCI World All Companies index which is the trust's own benchmark. They will be very similar, and it is the overall picture that matters, not the precision of the data. All this information can be downloaded and saved as a pdf too.

Key	Chart	Instrument	1m	3m	6m	1y	3y	5y	10y	Start of Data
A	✓	Mid Wynd International Investment Trust PLC Ord 5P	4.6%	0.9%	22.8%	16.8%	44.1%	111.4%	208.7%	1007.6%	✕
E	✓	FTSE World	2.6%	3.0%	20.0%	11.6%	27.8%	93.2%	193.6%	749.8%	✕
C	✓	Artemis Global Select R Acc	2.8%	1.8%	16.2%	16.2%	35.0%	90.2%	-	187.4%	✕
B	✓	IT Global	5.1%	2.6%	19.9%	9.8%	23.9%	86.5%	173.6%	802.4%	✕
D	✓	UK Consumer Price Index + 5%	0.9%	1.7%	2.9%	5.6%	21.3%	39.0%	97.9%	1009.7%	✕

Performance values rebased to Pound Sterling.

Source: Trustnet (www.trustnet.co.uk)

Step 8

Another useful step is to go to another of the data services to check up whether there is any news about Mr Edelsten or his funds. I would suggest Citywire (www.citywire.co.uk) for this purpose. Simply use the search box on the home page to type in either 'Simon Edelsten' or 'Mid Wynd' to see whether there have been any stories about the trust or the manager. This will throw up some useful news stories and in this case will also show that Mr Edelsten has written articles which have appeared in various publications. By now it will become apparent that he and his colleagues at Artemis took over management of the trust from Baillie Gifford in 2014.

Step 9

Now it is a good time to go back and take a more detailed look at the Annual Report and the trust's website. In the Annual Report, among other things, you will find that Mr Edelsten has a personal holding in the trust of 2.2 millon shares, which is worth nearly £15 million at the time of writing, and represents 5.89% of the issued share capital. The non-executive directors, who appear to have a strong Scottish flavour, own around a further 1 million shares of the trust, which is normally a good sign. You can read that the chairmanship is about to be handed over to a long serving non-executive director Russell Napier. There is more detailed commentary on the trust's performance.

Unlike some other trusts Mid Wynd does not have its own dedicated website, but has its own pages on the Artemis funds website. You can find your way there easily enough by entering 'Artemis Mid Wynd' in Google. There is a further chunk of information including a chart that compares the trust's performance since it took over management of the trust to its benchmark, and not just to a peer group. (Peer group comparisons are interesting but of less value than benchmark comparisons, since the majority of funds in a peer group will typically underperform the benchmark and may indeed have different benchmarks as well). Some trusts now offer regular videos in which the fund managers explain their approach and talk (invariably positively) about the future.

Step 10

By now you will have a good deal of information about the trust. A final step might be to check whether there is any additional useful research you can get access to on the trust. If you have a stockbroker, they may be able to provide some information, or you can try the other websites mentioned earlier. There is for example a regular yearly update on Mid Wynd on the Kepler Intelligence website, but bear in mind the caveats mentioned earlier. Check also to see if the platform you use has any views on the trust.

It is as well to be wary however of fund ratings and best buy lists, which have a mixed record and are generally not always of much value. A number of platforms provide short lists of funds that they like. A.J.Bell offers a "select list" of 17 investment trusts, for example, although its "favourite funds" section only includes open-ended funds. Hargreaves Lansdown provides some research notes on investment trusts, but only includes open-ended funds in its "Wealth short list" (formerly the Wealth 50). Fidelity has a select list of 50 funds chosen by its experts, but these too are open-ended funds only.

If you are getting the impression that the biggest platforms prefer to provide more guidance on funds than on investment trusts, you would not be wrong. A sceptic might say that this reflects the fact that platforms can make more money if their clients buy and sell the former. There is truth in this observation. While investors love the idea of having funds recommended, the FCA (Financial Conduct Authority) has found only limited evidence that they are of much value.

As for fund ratings, these can be found on many of the research and information websites I have already mentioned. Citywire, Trustnet and the Financial Times all provide fund ratings, as does Morningstar. You can search for these, but be aware that ratings are heavily influenced by past performance, and there is no clear evidence that you can make money by treating them as buy or sell recommendations. However they can be useful as an initial screening tool.

Armed with all this information you will now know that the trust has a good track record, is run by an experienced manager with two colleagues, has a growth-oriented style and invests in global equities. The investment style is thematic, with a bias towards such themes as technology and automation, and he has a significant stake in the trust's future. The board operates a discount control policy, aiming to keep the share price within 2% of the net asset value per share, and has fairly consistently traded at a premium, enabling it to issue new shares.

Don't forget scuttlebutt

Anything you can add to this picture through talking to friends, relatives and professional colleagues who know something about investment may throw up some additional insights. You will at least by now have enough information to ask sensible questions. It may also be a good idea to go back and find a better charting service to see how the trust has performed during different market conditions. However since there is only six years of data on how the trust has performed since Artemis took over the management, this is not really long enough for definitive conclusions to be drawn on these grounds alone.

GETTING HELP

Recognising that it takes some time to get the measure of the AIC's comprehensive statistics section, the AIC statistics department says it welcomes enquiries from private investors; just fill out the email enquiry form on the AIC website.

The largest equity sectors

CONVENTIONAL SECTORS	TOTAL ASSETS (£M)	MARKET CAP (£M)	NUMBER OF COMPANIES	AVG TOTAL ASSETS (£M)	AVG MARKET CAP (£M)	INDUSTRY TOTAL ASSETS
Global	32,577	29,261	15	2,172	1,951	14.8%
Flexible Investment	15,526	9,250	20	776	463	7.1%
UK Equity Income	10,891	8,943	24	454	373	5.0%
Global Emerging Markets	7,049	6,012	13	542	462	3.2%
Global Smaller Companies	5,722	5,200	5	1,144	1,040	2.6%
Country Specialist: Asia Pacific - ex Japan	5,804	4,644	10	580	464	2.6%
UK Smaller Companies	5,678	4,458	24	237	186	2.6%
Europe	4,103	3,495	7	586	499	1.9%
UK All Companies	4,245	3,305	11	386	300	1.9%
Asia Pacific	3,635	3,243	8	454	405	1.7%
Global Equity Income	3,376	2,946	5	675	589	1.5%
North America	3,667	2,941	7	524	420	1.7%
Japan	3,251	2,536	6	542	423	1.5%
Asia Pacific Income	1,948	1,782	4	487	446	0.9%
European Smaller Companies	2,142	1,725	4	535	431	1.0%
Japanese Smaller Companies	1,406	1,277	5	281	255	0.6%
Asia Pacific Smaller Companies	1,003	842	3	334	281	0.5%
North American Smaller Companies	351	294	2	176	147	0.2%
Country Specialist: Europe - ex UK	307	262	1	307	262	0.1%
UK Equity & Bond Income	397	233	2	198	116	0.2%

Source: AIC/Morningstar, data to 30/09/20

There are no fixed rules for what an investment trust can invest in. The trust's strategy does, however, have to be outlined in a prospectus and approved by shareholders if, as does happen, the board wishes to change that objective at a later date. For convenience, and to help comparative analysis, trusts are grouped into a number of different sectors, based primarily on their investment focus. These are listed here and on the following two pages. It has become conventional to list highly specialised investment trusts in separate categories.

The majority of the sector categories are self-explanatory. It is worth noting, however, that individual trusts within each broad sector category will often have somewhat different investment objectives and benchmarks. The 'flexible investment' sector is a relatively new one that includes a number of trusts which invest across a broad range of asset classes, not just equities. Most of these were previously included in the global sector.

These sectoral classifications are reviewed at regular intervals by a committee of the Association of Investment Companies. In 2019 the AIC introduced a number of changes to its categorisation of Asian trusts and specialist trusts in particular. In 2020 utilities was changed to infrastructure securities. By tradition the sectoral breakdown distinguishes between trusts that invest primarily in large cap stocks and those that focus on mid and smaller companies, whatever their regional focus.

The table on this page summarises the sectors which, together with healthcare, financials and technology, are known as conventional equity trusts, as opposed to alternative assets. With the latter proving very popular in recent years, the conventional trusts today account for only a fraction over 50 per cent of the industry's total assets. Before the global financial crisis, it would have been a significantly higher percentage.

A notable feature of the table is that only around 20% of these conventional equity trusts have the UK as their primary investment focus. Investment trusts from the very earliest days have always had a bias towards investment outside the UK. The aim of the very first trust to be launched, Foreign & Colonial (now known simply as F&C), was to enable its shareholders to diversify their portfolios by investing in bonds issued by companies outside the UK.

An external focus remains one of the key attractions of trusts today. It is one of the principal reasons why investment trusts have on average performed significantly better than the FTSE All-Share index since the coronavirus pandemic broke out in the first quarter of 2020. Combined with concerns about the future of the UK economy after Brexit, the UK stock market has underperformed most other countries' stock markets over the past four years and the associated sterling weakness has increased the value of investors' overseas holdings. ■

Specialist sectors

CONVENTIONAL SECTORS	TOTAL ASSETS (£M)	MARKET CAP (£M)	NUMBER OF COMPANIES	AVG TOTAL ASSETS (£M)	AVG MARKET CAP (£M)	INDUSTRY TOTAL ASSETS
Private Equity	20,751	17,489	16	1,297	1,093	9.4%
Infrastructure	11,105	12,242	6	1,851	2,040	5.1%
Renewable Energy Infrastructure	8,756	9,199	13	674	708	4.0%
Hedge Funds	11,086	7,339	8	1,386	917	5.0%
Biotechnology & Healthcare	6,136	5,980	7	877	854	2.8%
Technology & Media	4,225	4,005	4	1,056	1,001	1.9%
Debt - Direct Lending	4,168	3,216	10	417	322	1.9%
Debt - Loans & Bonds	2,153	1,618	11	196	147	1.0%
Debt - Structured Finance	3,238	1,589	7	463	227	1.5%
Growth Capital	1,511	1,372	3	504	457	0.7%
Royalties	1,147	1,174	1	1,147	1,174	0.5%
Commodities & Natural Resources	1,500	1,151	8	188	144	0.7%
Environmental	1,051	993	3	350	331	0.5%
Leasing	3,765	671	6	627	112	1.7%
Insurance & Reinsurance Strategies	309	255	2	155	128	0.1%
Financials	544	233	3	181	78	0.2%
Infrastructure Securities	289	202	3	96	67	0.1%
Liquidity Funds	9	9	1	9	9	0.0%

Source: AIC/Morningstar, data to 30/09/20

The specialist sectors are also clearly identified by their name. Unlike the conventional trusts, which are mainly defined by their regional focus, the specialist sectors are mostly grouped by industry. The specialist sector is worth looking at in more detail as it gives a flavour of the wide range of investment strategies which are available once you look beyond the conventional trusts.

It is these trusts, along with those investing in property, which are now commonly referred to as making up the majority of the 'alternative asset' sector. Private equity, infrastructure and renewable energy together have around a third more assets than they did two years ago, for example, although the ratings of two of these three have moved in opposite directions. Private equity trusts have moved out to large discounts, while the renewable energy trusts have in aggregate moved from a discount to a premium.

The biotechnology and healthcare sector has also seen a significant expansion in size and rating. These specialist sectors, along with financials, account for just 14 trusts between them, and are more usefully classified as conventional equity trusts, although by their nature they are less diversified than the equity markets where they are listed.

It is worth noting also that two new sectors have appeared since 2018. One is royalties, which currently consists of a single fast-growing trust, Hipgnosis Songs (SONG). The other is growth capital, a new category that includes three trusts which invest part or all of their capital in unlisted securities. These three trusts are Schroder UK Public Private (SUPP), formerly the Woodford Patient Capital Trust, Schiehallion (MNTN) and Merian Chrysalis (MERI).

The way the universe of listed trusts looks can and does change significantly from decade to decade. Note the significant difference between the total assets of the leasing sub-sector and its aggregate market capitalisation. The difference reflects both the amount of gearing involved and the level of discount of each trust. ∎

Property sectors

CONVENTIONAL SECTORS	TOTAL ASSETS (£M)	MARKET CAP (£M)
Property - UK Commercial	11,781	7,225
Property - UK Residential	2,707	2,215
Property - Europe	1,736	1,164
Property Securities	1,528	1,095
Property - UK Healthcare	895	795
Property - Debt	932	745
Property - Rest of World	369	132

VCT sectors

CONVENTIONAL SECTORS	TOTAL ASSETS (£M)	MARKET CAP (£M)
VCT Generalist	3,553	3,342
VCT AIM Quoted	814	738
VCT Generalist Pre Qualifying	155	153
VCT Specialist: Environmental	149	144
VCT Specialist: Media, Leisure & Events	28	21
VCT Specialist: Technology	11	7
VCT Specialist: Technology Pre Qualifying	3	4
VCT Specialist: Healthcare & Biotechnology	3	2

Source: AIC/Morningstar, data to 30/09/20

The main distinction in the property sector table is between trusts that invest directly in property (that is, buy and sell the bricks and mortar themselves) and those that invest primarily in the shares or debt of other listed property companies. The former by their nature are less liquid than the latter.

Another important distinction, which the pandemic has highlighted this year, is between generalist commercial property companies which allocate their money across multiple locations and types of asset (offices, industrial buildings and shops) and those which concentrate on a specific specialist type of property (such as supermarkets, social housing or medical surgeries). The closed-ended structure of investment trusts is well suited to commercial property. In poor market conditions, unlike open-ended property funds, the

NUMBER OF COMPANIES	AVG TOTAL ASSETS (£M)	AVG MARKET CAP (£M)	% TOTAL ASSETS
18	654	401	5.4%
6	451	369	1.2%
5	347	233	0.8%
1	1,528	1,095	0.7%
2	448	397	0.4%
4	233	186	0.0%
2	184	66	0.2%

NUMBER OF COMPANIES	AVG TOTAL ASSETS (£M)	AVG MARKET CAP (£M)	% TOTAL ASSETS
38	93	88	1.6%
8	102	92	0.4%
3	52	51	0.1%
5	30	29	0.1%
1	28	21	0.0%
4	3	2	0.0%
1	3	4	0.0%
1	3	2	0.0%

share prices of property investment companies will fall further and faster than the unit prices of equivalent open-ended funds, but the latter sometimes have to close their funds for a limited period of time after being swamped by sell orders. Such "gating" moves occurred in 2008 and again this year.

Venture capital trusts are specialist investment companies that exist to support companies at an early stage of their development, in return for which shareholders in the VCTs are offered some potentially attractive tax breaks. Most of these trusts will be investing in unlisted securities, although an exception are the AIM VCTs, which own mostly shares listed on the Alternative Investment Market. By their nature, most VCTs are relatively small and riskier. ■

Key sector metrics

AIC SECTOR	NUMBER OF COMPANIES	MARKET CAPITALISATION (£M)
Biotechnology & Healthcare	7	5,980
Japanese Smaller Companies	5	1,277
Global Smaller Companies	4	5,200
Japan	5	2,536
Global	15	29,261
North America	7	2,941
Private Equity	16	17,489
Europe	6	3,495
Infrastructure	6	12,242
UK Smaller Companies	21	4,458
Country Specialist: Asia Pacific - ex Japan	8	4,644
Private Equity (ex 3i)	15	7,791
VCT AIM Quoted	6	738
Asia Pacific	7	3,243
UK All Companies	12	3,305
Global Equity Income	5	2,946
Flexible Investment	25	9,250
Asia Pacific Smaller Companies	3	842
Property - UK Commercial	16	7,225
Debt - Loans & Bonds	12	1,618
UK Equity Income	26	8,943
VCT Specialist: Environmental	8	144
VCT Generalist	41	3,342
Hedge Funds	9	7,339
Global Emerging Markets	13	6,012
UK Equity & Bond Income	3	233
VCT Specialist: Technology	3	7
Commodities & Natural Resources	7	1,151

	10YR NAV TOTAL RETURN %	YIELD %	DISCOUNT / PREMIUM %	ONGOING CHARGE EXCL PERF FEE %	ONGOING CHARGE INCL PERF FEE %
	459.1	1.3	5.3	1.2	1.2
	357.4	2.9	-1.3	1.0	1.0
	293.8	0.3	-6.1	0.9	0.9
	273.2	1.1	-7.8	0.8	0.8
	254.1	1.1	-2.9	0.5	0.5
	231.4	2.7	-7.2	0.7	0.7
	205.0	3.5	-0.4	1.3	1.5
	170.3	2.0	-9.0	0.9	0.9
	162.2	4.7	13.1	1.1	1.3
	160.1	3.2	-12.7	0.9	1.1
	156.2	1.5	-11.1	1.4	1.5
	149.6	3.5	-21.6	1.3	1.7
	146.3	6.3	-9.0	2.2	2.2
	139.9	1.4	-6.9	0.9	1.0
	122.3	3.4	-12.8	0.6	0.6
	118.8	4.3	-0.8	0.7	0.7
	103.2	2.2	-14.2	1.1	1.6
	99.4	1.8	-12.8	1.1	1.1
	91.6	5.0	-10.7	1.5	1.5
	84.8	6.0	-6.7	1.2	1.2
	82.3	5.0	-5.9	0.6	0.6
	81.8	6.6	-3.3	3.0	3.0
	76.2	9.3	-5.6	2.4	2.9
	75.7	1.1	-21.9	1.8	2.7
	66.7	2.4	-11.2	1.1	1.1
	12.8	5.9	0.3	1.1	1.1
	-2.7	6.2	-33.3	2.4	2.4
	-14.2	5.6	-15.3	1.5	1.5

AIC SECTOR	NUMBER OF COMPANIES	MARKET CAPITALISATION (£M)
Environmental	3	993
Financials	4	233
VCT Generalist Pre Qualifying	7	153
Property - Europe	4	1,164
Insurance & Reinsurance Strategies	4	255
Renewable Energy Infrastructure	12	9,199
Leasing	7	671
Debt - Direct Lending	10	3,216
Debt - Structured Finance	6	1,589
Property - UK Residential	6	2,215
Technology & Media	4	4,005
Property - Debt	4	745

Source: AIC/Morningstar, all data to 30/09/20, base currency (figures ex 3i where stated)

Different sectors have very different characteristics, reflecting the different kinds of asset in which they invest. You can see this by looking at some of the key metrics for more than 40 sectors and sub-sectors. This table excludes most VCTs and the very large trust 3i. Trusts are ranked by their 10-year average share price total returns. Note that these figures are weighted averages, giving most impact to the largest trusts, and individual trusts within each sector may have significantly different characteristics.

Some interesting trends can be discerned, however. For example, the most expensive trusts, as measured by OCRs (ongoing charge ratios) are to be found in VCTs, hedge funds and private equity. The cheapest sectors on average are to be found in the two main UK equity sectors (equity income and all companies) and the global trusts.

The highest yields are also found among VCTs and in the equity income, property and infrastructure sectors. Looking at the performance figures it is evident that there is something of an inverse relationship between yield and NAV total returns over 10 years. Four of the five high yielding sectors have 10-year returns of less than 100%, while nearly all the others have higher returns.

	10YR NAV TOTAL RETURN %	YIELD %	DISCOUNT / PREMIUM %	ONGOING CHARGE EXCL PERF FEE %	ONGOING CHARGE INCL PERF FEE %
	-	0.8	0.0	1.1	1.1
	-	5.8	-17.1	1.7	1.8
	-	5.6	-5.5	2.5	2.5
	-	3.9	-18.1	3.1	3.3
	-	7.2	-17.2	7.7	7.7
	-	5.3	16.7	1.1	1.1
	-	21.4	-41.8	1.3	1.3
	-	7.0	-9.3	1.7	2.5
	-	7.9	-15.3	1.0	1.2
	-	5.1	-11.2	1.5	1.5
	-	0.0	-3.9	1.0	1.0
	-	8.4	-16.8	1.6	1.6

Even though trusts with higher yields have attracted a disproportionate amount of the capital that has flowed into the investment trust sector, the potential capital gains which are foregone by opting for higher yielding trusts has been significant in the last 10 years. However, this has been masked to a considerable extent by the tighter discounts on which higher yielding trusts tend to trade. Compare for example the average discount in the UK equity income sector (5.9%) with that in the UK smaller companies (12.7%) and the UK all companies sectors (12.8%).

Looking at the level of discounts more generally, it can be seen that more than 20 of the sectors were trading at a discount of more than 10% at the point this table was created (30 September 2020). Two sectors, infrastructure and biotechnology/healthcare, were trading on average at a premium, although for very different reasons – secure higher yields and exceptional growth rates, respectively. Renewable energy infrastructure trusts were also trading at a premium, although they are not directly comparable to the others in the table because of having less than 10 years history. ■

Largest management groups

MANAGEMENT GROUP	TOTAL ASSETS (£M)	MARKET CAP (£M)	NUMBER OF COMPANIES
Baillie Gifford	24,257	2,288	11
J.P. Morgan Asset Management	11,780	978	21
3i Group	8,924	970	1
Aberdeen Standard Investments	9,851	755	20
BMO Global Asset Management	10,026	730	10
Janus Henderson Investors	6,583	566	13
InfraRed Capital Partners	4,805	559	2
Pershing Square Capital Management	7,461	528	1
Frostrow Capital	5,017	486	4
Fidelity	4,848	381	5
Polar Capital Holdings	3,936	328	4
Tritax Management	4,258	305	2
RIT Capital Partners	3,352	291	1
Greencoat Capital	3,273	279	2
BlackRock Investment Management (UK)	3,429	274	8
Schroder Investment Management	3,341	269	5
Willis Towers Watson	2,976	262	1
Amber Infrastructure Group	2,350	261	1
3i Investments	2,228	258	1
Fundsmith	2,295	229	1

Source: AIC/Morningstar, data to 30/09/20

The management groups with the most trust mandates are listed here. The trust sector is a competitive one, in which no management group has a dominant position. There has however been some consolidation in the last few years. The 20 largest groups manage 61% of total industry assets, up from 50% five years ago, but only five firms out of roughly 400 in total manage more than 10 trusts. In 2018 Baillie Gifford, a private partnership based in Edinburgh, became the largest player in the investment trust sector for the first time, overtaking 3i and

AVG TOTAL ASSETS (£M)	AVG MARKET CAP (£M)	% TOTAL ASSETS 2020	TOTAL ASSETS 2015 (£M)	% TOTAL ASSETS 2015
2,205	208	11.9%	5,929	4.5%
561	47	5.8%	8,811	6.7%
8,924	970	4.4%	5,470	4.1%
493	38	4.8%	5,422	4.1%
1,003	73	4.9%	7,187	5.4%
506	44	3.2%	4,985	3.8%
2,402	279	2.4%	2,467	1.9%
7,461	528	3.7%	4,117	3.1%
1,254	121	2.5%	2,479	1.9%
970	76	2.4%	2,810	2.1%
984	82	1.9%	1,161	0.9%
2,129	152	2.1%	1,058	0.8%
3,352	291	1.6%	2,763	2.1%
1,637	140	1.6%	578	0.4%
429	34	1.7%	2,653	2.0%
668	54	1.6%	1,989	1.5%
2,976	262	1.5%	3,315	2.5%
2,350	261	1.2%	1,082	0.8%
2,228	258	1.1%	1,193	0.9%
2,295	229	1.1%	176	0.1%

J.P. Morgan, and has since further consolidated its lead through a combination of exceptionally strong performance and new mandate wins. J.P. Morgan has the largest number of trusts ahead of Aberdeen Standard Investments. The biggest firms typically launch and market their own trusts, as well as providing portfolio management and administrative functions, often centralising them. Smaller firms, by contrast, especially those managing specialist trusts, may only have one or more funds that they look after and will often sub-contract more services. ■

The largest trusts

COMPANY	MANAGEMENT GROUP	AIC SECTOR	TOTAL ASSETS (£M)	MARKET CAP (£M)
Scottish Mortgage	Baillie Gifford	Global	15,461	14,472
3i Group	3i Group	Private Equity	8,924	9,698
Pershing Square Holdings	Pershing Square Capital Management	Hedge Funds	7,461	5,277
F&C Investment Trust	BMO Global Asset Management	Global	4,528	3,677
RIT Capital Partners	RIT Capital Partners	Flexible Investment	3,352	2,914
Polar Capital Technology	Polar Capital Holdings	Technology & Media	3,057	2,836
HICL Infrastructure	InfraRed Capital Partners	Infrastructure	2,870	3,211
Alliance Trust	Willis Towers Watson	Global	2,976	2,624
Tritax Big Box REIT	Tritax Management	Property - UK Commercial	3,764	2,646
Monks	Baillie Gifford	Global	2,687	2,527
International Public Partnerships	Amber Infrastructure Group	Infrastructure	2,350	2,607
3i Infrastructure	3i Investments	Infrastructure	2,228	2,581
Templeton Emerging Markets	Franklin Templeton Investments	Global Emerging Markets	2,319	1,960
Tetragon Financial Group	Tetragon Financial Management	Flexible Investment	2,147	765
Worldwide Healthcare	Frostrow Capital	Biotechnology & Healthcare	2,076	2,098
Smithson	Fundsmith	Global Smaller Companies	1,946	1,989

	NET ASSETS (£M)	NET ASSETS 2015 (£M)	LAUNCH DATE	YIELD %	% SPREAD
	14,467	3,090	17/03/1909	32.8%	0.1%
	8,349	3,905	01/04/1945	351.2%	0.1%
	7,461	4,117	13/10/2014	146.3%	2.9%
	4,119	2,511	19/03/1868	169.8%	0.4%
	3,135	2,368	01/08/1988	188.4%	0.3%
	3,003	741	16/12/1996	0.0%	0.5%
	2,870	1,819	29/03/2006	497.6%	0.1%
	2,779	2,885	21/04/1888	176.7%	0.4%
	2,617	789	09/12/2013	451.6%	0.1%
	2,503	922	06/02/1929	22.2%	0.5%
	2,350	1,082	09/11/2006	456.0%	0.1%
	2,228	1,193	13/03/2007	338.5%	0.2%
	2,216	1,403	12/06/1989	229.5%	0.1%
	2,147	n/a*	19/04/2007	467.3%	3.7%
	2,076	856	28/04/1995	70.5%	0.3%
	1,946	n/a	19/10/2018	0.0%	0.1%

* Tetragon Financial Group obtained a listing on the Specialist Fund Market of the LSE on 09/11/15.

COMPANY	MANAGEMENT GROUP	AIC SECTOR	TOTAL ASSETS (£M)	MARKET CAP (£M)
Renewables Infrastructure Group	InfraRed Capital Partners	Renewable Energy Infrastructure	1,935	2,375
Finsbury Growth & Income	Frostrow Capital	UK Equity Income	1,880	1,829
Caledonia	Caledonia Investments	Flexible Investment	1,818	1,349
Fidelity China Special Situations	Fidelity	Country Specialist: Asia Pacific - ex Japan	2,239	1,711
Greencoat UK Wind	Greencoat Capital	Renewable Energy Infrastructure	2,276	2,035
HarbourVest Global Private Equity	HarbourVest Advisers L.P.	Private Equity	1,699	1,326
Witan	Witan Investment Services	Global	1,870	1,527
Sequoia Economic Infrastructure Income	Sequoia Investment Management	Infrastructure	1,739	1,729
Mercantile	J.P. Morgan Asset Management	UK All Companies	1,879	1,398

Source: AIC/Morningstar, data to 30/09/20

While a small minority of investment trusts are managed directly by the board of directors, the great majority delegate the management of their portfolios to specialist fund managers, employed on annual or multi-year management contracts with a mandate to meet the trust's investment objectives. Those objectives are set by the board of directors and need to be approved by shareholders before any significant changes can be made.

The investment trust with the greatest total assets, Scottish Mortgage (SMT), accounted for around 7.5% of the industry total as at 30 September 2020. The 20 largest individual trusts on this measure accounted for just over 40% of total industry assets. In contrast, more than 100 trusts had less than £50m in assets, although this figure includes a large number of venture capital trusts, which

NET ASSETS (£M)	NET ASSETS 2015 (£M)	LAUNCH DATE	YIELD %	% SPREAD
1,935	649	29/07/2013	494.9%	0.4%
1,843	674	15/01/1926	197.6%	0.2%
1,818	1,558	18/07/1960	248.4%	0.8%
1,802	786	19/04/2010	128.0%	0.3%
1,796	473	27/03/2013	529.9%	0.1%
1,699	883	06/12/2007	0.0%	1.1%
1,666	1,470	17/02/1909	287.2%	0.3%
1,639	144	03/03/2015	598.7%	0.4%
1,617	1,864	08/12/1884	373.7%	0.2%

Spread = (offer-bid)/mid(close)

are invariably much smaller on average. The largest trusts tend to have the best liquidity, meaning they are easy to buy and sell in size. The spread between bid and offer prices is typically well below 0.5%.

A majority of the largest trusts in the sector have been operating for many years, but that is by no means universally the case. Smithson (SSON), Pershing Square (PSH), Greencoat UK Wind (UKW) and Tritax Big Box (BBOX) have all been launched or listed on the London market in the last 10 years. At the same time there are regular departures from the investment trust universe, as funds either close down or return capital to shareholders, typically (though not invariably) as a result of indifferent performance or where the trust has a predetermined wind-up date. ■

Vintage investment trusts

COMPANY NAME	AIC SECTOR	LAUNCH DATE	MARKET CAP (£M)
F&C Investment Trust	Global	19/03/1868	3,677
Alliance Trust	Global	21/04/1888	2,624
Investment Company	UK Equity Income	01/01/1868	13
Dunedin Income Growth	UK Equity Income	01/02/1873	363
Scottish American	Global Equity Income	31/03/1873	693
JPMorgan American	North America	18/06/1881	1,031
Mercantile	UK All Companies	08/12/1884	1,398
JPMorgan Global Growth & Income	Global Equity Income	21/04/1887	499
Scottish Investment Trust	Global	27/07/1887	518
Henderson Smaller Companies	UK Smaller Companies	16/12/1887	562
Bankers	Global	13/04/1888	1,308
BMO Global Smaller Companies	Global Smaller Companies	15/02/1889	721
Merchants	UK Equity Income	16/02/1889	403
Edinburgh Investment	UK Equity Income	01/03/1889	766
AVI Global	Global	01/07/1889	782
Law Debenture Corporation	UK Equity Income	12/12/1889	596
City of London	UK Equity Income	01/01/1891	1,310
Aberdeen Diversified Income & Growth	Flexible Investment	05/01/1898	290
TR Property	Property Securities	05/05/1905	1,095
BlackRock Smaller Companies	UK Smaller Companies	02/05/1906	596
Witan Pacific	Asia Pacific	24/01/1907	251
Murray International	Global Equity Income	18/12/1907	1,226
Witan	Global	17/02/1909	1,527
Scottish Mortgage	Global	17/03/1909	14,472

NET ASSETS (£M)	TICKER	YIELD %	% SPREAD	1YR AVG DISCOUNT / PREMIUM %
4,119	FCIT	1.7%	0.4%	-4.80
2,779	ATST	1.8%	0.4%	-5.79
15	INV	4.6%	9.7%	-10.78
403	DIG	5.2%	1.6%	-6.59
661	SAIN	2.7%	0.2%	3.99
1,093	JAM	1.3%	0.6%	-5.49
1,617	MRC	3.7%	0.2%	-4.03
481	JGGI	3.8%	0.3%	2.50
581	SCIN	3.3%	0.4%	-9.78
657	HSL	3.2%	1.3%	-7.46
1,301	BNKR	2.1%	0.6%	0.08
802	BGSC	1.4%	0.7%	-7.78
417	MRCH	8.0%	0.9%	0.83
887	EDIN	6.5%	0.2%	-12.01
867	AGT	2.2%	0.3%	-9.75
627	LWDB	5.2%	0.7%	-4.81
1,331	CTY	6.0%	0.2%	1.37
349	ADIG	5.9%	1.1%	-13.11
1,269	TRY	4.1%	0.1%	-6.15
674	BRSC	2.7%	1.5%	-3.75
238	BGCG	1.7%	1.5%	-6.97
1,285	MYI	5.6%	0.7%	-0.49
1,666	WTAN	2.9%	0.3%	-4.87
14,467	SMT	0.3%	0.1%	-0.27

COMPANY NAME	AIC SECTOR	LAUNCH DATE	MARKET CAP (£M)
Hansa Investment Company (A share)	Flexible Investment	01/01/1912	205
Hansa Investment Company (Ord)	Flexible Investment	01/01/1912	197
Murray Income	UK Equity Income	07/06/1923	483
Finsbury Growth & Income	UK Equity Income	15/01/1926	1,829
Temple Bar	UK Equity Income	24/06/1926	437
Brunner	Global	01/01/1927	318
JPMorgan Japanese	Japan	02/08/1927	990
Monks	Global	06/02/1929	2,527
JPMorgan European Growth	Europe	15/03/1929	200
Shires Income	UK Equity Income	31/03/1929	66
Canadian General Investments Unit	North America	15/01/1930	553
Henderson Far East Income	Asia Pacific Income	30/05/1930	432
3i Group	Private Equity	01/04/1945	9,698
Henderson European Focus	Europe	01/01/1947	269
Keystone	UK All Companies	19/11/1954	157
Caledonia	Flexible Investment	18/07/1960	1,349

Source: AIC/Morningstar, data to 30/09/20

The first investment trust, F&C (FCIT), was formed in 1868 and continues in existence today. It celebrated its 150th anniversary in 2018. A number of other investment companies have also been around for many years. Twelve can trace their histories back to the 19th century. This is a list of some of the oldest vintage trusts which are still in existence.

A number of these trusts were started by wealthy families looking to invest their fortunes in a tax-efficient manner, but have since expanded to include outside investors as well. The first Scottish investment trust, Dunedin Income Growth (DIG), for example, was founded to provide a home for the savings of wealthy textile merchants in Dundee. Caledonia (CLDN) was founded by the Cayzer shipping dynasty.

NET ASSETS (£M)	TICKER	YIELD %	% SPREAD	1YR AVG DISCOUNT / PREMIUM %
314	HANA	1.9%	0.0%	-35.93
314	HAN	2.0%	6.1%	-36.33
525	MUT	4.8%	1.1%	-4.79
1,843	FGT	2.0%	0.2%	-0.13
509	TMPL	5.9%	0.8%	-6.23
383	BUT	2.7%	1.3%	-9.26
1,065	JFJ	0.8%	0.3%	-10.40
2,503	MNKS	0.2%	0.5%	3.19
238	JETG	3.3%	1.5%	-13.66
70	SHRS	6.2%	4.2%	-2.27
872	CGI	4.6%	2.4%	-31.75
425	HFEL	7.5%	0.3%	1.67
8,349	III	3.5%	0.1%	11.89
308	HEFT	2.5%	0.8%	-10.85
190	KIT	2.8%	0.8%	-14.95
1,818	CLDN	2.5%	0.8%	-20.23

Spread = (offer-bid)/mid(close)

There is no obvious correlation between age and size or quality of trust, although the mere fact of having survived for so long indicates that a trust has at least successfully established a niche in the market. The wide range of average discounts illustrates the disparity in liquidity, performance and popularity.

Note that a number of these trusts have changed investment manager in recent years. In 2020 alone the boards of Witan Pacific, whose mandate has moved to Baillie Gifford and is now Baillie Gifford China Growth (BGCG), Edinburgh Investment Trust (EDIN), Temple Bar (TMPL) and Perpetual Income and Growth (PLI) have all chosen to move from one management firm to a different one. ■

Long-serving managers

COMPANY NAME	TICKER	AIC SECTOR
Capital Gearing	CGT	Flexible Investment
Rights & Issues	RIII	UK Smaller Companies
Lowland	LWI	UK Equity Income
Aberforth Smaller Companies	ASL	UK Smaller Companies
City of London	CTY	UK Equity Income
Herald	HRI	Global Smaller Companies
JPMorgan Emerging Markets	JMG	Global Emerging Markets
Aberdeen Standard Asia Focus	AAS	Asia Pacific Smaller Companies
Schroder AsiaPacific	SDP	Asia Pacific
British & American	BAF	UK Equity Income
Atlantis Japan Growth	AJG	Japanese Smaller Companies
Atlantis Japan Growth	AJG	Japanese Smaller Companies
JPMorgan European Growth	JETG	Europe
BMO Capital & Income	BCI	UK Equity Income
JPMorgan Smaller Companies	JMI	UK Smaller Companies
JPMorgan European Smaller Companies	JESC	European Smaller Companies
Chelverton UK Dividend	SDVP	UK Equity Income
BMO Private Equity	BPET	Private Equity
Scottish Mortgage	SMT	Global
BlackRock World Mining	BRWM	Commodities & Natural Resources
Independent Investment Trust	IIT	UK All Companies
European Opportunities	JEO	Europe
Finsbury Growth & Income	FGT	UK Equity Income
HgCapital	HGT	Private Equity
Jupiter US Smaller Companies	JUS	North American Smaller Companies
Lindsell Train	LTI	Global
International Biotechnology	IBT	Biotechnology & Healthcare
Aberforth Smaller Companies	ASL	UK Smaller Companies
JPMorgan Russian Securities	JRS	Country Specialist: Europe - ex UK
Impax Environmental Markets	IEM	Environmental
Impax Environmental Markets	IEM	Environmental
Henderson Smaller Companies	HSL	UK Smaller Companies
Schroder UK Mid Cap	SCP	UK All Companies
Artemis Alpha Trust	ATS	UK All Companies

MANAGER NAME	EFFECTIVE FROM	YEARS IN SERVICE
Peter Spiller	01/01/1982	38 years 7 months
Simon Knott	01/01/1984	36 years 7 months
James H Henderson	01/01/1990	30 years 7 months
Alistair J Whyte	10/12/1990	29 years 8 months
Job Curtis	01/07/1991	29 years 1 months
Katie Potts	16/02/1994	26 years 6 months
Austin Forey	01/06/1994	26 years 2 months
Hugh Young	19/10/1995	24 years 9 months
Matthew Dobbs	20/11/1995	24 years 8 months
Jonathan Woolf	03/01/1996	24 years 7 months
Edwin C Merner	10/05/1996	24 years 3 months
Taeko Setaishi	10/05/1996	24 years 3 months
Stephen Macklow-Smith	01/01/1997	23 years 7 months
Julian Cane	01/03/1997	23 years 5 months
Georgina Brittain	02/01/1998	22 years 7 months
Francesco Conte	01/11/1998	21 years 9 months
David Horner	12/05/1999	21 years 3 months
Hamish Mair	01/02/2000	20 years 6 months
James K. Anderson	01/04/2000	20 years 4 months
Evy Hambro	01/09/2000	19 years 11 months
Maxwell Ward	18/10/2000	19 years 9 months
Alexander Darwall	22/11/2000	19 years 8 months
Nick Train	11/12/2000	19 years 8 months
Nic Humphries	01/01/2001	19 years 7 months
Robert Siddles	01/01/2001	19 years 7 months
Nick Train	22/01/2001	19 years 6 months
Kate Bingham	01/05/2001	19 years 3 months
Euan R MacDonald	14/05/2001	19 years 3 months
Oleg Biryulyov	09/01/2002	18 years 7 months
Bruce Jenkyn-Jones	22/02/2002	18 years 5 months
Jon Forster	22/02/2002	18 years 5 months
Neil Hermon	01/11/2002	17 years 9 months
Andy Brough	30/04/2003	17 years 3 months
John Dodd	01/06/2003	17 years 2 months

COMPANY NAME	TICKER	AIC SECTOR
Law Debenture Corporation	LWDB	UK Equity Income
Bankers	BNKR	Global
Standard Life UK Companies	SLS	UK Smaller Companies
EP Global Opportunities	EPG	Global
Miton Global Opportunities	MIGO	Flexible Investment
Murray International	MYI	Global Equity Income
Schroder Real Estate	SREI	Property - UK Commercial
Schroder Real Estate	SREI	Property - UK Commercial
BlackRock Greater Europe	BRGE	Europe
Aberdeen New India	ANII	Country Specialist: Asia Pacific - ex Japan
BMO Commercial Property	BCPT	Property - UK Commercial
Biotech Growth	BIOG	Biotechnology & Healthcare
JPEL Private Equity	JPEL	Private Equity
JPEL Private Equity	JPEL	Private Equity
JPMorgan American	JAM	North America
JPMorgan China Growth & Income	JCGI	Country Specialist: Asia Pacific - ex Japan
Invesco Income Growth	IVI	UK Equity Income
Schroder Oriental Income	SOI	Asia Pacific Income
BMO Global Smaller Companies	BGSC	Global Smaller Companies
JPMorgan European Income	JETI	Europe
JPMorgan European Income	JETI	Europe
JPMorgan European Income	JETI	Europe

Source: AIC, correct as of 30/09/20

Some individual trusts are also notable for having long-serving managers who have been running the trust's investments for many years. In some cases the managers also have significant personal shareholdings in the trust. This is typically regarded as a good omen for other shareholders, since it establishes a close alignment of interest between the manager and the shareholders. See the Skin in the Game page (page 224) for some examples.

Because fund management is an extremely well-paid profession, the fact that a manager continues to manage a trust after many years in harness can often be interpreted also as demonstrating exceptional commitment to the business. While some successful fund managers retire early to do other things, those who remain in post for decades are typically such enthusiasts for the challenge of investing that they cannot think of anything more interesting or rewarding to do with their time.

MANAGER NAME	EFFECTIVE FROM	YEARS IN SERVICE
James H Henderson	01/06/2003	17 years 2 months
Alex Crooke	01/07/2003	17 years 1 months
Harry Nimmo	01/09/2003	16 years 11 months
Sandy Nairn	15/12/2003	16 years 8 months
Nick Greenwood	06/04/2004	16 years 4 months
Bruce Stout	16/06/2004	16 years 2 months
Duncan Owen	15/07/2004	16 years 1 months
Nick Montgomery	15/07/2004	16 years 1 months
Sam Vecht	20/09/2004	15 years 10 months
Kristy Fong	09/12/2004	15 years 8 months
Richard Kirby	17/03/2005	15 years 5 months
Geoffrey Hsu	19/05/2005	15 years 2 months
Troy Duncan	30/06/2005	15 years 1 months
Gregory Getschow	30/06/2005	15 years 1 months
Eytan Shapiro	01/07/2005	15 years 1 months
Howard Wang	01/07/2005	15 years 1 months
Ciaran Mallon	28/07/2005	15 years 0 months
Matthew Dobbs	28/07/2005	15 years 0 months
Peter Ewins	31/07/2005	15 years 0 months
Stephen Macklow-Smith	02/08/2005	15 years 0 months
Michael Barakos	02/08/2005	15 years 0 months
Alexander Fitzalan Howard	02/08/2005	15 years 0 months

Against that sometimes situations arise where managers have such a large personal shareholding in a trust that they effectively control the running of the company, and as a result may not always make the interests of other shareholders as high a priority as they should. They are effectively being paid to look after their own money, often with a longer-term perspective that makes them worry less about short-term performance. These are exceptions however.

Note the wide range of sectors in which these trusts operate. From those included in this list a year ago, managers who have announced their retirements include Angela Lascelles of Value and Income (VIN), Jacob Rothschild at Rit Capital (RCP), Matthew Dobbs of Schroder Asia Pacific (SDP) and Schroder Oriental Income (SOI) and Robert Siddles of Jupiter US Smaller Companies (JUS). The longest serving manager still managing a trust now is Peter Spiller at Capital Gearing Trust (CGT). ∎

Skin in the game

A GOOD QUESTION FOR investors to ask about any company (not just investment trusts) is the extent to which the interests of the managers of the company are aligned with the interests of the shareholders.

In an ideal world it would be comforting to know that those managing the company stand to gain or lose in the same way as those providing the capital for the business (which is what shareholders effectively do).

In the case of investment trusts, the two parties whose interests you most want to have aligned with yours as an investor are the board of directors and the individual fund managers who make the investment decisions.

In both cases it is usually a positive if they have substantial personal investments in their trusts. One exception may occur if an individual or institution holds such a large shareholding in a trust that they effectively control the company and can do what they want with it, whether sensible or not.

Directors of trusts are required to disclose at least once a year in the company's annual report and accounts the extent of their holdings in the trusts on whose boards they serve. It is also a stock exchange listing requirement they notify the market within 24 hours of any further dealings in their trust's shares. All significant shareholders must also notify the market if they own more than 3% of the share capital in any trust.

While directors' interests are always available, it is less easy to discover how much the portfolio managers have invested in their trusts. They only have to disclose their shareholding if it exceeds 3% of the total issued share capital of the trust. Some choose to do so voluntarily.

Alan Brierley, investment analyst at Investec, does the industry a service by periodically compiling a summary of the shareholdings of directors and managers (where the latter can be ascertained). His last research on this topic, based on analysing 303 trusts, was published in October 2019, so the figures will have changed somewhat since then with market movements. Earlier reports appeared in 2018, 2017, 2014 and 2012.

These are some of his headline findings from the most recent survey:

- The total investment by boards and managers in the 2019 report was £3.39bn. While changes in the closed-end industry make comparisons of limited value, and equity markets have been strong, this is materially higher than the total of £1bn in 2014 and £687m in 2012.

- 50 chairmen/directors have an individual investment in excess of £1m, while 74 managers or management teams have a personal investment in excess of £1m.

- 39 investment companies, or 13% of those analysed, have chairmen or directors who all have shareholdings valued at more than one year of their director's fee.

- 16% of directors have no investment at all in their trusts (vs 14% in 2018 and 16% in 2014). Excluding those appointed in the past year, this falls to 10% (vs 9% in 2018 and 12% in 2014).

Board composition

The Investec report on board and manager shareholdings also provides some helpful data on board composition. Of the 303 trusts analysed, 94.6% of the directors could be classified as independent. Women accounted for 27.9% of investment company directorships, vs 22.3% in 2018, 15.2 % in 2015 and just 8% in 2010. This compares with 26.7% of FTSE 350 company directors. Notably there were still 43 all-male boards vs just two in FT 350 index companies. Given that the government has announced a voluntary target of 33% female directors by 2020, trust boards are becoming less "pale, male and stale", but were still lagging the corporate sector generally. These figures have improved further however since the date of the last Investec survey.

The following table highlights trusts in which the managers (or management teams) have shareholdings in excess of £10m:

Managers with a personal investment in excess of £10m at October 2019

COMPANY	MANAGER	VALUE (£'000)
Pershing Square Holdings	William Ackman and management	668,116
Tetragon Financial Group	Reade Griffith/Paddy Dear and team	256,966
Apax Global Alpha	Management team	193,985
Boussard & Gavaudan	Management team	129,251
North Atlantic Smallers	Christopher Mills	110,713
JZ Capital Partners	David Zalaznick/Jay Jordan	100,439
Manchester & London	Mark Sheppard	90,826
Scottish Mortgage	Management team	85,965
Third Point Offshore	Dan Loeb and family	70,981
New Star	John Duffield	48,514
Smithson Investment Trust	Terry Smith and team	34,557
Riverstone Energy	Management team	33,775
Lindsell Train	Michael Lindsell/Nick Train	28,420
HgCapital Trust	Management team	27,236
Value & Income	Angela Lascelles/Matthew Oakeshott	26,797
Aberforth Smaller Companies	Management team	24,676
European Opportunities	Alex Darwall	23,852
Finsbury Growth & Income	Nick Train	23,749
Syncona	Thomas Henderson	21,295
Independent Investment Trust	Max Ward	20,365
Primary Health Properties	Harry Hymen/Nexus Group	18,219
Capital Gearing	Peter Spiller	17,162
Mobius Investment Trust	Management team	15,886
Monks	Management team	13,600
Crystal Amber	Management team	13,176
Montanaro UK Smaller	Charles Montanaro and family	12,822
International Public Partnerships	Management team	12,532
Mid Wynd	Simon Edelsten	12,441
GCP Infrastructure Investments	Management team	11,572
Montanaro European Smaller	Charles Montanaro and family	10,626
Fundsmith Emerging Equities	Terry Smith/Mike O'Brien	10,186
Aberforth Split Level Income	Management team	10,032

Source: Investec

This year we also include a table showing which trusts have the most highly paid executive directors. By definition this is a relatively small group as most trusts outsource the management of the portfolio to external managers or advisers and most boards, as noted above, consist entirely of independent non-executive directors. Most but not all of those on the list are self-managed or specialist trusts therefore. Do not assume that the fund managers of trusts where the investment management function is delegated to a third party firm are necessarily suffering by comparison. Fund management is a very well-remunerated profession.

Highest paid executive directors

EXECUTIVE DIRECTOR	COMPANY	APPOINTED TO BOARD	TOTAL REMUNERATION (£)	VALUE OF INVESTMENT (£)
Christopher Mills, CEO	North Atlantic Smaller	1984	3,805,000	110,713,200
Will Wyatt, CEO	Caledonia Investments	2005	1,864,000	34,139,893
Jamie Cayzer-Colvin	Caledonia Investments	2005	1,165,000	11,173,452
Michael Morris, CEO	Picton Property Income	2015	851,000	49,308
Jonathan Murphy, CEO	Assura	2017	760,000	1,889,573
Denis Jackson, CEO	Law Debenture	2018	611,186	11,013
Tim Attlee, CEO	Empiric Student Property	2014	539,500	871,714
Andrew Bell, CEO	Witan	2010	497,881	1,501,500
Lynne Fennah, CFO	Empiric Student Property	2017	454,160	53,738
Tim Livett, CFO	Caledonia Investments	2019	375,000	-
Andrew Dewhirst, FD	Picton Property Income	2018	350,000	26,220
Jayne Cottam, CFO	Assura	2017	344,000	68,955
Max Ward, MD	Independent IT	2000	200,000	20,364,960
Robin Angus	Personal Assets	1984	200,000	2,038,816

Source: Investec

Returning capital

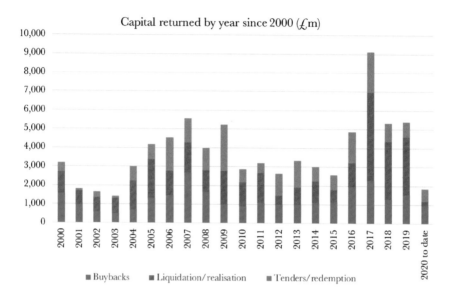

Capital returned by year since 2000 (£m)

■ Buybacks   ■ Liquidation/realisation   ■ Tenders/redemption

Source: AIC/Morningstar (Buybacks from Winterfloods Monthly).
Like the Numis chart from last year this does not include capital dividends.

There can be a number of reasons why a trust decides to return capital to its shareholders. One is to try and limit the discount at which the shares in the trust are trading. Another is because a trust has decided to liquidate itself or offer an exit to shareholders, typically because of a run of poor performance. In some other cases a trust may decide to make a distribution of capital because of the sale of a significant asset it owns.

Many investment companies now have measures in place with which they attempt to control the discount and/or reduce discount volatility. Some trusts give a specific discount target, a level at which they promise to take remedial action. Others content themselves with a more modest statement of intent to keep the discount in mind.

These measures include buying back shares in the market, making tender offers at periodic intervals (enabling those who wish to sell their shares to do so at a price close to NAV) and agreeing to hold a continuation vote at some date in the future. It is fairly routine these days for investment companies to adopt the power to buy back their own shares. This requires shareholder approval at a general meeting and more than two-thirds of the companies in the sector have obtained this approval.

There is no doubt that many boards of investment companies are taking discount controls more seriously than in the past. In 1999 it became possible for investment companies to hold shares they have bought back in treasury, meaning they can be retained without being cancelled and so can be reissued later if and when demand for the shares has grown again. Buybacks have been running at an average rate of around £1.2bn a year over the past 20 years.

As the chart shows, overall figures for the return of capital have been trending higher in recent years. One reason is the emergence of so-called professional 'activist investors' who buy a block of shares and use that as leverage in trying to force the board of poorly performing trusts to take some action. Trusts whose boards have committed to continuation votes or tenders at fixed intervals, or have suffered sustained periods of poor performance, can decide to liquidate the company if they judge it is too small or too out of favour to remain viable. ■

New issues

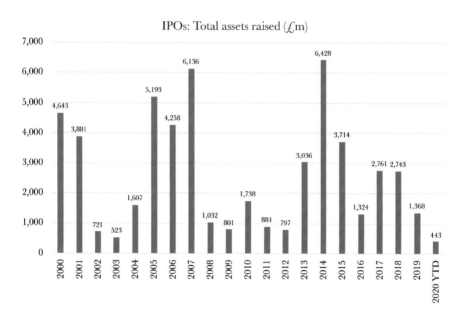

IPOs: Total assets raised (£m)

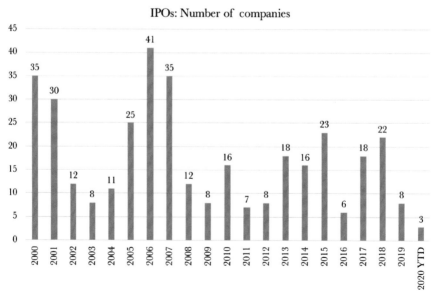

IPOs: Number of companies

Source: AIC/Morningstar, company details and total assets at launch. Data to 31 October 2020

Whereas buybacks and tender offers reduce the amount of capital invested in the trust sector, in any year they will be offset by a combination of new and secondary issues by other trusts. New trusts are launched on a regular, if cyclical, basis. Certain periods are characterised by a spurt of new issues in a particular segment of the market. Property trusts and hedge funds, for example, were popular in the run up to the financial crisis in 2008. Income-generating trusts from alternative assets, such as infrastructure, have been particularly popular since then. After two good years for IPOs in 2017 and 2018, the last two years have been disappointing with just eight new launches successfully completed in 2019 and only three in 2020 at the time of writing (mid-October).

The successful IPOs so far in 2020 were Nippon Active Value (NAVF), which raised £103m in January to pursue an equity activist strategy in Japan, Home Reit (HOME), which raised £264m in September to build homeless and sheltered accommodation, and Triple Point Energy Efficiency Infrastructure (TEEC), which raised £100m in October. Nippon Active Value was the first equity IPO to be launched since October 2018.

At the same time there are regular departures from the investment trust universe, as funds either close down or return capital to shareholders, typically (though not invariably) as a result of indifferent performance or where the trust has a predetermined wind-up date. The way the universe of listed trusts looks can therefore change significantly from decade to decade.

Some big-name fund managers with strong personal followings have been behind some of the largest recent new trust launches, showing the power of a star name. Examples include Anthony Bolton in 2010 (Fidelity China Special Situations, FCSS), Terry Smith in 2014 (Fundsmith Emerging Equities, FEET) and 2018 (Smithson, SSON) and Neil Woodford in 2015 (Woodford Patient Capital, WPCT). Each one of these raised several hundred million pounds at launch.

A star name is not an automatic guarantee of success, as the Woodford example illustrates. The trust was the worst performer of all trusts in 2019 and the investment manager Woodford Investment Management resigned as manager after being forced out of business following a series of liquidity issues in its open-ended Woodford Equity Income fund. The trust has since been taken over by a new management team at Schroders and renamed the Schroder Public Private Trust (SUPP). ∎

Secondary issuance

COMPANY NAME	SECONDARY FUNDRAISING (£M) 01/10/19-30/09/20
Hipgnosis Songs	657
Greencoat UK Wind	400
Renewables Infrastructure Group	348
Sequoia Economic Infrastructure Income	300
Smithson	286
SDCL Energy Efficiency Income	264
Supermarket Income REIT	240
HICL Infrastructure	237
3i Infrastructure	223
International Public Partnerships	192
Personal Assets	170
Worldwide Healthcare	165
Warehouse REIT	153
Finsbury Growth & Income	140
Urban logistics REIT	137
City of London	134
Greencoat Renewables	113
Edinburgh Worldwide	112
Allianz Technology	112
Capital Gearing	88
HgCapital	78
Impax Environmental Markets	77
GCP Student Living	76
Gresham House Energy Storage	73
BB Healthcare	66

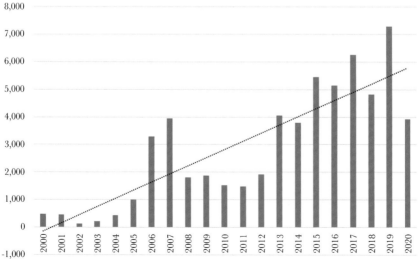

Secondary fundraising (£m)

Source: AIC/Morningstar, excludes company issuance from treasury

One important difference in the last two decades is that it has become easier for trusts to grow through a process known as 'secondary issuance'. Essentially trusts that are popular with investors can now, provided they have the necessary shareholder approvals, more readily issue additional shares without the need to produce an expensive legal prospectus.

It is nothing like as simple as the daily process by which open-ended funds can issue or cancel units in their funds, but it does enable trusts to tap into additional demand on a regular basis. Scottish Mortgage is the most striking example: it has raised an additional £700m of capital in this way since January 2017. Many of the infrastructure funds have also grown rapidly through this route.

Secondary issues can take a number of different forms. The most common are placings of new shares and so-called 'C-share issues'. These two mechanisms, which are less cumbersome and time-consuming than a new issue, both have the effect of allowing an existing trust to expand its capital base by growing the number of shares in issue. A C-share issue is used when it may take some time for the capital raised to be invested. The shares are then traded separately until the investment process is largely complete and the two shares classes are consolidated into one. Placings are more common when a trust has already identified where it wants to invest the money and can complete the transactions in quick order.

Boards that have bought back their own shares also have the option of reissuing shares that they have not yet cancelled. A number of well-known trusts whose performance or style of investing have become popular in recent years have been able to issue a steady stream of new shares at a premium to NAV. Issuing shares at a higher price than the current NAV per share enables the trust to grow in size without penalising existing shareholders.

All issues of new shares have to be approved by existing shareholders, so as to avoid dilution of their interests. Many companies seek approval at their AGMs for the flexibility to issue new shares up to certain annual limits. More than £60bn of new capital has been raised through secondary issuance since 2000. 2019 was a record year for such issuance. The total issued up to 30 September 2020, £4.8bn, was running 18% below the same period a year earlier. The largest issuers are listed in the table. ■

Closed-end funds vs open-ended funds

Performance of Closed-End Funds vs Open-Ended Funds (Equity & Property Mandates)

	NAV total returns (annualised) Open-Ended funds			NAV total returns (annualised) Investment Cos		
	1 yr	5 yr	10 yr	1y	5y	10y
UK - Equity Income	(17.4)	1.1	5.3	(16.8)	1.7	7.1
UK - All Companies	(12.8)	3.2	5.7	(13.6)	3.5	7.8
UK - Smaller Company	(0.0)	6.8	10.2	(6.7)	5.1	11.9
US - General	9.3	16.1	13.8	14.8	14.7	12.5
US - Smaller Company	4.7	14.5	13.3	(5.9)	12.3	12.8
Global - Equity	6.8	12.9	9.6	35.1	19.4	14.0
Global - Equity Income	(3.9)	9.3	8.6	(4.1)	11.0	8.7
Europe - General	3.2	9.3	8.1	5.7	11.9	11.4
Europe - Smaller Company	9.9	10.7	10.4	16.9	14.5	12.9
Asia Pacific - Ex Japan	8.1	13.5	7.3	17.2	16.5	10.4
Japan - General	5.7	12.2	9.3	15.7	17.2	12.9
Japan - Smaller Company	9.7	16.1	13.6	24.2	21.4	14.0
Emerging - Global	1.6	11.5	4.1	4.4	14.3	6.4
Technology	34.8	24.0	17.0	43.3	27.3	19.9

It is not uncommon for the investment managers of trusts to manage other funds outside the investment trust sector at the same time. In fact, a number of fund managers start their careers managing different kinds of fund (typically unit trusts and OEICs, though also hedge funds) and if successful are encouraged to take over or start an investment trust with a broadly similar investment objective.

Adding an investment trust to their responsibilities gives successful fund managers the opportunity to take advantage of the benefits of the investment trust structure, including the use of gearing and freedom from unhelpful forced selling as a result of fund flows. They can also use derivative securities such as futures and options for investment purposes.

These advantages show up regularly in comparisons between the long-term performance of investment trusts and that of open-ended funds with either the same manager or the same investment objective. Where trusts and similar funds can be directly compared in this way, trusts typically show up with superior performance records. Where a trust and an open-ended fund with the same mandate are managed by the same individual, it is rare for the trust not to do better over the longer term.

Note: Data to 30 September 2020. Blue shading indicates outperformance by ICs relative to open-ended funds.
Source: Morningstar, Numis Securities Research

Price total returns (annualised) Investment Cos		
1y	5y	10y
(19.1)	0.6	5.8
(17.2)	2.6	7.1
(10.4)	5.1	11.2
12.5	14.4	11.3
(9.4)	11.7	10.6
34.3	19.2	14.3
(6.5)	10.9	7.9
4.6	10.6	11.2
15.1	14.0	12.6
18.8	17.7	10.5
16.2	16.8	14.8
26.7	22.5	10.5
3.2	14.8	5.1
43.4	27.6	18.7

The degree to which comparable trusts outperform does vary markedly however from sector to sector and is not true every year (2019 being an example when the effect was less marked). The table summarises the difference in the performance of directly comparable trust and open-ended equivalent sectors as at 30 September 2020. The blue-shaded cells show the periods over which trusts in each sector have outperformed.

While the general trend of outperformance continued to hold, the table highlights the relatively poor share performance of UK equity trusts over one and five years, together with trusts in the US smaller companies and global equity income sectors. On a NAV basis, the relative performance is a little better, although the US market remains an exception.

It is fair to point out that such simple comparisons can be criticised by statisticians on the grounds that the two samples are very different in size and also may display what is called survivorship bias. In 2018 academics at Cass Business School in London reported that a detailed analysis of investment trust returns between 2000 and 2016 appeared to support their superior performance. However, the study has now been abandoned because of 'data issues', principally the sample size and survivorship bias problems. ■

Interpreting performance data

There is a reason why the regulators insist that every piece of marketing literature issued by any kind of fund provider includes the phrase "past performance is no guarantee of future performance". The reason is that it is true. Performance data – how much money a trust has made for its shareholders in the past – does give you useful information about an investment trust's track record, and the way that it has been investing your money, but that information in isolation is insufficient to tell you whether you should buy or continue to own that trust. It is a starting point for analysis, but not in itself conclusive about the likelihood the past success, or past failure, will repeat.

There are several reasons for that. They include:

- markets move in cycles and are unpredictable

- styles of investing come in and out of fashion

- superior performance in one period often does not repeat in the next

- managers of trusts can be and often are changed, making direct comparisons with earlier periods difficult

- unexpected events, such as political shocks and natural disasters, may throw a hitherto successful strategy off course.

What the regulators are keen to ensure is that less-sophisticated investors are not misled into thinking that a trust which has done particularly well in the past will continue to do so in the future. Their perspective is underpinned by many academic studies. However, that is not the same as saying that past performance information has no value at all. Clearly it is still important for any investor to understand how a trust has performed in the past and to seek to establish why it has the track record it does.

At the very least it is important to understand the following:

- whether (and if so why) the trust's investment manager has changed over the track record period being looked at

- how far the performance of the trust has been affected by gearing

- how the trust performed during periods when markets were rising and when they were falling – it may be very different

- whether or not the trust has done better than a suitable benchmark, including the one chosen by the board

- how much risk the trust is taking relative to other comparable trusts and the markets in which it is investing.

The performance tables that follow should be studied with those factors very much in mind.

The dangers of relying on past performance figures has ironically been underlined by the experience of Key Information Documents (KIDs). These became compulsory for investment companies to issue in 2018 under new fund regulations introduced by the European Union. Despite the regulatory mantra about past performance mentioned earlier, KIDs still require investment companies to illustrate how a trust might perform under a number of different forward-looking scenarios.

Closer analysis revealed that the projections which companies are required to produce are based on a formula which appears in part to be an extrapolation of how the trust in question performed at different points in the past. Not only that, but they also produced very different projected outcomes for similar kinds of trusts, and statements about risk which in places appeared to defy both logic and common sense. The AIC's official response was to advise potential shareholders to "burn before reading".

Given that one scenario trusts were mandated to provide, using a formula over which they had no say, included a market decline similar to that seen in 2008-09, the market fall in March 2020 has provided an obvious opportunity to compare the results indicated in the KIDs with what actually happened. There was very little correlation between the outcome foretold by the KID and the actual share price response. The KIDs appear to be both poorly constructed and potentially misleading, but, although the UK government has promised to review the regulations after the Brexit transition period is complete, they remain in force for now.

The Financial Conduct Authority has also conducted a number of studies into the best buy lists which are produced by a number of investment platforms and broking firms. Its conclusion is that there may be some value in them, but investors would be unwise to rely solely on them when making decisions on which funds to buy. Their conclusions can be found on the FCA website.

KEEP UP TO DATE

Join Jonathan Davis and Simon Elliott for the free *Money Makers* weekly investment trust podcast, reviewing all the week's news, results and market movements in the investment trust sector. Every Saturday from *Money Makers* (www.money-makers.co).

Best long-term performers

10 years

COMPANY NAME	TICKER	AIC SECTOR
Baillie Gifford Shin Nippon	BGS	Japanese Smaller Companies
Scottish Mortgage	SMT	Global
Biotech Growth	BIOG	Biotechnology & Healthcare
Allianz Technology Trust	ATT	Technology & Media
International Biotechnology	IBT	Biotechnology & Healthcare
Lindsell Train	LTI	Global
Polar Capital Technology	PCT	Technology & Media
Worldwide Healthcare	WWH	Biotechnology & Healthcare
Baillie Gifford Japan	BGFD	Japan
Edinburgh Worldwide	EWI	Global Smaller Companies

20 years

COMPANY NAME	TICKER	AIC SECTOR
Aberdeen New Thai	ANW	Country Specialist: Asia Pacific - ex Japan
Scottish Mortgage	SMT	Global
Scottish Oriental Smaller Cos	SST	Asia Pacific Smaller Companies
Aberdeen Standard Asia Focus	AAS	Asia Pacific Smaller Companies
Pacific Horizon	PHI	Asia Pacific
HgCapital Trust	HGT	Private Equity
JPMorgan Russian Securities	JRS	Country Specialist: Europe - ex UK
TR Property	TRY	Property Securities
Rights & Issues Investment Trust	RIII	UK Smaller Companies
Aberdeen New Dawn	ABD	Asia Pacific

MANAGEMENT GROUP	£100 INITIAL INVESTMENT	ANNUALISED %
Baillie Gifford	931	25.0
Baillie Gifford	872	24.2
Frostrow Capital	853	23.9
Allianz Global Investors	835	23.6
SV Health Managers	706	21.6
Lindsell Train	668	20.9
Polar Capital Holdings	657	20.7
Frostrow Capital	580	19.2
Baillie Gifford	551	18.6
Baillie Gifford	550	18.6

MANAGEMENT GROUP	£100 INITIAL INVESTMENT	ANNUALISED %
Aberdeen Standard Investments	1,629	15.0
Baillie Gifford	1,523	14.6
First State Investments	1,499	14.5
Aberdeen Standard Investments	1,470	14.4
Baillie Gifford	1,436	14.3
Hg	1,316	13.8
J.P. Morgan Asset Management	1,215	13.3
BMO Global Asset Management	1,127	12.9
Discretionary Unit Fund Managers	1,054	12.5
Aberdeen Standard Investments	1,022	12.3

30 years

COMPANY NAME	TICKER	AIC SECTOR
Rights & Issues Investment Trust	RIII	UK Smaller Companies
Scottish Mortgage	SMT	Global
HgCapital Trust	HGT	Private Equity
Canadian General Investments Unit	CGI	North America
ICG Enterprise Trust	ICGT	Private Equity
Templeton Emerging Mkts Invmt Tr TEMIT	TEM	Global Emerging Markets
BlackRock Smaller Companies	BRSC	UK Smaller Companies
Pacific Horizon	PHI	Asia Pacific
Finsbury Growth & Income	FGT	UK Equity Income
Invesco Perpetual UK Smaller	IPU	UK Smaller Companies

Source: AIC/Morningstar, data to 30/09/20

Although the turnover in surviving trusts from one year to the next is high, a good number of trusts have survived long enough to post 20- and 30-year track records. These tables list the best performing trusts over both those periods, as well as the past 10 years, measured as both the value of £100 invested and as a compound annualised rate of return, with dividends reinvested.

Of just under 400 trusts whose data is recorded by the AIC, around a third have been launched in the last 10 years. There are 271 trusts with a 10-year track record, 157 with a 20-year record and just 82 with a 30-year record. This is another indication that there is a Darwinian process at work in the sector, with the weakest trusts eventually being either liquidated, taken over and renamed, or absorbed into another investment trust.

The average annualised rate of return achieved by the top trusts that have survived this long is 21.6% per annum over 10 years, 13.7% over 20 years and 13.5% over 30 years, although this includes a wide range of outcomes and risk

MANAGEMENT GROUP	£100 INITIAL INVESTMENT	ANNUALISED %
Discretionary Unit Fund Managers	7,877	15.7
Baillie Gifford	7,323	15.4
Hg	5,948	14.6
Morgan Meighan & Associates	5,219	14.1
Intermediate Capital Group	4,416	13.5
Franklin Templeton Investments	3,565	12.7
BlackRock Investment Management (UK)	3,503	12.6
Baillie Gifford	3,309	12.4
Frostrow Capital	3,203	12.3
Invesco Asset Management	3,195	12.2

profiles. Because of the magical effect of compounding, any trust that can grow at 10% every year will at least double in value every seven years.

The longer the period, however, the harder it is to sustain a double-digit rate of return. The 30-year period for example includes three significant bear markets (1990-91, 2000-03 and 2007-09), while the past 10-year performance figures include none of them. The global financial crisis has been followed by what by historical standards is one of the longest and most impressive bull markets, so the 10-year figures are flattered by that.

It is notable also how little commonality there is between the three tables. Only one trust, Scottish Mortgage, appears among the top 10 in all three periods. The 30-year period includes trusts from no fewer than eight different sectors, suggesting that these trusts do have something special about them, not just the good fortune of operating in the sectors that have performed particularly well. It is also a testament to the breadth and diversity of the investment company sector as a whole. ∎

Sector returns by year

Average share price total returns (unweighted)

01/10/2019 – 30/09/2020		01/10/2018 – 30/09/2019		01/10/2017 – 30/09/2018		01/10/2016 – 30/09/2017	
TICKER	SPTR	TICKER	SPTR	TICKER	SPTR	TICKER	SPTR
Other alternatives	3.79	Global Equities	5.61	Private equity	12.80	Global Equities	20.97
Global Equities	3.55	VCTs	3.34	Global Equities	8.54	Private equity	19.08
VCTs	-1.72	Private equity	3.25	UK Equities	6.43	UK Equities	17.05
Flexible Investment	-10.53	Other alternatives	2.47	Other alternatives	6.39	Property	13.69
Private equity	-10.66	Flexible Investment	2.22	Flexible Investment	5.01	Other alternatives	13.31
Debt	-12.51	Property	0.04	Property	4.91	Flexible Investment	13.16
Property	-12.61	Debt	-0.56	Debt	4.80	Debt	8.59
UK Equities	-14.14	UK Equities	-5.13	VCTs	4.36	VCTs	6.01

NAV per total returns (unweighted)

01/10/2019 – 30/09/2020		01/10/2018 – 30/09/2019		01/10/2017 – 30/09/2018		01/10/2016 – 30/09/2017	
TICKER	SPTR	TICKER	SPTR	TICKER	SPTR	TICKER	SPTR
Other alternatives	5.11	Private equity	9.02	Private equity	10.09	Global Equities	17.72
Global Equities	5.07	Property	5.16	Global Equities	8.86	UK Equities	16.80
Property	-0.42	Global Equities	5.04	Property	8.25	Property	9.99
VCTs	-2.33	Flexible Investment	4.50	Other alternatives	7.55	Other alternatives	9.11
Private equity	-3.48	Other alternatives	3.43	Flexible Investment	6.85	Private equity	9.10
Debt	-4.87	Debt	2.89	UK Equities	5.05	Debt	8.09
Flexible Investment	-5.52	VCTs	-1.50	VCTs	5.05	Flexible Investment	7.92
UK Equities	-10.55	UK Equities	-2.99	Debt	4.34	VCTs	5.42

Average share price total returns (unweighted)

01/10/2011 – 30/09/2012		01/10/2010 – 30/09/2011		01/10/2009 – 30/09/2010		01/10/2008 – 30/09/2009	
Debt	20.71	Private equity	12.34	Debt	46.94	Global Equities	21.35
UK Equities	16.66	Flexible Investment	7.42	Flexible Investment	21.96	Other alternatives	16.19
Global Equities	13.85	VCTs	5.32	UK Equities	20.29	Property	11.20
VCTs	13.40	Property	5.25	Global Equities	18.17	Debt	11.14
Private equity	8.05	UK Equities	5.00	VCTs	15.81	UK Equities	8.23
Other alternatives	4.23	Other alternatives	4.90	Other alternatives	15.71	Flexible Investment	-5.03
Flexible Investment	3.82	Debt	4.47	Private equity	14.30	VCTs	-11.00
Property	0.34	Global Equities	-6.31	Property	7.40	Private equity	-11.54

NAV per total returns (unweighted)

01/10/2011 – 30/09/2012		01/10/2010 – 30/09/2011		01/10/2009 – 30/09/2010		01/10/2008 – 30/09/2009	
Debt	20.95	Private equity	12.56	Debt	30.69	Global Equities	19.67
UK Equities	18.70	Flexible Investment	5.19	UK Equities	19.27	Other alternatives	18.85
Global Equities	14.57	VCTs	2.92	Global Equities	17.93	UK Equities	8.94
VCTs	9.46	Other alternatives	2.67	Flexible Investment	15.84	Debt	4.13
Flexible Investment	7.60	Debt	2.45	Property	15.45	Flexible Investment	-0.24
Other alternatives	7.00	UK Equities	1.61	Other alternatives	13.39	VCTs	-4.06
Property	5.50	Property	0.64	Private equity	12.14	Private equity	-10.03
Private equity	2.67	Global Equities	-6.57	VCTs	3.71	Property	-18.03

01/10/2015 – 30/09/2016		01/10/2014 – 30/09/2015		01/10/2013 – 30/09/2014		01/10/2012 – 30/09/2013	
TICKER	SPTR	TICKER	SPTR	TICKER	SPTR	TICKER	SPTR
Global Equities	30.49	Property	10.57	Property	14.96	UK Equities	37.39
Private equity	19.62	UK Equities	9.40	VCTs	12.53	Property	24.70
Flexible Investment	18.80	VCTs	6.61	Private equity	11.94	Private equity	23.43
Other alternatives	18.30	Private equity	3.85	Global Equities	8.96	Global Equities	22.31
UK Equities	8.77	Flexible Investment	-0.32	Flexible Investment	8.18	VCTs	17.32
Property	7.65	Debt	-0.85	Debt	8.06	Debt	16.00
Debt	7.33	Global Equities	-1.54	Other alternatives	7.66	Flexible Investment	11.65
VCTs	5.45	Other alternatives	-1.86	UK Equities	7.10	Other alternatives	10.63

01/10/2015 – 30/09/2016		01/10/2014 – 30/09/2015		01/10/2013 – 30/09/2014		01/10/2012 – 30/09/2013	
TICKER	SPTR	TICKER	SPTR	TICKER	SPTR	TICKER	SPTR
Global Equities	32.40	Property	11.77	Property	14.31	UK Equities	28.40
Flexible Investment	22.55	Private equity	8.94	VCTs	9.55	Global Equities	18.13
Private equity	20.60	UK Equities	8.52	Global Equities	8.78	Debt	14.70
Other alternatives	17.48	VCTs	5.40	Private equity	8.37	VCTs	10.57
Debt	13.10	Flexible Investment	1.52	UK Equities	8.23	Flexible Investment	9.09
UK Equities	10.08	Debt	0.65	Other alternatives	7.82	Property	8.95
Property	7.75	Other alternatives	0.23	Flexible Investment	7.64	Private equity	8.71
VCTs	5.80	Global Equities	-0.94	Debt	7.22	Other alternatives	7.46

01/10/2007 – 30/09/2008		01/10/2006 – 30/09/2007		01/10/2005 – 30/09/2006		01/10/2004 – 30/09/2005	
Other alternatives	-9.26	Other alternatives	24.34	Property	24.63	Global Equities	44.50
VCTs	-9.50	Global Equities	22.07	UK Equities	19.07	Private equity	43.94
Private equity	-16.29	Private equity	15.71	Private equity	18.85	Flexible Investment	42.38
Flexible Investment	-16.90	Flexible Investment	11.48	Global Equities	12.62	UK Equities	34.11
Debt	-26.19	UK Equities	10.92	Flexible Investment	11.98	Other alternatives	31.57
Global Equities	-26.34	VCTs	3.61	Other alternatives	11.59	Property	22.76
UK Equities	-29.66	Debt	2.55	Debt	4.44	VCTs	12.77
Property	-32.09	Property	-9.25	VCTs	4.02	Debt	11.94

01/10/2007 – 30/09/2008		01/10/2006 – 30/09/2007		01/10/2005 – 30/09/2006		01/10/2004 – 30/09/2005	
Private equity	7.69	Other alternatives	27.84	Property	29.71	Global Equities	35.61
VCTs	-6.96	Global Equities	23.73	Private equity	22.97	Flexible Investment	31.67
Other alternatives	-7.28	Private equity	22.01	UK Equities	18.99	UK Equities	30.12
Flexible Investment	-12.46	Flexible Investment	14.33	Global Equities	13.49	Private equity	28.33
Property	-15.84	UK Equities	11.15	Flexible Investment	12.73	Property	25.29
Global Equities	-22.97	VCTs	6.37	Other alternatives	9.86	Other alternatives	24.28
Debt	-24.36	Debt	5.82	Debt	5.75	Debt	14.47
UK Equities	-27.43	Property	2.45	VCTs	5.27	VCTs	6.44

243

Average share price total returns (unweighted)

01/10/2003 – 30/09/2004		01/10/2002 – 30/09/2003		01/10/2001 – 30/09/2002		01/10/2000 – 30/09/2001	
Property	49.72	Other alternatives	59.86	Property	9.36	Property	-1.40
Flexible Investment	24.41	Debt	45.30	VCTs	-5.36	Flexible Investment	-16.71
Debt	23.76	Global Equities	35.87	Global Equities	-9.48	VCTs	-16.89
Private equity	18.18	Property	33.74	Flexible Investment	-10.16	UK Equities	-19.38
Global Equities	16.29	UK Equities	27.33	UK Equities	-15.93	Debt	-27.44
UK Equities	15.04	Flexible Investment	20.66	Private equity	-16.37	Private equity	-28.00
VCTs	10.42	Private equity	19.97	Other alternatives	-31.44	Global Equities	-31.21
Other alternatives	8.28	VCTs	-5.01	Debt	-32.38	Other alternatives	-47.23

NAV per total returns (unweighted)

01/10/2003 – 30/09/2004		01/10/2002 – 30/09/2003		01/10/2001 – 30/09/2002		01/10/2000 – 30/09/2001	
Property	46.35	Debt	91.11	Property	6.07	Property	2.86
Flexible Investment	20.23	Other alternatives	41.14	Private equity	-7.56	VCTs	-2.78
UK Equities	17.31	Global Equities	29.10	Global Equities	-8.00	Private equity	-13.45
Global Equities	13.77	Property	28.44	VCTs	-8.77	Flexible Investment	-15.88
Private equity	12.66	UK Equities	23.56	Flexible Investment	-12.11	UK Equities	-19.58
Other alternatives	5.82	Flexible Investment	18.44	UK Equities	-14.44	Global Equities	-29.67
Debt	5.20	Private equity	3.22	Debt	-23.37	Debt	-33.03
VCTs	4.57	VCTs	-2.25	Other alternatives	-25.10	Other alternatives	-41.26

These coloured charts show, in reverse order, the best and worst performing sectors over the past 24 years. Each category aggregates a number of component sectors and subs-sectors into broad asset class groupings. The purpose is to give a broad perspective on the fluctuations that investors inevitably face from year to year.

The data shows the share price and NAV per share total return for each 12-month period ending on 30 September going back to 1996–97. The charts underline not only how sectors rise and fall in popularity from one year to the next, but also illustrate the importance of asset allocation and the benefits of diversification.

To take the most extreme (but impractical) example if an investor had the foresight to know which sector was going to perform best in the following

01/10/1999 – 30/09/2000		01/10/1998 – 30/09/1999		01/10/1997 – 30/09/1998		01/10/1996 – 30/09/1997	
Other alternatives	206.64	Global Equities	76.30	Private equity	14.17	Property	31.10
Private equity	39.63	Other alternatives	66.86	Debt	12.49	Private equity	23.55
VCTs	36.13	Private equity	29.66	Flexible Investment	-0.27	UK Equities	16.61
Global Equities	30.48	UK Equities	28.54	UK Equities	-4.03	Debt	15.83
Flexible Investment	29.22	Property	28.16	VCTs	-7.57	Flexible Investment	13.35
UK Equities	28.27	Flexible Investment	22.35	Property	-10.80	Other alternatives	7.98
Property	24.57	Debt	14.82	Global Equities	-28.16	Global Equities	5.36
Debt	4.96	VCTs	5.29	Other alternatives	-39.36	VCTs	4.13

01/10/1999 – 30/09/2000		01/10/1998 – 30/09/1999		01/10/1997 – 30/09/1998		01/10/1996 – 30/09/1997	
Other alternatives	165.85	Global Equities	59.43	Private equity	20.01	Property	27.65
Private equity	29.41	Other alternatives	53.48	Debt	11.57	UK Equities	24.74
Global Equities	28.43	UK Equities	28.05	VCTs	6.58	Private equity	22.61
Flexible Investment	28.34	Flexible Investment	24.01	Property	-0.40	Flexible Investment	19.89
VCTs	28.08	Property	23.77	Flexible Investment	-1.92	Other alternatives	15.43
UK Equities	21.96	Private equity	18.38	UK Equities	-2.96	Global Equities	10.52
Property	20.66	Debt	12.83	Global Equities	-24.22	Debt	10.16
Debt	0.57	VCTs	2.36	Other alternatives	-25.29	VCTs	9.11

year and allocated all his or her capital to it at the start of the year, an initial investment in 1997 of £1,000 would have grown to £305,000 by this year. If instead he or she had chosen the asset class which was going to perform worst each year, that £1,000 would have shrunk to just £149 – quite some difference. Note also how asset classes which do well in one year inevitably also have years when they do poorly, and vice versa.

It is worth studying the behaviour of different types of asset during bad bear markets (as we experienced from March 2000 to March 2003 and from late 2007 to March 2009). The difference between the share price total return and NAV per share total return is largely explained by movements in discounts. ■

Sector focus

Property

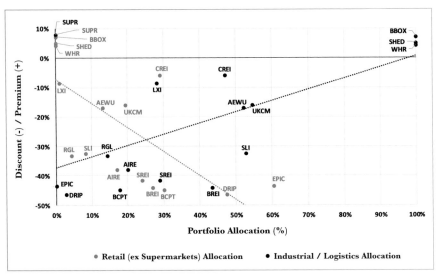

Source: Winterflood Securities, The Funds. Discount/premium data as at 12 October 2020. Allocation data as at latest available date.

Key: SUPR Supermarket REIT; BBOX Tritax Big Box REIT; SHED Urban Logistics REIT: WHR Warehouse REIT; CREI Custodian REIT; LXI LXI REIT: AEWU AEW UK REIT; UKCM UK Commercial Property; RGL Regional REIT; SLI Standard Life Property Income; EPIC Ediston Property; AIRE Alternative Income REIT; SREI Schroder Real Estate; DRIP Drum Income Plus REIT; BCPT BMO Commercial Property.

A key theme in the UK commercial property sector for a number of years has been the polarisation of returns between different sub-sectors, and in particular the outperformance of industrial and the underperformance of retail. 2020 has been no different, with the Covid-19 pandemic and associated lockdown measures accelerating the growth in e-commerce that was already driving this trend. The impact of the coronavirus is also reflected in rent collection figures, with funds that focus purely on industrial assets, such as Tritax Big Box REIT, Urban Logistics REIT and Warehouse REIT, reporting almost 100% collection rates, while those with a high retail weighting, such as Ediston Property Investment Company and Drum Income Plus REIT, struggled with rent collection during the lockdown period and were forced to cut or suspend dividend payments as a result.

The chart shows each trust twice, comparing its rating (discount or premium) to the proportion of its portfolio allocated to retail property (shops) and industrial/logistics property (warehouses and factories). The retail allocation is in green and the industrial/logistics allocation in red. The arrows show the trend – those with high retail allocations have the worst ratings, while those with high allocations to industrial/logistics are significantly better. Note that trusts investing in supermarkets are an exception to this trend, reflecting their strong business performance during lockdown.

While capital has been flowing out of retail and into industrial assets for some time, the likelihood that this will continue is reflected in their ratings. As shown in the chart, investment trusts with a high industrial/logistics allocation and/or a low retail exposure tend to be trading at narrower discounts or even at premiums to NAV, while the reverse is also generally true. The demand for funds investing in industrial assets has enabled Urban Logistics REIT (£92m raised) and Warehouse REIT (£153m) to raise significant equity since the end of March.

EMMA BIRD, *investment companies analyst, Winterflood Securities.*

Infrastructure

Infrastructure sector rating and equity issuance

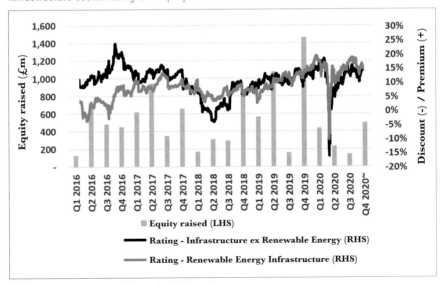

Source: Winterflood, Morningstar. Data to 14 October 2020

The infrastructure peer group has been among the most resilient in 2020 with the vast majority of funds continuing to pay dividends in line with targets set prior to the onset of the pandemic. In addition, capital values have held up well, particularly relative to some other asset classes. The contrast of this resilience with dividend cuts elsewhere in the UK equity market and lower interest rates has, in our view, increased the attraction of the asset class for investors. It also has strong ESG credentials, which is becoming increasingly important for investors.

The result is that the sector is one of the few to see its shares trade on a premium to net asset value. This demand has enabled funds in the sector to continue to raise equity from investors, with more than £700m raised for existing funds since the onset of the pandemic. In addition, the sector saw a new fund launch – one of only a handful of investment company IPOs in 2020 – as Triple Point Energy Efficiency Infrastructure raised £100m in October.

However, the sector has not been immune to the economic impacts of the pandemic. Revenues for the renewable energy infrastructure funds were reduced to varying degrees by lower electricity prices resulting from lower demand as the world went into lockdown as well as the oil price war between Saudi Arabia and Russia. The electricity price recovered in the third quarter of 2020. The longer-term electricity price forecast continued its downward trajectory in the first half of the year as a result of a variety of factors including expectations of greater renewable energy deployment and lower gas prices. The impact of this on capital values was offset in many funds by positive impacts including extended asset life assumptions, cost savings and increased market demand for infrastructure assets.

Outside of the renewable energy infrastructure sector assets with availability-based revenues, such as PFI school projects, fared relatively well, while economically sensitive assets with demand-based revenues, such as toll roads, faced greater uncertainty.

KIERAN DRAKE, *Investment Companies Analyst, Winterflood Securities.*

———

"THE INFRASTRUCTURE PEER GROUP HAS BEEN AMONG THE MOST RESILIENT IN 2020 WITH THE VAST MAJORITY OF FUNDS CONTINUING TO PAY DIVIDENDS IN LINE WITH TARGETS SET PRIOR TO THE ONSET OF THE PANDEMIC."

Debt

Debt subsector ratings in 2020

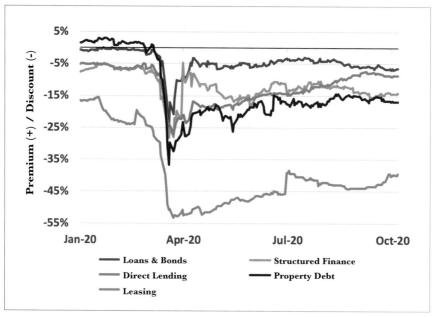

Source: Morningstar. Data to 14 October 2020

The debt sector has seen significant growth over the last decade, both in terms of the number of funds and assets, driven largely by the demand for income in a low interest rate environment. Mandates within the sector are diverse with portfolio investments ranging across asset classes including corporate bonds, loans, CLOs, royalties and aircraft leasing.

While many of these funds offer attractive yields, in some cases they invest in higher risk and/or illiquid areas of the market. In the past few years this has become apparent as a number of funds have had difficult periods of performance driven by problem assets and have either been wound down, are in the process of being wound down or have been subject to corporate action.

In 2020 the sector has felt the economic impact of the pandemic with the majority of funds seeing negative share price total returns in the nine months to 30 September. Several funds suspended their dividend in response to the pandemic, while some others took less drastic action and reduced dividend payments. The reason behind suspensions/cuts were varied but included reduced income, wanting to retain cash to shore up balance sheets, the lower interest rate environment, and wanting liquidity to take advantage of investment opportunities during the market dislocation at the height of the crisis. As markets have stabilised and the economic outlook has become slightly clearer some of the funds that made changes to their dividends have reinstated them or increased them closer to their previous targets.

While NAV performance for most funds has been resilient so far, the difficulties seen by some combined with dividend cuts has created investor uncertainty, which has spread across the sector. This has seen discounts widen across the board. As the chart shows, ratings across the subsectors have partially recovered since March 2020, but remain below their pre-pandemic levels. This has potentially created an investment opportunity. However, with the economic outlook still uncertain, discounts for funds in the sector that invest in more economically sensitive areas of the market and those impacted by social distancing measures are likely to persist while investors wait to see how the impact on underlying portfolios unfolds.

KIERAN DRAKE, *Investment Companies Analyst, Winterflood Securities.*

Z scores

Z Scores

(current discount - average discount) / volatility of discount

1 year

| Fund | Ticker | Discount | | |
		Current	Average	Z Score
Honeycomb IT	HONY	3.4	10.7	-4.4
GRIT Real Estate Income	GR1T	-8.1	2.3	-4.1
US Solar Fund - $	USF	0.6	4.3	-3.7
Riverstone Energy	RSE	-42.2	-28.1	-3.2
Keystone IT	KIT	-17.6	-12.8	-2.7
ICG Longbow Senior Secured UK Pro|	LBOW	-0.9	1.7	-2.6
Highbridge Tactical Credit	HTCF	-7.1	-3.0	-2.5
Aberdeen Standard European Logistic	ASLI	-5.6	3.6	-2.5
CVC Credit Partners Euro Opps - £	CCPG	-5.7	-0.6	-2.5
TwentyFour Income	TFIF	-3.2	1.4	-2.5
Aberforth Split Level Income	ASIT	-13.6	-4.0	-2.4
Scottish Mortgage	SMT	-2.4	1.9	-2.4
Mobius IT	MMIT	-7.4	-0.1	-2.3
JPEL Private Equity	JPEL	-20.0	-17.9	-2.3
UK Mortgages	UKML	-16.9	-2.2	-2.3

| Fund | Ticker | Discount | | |
		Current	Average	Z Score
Carador Income Fund Redeemable	CIFR	35.9	0.9	4.5
Global Resources	GRIT	202.1	-22.5	3.6
Chenavari Capital Solutions	CCSL	-9.3	-15.7	3.5
Sirius Real Estate	SRE	6.8	-6.0	3.5
BB Biotech	BION	26.0	12.4	3.4
GCP Student Living	DIGS	6.9	1.7	2.7
Carador Income Fund	CIFU	0.2	-12.7	2.5
LMS Capital	LMS	-23.3	-33.0	2.3
JPMorgan Russian	JRS	-9.8	-15.1	2.3
Secure Income REIT	SIR	9.8	3.5	2.2
Greencoat UK Wind	UKW	16.5	12.0	2.2
Globalworth Real Estate	GWI	10.9	0.0	2.0
Foresight Solar	FSFL	13.1	6.0	2.0
RDL Realisation	RDL	-21.7	-55.5	2.0
Fondul Proprietatea GDR	FP/	-20.1	-31.2	1.8

Z-scores measure mathematically how far a trust's current discount or premium has diverged from its average over some previous period (days, months or even a year can be used). Brokers and other professional investors calculate the figures regularly in order to look for trading opportunities or good entry/exit points. A minus figure for a z-score suggests that a trust looks 'cheap' relative to its past discount history; and a positive figure the reverse.

There may, however, be a good reason for the change in sentiment towards a particular trust, so they are a blunt instrument without specialist knowledge and should never be used or relied on by inexperienced investors. If you already have a specific investment trust on your watchlist and are looking for a good moment to buy, then checking the z scores can be a useful guide to timing your purchase. Bear in mind however that discounts widen for a reason; if the z-score is looking attractive, it is often because there is some negative story or headline out there.

If the story is essentially transient, as it often will be, and your belief in the investment trust is that it has a sound strategy for the longer term, then these will be good moments to take the plunge. By the same token, if you are thinking of selling part or all of your holding in a trust, then at the margin it makes most sense to do so when the trust's shares are showing up as 'dear' in the z-score rankings. Since most investors tend to hold the trusts they own for a number of years, these opportunities do not arise very often in practice.

The table that is shown opposite (source Numis Securities) is for illustration only. The data dates from 2019 and is therefore not current. Z-scores by their nature tend to be volatile. Looking at the upper part of the table, which shows the trusts which were looking "cheap" at that point on the basis of a negative one-year z-score, buying Scottish Mortgage trust at a rare discount would have been a very smart move, given its subsequent spectacular performance, but buying Riverstone Energy would equally have been a disaster. If you see this kind of information, handle with care! ■

Platform costs

	£5,000	£15,000
AJ Bell Youinvest	1.05%	0.47%
Barclays	1.44%	0.48%
Bestinvest	1.00%	0.60%
Charles Stanley Direct	1.40%	0.66%
Close Brothers A.M. Self Directed Service	0.97%	0.49%
EQi	1.09%	0.36%
Equiniti Shareview	1.50%	0.83%
Fidelity Personal Investing	1.70%	0.57%
Halifax Share Dealing	1.25%	0.42%
Hargreaves Lansdown	1.41%	0.62%
iDealing	1.19%	0.40%
IG	0.64%	0.21%
Interactive Investor (Investor Product)	2.40%	0.80%
iWeb	0.90%	0.30%
Sharedeal	0.76%	0.25%
Strawberry	1.56%	0.67%
The Share Centre (standard)	1.80%	0.80%
The Share Centre (frequent)	3.72%	1.24%
Willis Owen	1.00%	0.60%
X-O	0.48%	0.16%

Source: AIC/the Lang Cat consultancy

How much does it cost to hold shares in investment trusts on a private investor platform? The table gives an illustrative estimate for most of the largest platforms. The costs are shown as an annual percentage of the value of your portfolio, based on the amount you have invested. The data is collected by the Lang Cat consultancy and published on the AIC website. It is a valuable source of information, albeit with some important caveats.

It is important to note that your investment is assumed to be within an ISA tax wrapper. The figures shown only include ongoing platform fees, additional wrapper charges (if any) and trading charges (where applicable). Other charges involved in investing in investment companies, for example the management charges of the investment companies themselves, are excluded. The data is

£25,000	£50,000	£100,000	£250,000	£500,000	£1,000,000
0.28%	0.14%	0.07%	0.03%	0.01%	0.01%
0.29%	0.15%	0.12%	0.11%	0.10%	0.10%
0.52%	0.46%	0.43%	0.41%	0.31%	0.25%
0.53%	0.44%	0.29%	0.11%	0.06%	0.03%
0.39%	0.32%	0.29%	0.26%	0.26%	0.23%
0.22%	0.11%	0.05%	0.02%	0.01%	0.01%
0.56%	0.28%	0.14%	0.06%	0.03%	0.01%
0.34%	0.17%	0.09%	0.03%	0.02%	0.01%
0.25%	0.13%	0.06%	0.03%	0.01%	0.01%
0.37%	0.19%	0.09%	0.04%	0.02%	0.01%
0.24%	0.12%	0.06%	0.02%	0.01%	0.01%
0.13%	0.06%	0.03%	0.01%	0.01%	0.00%
0.48%	0.24%	0.12%	0.05%	0.02%	0.01%
0.18%	0.09%	0.05%	0.02%	0.01%	0.00%
0.15%	0.08%	0.04%	0.02%	0.01%	0.00%
0.54%	0.45%	0.35%	0.29%	0.27%	0.26%
0.64%	0.52%	0.46%	0.42%	0.41%	0.41%
0.74%	0.37%	0.19%	0.07%	0.04%	0.02%
0.52%	0.46%	0.38%	0.27%	0.21%	0.18%
0.10%	0.05%	0.02%	0.01%	0.00%	0.00%

based on publicly available charging structure information, with some details verified in conversations with platforms.

This table assumes that you only hold investment trusts on the platform. A separate table on the website shows how the figure might vary if you also hold open-ended funds on the platform. The platform charges will generally be higher, at least for portfolios of £50,000 or more, as the platform charges for holding investment trusts are typically lower. Bear in mind however that charges are not the sole, or even the most important, criterion for choosing a platform. The quality of the service – the range of options, the quality of the research and how smoothly and efficiently the platform works – are every bit as relevant. ■

PARTNERS

Aberdeen Standard
Investments

Aberdeen Standard Investment Trusts

Searching widely to discover more investment opportunities

Aberdeen Standard Investments is a leading global asset manager dedicated to creating long-term value for our clients. We manage assets worth £455.6bn on behalf of clients in 80 countries (as of 30 June 2020). In managing these assets, we employ over 1,000 investment professionals and provide client support from 48 client-relationship offices globally. This ensures we are close to our clients and the markets in which they invest.

We are high-conviction, long-term investors who seek to realise the value of our investments over time. In our view, teamwork and collaboration between investment managers and across asset classes is key to delivering repeatable, robust investment performance. We are also resolute in our commitment to active asset management.

If you're keen to capture the potential offered by global investment markets, turn to Aberdeen Standard investment trusts. Managed by teams of experts, each trust is designed to bring together the most compelling opportunities we can find to generate the investment growth or income you're looking for.

You can choose from trusts investing in the UK, in specific overseas regions, such as Asia or the Americas, or that give you a global spread of investments. With a flexible multi-asset fund, a diversified private-equity trust, three property funds and two UK smaller-companies funds to choose from too, there's plenty of choice to target your specific investment goals.

Find out more at www.invtrusts.co.uk

About Allianz Global Investors

Allianz Global Investors is one of the world's leading active investment managers. Understanding our clients' needs in order to act to their best advantage is embedded in our business, using our insightfulness to partner with clients and to drive performance.

Allianz Global Investors works for many clients around the world. From pension funds, large and small, to blue-chip multinationals, from charitable foundations to families, individuals and their advisers. We have created a business that enables us to meet the demands of our clients on a local basis and that empowers our investment managers to focus on achieving strong and consistent investment results.

Allianz Global Investors and its predecessors have been managing investment trusts since 1889, providing investors with access to investment opportunities around the world. Each trust is a company listed and traded on the London Stock Exchange, and has its own independent board of directors whose duty it is to look after your interests as an investor.

Established in 1889, The Merchants Trust PLC has, throughout its history, provided shareholders with an opportunity to benefit from investment in a diversified portfolio of leading companies with strong balance sheets and the potential to pay attractive dividends. Merchants aims to provide its investors with an efficient, competitive and cost-effective way to achieve an above average level of income and income growth together with long-term capital growth through a policy of investing mainly in higher yielding large UK companies.

The Brunner Investment Trust PLC aims to provide growth in capital and dividends over the long term by seeking out the world's most exciting growth opportunities. We believe that it's the quality of the company that matters, not its location – so through Brunner, investors can access a spread of high-quality growth companies operating in different sectors and countries in a single portfolio. The Trust favours large, well-financed businesses with global reach, pricing power and brand strength.

Allianz Technology Trust invests in a diversified, but focused portfolio of companies that use technology in an innovative way to gain a competitive advantage. Particular emphasis is placed on companies that are addressing major growth trends with innovation that replaces existing technology or radically changes products and services and the way in which they are supplied to customers. The Manager aims to invest in the most attractive technology shares globally, seeking to identify the leading companies in emerging technology growth sub-sectors.

About Axiom Alternative Investments

Axiom AI was created in 2009 and is a boutique asset manager specialising in financial institutions (banks and insurance companies).

The team combines the complementary expertise of credit portfolio managers and former investment bankers specialised in regulatory capital. With six investment professionals covering financials, Axiom has one of the largest research and portfolio management teams dedicated to financials in Europe.

The company manages $1.9bn through a range of UCITS funds, closed-ended funds, dedicated funds and managed accounts covering the full spectrum of financial debt (senior debt, non-preferred senior debt, subordinated debt and equities). Axiom markets its funds to institutional clients, private banks, family offices and IFAs across Europe. Its financial debt funds range counts seven funds with different risk/reward profiles to meet its clients' needs and target returns.

Since its inception in 2009, Axiom has become reputed for its knowledge in European financials and is often solicited by the media to discuss the sector and bank regulation. The company has developed strong partnerships based on its expertise on financial credit.

Since 2018, the company has developed its alternative investment capability by launching two strategies in this space.

The company is independent and is regulated by the AMF, FCA and SEC.

Independent Global Investment Managers

Baillie Gifford has been managing investments since 1908. As a wholly independent partnership, with no external shareholders demanding short-term gains, we can focus on what we do best, seeking out long-term investment returns for our clients.

We are the largest manager of investment trusts in the UK with a range of 11 trusts. We have an extensive range of OEIC sub-funds and manage investments globally for pension funds, institutions and charities.

Curious

The best investment ideas spring from thinking about future possibilities, not short-term probabilities. From Edinburgh, our research covers the globe. We set no barriers to the imagination of our investors, encouraging fresh perspectives and the use of diverse sources of information.

Active

The world is complex. We believe that the way to generate returns for our clients is to focus on the deceptively simple task of identifying and investing in those companies which have the potential to grow at a faster rate, on a more sustainable basis, than their peers. We conduct rigorous qualitative research to establish whether prospective investments have the competitive, financial and strategic advantages to deliver on that potential.

Long Term

We are long-term investors, not speculators. Our investment philosophy focuses on growth, while our universe is global. Over a century of global investment experience has taught us that patience is vital and we are not interested in following fads and fashions or pursuing short-term performance. It's a philosophy that has guided our investment strategy for over 100 years.

The value of a stock market investment and any income from it can fall as well as rise and investors may not get back the amount invested. Your capital is at risk. Baillie Gifford & Co Limited is authorised and regulated by the Financial Conduct Authority.

BB Healthcare Trust
Bellevue Investments

Bellevue Asset Management

With over £6.5bn AUM in healthcare strategies, Bellevue Asset Management is very much a specialist healthcare asset management company. Our distinct specialisation, coupled with entrepreneurial efforts and strong sense of independence, makes our Group what it is today. As a standalone asset manager with a multi-boutique profile, we specialise in investment themes offering attractive return potential that can be unlocked through our active investment strategies and we are benchmark agnostic in doing so.

A strong commitment to excellent investment performance sustained by competence, specialisation and innovation is a key driver of our success. Our well-defined product range helps investors balance specific investment themes with effective diversification and gives them access to enduring growth stories.

Committed To Active Asset Management

Our employees are both investment experts and entrepreneurs, and they have a stake in the success of their own clients. This culture goes hand in hand with a strong conviction in active management with a high degree of discipline. Bellevue's basic business philosophy gives the portfolio management teams the entrepreneurial freedom they need to deliver what we promise. There are no high-level investment committees or CIOs. All of our expert teams within the various product areas, which operate independently, are distinguished by a high degree of responsibility, respect and visionary leadership.

This has kept us and our clients one step ahead of the broader investment community since 1993. Creating value for our clients, employees and shareholders is our mission.

About Fidelity International

Fidelity International provides world-class investment solutions and retirement expertise to institutions, individuals and their advisers – to help our clients build better futures for themselves and generations to come. As a private company, we think generationally and invest for the long term. Helping clients to save for retirement and other long-term investing objectives has been at the core of our business for 50 years.

We offer our own investment solutions and access to those of others, and deliver services relating to investing. For individual investors and their advisers, we provide guidance to help them invest in a simple and cost-effective way. For institutions, including pension funds, banks and insurance companies, we offer tailored investment solutions, consultancy, and full-service outsourcing of asset management to us. For employers, we provide workplace pension administration services on top of, or independently from, investment management. We are responsible for total client assets of £457.3bn from 2.5m clients across Asia Pacific, Europe, the Middle East and South America.

Our Investment Approach

Investing requires a continuous research commitment to build a deep understanding of what is driving industries and individual businesses. This is where our global research capabilities with 406 investment professionals and research support staff around the world come in: Fidelity International is committed to generating proprietary insights and our analysts work together across asset classes, e.g. combining insights from equity, credit, macro and quantitative research, to form a 360-degree view on the health and prospects of companies.

Our analysts carry out their research on the ground – visiting the shop floor, speaking to customers, competitors, suppliers, and independent experts to form conviction.

Over the course of a year, we estimate across the entire Fidelity research group, covering fixed income and equities, that we conduct in excess of 15,000 company meetings each year – or one every eight minutes on average between them.

We commission a number of bespoke projects and surveys to understand the market potential of companies' product and service innovations. As part of our fixed income research, we run 15 top-down systematic overlay models as well as generating a wide range of quantitative tools and nudges to complement our fundamental credit analyst output.

Our UK Investment Trust Business

Fidelity has over 25 years' experience managing investment companies and manages around £4.1bn in assets across five investment trusts. These are all focused on equity growth strategies.

As a major platform distributor, Fidelity is able to offer its own investment trusts and those managed by third parties to professional investors and retail investors alike through a range of different product wrappers. Fidelity also promotes its range of trusts directly to institutions and wealth managers through its highly experienced in-house sales teams.

J.P.Morgan
Asset Management

About J.P. Morgan Asset Management

J.P. Morgan Asset Management, with assets under management of USD 2.2trn (as of 30 June 2020), is a global leader in investment management. J.P. Morgan Asset Management's clients include institutions, retail investors and high net worth individuals in every major market throughout the world. J.P. Morgan Asset Management offers global investment management in equities, fixed income, real estate, hedge funds, private equity and liquidity.

J.P. Morgan Asset Management Investment Trusts

With more than 150 years of investment experience, J.P. Morgan Asset Management is one of the UK's leading investment trust providers. The company combines global investment resources with local expertise to offer more than 20 investment trusts – each designed to help investors build stronger portfolios.

Thanks to its worldwide network of experienced investment professionals, J.P. Morgan Asset Management has the scale and expertise to invest successfully across all major asset classes and regions, and through multiple market cycles.

Investment trusts are a well-established part of J.P. Morgan Asset Management's comprehensive range of investment solutions, with some of its key trusts offering a track record stretching back more than a century – a testament to the company's long-term view and ongoing commitment to its clients.

QuotedData

BY MARTEN & CO

Free, reliable research for everyone

QuotedData publishes free, reliable educational resources, research and news on carefully selected sectors and companies, some of which is sponsored. In addition, we provide data, including performance charts and statistics, across the full spectrum of pan-European equities. Our team of expert analysts write with a balanced view and our goal is to provide you with all the information you need to make your own investment decisions, or to understand in more detail what your adviser is recommending to you.

Founded in 2013, QuotedData is part of Marten & Co, our financial services business that specialises in the provision of high-quality equity investment research to professional investors, as well as offering corporates expertise in access to capital and investor relations.

Our services

- Daily news digest
- Company research
- Monthly/Quarterly sectoral round-up
- Investor guides
- Glossary of investment terms
- 'Helpful stuff' section – general tips on investing
- Data bank and performance statistics for all pan-European equities
- Investor events near you database

About Polar Capital

Polar Capital is a specialist, investment-led, active fund management company offering investors a range of predominantly long-only and long/short equity funds, including three thematic investment trusts.

The company's open-ended, closed-ended and alternative investment strategies are all based on long-term investment themes, specialist sectors and global, regional or single country geographies. They have a fundamental, research-driven approach, where capacity is rigorously managed to enhance and protect performance.

The investment trusts are in the specialist sectors of technology, healthcare and financials with the newest – launched in July 2013 – being Polar Capital Global Financials Trust (PCFT), which invests in one of the largest investable equity sector globally. The financials' sector oils the wheels of the worldwide economy and includes banks, insurance companies, asset managers, stock exchanges, specialty lenders and fintech companies. Technological developments and regulatory changes post the global financial crisis are leading to profound changes which are providing attractive investment opportunities in a sector with companies in different stages of recovery and within underpenetrated emerging markets.

Polar Capital was founded in February 2001 and the Polar Capital Technology Trust (PCT) was the first portfolio it managed. PCT has access to the growth potential of companies in the global technology sector and is managed by one of the largest technology investment teams in Europe. The Trust's longevity has seen it enjoy a multi-cycle/multi-year track record.

Polar Capital Global Healthcare Trust (PCGH) is run by an investment team of five senior fund managers looking at healthcare's long-term, secular growth. Its long-term driver is an ageing global population driving the demand and the need for increased healthcare provision – something for us all to consider as we all live longer. The shorter-term focus has been on diagnostics, drug development and vaccines to counter Covid-19.

The company's principal location is in London, with investment staff in offices in Los Angeles, Connecticut, New York, Edinburgh, Jersey, Paris, Germany, Spain and Shanghai.

FAR FROM THE LAND

A story of Irish betrayal

John Sanders

PAN BOOKS

"She is far from the land where
her young hero sleeps."

Thomas Moore, 1779-1852

First published 1997 by True Crime Library

This edition published 2005 by Pan Books
an imprint of Pan Macmillan Ltd
Pan Macmillan, 20 New Wharf Road, London N1 9RR
Basingstoke and Oxford
Associated companies throughout the world
www.panmacmillan.com

ISBN 0 330 42110 7

A CIP catalogue record for this book is available from
the British Library.

Printed and bound in Great Britain by
Mackays of Chatham plc, Chatham, Kent

CONTENTS

INTRODUCTION

This is a true story about corruption and murder set against a background of Ireland's struggle for liberty. The events predate by approximately a quarter of a century the genesis of the Irish Republican Army, which was an offshoot of the Irish Volunteers formed in 1913. The main objective of the IRA today may be historically linked with these events, but that objective is quite different from the main aim of the people in this book. The quest of Irishmen from the 1870s until the early 1920s was for Home Rule – the right for Southern Ireland (then a part of the United Kingdom) to have control over her internal affairs.

The nineteenth-century struggle for Home Rule depended heavily upon financial support from Irish-Americans living in the United States. They operated through a secret society, the Clan-na-Gael, and during the 1880s, frustrated by the British government's waywardness, took a decision – the first such decision ever taken – to wage war on England through terrorism.

A light sketch of Irish affairs – some of which are touched upon in the story of Dr Patrick Cronin, the central character in this book – as seen from Victorian Westminster during that turbulent decade, might help the reader to put the events in the story in perspective.

During the 1880s unrest in Ireland was a major political

problem for the British Parliament. When the decade opened violence in the Irish countryside was rampant. In 1880 there were 2,590 outrages ranging from cattle-maiming to murder – a tenfold increase within three years. In politics, the same year saw the beginning of Liberal Prime Minister William Gladstone's second administration.

The leader of the Irish party at Westminster was Charles Stewart Parnell, a Protestant country gentleman of Wicklow who dominated the decade. Parnell helped rural Irishmen to set up a society of tenants called the Irish Land League, which quickly became a militant organisation. Violent speeches were made, and tenants were urged to stop paying rent altogether.

The hand of the Land League was everywhere, and people were punished merely for not belonging to it. The movement added the word boycott to the English language, derived from Captain Boycott, a Mayo landlord and agent, one of the first against whom the practice of boycotting was put into force. Boycotting was instituted against landlords who were disliked by their tenants, against tenants who had paid their rents to unpopular landlords, and against anyone else who incurred the hostility of the Land League.

People who were boycotted were rigidly isolated from family, friends and neighbours as though they were lepers. They were unable to get servants; their crops went ungathered, often they couldn't even buy the essentials of life in the shops. Medicine was sometimes refused by a chemist to the sick children of the boycotted, and no one could be found to dig a grave for them. Boycotting continued to be practised in Ireland even at the beginning of the twentieth century, especially in the southern counties.

In the struggle for Irish self-determination Charles Stewart Parnell and his Irish Nationalist Party needed both the funds of the Irish-Americans and the sympathy of the Roman Catholic Church in Ireland. To the former he had to show that he was militant, and possibly even revolutionary; to the latter he had to demonstrate that he would

Charles Stewart Parnell

use only lawful means to attain his objectives. The way forward between these two polarised interests, he decided,
was by parliamentary agitation in the House of Commons.

The British government was meanwhile attempting land
reforms and coercive legislation in Ireland, and when
Parnell and other Irish MPs were seen to be breaking the
law they were arrested and imprisoned without trial. It
was an odd commentary on parliamentary government
that a Liberal ministry should be in power and that Irish
members should be in prison, and early in 1882
Gladstone determined to liberate them on terms. In a
secret meeting with Parnell the Prime Minister worked
out a gentleman's agreement and had him released.

Suddenly Britain was stunned by the horrific murder of Lord Frederick Cavendish and Mr T. H. Burke, the Secretary and Under-Secretary for Ireland. This was then a crime without parallel in the history of England and Ireland at that time and it was as unexpected as it was terrible.

On May 6th, 1882, Lord Frederick Cavendish had arrived in Dublin to be present at the entry of the new Viceroy, Lord Spencer. After the ceremony he walked with Mr Burke through Phoenix Park. It was a bright summer evening between seven and eight o'clock, and there were lots of people in the park.

The two statesmen were walking along the principal road, which had grassy stretches on either side, with trees here and there, when they were attacked by four men who belonged to an Irish terror group calling themselves the Invincibles. Wielding long surgical knives, the gang set upon the statesmen and cut their throats. Despite all the strollers in the park, the four escaped without being challenged.

A number of people saw the murders. Lord Spencer, the new Viceroy, was himself looking out of one of the windows of the viceregal lodge and watched unconcerned the scuffle on the road about a hundred yards away. He had no idea he was a spectator at the murder of two colleagues; he thought he was merely looking at the antics of a few boisterous young men.

It subsequently emerged that the Invincibles had decided to murder only Mr Burke, who had been sent to Ireland to carry out the provisions of the recently passed Irish Coercion Act for the preservation of peace and the protection of Irish life and property. He was killed according to plan, but Lord Frederick Cavendish – who was a son of the Duke of Devonshire, and against whom there was no ill-feeling – was simply unlucky to be in his company, and shared his fate for no reason at all.

Parnell and the Irish Nationalist Party leaders were as appalled by the murders as the British public. Immediately they issued a manifesto which stated, "We feel that no act has ever been perpetrated in our country during the exciting struggles for social and political rights in the last fifty years that has so stained the name of hospitable Ireland as this cowardly and unprovoked assassination of a friendly stranger, and that until the murderers of Lord Frederick Cavendish and Mr Burke are brought to justice that stain will sully our country's name."

But murder and agitation still continued. On January 13th, 1883, the police raided selected houses in Dublin and arrested seventeen men, among whom was James Carey, a builder and contractor, who had just been elected a member of Dublin Town Council. The seventeen were tried for conspiracy; five were hanged, three were sent to penal servitude for life and others to penal servitude for long periods.

Carey turned informer and was allowed to escape. He took ship for Cape Town, unaware that also on board was a man named O'Donnell who was travelling out with the express purpose of killing him. O'Donnell shot Carey dead in Cape Town; the murderer was then brought back to England and executed.

The Phoenix Park murders caused an outcry in Britain and the government had no hope of survival unless it toughened up its policy towards Irish terrorism. Gladstone had already decided that some form of Irish Home Rule was needed, but he had failed to convince his colleagues, who would have no truck with a policy that hinted at a surrender to terrorism. At last, on April 8th, 1886, he introduced a Home Rule Bill to the Commons, and for the next sixteen days his proposals were brilliantly debated. Despite all the splendid oratory however, they were defeated, and the Prime Minister accordingly called a General Election to be fought on the issue of Irish Home Rule. Again Gladstone and his Liberal Party lost. The vengeful British electorate was not going to forget Phoenix Park in a hurry, and the only course of action for Gladstone now was to resign. His government was followed by a Conservative administration (1886) under Lord Salisbury which took a tough line on Irish crime but introduced agrarian reforms – a policy of "killing Home Rule with kindness."

On April 18th in the year after Salisbury took office *The Times* published a letter purporting to be from Parnell, in which he apologised for his earlier condemnation of the Phoenix Park murders. That same evening Parnell rose from his seat in the Commons and told MPs the letter was a forgery. The House did not believe him, but after considerable Irish pressure a commission was set up in September 1888 to inquire into the letter and other charges advanced by *The Times*. One of the witnesses at the Parnell Commission – as this state trial was called – was the British government spy Le Caron, who appears as something of a mystery man in the story of Dr Cronin.

Le Caron's real name was Thomas Beach, and he was born in Colchester in 1841. He went to America, fought for the North in the American Civil War and, styling himself Major Henry Le Caron, joined the Clan-na-Gael as a British spy, rising to the rank of "Senior Guardian" in one of the organisation's "Camps." For 25 years this non-Irishman was a trusted friend of the Clan-na-Gael's leadership while he was passing on all the organisation's plans to Sir Robert Anderson, of Scotland Yard, and thus enabling the British police to defeat the dynamite campaign, as the terrorist action was styled. He was recalled to London to give evidence against Parnell, where the revelation of his real identity stunned Irish freedom fighters all over the world.

The Parnell Commission largely vindicated the Irish leader, and the letter to *The Times* was proved to be a forgery. It was in fact bought with other documents from one Richard Pigott, a needy and disreputable Irish journalist. While the commission was still sitting, Pigott fled to Madrid, where he blew his brains out. Parnell subsequently sued *The Times* for libel, claiming £100,000, but the action was compromised without going into court by a payment of £5,000.

Then in November 1890 disaster struck Home Rule hopes when Parnell was revealed as an adulterer in a divorce case. The respondent was Kitty O'Shea, wife of Parnell's friend Captain O'Shea. That was too much for the Roman Catholic Church and for Gladstone's Liberal Party, both of which announced withdrawal of their support for Home Rule unless Parnell resigned. This the Irish leader flatly refused to do, with the result that the Home Rule party was irrevocably split.

Gladstone came back to office in 1892, the year after Parnell died, and brought in a new Home Rule Bill. But there was a revolt in the Liberal ranks; the House of Lords rejected the Bill, and the Irish party in the House of Commons, hopelessly split by Parnell's fall, went into the wilderness.

Thus the struggle for Irish self-determination, which spans three centuries, was reaching a climax during the 1880s, when the drama surrounding Dr Patrick Henry Cronin, fervent Irish-American supporter of Ireland's freedom, was being played out.

That drama took place in Chicago which in the 1880s was unrecognisable as the cellular skyscraper metropolis of today. Only eighty years earlier the United States government had built a frontier post, Fort Dearborn, near the southern end of Lake Michigan on the site of the future city. The settlement did not grow at once. In 1812 the fort's garrison was massacred by Indians. Forty years before the events in this book Chicago covered an area of only two and a half square miles and had a population of 4,170. The town started to become commercially important in mid-century, and was growing phenomenally when, in 1871, it was largely destroyed by fire. Its rebuilding programme was spectacular, but in the late 1880s its population was still just under a million, and approximately half of these were foreign-born settlers who had little interest at that time in Chicago society. So while the modern Chicago with its vista of skyscraper silhouettes along the front of the lake is an impressive embodiment of the modern American commercial spirit, during the time of these events it was still a town where possibly only about 500,000 people spoke fluent English, many of whom would have been able to recognise its prominent citizens, such as Dr Cronin, whose misfortunes were thus the subject of universal interest.

1
ENTER A DARK STRANGER

Napier Moreland, hostler, was sweeping the yard at Paddy Dinan's livery stable when the stranger came in.

The stranger had on a faded brown coat, the two top buttons fastened, the collar turned up, but not high enough to cover his cheeks. He wore a soft hat with a round crown, a little flattened in on top, with the wide rim pulled low over his eyes. Even by the light of the yard's single gas-lamp Napier Moreland could tell the stranger didn't want to be recognised.

"I've called for the rig Dan Coughlin ordered this morning," the stranger said. "It was for collection by Mr Smith."

"Don't know nothing about any horse," Napier Moreland said tersely, continuing to sweep. "You'll have to see the gaffer when he comes back. Shouldn't be long." He looked sideways beyond the yard to the suddenly clanging gate that led on to Chestnut Street. "You're lucky. He's just come in. He's out front now with Blacksmith Jones."

The stranger glanced up briefly, following the hostler's gaze towards the gate. Now the hostler, alert with curiosity, could see the stranger's face for the first time. He was a young man with a dark beard and a light brown, almost auburn moustache. His face was dirty; he looked as if he hadn't shaved for the best part of a week. The hostler thought, he's probably a mechanic just finished work.

The stranger disappeared through the stable barn. From somewhere inside the gaslight-blurred barn Paddy Dinan, the newly arrived gaffer, hollered across the yard, "Napier! Take that harness off the bay. You know that animal ain't never been driven single." The livery-stable owner appeared framed in the doorway of the barn, with Blacksmith Jones and the stranger behind him. "And Napier, get the old white horse* out for Mr Coughlin's friend, and harness it to the Whitechapel buggy, will ya now."

The hostler took the harness off the bay and led the horse to Blacksmith Jones. Then he led the white horse into the yard.

The stranger said at once, "I don't want a white horse."

Paddy Dinan turned to his hostler. "Napier, take that horse back and bring the other one."

The other horse was also a white. If anything it was whiter. Again the stranger objected.

"I don't want a white one," he insisted. He pointed across the yard to the bay, which Blacksmith Jones had tied up to a stable door. "Why can't I have that one over there?"

"The bay's worked out," Paddy Dinan said patiently. "This white's all I've got left this evening."

They watched Napier harness the old white horse to the buggy.

"I don't like that buggy either," the stranger said. The buggy was an old one, pretty well worn, with no side curtains.

"It's the only one I've got," Dinan said. There was a hint of tired exasperation in his voice now. "It's a dark night, anyways, so your customer won't be recognised from the street, if that's all he's worried about."

---

*Throughout the documents relating to this story, Paddy Dinan's white horse was never referred to as a grey, the term used today for a white horse.

The stranger climbed into the buggy, took the reins and drove out of the barn. Paddy Dinan went out to the gate to watch the horse as it trotted off down Chestnut Street, checking to see it was working and in good form. Dan Coughlin, who had given him the order for the rig for Mr Smith that morning, was a senior Chicago detective and a good customer of the stable, too good a customer to disappoint. Satisfied, Paddy Dinan turned back to the barn. It was, he later remembered, ten minutes past seven on the evening of Saturday, May 4th, 1889.

*　　　　*　　　　*

Saturday, May 4th, 1889 had so far been a hectic day for Dr Patrick Cronin and the evening threatened to be as crowded. He had been on call all day; now at 5 p.m. he was back at his apartment in the Windsor Theatre Block, 470, North Clark Street, Chicago. His receptionist and housekeeper Mrs T. T. Conklin, who lived with her husband in the next-door apartment, came to greet him in the hallway.

"I'm hoping there won't be any calls tonight," Dr Cronin said wearily. "I could do with a glass of sherry before dinner and a few moments rest." A confirmed bachelor, the doctor was accustomed to having his wishes interpreted as commands.

"Of course you could!" exclaimed Mrs Conklin. She was a motherly woman whose figure was lost in the ballooning fashion of the last half of the Victorian century. "People give you no peace at all." She hurried off to fetch a glass and the sherry bottle and to see to the doctor's dinner.

Dr Cronin drank his sherry, ate his dinner quickly, and went out again, returning shortly after 6 p.m. A number of patients had arrived at the surgery, and he had less than ninety minutes to treat them before going on to a

DR PATRICK CRONIN

meeting with the leading shareholders of the *Celtic-American*, an Irish-American newspaper he had founded some years earlier.

A naturalised American citizen, Patrick Henry Cronin was born in Buttevant, Ireland, arriving in the New World with his parents as a boy. Now, aged 43, he was as well known in Chicago as an Irish patriot as he was renowned as a physician. As a patriot he had campaigned since his youth for self-government for Ireland, growing into the cause like root-ivy. As a physician he had an extensive list of patients and an army of friends. But that Saturday night Dr Cronin was not a happy man. He was uncomfortably aware of the troubles heaping up around him. Lately some people in the Irish-American secret societies were saying that he was more trouble to the cause than he was worth; others even maliciously hinted he was a British spy. His Irish-American enemies were growing by battalions - once some of them had tried to kill him, and the memory of that horrific night when he escaped by a hairs-breadth had prompted him to write to a friend, naming names if ever he should be found dead in suspicious circumstances. So it was that as he hurried about his business on that evening of May 4th there was some tension in Dr Cronin's movements, some exasperation in his voice, some sense of preoccupation in his manner, for lately there was a perpetual dark notion in his mind that his life was in constant danger.

Mrs Conklin, wearing a stiff white gown now in her role as the doctor's receptionist, called, "Next, please!" and Agnes McNearney rose from her seat and followed her into the surgery. Behind her in the waiting-room Agnes left her sister Sarah and her mother, with whom she lived at 80 Locust Street, Chicago. Both of them had decided to accompany her to the doctor's.

Dr Cronin closed the door and Agnes began to recite her problem. Outside, Sarah McNearney and Mrs McNearney settled down to wait. Agnes had not long been with the doctor when there was a ring at the door-bell. Mrs Conklin opened the door and a stranger, breathing heavily as if he had been running, stood on the threshold. Sarah McNearney and her mother looked up inquisitively.

"Is the doctor at home?" the man asked.

"Yes," said Mrs Conklin. "He's busy at the moment though, with a patient."

"Can I see him? It's urgent."

"Come in."

The stranger hesitated on the doorstep. Mrs Conklin said gently, "You'll have to come in if you want to see the doctor."

The man followed her into the waiting-room. "I can't wait here," he said, looking around anxiously. "I'm in a hurry. The doctor's needed right away – it's an accident case."

"Sit down," said Mrs Conklin. The stranger went to the far end of the waiting-room, watched attentively by Sarah McNearney. He sat on the edge of a chair, she afterwards remembered, and everything about him betrayed his nervousness. When their eyes met briefly Sarah shuddered involuntarily; that first full look was incised on her mind, and later she was to recount it vividly: "He had a stare that you would not see in many persons. It was a stare that was just piercing. He looked at me so sharp that I had to throw my eyes off his face. Every time I looked up he looked straight at me, and wouldn't take his eyes off."

Sarah was also to remember that the stranger was about five feet seven, with a thin face, not cleanly shaven, and a dark moustache. His faded black topcoat was unbuttoned, and he wore a flat soft felt hat. His boots were rather rough-looking, muddy and unpolished, and looked as if they had been wet.

Mrs Conklin went to the surgery door and knocked. She called out, "There's a gentleman here who has an accident case. He wants you right away."

From inside Dr Cronin replied, "In a minute."

PATRICK O'SULLIVAN

In much less than a minute the doctor came into the waiting-room. The stranger got up and advanced towards him.

"Are you Dr Cronin?" the stranger asked.

"Yes."

"There's been an accident, doctor. A man's been run over by an ice wagon. His leg's smashed. He's one of Patrick O'Sullivan's men."

Patrick O'Sullivan. The name did not seem to register at once with Dr Cronin, despite the fact that a few weeks previously he had signed a contract with O'Sullivan, a local ice-manufacturer, to provide medical care for his employees.

"Why didn't you get another doctor?" he asked irritably, some of the inner tension beginning to surface.

The stranger took a card from his pocket and pressed it into the doctor's hand. "Mr O'Sullivan's out of town," he said. "He told us if anything happened we should go to Dr Cronin."

Fingering the card, Dr Cronin seemed to remember the contract. The agreement was that if any of O'Sullivan's men were hurt a messenger would present him with the boss's card and he would attend the injured man right away. He put the card on the mantelpiece, sat down at a table, and wrote a prescription for Agnes McNearney. He walked back into the surgery and talked to Agnes while he put on his overcoat. "Come back at three o'clock on Monday afternoon," he told her. He got out his surgical bag and remembering that the stranger had said it was a smashed leg, opened the catch and put in an ample supply of cotton wadding. From a cupboard he took a rectangular metal box in which he kept his splints.

The McNearney ladies left the surgery a few seconds ahead of the doctor. They remembered that it was just after 7.15 p.m.

Outside in North Clark Street, Frank Scanlan, shipping clerk with W. M. Hoyt and Co., had stopped on his way home for supper to talk to the owner of a candy store outside the Windsor Theatre building. Scanlan remarked upon the splendid weather – the warmth that early May evening was filling the streets with walkers. He glanced up as he saw Dr Cronin, whom he knew, getting into a buggy. A stranger, walking just in front of the doctor, climbed into the buggy's driving seat.

Scanlan was surprised, for he too was due at the meeting of the *Celtic-American* shareholders that evening. From what he could see Dr Cronin was in a hurry and it didn't look as if the meeting was on the doctor's mind at that moment. So as the driver picked up the reins Scanlan called out, "Hello, doctor, where are you going?"

Dr Cronin said, "I've got to go to an accident at the ice house up North."

"You know there's a meeting at your office tonight?" Scanlan asked.

Just as he spoke the driver asked Dr Cronin to change seats. The driver got up and the doctor slid over, moving to the right, on the side where Scanlan was addressing him. Leaning down, Dr Cronin said, "It's a good thing you came along. You can take the keys." He reached into his pocket and produced a large bunch of keys.

"Which one unlocks the door?" Scanlan asked.

As the doctor selected the key and passed the bunch through the side of the buggy, keeping his thumb and forefinger on the appropriate key, the driver started up the horse and Scanlan lost the key. In desperation he began to run alongside the moving buggy, calling out, "When will you be back?"

Over his shoulder Dr Cronin shouted, "God knows. I've no idea how long this will take." As the horse broke into a fast trot Dr Cronin shouted back, "You'll find some papers down there for the men to sign..." The rest of the conversation was reduced to shreds as the horse and buggy sped off down the street.

Frank Scanlan remembered the driver. He recalled later that the man looked as if he hadn't shaved for a week. His moustache was dark, his eyes were very dark. "He had a fierce look in his eyes, and I rather thought it was on my account," Scanlan recalled. The driver had a soft felt hat pulled down over his forehead and an old dark brown overcoat. Scanlan remembered, also, the horse and buggy. The horse was white, and the buggy was old. And Scanlan remembered the time. It was 7.25 p.m.

*   *   *

Mr T. T. Conklin shook his wife awake and set a cup of coffee down on her bedside table. "The doctor didn't come back from that call last night," he whispered urgently. "There's no sign of him anywhere in his apartment."

Blinking at the light, Mrs Conklin said, "What time is it?"

"Eight o'clock. You said the man brought a card. Where is it?"

"The doctor put it on the mantel in the waiting-room." She struggled up, suddenly afraid. "Something bad has happened to him. What are you going to do?"

"I'm going up to Lakeview to see that ice man and find out what's happened to Patrick."

"I'm coming too," Mrs Conklin said.

Half an hour later the Conklins were rattling northwards through the empty Sunday morning streets of Chicago. Out to their right, silvery Lake Michigan gleamed like a mirror, reflecting the start of another fine spring day. Huddled in their buggy, the Conklins, oblivious to their surroundings, discussed in snatches of conversation the possibility that the doctor might be sitting beside some desperately injured workman. But then, they reasoned, Patrick Cronin was a thoughtful man – somehow he would have let them know. Mr Conklin kept his darker thoughts to himself. He was the friend to whom Dr Cronin had recently confided that his life had been threatened by his enemies in the Irish secret societies, and that he was increasingly fearful for his personal safety.

An hour's drive brought them to Lakeview, a fashionable suburb of nineteenth-century Chicago. They found the home of ice-dealer Patrick O'Sullivan, whose message the previous evening had taken Dr Cronin out of his surgery, at the junction of Bosworth and Roscoe Avenues.

O'Sullivan's housekeeper, Mrs Tom Whelan, still in her nightcap and dressing- gown, answered the door. "Mr O'Sullivan's gone out," she announced. "I'm sure I don't know when he'll be back."

More anxious than ever, the Conklins drove back south to central Chicago. On the way they stopped at the office of the Pinkerton Detective Agency* and spoke to a Mr Murray, who was on duty at the office. He listened to their story and promised to investigate immediately. Mr Conklin took his wife home, then went to East Chicago Avenue police station where he met for the first time the police officer who was to loom large in the Dr Cronin mystery.

Captain Michael Schaack, a beefy German, was a remarkably slow-witted man for his position, which he had reached by a combination of years of service and political wire-pulling. At midday that Sunday, with his lunch at the forefront of his mind, he was not in a humour for this whingeing little fellow's complaint about his missing buddy. When Mr Conklin had finished his story, laying heavy emphasis on Dr Cronin's enemies, Schaack remarked with a non-committal shrug, "I don't see you've got anything to worry about. The doctor's probably with a patient."

Mr Conklin was persistent. "He told me he once sent you a letter in which he asked to be protected in regard to his troubles," he reminded Schaack. "That should suggest to you that he could be in danger."

"Well, I can't do anything about it until six o'clock," Schaack replied. "That's when the night men come on

*The Chicago-based Pinkerton Detective Agency was founded in 1852 by Allan Pinkerton.

duty. I don't have anyone here to make inquiries at this time."

When the unhappy Mr Conklin left the police station Captain Schaack gazed after him in disbelief, incredulous that the silly old fellow should want to bother him on a Sunday about a single, middle-aged man who hadn't come home like a good boy on his Saturday night out. Still shaking his head, Schaack pulled on his coat, planted his cap on his large cropped head, and set out with slavering anticipation for his lunch.

2

THIS LAWYER SHOOTS TO KILL

Patriotism seldom recognises class distinctions. Daniel Coughlin the detective, Paddy Dinan the liveryman, Frank Scanlan the shipping clerk, the staring-eyed buggy-driver with a week's growth of beard, and Dr Patrick Cronin, the prosperous medical practitioner, were bonded together in the common cause of freedom for their motherland, the more so since they were in self-imposed exile. In that cause the new Irish immigrants, bred in poverty, illness, banishment and sorrow, were blood-brothers to the established Irish-Americans whose ancestors had also known all that same deprivation and shabbiness, and had passed down the memory of it by word of mouth, like relay runners passing a baton, and with the same resolution, for the baton was not to be dropped.

In that common cause all of them were members of a secret society, the Clan-na-Gael, which roughly translates to the name by which it was also known by its members, the United Brotherhood. The organisation was founded in the United States in 1869 with three principal objectives – to assist similar organisations in Ireland and England to establish an Irish republic, to bring about fraternal feelings among Irishmen in America, and "to assist in the elevation of the Irish race." Its doors were open only to Irishmen or Americans of Irish descent – and since around four million Irishmen left their native land to settle in America during the second half of the nineteenth century, it isn't surprising that membership of the Clan-na-Gael in the twenty years from its founding to the mysterious disappearance of Dr Cronin that Saturday night in 1889 grew so fast that it stretched across America from ocean to ocean.

In that year one estimate was that there were 15,000 members. Each paid a small fee to join and thereafter a small annual subscription; the organisation was further supported by donations from wealthy Irish-Americans. These funds paid for the setting-up of the organisation's biennial conventions, the caring for families of members who were in need, and various other expenditures, but there were no paid officials and the size of the membership and the number of donations meant that between 1881 and 1884 there were funds surplus to requirements of around $250,000 – worth well over five million pounds by today's standards.

The organisation was divided into districts, each with its District Member and District "Camps." Each Camp had a public name – the only name by which it was known to outsiders. Thus Camp 20, the Camp in which events in the Cronin affair were focused, was called the "Columbia Club"; other camps were known as literary clubs or sporting clubs. With one remarkable exception – Alexander Sullivan, whose story we are about to tell – any non-Irishmen with a literary or sporting bent who tried to join these clubs found the door slammed in their faces, for neither books nor sport were on any of their agendas, which were reserved almost exclusively for discussions on how to liberate Ireland from the British yoke.

For the first twelve years of its existence the Clan-na-Gael was governed by an Executive Board composed of its District Members. In 1881 there were fifteen District Members on the Board but in 1881 too, all that was changed.

In that year a National Convention of the organisation

decided to reduce its Board to just five members. Three of the five elected – Alexander Sullivan of Chicago, Dennis Feeley of Rochester, New York, and Colonel Michael Boland, of Kansas City – appeared to share the same policy views, and since they constituted a majority of the Board they took charge of it.

Two years later this triumvirate persuaded the biennial convention to reduce the Executive Board to just the three of them, for, they announced, the time had come to begin "active work" on behalf of Ireland which, put simply, meant the murder of innocent people and the destruction of property in the United Kingdom. History labelled that decision the dynamite policy and its front-line protagonists "the dynamiters". Since its inauguration by Sullivan, Feeley and Boland in 1883 the dynamite policy has been with us on and off right down to the dying embers of the twentieth century; only the nomenclature has changed, to terrorism and terrorists.

To ensure that their policy was carried out with the ruthless efficiency which they claimed it needed, the restyled Executive Board drew up a new oath for the organisation's members, binding them all to obey the Board without comment or question. What this meant was that if they directed a man to go and kill another man in England it had to be done; no one had any right to question the order.

Alexander Sullivan, an archetype of the urban cowboy who proliferated across America's Mid-West in the second half of the Victorian century, held the central role in the triumvirate. Sullivan was a self-styled lawyer, an amateur politician, and an unconvicted murderer; he was eventually to become, in the words of a senior policeman, "the most thoroughly watched man in Chicago." He began his working life in Detroit with a job in a shoe-shop. Selling shoes inspired him to some sort of ambition, for he next opened his own shoe-shop. It wasn't successful, the shop burned down, and it was generally thought that Sullivan was the arsonist, although nothing could be proved.

Sullivan turned to politics and made himself conspicuous as an advocate for labour rights, working for the Republican Party in the political campaign of 1868. Forty years earlier President Andrew Jackson had declared as his new Democratic Party was swept into office by a huge majority, "To the winner belongs the spoils," and since that time the "Spoils System" – presidential patronage for those who work to get the party elected – has been a feature of the American political scene. The spoils that Sullivan the ex-shoe-salesman received for his polished and forcible oratory was his appointment as collector of Internal Revenue at Santa Fe in New Mexico. The Senate, however, must have heard a thing or two about Sullivan, for they refused to confirm the appointment, although subsequently they did allow him to become Secretary of the Territory of New Mexico.

New Mexico, still some years away from the status of statehood, was virgin country for an entrepreneur. Sullivan started a newspaper, the *Santa Fe Post*, and wrote an article which reflected upon the integrity of one General Heath. The furious general cornered Sullivan in a shop and fired two shots at him, both of which missed. Several days later, as Sullivan was passing General Heath's house, the general fired at him again, and Sullivan, now armed, drew his revolver and fired back. Both men were arrested and bailed. Heath decided to leave town; Sullivan, in this first brush with the law, was tried and acquitted.

On April 18th, 1872, Sullivan left Santa Fe and the New Mexico Territory for Washington, D.C. From there he went to New York, and in the spring of 1873 arrived in Chicago, where he became engaged to marry a Miss Buchanan. In an article for a Chicago newspaper intriguingly entitled "Unsexed Women" a journalist named Fitzgibbons made an unkind reference to Miss Buchanan, whereupon Sullivan put a revolver in his pocket and went off to Fitzgibbons's office "to see him about it." Nothing, it seems, came of the encounter.

Sullivan worked as a departmental editor on the *Chicago Post*, and as a reporter on the *Inter Ocean*, and the *Chicago Times*. On February 14th, 1876, he was appointed secretary of the Chicago Board of Public Works. This was the sort of important municipal appointment that should have been sufficient to bring any truculent spirit to his senses, but not so Sullivan. Six months later he shot and killed Francis Hanford, a high-school headmaster.

Hanford's crime was that he had written a letter to the city council charging Mrs Sullivan (the former Miss Buchanan) wife of the Secretary of the Board of Public Works, with using her influence with Mayor Colvin to get the previous Secretary fired and her husband appointed in his stead. When Sullivan heard about this he left his office, ordered a carriage and drove with his wife to Hanford's house, where he found the headmaster sitting on his front steps. Sullivan, who had never met Hanford before, demanded an apology for the letter, which was peremptorily refused. Sullivan knocked him down. Sullivan was to claim that another man, named McMullen, joined in the ensuing fight on the side of Hanford, leaving the headmaster free to attack Mrs Sullivan, striking her in the face. At this Sullivan drew his revolver and shot Hanford dead.

The killer spent two months in jail and then, in October 1876, faced a carnival trial. The prosecutor was later arrested in New York for theft, and it was freely claimed that the judge, W. K. McAllister, had prejudiced the case so much in Sullivan's favour that a number of the city's influential citizens asked him to resign. The jury was discharged after announcing it could not agree – eleven jurors were for acquittal and one for conviction. The obstinate juror was one F. J. Berry, who received almost a public ovation when his action became known.

Thanks to Mr. Berry, Sullivan faced his second trial for the murder six months later. He was defended by W. J.

Hynes, whom he later condemned to death through the Clan-na-Gael. The second trial lasted a week; the defence was justifiable homicide, and the verdict was not guilty.

Now Sullivan became a lawyer. Although totally untrained, during the next few years he built up a substantial practice with a client list mostly from the Clan-na-Gael. In 1881 he was elected to the organisa-

DETECTIVE DANIEL COUGHLIN

tion's reduced Board, and two years later he effectively controlled it. It gave the Irishmen in Chicago a sense of well-being and importance if when they had a legal problem they could brief the great man who was their national leader. Yet here, in the rag-tag life of Alexander Sullivan, soap-box orator turned Irish-American dictator, was the most extraordinary of all the deceptions he had so far practised. For Sullivan was not an Irishman at all, nor was he of Irish descent, and he hadn't the slightest interest in old Erin. He was in fact born in Amherstburg, Ontario, the son of a British soldier. While the Clan-na-Gael was turning somersaults to avoid the halogen glare of publicity, shrouding itself in secrecy, fearful of infiltration by British spies, it had allowed its leadership to be usurped by an outsider whose sole ambition was to steal its considerable funds.

Sullivan and his confederates Feeley and Boland began their thieving three years after they had seized office at the 1883 Convention. Arrogantly demonstrating that three and only three was going to be the permanent number of the Executive Board, they adopted the symbol of the Triangle, and issued orders under that designation. Freeing themselves of all sumptuary constraints, the Triangle announced that great sums of money provided from the funds in the organisation's treasury were being expended on "active work," and to lend colour to this fiction they produced a certain amount of this work which had to be done by sending dynamiters to England. Very few of these emissaries of terror were given the monies which the Triangle claimed they were given, and which were essential for their personal safety. When they arrived in the United Kingdom they were met by an agent of the organisation who had been briefed by the Triangle to get rid of the dynamiter as quickly as possible. Either the agent or someone else then made known to the English police who the dynamiter was, and he was arrested and jailed, almost always for life. It was eventually estimated that the prison doors of England were locked against twenty or more dynamiters who were sent by the Triangle and betrayed by it.

The extent of the embezzlement can be gauged from the fact that when the Triangle took hold of the organisation there was the known fund of $250,000 in the treasury. Because all records were methodically destroyed it is not clear exactly whether the thefts began after the Board was reduced to five members in 1881 or after the coup of 1883, but in 1885 the Triangle announced to the stunned Brotherhood that the treasury was empty and the Clan-na-Gael was in debt to the Triangle for $13,000, which Sullivan, Feeley and Boland had personally loaned it.

But now, how to stifle the furore which they knew must break like a tidal wave in this organisation that spanned America from ocean to ocean? The device they chose was to circulate a rumour that Scotland Yard was watching the Clan-na-Gael, and for that reason the biennial Convention, the forum at which the accounts would be openly discussed, must be postponed. Further, because of that English surveillance, they must destroy every vestige of the work they had done, their books and every written record.

So, when the tidal wave arrived the Triangle had erected a seemingly unassailable defence to meet it. Under the rules no one was entitled to question their decisions – and no one could anyway, because all financial and work records had been burned for "security reasons." But the strongest barrier against a storm may be breached, and a strong man might attack this one if he cared sufficiently for honesty and truth and not at all for the consequences of his actions. The strong man who decided to assault the Triangle's defence was Dr Patrick Henry Cronin.

3

DEADLY ENEMIES

Although some information gaps now appear for a time in the workings of the Clan-na-Gael, it is possible to trace at least in outline the proceedings that brought Alexander Sullivan and Dr Cronin into the head-on collision which was the genesis of so much enmity and hate that violence was bound to happen.

As soon as the debt of $13,000 became known, the camps met to discuss it. Many members were sickened by the Triangle's statement, and contrary to the rules, began to attack the Executive Board, charging it with inefficiency and corruption. Sullivan and his two acolytes would have none of it. They expelled Camp after Camp for daring to criticise them, to the point that very soon just the name of the United Brotherhood could be styled the misnomer of the century.

It was at this point, just as the Triangle felt that something must be done to quell dissension, that Dr Cronin stood up to address Camp 95, his Camp on Chicago's North Side. The doctor began by reading a circular from another Camp protesting against the action of the Executive Board, and when he finished reading it he added some comments of his own which were never recorded.

A few days later – we are still in 1885 – Dr Cronin received a note summoning him to be tried as a traitor to the cause. The charge was that he had publicly aired criticism of the Triangle. All written records of that trial – if indeed there were any – have vanished. All that is known is that the prosecutor was Alexander Sullivan and the committee that sat in judgment on Dr Cronin included the Chicago detective Dan Coughlin – the same detective who ordered the horse and buggy from Paddy Dinan's livery stable – and the Clan-na-Gael executive Major Henry Le Caron, then a trusted member of the organisation but in reality a spy in the pay of the British and, some believed, in the pay of Alexander Sullivan too. The result of their deliberations was that Dr Cronin was found guilty of treason and expelled from the Clan-na-Gael.

By now, however, the many hundreds of seceding members of the organisation were forming their own Irish Brotherhood, and it was this breakaway group that Dr Cronin now joined. For the next three years the two factions existed in common cause and simmering enmity, both of them too weak to be of much use in furthering their aim of Irish nationalism. In the upheaval that followed the secession Sullivan, Feeley and Boland resigned from the Clan-na-Gael – either because of pressure from the remaining members or because, the treasury now being empty, the organisation served no further purpose for them. One thing that was abundantly clear from subsequent events however, was that the mutual hatred between Sullivan and Dr Cronin was not mitigated by the passage of time. It is equally clear that a more democratic style of leadership was in command of the Clan-na-Gael, for in 1888 the two factions had talks, as a result of which it was decided to bring both sides together in a convention held at Chicago with the object of a reunion.

There was, the breakaway group declared, much sorting out to be done. Two secessionists, Luke Dillon and John Devoy, told the meeting that everyone knew that there had been misappropriation of funds and that patriots had been sent to their doom in England, with the result that there could be no union until those responsible were tried and punished. The convention appointed a committee of ten of its members to investigate the charges against the Triangle, among them Dr Cronin. The ten members then decided there were charges to answer, and six of them, three from each faction, were selected to try Sullivan, Feeley and Boland. Again one of the six was Dr Cronin, so that now, three years after being put in the dock and branded a traitor to Irish nationalism at a secret kangaroo court, the doctor was back in another kangaroo court as a judge, with one of his former judges in the dock. The difference this time was that Dr Cronin was determined that the proceedings would not be secret, that every Irish-American patriot in the land would be given a full account of the crimes of Alexander Sullivan and his two confederates.

To accomplish that aim Dr Cronin made three hundred pages of notes during the 12-day trial of the former members of the Triangle, with the intention of publishing them at the next convention of the Clan-na-Gael.

A few weeks before the proceedings began, Dr Cronin noted, its six judges met at the Westminster Hotel, New York, on July 20th. They elected J. D. McMahon, a New Yorker, as trial chairman and P. A. O'Boyle as secretary. The other four members were Cronin himself, Dr. P. McCahey, C. F. Burns and J. J. Rogers.

The trial of the former Triangle members, which was to cost the organisation $2,700, mostly in expenses paid to witnesses brought from all over the United States, opened at Genesse House, Buffalo, N.Y., on August 29th, 1888. The first day began with a vigorous protest from Alexander Sullivan that Dr Cronin should not be allowed to sit in judgment on him.

"One of your committee is a malignant enemy of mine," he declared. "The party I refer to is Dr Cronin. He has recently made statements through a newspaper in regard to me that he knows to be false. For this and many other reasons I object to being tried by the committee as constituted."

Feeley and Boland both added their voices to this objection. Boland said that although personally he had some objections to Dr. McCahey, he would waive them and join with Sullivan and Feeley in asking that Dr Cronin retire from the committee, they being willing to accept anyone in the room in preference.

What happened next may be gleaned only from Dr Cronin's copious notes of the trial. Each of the six members of the committee made notes, none more than Cronin and McCahey, but there was to be no central report; each member was to cast his vote at the end of the trial. Only Dr Cronin's notes remained extant for any length of time, as he was determined they should be. After the defendants' outburst he recorded:

"Dr Cronin replied to this; said he thought it very strange that Mr Sullivan should speak of him as a malignant enemy. Dr Cronin had never characterised Sullivan personally as an enemy; anything said by him, Cronin, was directed towards the men who, he was given to understand, had wrecked the organisation. Sullivan was one of them, he understood, and only in connection with certain developments pertaining to the order did he say anything of Sullivan. If Mr Sullivan believed everything told him by gossip he, the doctor, could not help it.

"' Indeed,' the doctor continued, 'why should I be the enemy of Mr Sullivan? What has he done to me that I should, as he says, single him out for personal enmity?'

"To this Mr Sullivan replied that he could prove by a dozen men who would not believe the doctor under oath that Cronin was an expelled member of the organisation.

"Dr Cronin said, interrupting Mr Sullivan, that the gentlemen evidently meant to irritate him or intimidate the committee. Mr Sullivan said he did not wish to intimidate the committee."

If there was any doubt left in anyone's mind that the irresistible force had met the immovable object, it was surely dispelled by Dr Cronin's next and final statement: "Then you probably mean to intimidate me. That you cannot do, sir, and you ought to know it by this time. All the objections you urge were made at the convention, and by an almost unanimous vote. As the selection of that convention I am the peer of anyone here, and doing my duty by the body that created me. I would not leave if I could."

The objections of the defendants were overruled by five votes to one (Secretary O'Boyle was the abstention). But the chairman, J. D. McMahon, seemed to think that notwithstanding the committee's ruling, Sullivan ought to put his objections to Dr Cronin's participation in writing at the end of the trial. The merit of this is not quite clear, since the verdict was going to be announced before Sullivan's protest letter could be written. Sullivan certainly made a point later on of circulating his protest among the Clan-na-Gael membership, but he would probably have done that anyway without the chairman's suggestion. The protest letter, written from New York and dated September 15th (a suggestion was made later that although the letter was dated 15th September, it was not written until six months later, for reasons which will become obvious) was addressed to the secretary, O'Boyle, and testified to Sullivan's vehement dislike, and perhaps now his very real fear, of Dr Cronin:

"First, he is a personal enemy, second, he has expressed opinions in this case; third, he is a perjurer and scoundrel, unfit to be placed on any jury.

"To the first objection I cite the men of the United Brotherhood organisation in Chicago, from which he was expelled in a case where I conducted the prosecution. There is no question in Chicago of his personal hostility [...] his was one of the signatures to a circular assailing me, and he was a regular attendant at meetings hostile to me.

"In support of the second objection [...] Cronin was one of those who circulated charges against my former associates and myself. He therefore not only expressed opinions, but [...] caused those opinions to be published and circulated.

"Your committee is chosen from two bodies whose members differ on many points, but who all agree, or profess to agree, in denouncing unfair trials, biased juries and prejudiced jurors in Ireland, and yet I am asked, after a period of four years has elapsed since I was a member of the organisation, to come for trial before a committee chosen in my absence at a place where I was given no opportunity to be heard ...

"While you ask the world to believe that you want a fair trial on one side of the Atlantic, you ask me to accept as a juror one who would be excluded in any civil court from a jury in a trial; of a case in which I had an interest however trivial... Had he [Cronin] as much decency as an ordinary dog he would not sit in a case in which I was interested.

"As to the third objection to Cronin, I charge that the brand of perjury is so burned into the scoundrel's brow that all the waters of the earth would not remove the brand. [...] Cronin was expelled, a convicted liar, who added perjury to his slander. I have further investigated his record, and I find that in several matters outside of the organisation he is also a perjurer. Cronin swears that he lived at St. Catharines, Canada, until after the assassination of President Lincoln, April 14th, 1865. Captain McDonald, of No 2 Company, Nineteenth Battalion of the Canadian militia, says that in 1862 or 1863 he had P. H. Cronin in his company. He was known as 'Singer Cronin', and at the time of joining he took the oath of allegiance as follows: 'I swear that I will bear true and faithful allegiance to Her Majesty the Queen, her heirs and successors.'

"The record shows that Dr Cronin's father, J. G. Cronin, was a British subject and lived in Canada up to the time of his death, so that P.H. Cronin, until 1865 or 1866, when he left Canada, was a British subject [...]. Yet this creature swore in his name as a voter in St. Louis and voted in that city..."

The protest then rambled on with a rather convoluted suggestion that Dr Cronin had falsified his age at the time of his arrival in the United States in order to obtain the franchise, "a side of his character which should be considered in connection with any report his malice and prejudice may dictate."

Sullivan concluded: "I have not made any formal protest against the presence of Dr McCahey on the trial committee, but it is well known that he has been active in publishing documents and interviews hostile to me, and it is at least strange that one who has been so engaged should be willing to serve on such a committee."

This, then, was Alexander Sullivan's protest about the presence of Dr Cronin as a judge, and, because it was written after the verdict was announced, it could not have had any material effect on the outcome of the trial. Sullivan and his two Triangle confederates faced two sets of charges, one made by John Devoy, alleging they fraudulently spent, or misappropriated, $128,000 without the knowledge of the membership, and the other made by Luke Dillon, alleging they spent $87,000 during the years 1885 to 1887 and failed to account for it.

The charges alleged that all the "active work" claimed by the Executive Board and its agents had not been performed, because there was no proof, no vouchers, contracts, or receipts to support those claims; that men on dynamiting "errands" for the Brotherhood had been basely neglected, and their families left without support; that bogus transfers of cash to members of the organisation had been issued as coming from Ireland; that a district convention was falsely instituted at Pittsburgh and that Executive Board members and proxies sat as delegates in that convention in direct violation of the constitution, in order to get votes to support the Triangle.

The notes of the evidence, written in Dr Cronin's neat handwriting, constitute a startling document and present a fascinating insight into the workings of a corrupt terrorist organisation. Four principal witnesses were examined; two of them male, who were not named for security reasons, and two women.

The first witness, a male dynamiter, sketched a picture of how the dynamiters arriving in England found themselves friendless and penniless, how they "became incensed to the last degree, deeply wounded in their pride and self-love and gripped in a coil of angry passions as the extent of their almost total neglect in the face of the enemy overwhelmed them." The dynamiter said that after the Boston Convention of 1884 a man named Donovan, who was acting as an agent for the Executive Board and who "was then in the employ of General Kerwin," asked him if "he could furnish enough men to accomplish a certain amount of active work." General Kerwin was the District Member for New York. The witness found one recruit. Donovan and a District Member, John Moroney, paid the steerage fare of this recruit and the witness to England, which was $18 each, and gave them $100 each "to carry on work." For further funds they were referred to "the agent on the other side."

"Donovan said that his reason for not giving me more before leaving was that men engaged in similar work had been arrested on landing on the other side – that my carrying a large sum might excite suspicion. That was satisfactory to me, especially as I was given the name of the agent on the other side who was to furnish funds as needed.

"On the way over I had to pay £2 for accommodation on the steamer, and after I had been on the other side nine days I had only £10 left. I then went to meet the man who I was told was the agent and told him I was short of funds and needed £10. He said he had no money to give me, he had hardly enough money for his own expenses. He said he had received only $200 himself when he landed in England and that he might have to stay there for a year living only on that money.

"I said I would return at once to America, to which the agent replied that he would ask the Executive Board for money for me. I told him that if the funds were not forthcoming I would go back. I then asked him where it would be necessary to do the work. He said he didn't know; things were looking queer; he was sure he had been betrayed by someone because two men who he suspected were detectives had called at his lodgings and asked for him under his assumed name."

Believing he was under surveillance, the agent, said the witness, was in a state of considerable alarm, and asked that the dynamiters should do nothing for six weeks. During that time the witness met two other dynamiters, both of whom wanted to get on with their work but "the agent was so careful that we thought it was cowardice." The agent changed his lodgings several times, moving on each time because he thought he was being watched. In the meantime, no more money was forthcoming from America.

"I finally induced him to give orders to do the work," the witness said. "This was on Thursday. On Saturday we did it. After the work was done I met him that same evening. I was so reduced for funds that I prevailed upon him to give me £4 of the £16 he had left. Shortly after that he was arrested, and is now in prison."

The witness had no bed or bedding on the ship on his return trip, and slept on a plank. When he got back to America he complained to Donovan and Moroney and through them to the Executive Board of their "culpable neglect." As a result Donovan gave him $10 for his travelling expenses to get home.

The witness went on two more terrorist missions to England with various other dynamiters. "We always bade each other good-bye after each meeting, thinking it might be our last meeting on earth." He had heard that in order to return to America one of his accomplices had to sell his clothes to raise the fare.

The witness knew a dynamiter named Cunningham who had been arrested in England and sent to penal servitude for life. When the witness heard that Cunningham's mother was destitute he complained to John Moroney that it was "shameful." Moroney said he would speak to General Kerwin about it, to which the witness said that if the organisation would not help Mrs. Cunningham he would do so himself. Later General Kerwin came to the witness's home and upbraided him, telling him he ought to be expelled from the Clan-na-Gael for suggesting that the organisation would not help a dynamiter's family. None the less the organisation did nothing. The witness continued to campaign on behalf of Mrs Cunningham, who was finally sent $100 by the Executive Board.

The witness went on making himself unpopular with the senior members of the Clan-na-Gael. Some months later he met a woman in Detroit who told him that the wife of Captain Mackey Lomasney, a dynamiter who was killed in London in 1884, was destitute, and this after Lomasney had been told before going on his mission that if he died his family would never want. The witness began campaigning for Mrs Mackey Lomasney, and "at once $1,025 was raised, and was sent to her in Detroit, where matters were found to be even worse than they had been represented."

The witness then discovered that the relatives of Dr Gallagher, another dynamiter serving a life sentence in England, were in want. The witness raised $100 for Mrs Gallagher.* Then came a statement which indicated that terrorists could expect to be coldly abandoned to their fate if their "heroism" landed them in the dock. "I requested," said the witness, "that the men on trial on

---

* Dr. Gallagher was serving his sentence in Chatham Prison, where he met the American Austin Bidwell, serving life for a fraud on the Bank of England. In his book "From Wall Street to Newgate" (*True Crime Library*, 1996) Bidwell describes the punitive regime of Victorian prisons, which were designed to break a man, and says: "I got to know all the Irish dynamiters – Dr Gallagher, Daily, Eagan and others. They were paying dearly for their zeal in wanting to serve their country. The one I pitied most was poor Gallagher. The strain on his spirit was too great; he soon broke down, and his dejected, forlorn looks, his stooping shoulders and listless walk made me think his days were numbered. He still lived some years later, when I last heard of him, but if he is to breathe the air a free man then his friends must agitate for his release, for he was then slowly sinking into his grave." Dr Gallagher was released in 1896 and found to be insane.

the other side should be defended. General Kerwin said that friendless men were better off in such cases."

Dealing with the allegation that the Triangle packed the Pittsburgh convention with phoney delegates in order to secure favourable votes, the witness said he himself was a delegate to that convention. Just before the convention opened he received a visit from two elected delegates. They told him that despite the fact that they represented eleven districts between them they had been thrown out of the convention in order to seat two nominees of the Triangle, Michael Boland and a man named Miller.

The witness made a protest at the convention, and urged that the two elected delegates should be allowed to take their seats. He also objected to other proxies at the meeting, one of them representing Father Dorney, who was unable to attend "because he was having trouble with his bishop."

The witness was surprised to hear from the platform that District S, which was supposed to be in Australia, had asked by cablegram to be represented by proxies. In fact, the witness claimed, there was a good deal of evidence to suggest that no such cablegram had been sent and no such request had been received, but District S was none the less represented by two proxies, and both of them happened to be friends of Alexander Sullivan and Michael Boland.

Cross-examined by Michael Boland, the witness said that in common with other district delegates he left the convention before it was over, claiming it was not a properly constituted meeting of the organisation.

Michael Boland: "You don't of course know of any operations outside of your own?"

Witness: "That is correct."

Witness No. 2 confirmed the evidence of Witness No. 1 with regard to the organisation's treatment of Mrs Cunningham. In July 1885 Witness No. 2 succeeded John Moroney as a District Member and three months later went out to the West as a regional organiser for the Clan-na-Gael. At the Pittsburgh Convention in November that year several senior members mentioned an "active worker" who was in straitened circumstances, and Witness No. 2 promised to take up the matter. He later spoke to General Kerwin. The general, however, said "he had no power; that this was not an organisation to grant pensions." Witness No. 2 was later referred to Michael Boland, who after at first refusing to do anything then authorised the witness to pay $200.

Witness No. 2 later saw General Kerwin again. "I told him that he should send money to Mrs Cunningham, that the lady was hurt on the subject of being neglected by us. He said he would send it."

Like Witness No. 1, Witness No. 2 objected at the Pittsburgh Convention to the proxies for the Australian District S. When he asked if in fact the Clan-na-Gael had an organisation in Australia he received the fairly startling reply from the Convention Secretary: "There is one in contemplation." Not content with chucking out bona-fide delegates to put in their own men, it seemed, the Triangle actually invented the District of Australia in order to put in two more of their own supporters. The witness said that Boland had voted for the Australian "representatives" to attend the convention, and had personally advised the witness not to oppose their appointment.

Witness No. 3, "a member since the beginning of the old organisation," recalled his friendship with Mackey Lomasney and remembered his departure for England on his last mission in August 1884 with his brother Jim and a third dynamiter, whom he rather quaintly referred to as "Mr So-and-So."

Lomasney's orders were to make reprisals "to avenge wrongs that had been practised on certain Irish leaders." The trial was told that that mission was doomed from the start, for a spy in the organisation relayed Lomasney's orders to Scotland Yard, who arrested him as his ship docked.* In fact, that story was false – Lomasney not only landed safely, but wandered around London for the next four months. The story of his immediate arrest on arrival in England had been circulating in the Clan-na-Gael for some time, although quite a number of the members had refused to believe it. They pointed out that there appeared to be no record in England of his arrest or imprisonment. Lomasney, they concluded, had never left America, and he was probably a traitor to the cause. There were apparently enough incidents in Lomasney's buccaneering life to give colour to these suspicions, so an alternative report of the fate of Lomasney was then published. This said that he had been found one night at his home in Detroit, had been summarily tried and sentenced to "removal." How he was "removed" and what disposition was made of his body was a mystery, for not a vestige of him was ever found. Dr Cronin undoubtedly had this story in the back of his mind as he listened to the witnesses – his notes made it clear that he felt he had to be sure that Lomasney was actually sent on his dynamite mission to England. What is interesting about this is that it shows that even Dr Cronin, a senior official of the organisation, was ignorant of the dynamiter's true fate, which was that in December, 1884, he blew himself and another man to fragments in an attempt to destroy London Bridge.

Mackey Lomasney had a wife and five children and an aged father. After his death his widow's condition was "a most outrageous case of neglect – she was destitute, without coal or clothing, without anything but her poverty and pride, until August 1886." Witness No. 3 saw several senior members of the organisation about her beggared misery, including Michael Boland, who "denied all responsibility" and alleged that Mrs Lomasney had been supplied with plenty of money. Another senior official of the organisation had offered the witness $100 to give to

---

* While it was known in August, 1888, the time of these events, that there was a spy in the organisation, it was not known who he was. Le Caron's role was revealed for the first time at the Parnell Commission in September.

Mrs Lomasney, but the witness refused it and told the official to "do your duty properly."

Answering a question from Dr Cronin, the witness said Mackey Lomasney was "the soul of honour, he despised trickery; he did not care for office and never held any in his life except in danger." In 1887, three years after Lomasney disappeared, his widow was put out on the street.

Witness No. 4 was Mrs Susan Lomasney, the widow of the dynamiter. Alexander Sullivan told the court that she need not be sworn – a request made presumably to show his reliance on the bare word of a dynamiter's wife. Since her husband went away, she said, she had received about $1,000 from the organisation.

In August 1886 she was so hard up that she had to borrow a dress to go and visit Sullivan. "After advising me to sell my little store he asked me for a schedule of my liabilities. I told them they were $200 and he said he would attend to it. At that time he gave me no money nor offered me any." Sullivan told Mrs Lomasney not to mention his name to anyone.

Several weeks after that visit she met Sullivan again and asked him for a loan of $100, which he gave her. That was all the money she ever got from him. Cross-examined by Sullivan she agreed that her husband had written to her from England saying he had received some money from Mr. Sullivan, but she didn't know how much it was. Dr Cronin must have been waiting for this point; here, he noted, Sullivan was actually admitting that Mackey Lomasney was sent to England by the organisation, so that the story of the Detroit execution was a fabrication.

The trial committee heard one more witness after Susan Lomasney, then all six of them went home to write up their reports. Several more weeks were to pass before their verdict was known.

4

THIS MUST REMAIN SECRET!

Three men controlling an organisation of 15,000 members spread across a width of 3,000 miles in an era of undeveloped communications would be a severe test of the best management ingenuity. The Triangle was far from the best, but it inspired a certain respectful awe in its membership – at least until the discovery that most of its decisions were corrupt. After its departure, with the membership configuration remaining unchanged, chaos arrived. The members hurried this way and that, directed by a variety of different voices, including often their own. This lack of cohesion, this absence of any central direction, was nowhere better manifested than in the trial of the Triangle.

Before the trial began it was decided that the verdict would be that of the majority of the committee, who would make their report to the Executive Board. If the minority so wished, however, they too could write a report and submit it to the Executive Board. No provision seems to have been made for a tie. If all six judges agreed on an acquittal there would be no problem, but if all six agreed on a conviction there was no fathoming what the next step might be. They couldn't expel Sullivan, Feeley and Boland because they had already left the organisation. They couldn't take their report to the police, for that would be to declare overtly that while the

Triangle was violating the laws of America, the whole organisation was violating the laws of Great Britain. The Triangle's crimes, which everyone knew had happened anyway, were unpunishable except by public shame within the ranks of Irish-Americans. That was scarcely likely to have much effect on such men, and might ricochet alarmingly on the organisation if they were given a wider airing than the Irish-American fraternity.

Undoubtedly this was the reason why four of the judges – one of whom had actually left the Clan-na-Gael and joined the splinter organisation because of his revulsion over the Triangle's crimes – opted for acquittal. Having heard all the evidence, in the knowledge that there was nothing more they could do they now preferred to bury this revealed blot on their escutcheon and start a fresh page in the history of their organisation.

The minority report, signed by Dr Cronin and Dr McCahey, was for a conviction on the principal charges, and in particular on the charges of "scandalous and shameful neglect of the family of one who lost his life in the service of this Order," and the charge of issuing a fraudulent financial report and squandering the funds.

As Dr Cronin gathered up his thick sheaf of papers at the end of the trial he had already made up his mind what the next stage must be. The majority might wish to acquit the Triangle; nevertheless, he and McCahey would hold out for the evidence, rather than their minority report, to be published in every Camp in the Clan-na-Gael, so that every member would know that the Triangle had robbed the organisation of its members' funds, and robbed brave men of their liberty, and every member could then judge for himself.

"I insist that the evidence is published," Dr Cronin said when the six judges met to consider each other's reports some weeks after the trial.

The four signatories to the majority report, who had decided upon a not guilty verdict, shook their heads. "The matter is now closed," said the chairman. "All the reports are secret. The Executive Board has ruled that they must remain under lock and key."

Dr Cronin stared silently at the floor. Those who imagined that this implied disagreement but acceptance were wrong. The evidence, as set down in his notes and written up in the minority report, was going to be given a very public airing. His intention, he later told friends, was that when the Irish National League assembled in Philadelphia in 1889, he would read a full report of the secret proceedings just concluded, so that everyone would know about the treachery of the Triangle.

* * *

No one who went to the monthly meeting of Camp 20 on Friday February 8th, 1889, expected it to be anything more than a routine assembly. In the chair the "Senior Guardian," John Beggs, 37, welcomed the gathering and was about to launch into the business of the evening when a member named Andrew Foy stood up, cleared his throat, and said he had a suggestion to make.

"It is my belief that there are four British spies in our organisation," Foy began. Just the mention of British spies was enough to break the humming stillness of the meeting-room, freezing the Irishmen into statues. "We cannot continue to function in this manner, with everything we say or do being referred straightway back to London. Therefore I propose that we reorganise this society and give it a new name, and that everyone upon whom rests a taint of suspicion should be expelled and debarred from all contact and association with the body."

Sitting at the back of the hall was Captain Thomas F. O'Connor, a member of the Clan-na-Gael for nearly twenty-five years, and connected with Camp 20 for nearly sixteen years. Six or seven weeks previously Captain O'Connor had paid a visit to Camp 95, Dr Cronin's Camp, and had heard the doctor read a report relating to the trial of the old Executive Committee, the Triangle, with its strong insinuations of corruption and embezzlement. Its disclosures had grieved and angered him.

Now, at this Camp 20 meeting, he knew at once why Andrew Foy was making his proposition and at whom his covert insinuations were directed. The dissolution of the existing order and its reorganisation was being mooted deliberately to cover up any Triangle misdeeds that were likely to be unveiled. Foy – or rather those who had prompted him to make the suggestion – reasoned that if the organisation was dissolved no one would be able to ask awkward questions of it, and the way of getting its dissolution approved was to attack its innocent members, calling them traitors. In one stroke Andrew Foy was branding Dr Cronin and his patriotic friends as British spies, while at the same time doing a whitewash job on the Triangle. And Captain O'Connor didn't think he had to look too far to determine who had put Foy up to it.

As Foy sat down Captain O'Connor rose. He was a big man, the kind whose words came from his heart as well as his lips. Soldier was written in his face, and it told in his bearing.

"I'm not one jot surprised to hear that sort of proposition!" he bellowed from the back of the hall. "I know positively that this organisation is controlled by a clique of rogues known as the Executive Board, or the Triangle, and that they have squandered the funds of this society to the amount of at least $100,000. Not only that, they've sent brave, unselfish men to England, under orders to carry out their projects, and betrayed those same brave men into English prisons.

"And I'll tell you something else, fellow-Irishmen. The English spy Le Caron has been an agent of that same Executive Board, and he has received pay from them. We've no need to break up this organisation and reorganise it. What we need to do is to investigate what the Triangle were up to when they were in office for several years. Like robbing us of our money, of our organisation's funds."

Pandemonium broke out in the meeting-hall. Amid the yells of rage and hate Senior Guardian Beggs, who described himself as a lawyer and was a close friend of Alexander Sullivan, visibly stiffened. The information upon which O'Connor was basing his outrageous claim could have come only from Dr Cronin's minority report, which was secret. No one was supposed to know the result of the deliberations of the Triangle trial committee. Where had this insolent, inquisitive fellow picked this up from? Beggs lay back in his chair and whispered to Detective Dan Coughlin, a committee member sitting next to him, and also a close friend of Alexander Sullivan. Holding up his hand for silence, Coughlin leaned forward and addressed Captain O'Connor tersely.

"I demand to know your authority for the statement you've just made," he said.

From around the room there was a chorus of "Yes! Yes! Give us your authority for it!"

"You demand nothing!" O'Connor roared back. Shaking his finger towards John Beggs, he added, "If you demand that information from me, I'll reply to you."

More angry shouts and counter-insinuations spread rapidly around the hall, while the platform stared at Captain O'Connor with distrustful vigilance. Three times O'Connor shouted above the uproar, asking Beggs to challenge him about the source of his statement. But Beggs stayed silent, refusing to be drawn. Then, "You know my authority for it, all of you up there," O'Connor roared. " I'll tell you of my own free will. I was in another Camp. I heard part of the secret trial report read out to the members. The Camp was Dr Cronin's, and he was on the trial committee."

That was too much for John Beggs. He was a slightly built man with light-coloured hair and a large, light-coloured moustache. He didn't look like the sort who would inspire much fear in others, but that evening there was no mistaking his fury at this indirect assault on his friend Alexander Sullivan. He got slowly to his feet, and the numbness, the rigidity brought on by the taunts, was wearing away quickly, to be replaced by quietly swelling rage.

"I won't have these attacks made on our leadership," he snarled, beginning to shake with animal wrath. His voice rose to a gradual crescendo with its resistance to the wrongs done to the organisation. "There is a core of rottenness, an enemy within, a determination to destroy, among some of the rank and file of this organisation." Ingeniously he twisted his text into all kinds of shapes. "We elected these men and they've done their best and they are doing their best for us and for Ireland. These dirty hole-in-the-wall attacks on their integrity by yellow traitors to our cause must cease." He paused and seemed to compose himself. Quiet rage was his uppermost emotion as he added slowly, vehemently, "They must stop even if it takes blood."

As Beggs sat down, drying his lips with a handkerchief, a mutual, burning sense of injury reddened the room. Dan Coughlin jumped to his feet. "I move through the chair that as stated in the rules the Senior Guardian appoints a committee to investigate this slander of Dr Cronin, and inflict a suitable penalty on him," he shouted.

Caught up in a sudden infection of excitement, the members began to chorus their approval at the tops of their voices. As must now be well known, there was nothing the Clan-na-Gael liked better than a secret committee, a kangaroo court to clear up its more unhealthy problems. Being secret it could be tucked away and forgotten; it would not interfere with their engaging candour, their genial way of tossing their more mundane problems about. The rules, which had been framed by others who also had a love of secret inquiries, authorised the Senior Guardian to appoint a committee and allowed him to keep the names he chose an absolute secret. He could select who he pleased, and no one would be any the wiser.

Amid all the tumult Coughlin's motion was speedily carried, while at the back of the hall Captain O'Connor was already forgotten. Beggs announced that he would appoint the committee by handing a piece of folded paper to each member as he left the room that evening. Four of the papers would have a cross on them, the rest would be blanks. Anyone drawing a paper with a cross was appointed a member of the committee, and should return to the room for a briefing.

So, shortly after the last member filed out, four men came back into the room. The excitement was gone, the atmosphere was now sinister. As they slipped back through the door its hinges did not creak, nor were their steps heard upon the floor. The four men were Daniel Coughlin, Patrick Cooney, Martin Burke, and John Beggs – the Senior Guardian having made sure he retained a marked paper for himself. From the subsequent actions of Coughlin, Cooney and Burke it could be deduced that Beggs had ensured that they too had had marked papers deliberately slipped into their hands. They betrayed no knowledge of this, however, as they listened composed and quiet to Beggs's briefing on his arrangements for the trial committee meeting and the need for secrecy.

Later that night, on his way home, the Senior Guardian began to have second thoughts about the events of that evening. Had he gone too far, he wondered? He knew the full significance and the possible consequences of appointing a trial committee – if they found against Cronin, branded him a traitor to the cause, that meant the doctor would have to die. And the Senior Guardian didn't fancy being so obvious an accessory to murder.

For John Beggs knew that the Chicago police were fully aware of his past. Recalling on his way home that night the events in his life seven years ago, Beggs shuddered involuntarily ...

In the summer of 1882 three Irish informers named Carey, Kavanagh and Farrell told the English police that one of the gang that murdered Lord Frederick Cavendish and Mr T. H. Burke, the Secretary and Under-Secretary for Ireland, in Phoenix Park, Dublin, in May that year* was in hiding in Manchester. He was a man who, they said, held a prominent position in an organisation of militant Irish patriots in Ireland who called themselves the Invincibles. His name was John F. Beggs, an American citizen, born in Lowell, Massachusetts.

By the time Manchester police got on to Beggs's tail they discovered he had left his hiding place two days previously, and was now on his way to America.

The celebrated Manchester detective Inspector Jerome Caminada went to America in pursuit of him and traced him to lodgings in Boston, but when Inspector Caminada arrived there Beggs had left and was on his way back to England. He was next found in Ireland, where an English detective shadowed him for some time. He left Ireland for Manchester again, where Caminada got on his tail, and followed him for six weeks. One Thursday he suddenly disappeared. It was known he had gone to London, and on the following Saturday two explosions occurred in two public buildings in the capital. In the next few days Beggs took lodgings near one of the royal palaces in London and was so closely watched that he evidently became aware of it and hurried off back to Manchester, where he had a number of Irish friends. From there, still hampered by the strict police surveillance and doubtless despairing of it, he left for America, where he was watched by detectives right up to the moment the ship sailed. He had been in America ever since.

He did not exactly go to ground there. A short time after his return he was convicted of theft in Ohio and sent to the penitentiary. He left his wife and went to live with another woman, which in the America of the late Victorian century made him a moral bigamist. He also collected a string of convictions for petty fraud and theft.

Beggs knew that only lack of evidence had prevented

* See Introduction.

his arrest in Manchester; he doubtless also knew that English juries were loath to accept the evidence of informers unless it was corroborated. He knew too that the English police would have passed on all the information they had about him to their American counterparts. His source of course was Senior Detective Dan Coughlin, who would also have counselled him to confine his conspiratorial work for the foreseeable future out of sight of the multitude, for the English would not be likely to forget Phoenix Park in a hurry, and the Americans would not take kindly to a man with his reputation turning to murder on American soil. Now, as he walked to his home at 417 West Madison Street, Chicago, Beggs was frightened. He was suddenly aware of the consequences for himself of the act he had set in motion.

After a sleepless night he wrote to his superior, Edward Spellman of Peoria, who was District Officer of the Clanna-Gael. He told Spellman that the Camp had asked for a secret trial committee, and would the District Officer like to appoint one himself?

Spellman wrote back at once. "Read your constitution," he said. "It authorises the Senior Guardian to appoint trial committees."

Beggs, desperate, wrote again. He said, "There is an unwritten law of the order as well as a written law, and according to the first it devolves on you to appoint this committee. The risk is too great for me, and I will not assume it."

But Spellman, who perhaps did not comprehend the full significance of the trial committee in this instance, flatly refused to be Beggs's tool. He would abide by the constitution.

Beggs was crushed with anxiety. About this time, it was noticed, he began to be closeted for long periods with his friend Alexander Sullivan, sometimes at Sullivan's office, which was in the Opera House block, where Dr Cronin had his second surgery, but more frequently at his home,

No. 378 Oak Street. Possibly these conferences succeeded in strengthening Beggs's resolve; in any event he now shouldered his official burden with no more visible misgivings, and in the middle of February his secret committee began work on the case of Dr Cronin, accused of reading the minority report of the trial committee which had tried the Triangle.

So for the second time Dr Cronin was tried in his absence and behind closed doors by his confrères of the Clan-na-Gael. On the first occasion he was expelled, and later joined the splinter organisation. No report of his second trial, which must have been all over in a couple of hours, has ever been found, but its undoubted conclusions were soon to become terrifyingly self-evident.

MARTIN BURKE

5
THE CARLSON COTTAGE

Real-estateman James Marshall, boss of Knight and Marshall of Chicago, called "Come in" in answer to the knock on his office door. It opened to admit the company's cashier, Edward Throckmorton.

"There's a customer waiting outside, Mr Marshall," Throckmorton said hesitantly. "A Mr J. B. Simmons. He wants to rent the top floor rooms at 117 Clark Street for only a few weeks. I'm wondering if it's wise to let that property for so short a time?"

"Has he seen the place?" Mr Marshall asked.

"The janitor apparently showed him all the rooms on the upper floor before he called on us," Throckmorton explained. "You remember those rooms are arranged for living purposes and we generally rent them to people with families."

"Ask him to come in," Mr Marshall said.

Accustomed to appraising potential customers quickly during the greetings formality, Mr Marshall decided that J. B. Simmons was an ordinary-looking man in comfortable circumstances; medium-sized and fairly well-dressed.

"What I'm looking for is a nice quiet place for a few weeks, and that set of rooms fits my bill," Simmons said. "I've a sick friend who's coming to Chicago for treatment and I need this nice quiet place for him. I'm willing to take the whole floor if the rent isn't too high."

"Can you supply us with the usual references, Mr Simmons?" Mr Marshall asked pleasantly.

"I'm afraid I can't. You see, I'm a stranger in this city. But I can pay cash in advance."

Mr. Marshall studied his blotting pad for a moment. It was near the end of the renting year, and it was tempting to take cash up front for the remaining few weeks. He could make a quick deal, and the firm could lose nothing by it. He did some quick arithmetic, then said, "There are six rooms. I can let you have them for forty-two dollars a month."

"That's all right, then," Simmons replied.

Mr Marshall smiled at his customer, then at his cashier. "Today is February 19th." he said. "Mr Throckmorton will make you out a lease to April 30th."

As soon as the paperwork was finished Simmons took a bankroll from his pocket. It occurred to Throckmorton, unaccustomed to seeing such a large amount of cash being handled in what appeared to him to be a cavalier, almost negligent fashion, that this customer was even better heeled than his appearance suggested. His view was confirmed when Simmons peeled off six bills – four of them ten-dollar bills. While Simmons signed each page of the lease, the observant cashier watched him from the corner of his eye. The customer, he noted, was about five feet seven inches tall, weighed probably around 150 lb, and was about 35 years old. His complexion was neither dark nor fair, he had a rather heavy reddish-brown moustache, his forehead was high and his drab-coloured hair was thin. He wore a dark cutaway coat, dark trousers, a heavy, brown overcoat and a Derby hat.

The description that Mr Throckmorton memorised was one day to prove important because it exactly fitted Patrick Cooney, one of the four members of John Beggs's secret trial committee which had just finished sitting in judgment on Dr Cronin. But on February 19th, the day the lease was signed, Edward Throckmorton had no reason to know that, neither had he any reason to guess that J. B. Simmons was far from being a stranger in Chicago. He had no sick friend; he wanted the rooms because they were exactly opposite the Opera House building where Dr Cronin had his second surgery, and because they were so positioned that anyone living in them could use them as an observation post to see straight into the office of Alexander Sullivan in the same Opera House building.

An hour later Patrick Cooney, alias J. B. Simmons, called at the furniture store of Alexander H. Revell and Co., at the corner of Fifth Avenue and Randolph Street, Chicago. Approached by a salesman, William Hatfield, Simmons asked to see some furniture, carpets, and a large trunk.

"Give me the cheapest kind of furniture you've got," he said. "They're only for temporary use. But I want the trunk to be the very largest you have."

He took the first things he was shown, and did not question the prices asked. Like Edward Throckmorton, Mr Hatfield was impressed when the customer produced his fat roll of large-denomination dollar bills. Everything was listed, and this bill of sale, showing J. B. Simmons's purchases, was retained by the store:

32 yards of carpet at 35 cents		$12.80
1 trunk		$3.50
1 out-door mat		$1.00
1 small hand-satchel		$1.00
1 chamber set		$14.50
1 "solid comfort" spring		$1.50
1 mattress, excelsior top		$2.75
1 pair of pillows		$2.00
1 bowl, pitcher, etc.		$1.35
1 lamp		$0.50
1 comforter		$1.00
1 cane chair		$0.65
1 cane rocker		$1.95
1 trunk strap		$1.00
	Total	$45.50

Mr Hatfield was slightly perplexed because J. B. Simmons couldn't say how large his room was for the carpet, a cheap ingrain. "I guess thirty-two yards will be plenty," Simmons decided, after reflecting upon it.

The salesman was even more perplexed by the answer to his next question, asking where the goods should be sent.

"I don't know," replied J. B. Simmons. "You keep them here and I'll take a memorandum of them."

The reason he didn't know the address was that he had to return later that day to Mr. Marshall's real-estate office to sign the lease on 117 Clark Street. He couldn't have the goods sent to a place which he hadn't yet leased, so he said, "I'll come here tomorrow or the next day and give you my address."

Simmons returned to the furniture shop next day and told Mr Hatfield to deliver his purchases to 117 Clark Street, rooms 12 and 15. The other four rooms, it seemed, would have to remain unfurnished. "Send along a man to put the carpet down," Simmons added.

The day after that he went back to the shop again and said the trunk strap wasn't large enough for his purposes. He was given another, very large and very heavy, for which he paid an additional fifty cents.

The shop's carpenter, Fred Allen, accompanied J. B. Simmons's furniture and household goods to Clark Street. The first thing Mr Allen noticed was that there were two rooms in the building with the number 12. The door of the first one was covered with Turkish characters and was on the second floor. This was not the room occupied by J. B. Simmons. To reach Simmons's suite of rooms Mr Allen had to climb the second staircase. In room No. 15 the carpenter found a short, rather well-built man, with a dark complexion and a close-cropped black moustache. This man who had no noticeable accent in his speech and seemed to be an American, told Mr Allen to go ahead with his work.

The man did not say who he was, but his description

tallied with that of another calling himself Frank Williams, who we shall meet elsewhere in a moment. And the description of Frank Williams exactly fitted Martin Burke, who was also one of the four members of John Beggs's secret trial committee. So now, although no one other than Detective Dan Coughlin and Senior Guardian John Beggs would have been in the know, two members of the trial committee, Martin Burke and Patrick Cooney, were setting up in residence at 117 Clark Street under assumed names, right across the road from Dr Cronin's offices.

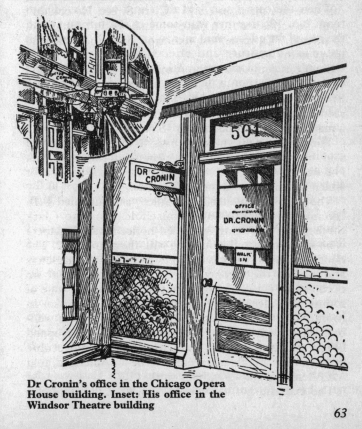

Dr Cronin's office in the Chicago Opera House building. Inset: His office in the Windsor Theatre building

Frank Williams, as we shall call him (since that was his current preference), supervised the laying of the carpet and talked in a friendly fashion to the carpenter Mr Allen. He smoked a cigar, and his amiability even led him to offer the carpenter a cigar too. The carpet proved to be too long by several yards for the room. "I'll cut it off," Mr Allen said.

"Oh, no, don't do that," Frank Williams protested. "Turn it under. I'd much rather have it that way. You see, this is only temporary anyway. I may move at any time."

When the carpet was laid the trunk was moved into room No. 12, together with some of the furniture, and the rest of the effects went into room No. 15. There, with its sparse furniture and effects, and its view of Dr Cronin's office block, we shall leave No 117 Clark Street and move on a month to survey another vacant property for lease, farther out of Chicago at Lakeview.

The house of the iceman Patrick O'Sullivan, whose emissary called so urgently on Dr Cronin on the evening of May 4th, faced east and was surrounded by ample grounds, with a barn and out-houses in the rear. The plot at the back of his residence was vacant, but immediately next to it, facing Ashland Avenue and almost in the rear of Patrick O'Sullivan's house, was an empty cottage, No. 1872 Ashland Avenue.

It was a two-storey structure with a narrow frontage and fenced on all sides. It had six rooms, a large basement and an attic, and it was altogether a gloomy-looking place. Behind it, cramped into this same ill-favoured and ill-savoured patch in an otherwise pleasant neighbourhood, was an even smaller house, the home of Mr and Mrs Jonas Carlson, two elderly immigrants from Sweden who were in such penurious circumstances that their only means of livelihood was the rent of the cottage, which they owned.

John Carlson, the 25-year-old son of the Carlsons who with his wife Annie was staying with his parents, answered the door knock at his father's house on March 20th when a fairly well-dressed man, "who might have been a working man," introduced himself as Frank Williams and asked if the empty cottage was for rent. He was told that it was vacant, that the price was $13 a month. He expressed interest, and John's father, old Jonas Carlson, showed him over the premises. Williams immediately agreed to rent it, paying over his $13.

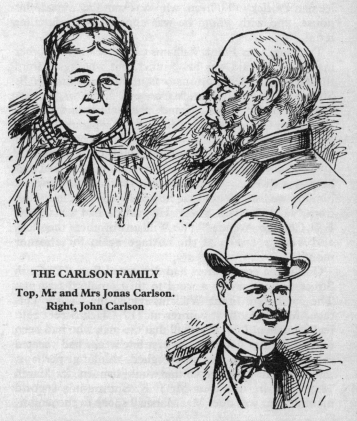

THE CARLSON FAMILY

Top, Mr and Mrs Jonas Carlson.
Right, John Carlson

While old Mr Carlson was making out the receipt in his sitting-room, John Carlson asked Williams what his business or profession was. Annie Carlson, who was also in her father-in-law's sitting-room, remembered that the question didn't suit Williams. "He looked sullenly at my husband, and all of us, and then, lowering his eyes, said, 'I am employed downtown.' I remarked after he'd left that he seemed mad at the question." Both she and her father-in-law noticed that when Williams left he didn't go towards Ashland Avenue but went over to talk to the iceman Patrick O'Sullivan, who was standing outside his house, and with whom he was apparently on familiar terms.

Two days later Frank Williams came back with another man, who he said was his brother, but who again from the Carlsons' descriptions was almost certainly J. B. Simmons (in reality Patrick Cooney), and a wagon carrying a bureau, a wash-stand, a bedstead and several rugs. John Carlson was still staying at his parents' house. He remembered that the driver of the wagon remained seated and did not help the Williams brothers to unload.

"I casually stepped up to the driver and discovered that he was a Swede," young Carlson recalled. "I spoke to him in Swedish. He told me he had brought the furniture from No. 117 Clark Street. He said he had a stand on East Chicago Avenue." The Williams brothers then left, and were not seen at the cottage again for another month.

Oddly, the conspirators had decamped from 117 Clark Street without saying a word to their landlord's agents. The day before Frank Williams rented the Carlson cottage, March 19th, a painter at 117 Clark Street told real-estateman John Marshall that the man who had been renting the top floor for the past few weeks had vacated the premises. Mr. Marshall sighed, thinking, perhaps, that he might have known this would happen, for March 19th was the day that Mr J. B. Simmons's second month's rent was due. Mr. Marshall spoke to the janitor, who didn't know when Mr Simmons had moved out, but the doors were unlocked and the rooms were empty. The janitor thought Mr. Simmons might have been gone three or four days.

As it happened, Mr Marshall had no difficulty in reletting the rooms. Unfortunately for the Chicago police whose eventual task it was to try to make something tangible out of these labyrinthine comings and goings, the name of the quite innocent new tenant at 117 Clark Street was Mr Williams – a name that set all the alarm bells ringing until it was determined that this Mr Williams was nothing to do with Frank Williams.

But why, we may well ask, had the birds flown? What caused Patrick Cooney and Martin Burke – alias J. B. Simmons and Frank Williams – to up sticks from No. 117 Clark Street, carrying probably under cover of night their pathetic bits of cheap furniture, including the over-sized carpet, to some outhouse for a day or two before renting the Carlson cottage? The answer is that the sentence of the secret trial committee on Dr Cronin was that the doctor was to be kidnapped and murdered. A day or two after that decision was taken No. 117 Clark Street was rented either as an observation post or as a murder house, or possibly as both, and subsequently it was found to be unsuitable for either purpose – J. B. Simmons and Frank Williams clearly failing to find any reason to lure Dr Cronin inside. After a few weeks they gave up, rented the Carlson cottage which they thought was a better execution place, and for the next month, during which nothing continued to happen, again failed to devise any kind of plan that would persuade Cronin to come near the place.

It isn't difficult to imagine the storm of criticism that Patrick Cooney and Martin Burke must have been facing from the Clan-na-Gael's murderous conspirators, Alexander Sullivan, John Beggs, Detective Daniel Coughlin and iceman Patrick O'Sullivan – criticism such as, "You've been hanging around in Clark Street a month, and all you've done is spend money on cheap furniture and rent. How long's this going on for?" And after listening to Cooney and Burke's heated excuses for non-action, a suggestion from O'Sullivan, "There's an empty cottage near my house that's much better suited for this job. You'd better get moving there." And then for a month after that more differences of opinion, for it was noticed by sharp-eyed neighbours that although the "Williams brothers" did not physically move into the rented Carlson cottage, they spent a long time going in and out of iceman O'Sullivan's house, mostly at night.

The Carlson cottage

The gossip got to the Carlson family. Old man Carlson was uneasy that his cottage wasn't being occupied. He wanted a reliable tenant, and when one day in mid-April he saw O'Sullivan he told him that the tenant was a strange fellow, not living in the house he had rented.

"I'm worried about my rent and whether he's going to stay," Carlson grumbled.

"Who are you talking about?" O'Sullivan said.

"My tenant Frank Williams. He's a friend of yours."

"I don't know anyone named Williams," O'Sullivan said. "I've never seen your tenant."

"But I've seen you talking to him!" Carlson protested.

At this point Carlson was aware that O'Sullivan rapidly changed tack, and he was certain that the reason was that he told O'Sullivan he had seen him with Frank Williams.

"Ah, your tenant," the iceman said. "Yes, of course. Don't worry about him. He's all right. He'll pay you all right when the month is up."

Mr Carlson went home and told his wife about the

conversation. The two old Swedes sat at their kitchen table ruminating uneasily. Mrs Carlson, an upright and very religious Scandinavian, sensed that something was morally wrong. Although she depended on the rent for her living, she was determined to have only "respectable" tenants; they must not let the cottage again to the "Williams brothers," she said. The previous year, she reminded her husband, they had had an unfortunate experience with a tenant, a Mr King, who had rented the cottage with his wife, or a woman he called his wife. Mr. King was a book-keeper in the city, and she remembered that something must have gone badly wrong with his books, for he was arrested and had only recently been released from the penitentiary. We shall be meeting Mr King presently, for even he has his place in the Dr Cronin saga.

Mrs Carlson was alone in her house when the "Williams brothers" knocked on her door on April 20th, tipped their hats respectfully, and said they had come to pay the second month's rent.

"I'm afraid I can't let you have the cottage any more," Mrs Carlson replied sternly. "I'm putting the place up for sale."

"What's your price?" one of the men asked.

"Three thousand dollars."

"Wow! That's far too much. I wouldn't give you more than $2,500 for it."

Metaphorically wringing their hands, the "Williams brothers" told her that their sister who had been very sick would soon be leaving hospital and it would have been their plan to move her into the cottage, where they hoped with the help of the Almighty she would win back all her good health. For a doorstep tale probably conceived on the spur of the moment it was evidently convincing, for Mrs Carlson relented and the thirteen dollars for the second month's rent was thrust into her outstretched banana fingers.

The Carlsons could scarcely have guessed at that

moment that there never would be a third month's rent, and that in a very short time their cottage was to become the focal point for a mystery that was to set the English-speaking world by the ears.

6
A BLOODY TRUNK

Patrolmen Smith and Hayden, of Lakeview police, were on separate beat duty in Chicago on the night of Saturday – Sunday, May 4th – 5th. They had instructions to meet every so often and to report to each other any unusual happening. Now at 2 a.m., yawning at the fresh black night, they came together at the corner of deserted Clark and Diversey streets, and huddled in the doorway of a store. The beat duty had so far been uneventful and there were still five hours to the chilly dawn. A laggard mist hung over Lake Michigan, a searching, damp cold pervaded the abandoned streets. The two patrolmen had reached that point in their shift when possibly only the Archangel Gabriel might have thought it was fun to be a Chicago cop on weekend night duty.

Smith cocked his head on one side. "Listen!" he said.

From down the empty ribbon of Clark Street came the furious rumble of a wagon, seemingly being driven northwards at high speed. Smith stepped out from the shadows to the edge of the pavement, for officers of Lakeview were under instructions to hail passing vehicles and prowlers after midnight. But when the wagon came into view it was travelling so fast that Smith's attempt to flag it down went unheeded; in the darkness, and at the rate they were going, the occupants, Smith thought –

wrongly as it turned out – might not have seen him. But Patrolman Smith had time to notice four things as the wagon raced noisily past him. The vehicle, he thought, was an old "carpenter's wagon;" it was being pulled by an old bay horse; there were three men in it; and behind them was a large trunk.

"What did you make of that?" Smith said to Hayden. "I reckon it's mighty suspicious."

Hayden shrugged. The only reason he could think why a wagon was being driven at high speed down an empty street in the middle of the night was that its occupants were tired after a long day and wanted to get to bed. The two policemen went off on their separate beats again, and an hour and a half later, at 3.30 p.m., they met for the second time that night at the corner of Clark and Diversey streets. They had been there only a minute or two when Smith again cocked his head on one side and bade his fellow-officer listen.

"It's another wagon," Smith said. "It's coming from the opposite direction."

A wagon in Clark Street in the small hours of Sunday morning was rare but not extraordinary. This time Patrolman Hayden moved to the edge of the pavement to look at the vehicle, travelling southwards towards the centre of Chicago, as it clattered furiously past them – he did not attempt to stop it, nor, he thought afterwards, would he have been able to. He had time to notice that it was the same "carpenter's wagon," that it had only one occupant, the driver, and the same old bay horse was pulling it.

The officer noticed too that the driver wore a soft hat. He was young and muscular. There was no name on the wagon. Officer Hayden saw all this, and although he couldn't get a good look at the man he distinctly remembered that this time there was no trunk in the wagon.

Before the two officers split up again for another solitary spell of beat work and again when they came together for a third time that night, Patrolman Smith expressed his concern about the wagon. There was something fishy about it, he insisted, and they ought to report it. But why, Hayden challenged him. What could they report about a wagon travelling fast in the middle of the night? Smith saw the point, but remained unconvinced.

A few hours later, at 7.30 a.m. on Sunday morning, Alderman Chapman of Lakeview was driving along Evanston Avenue, between Graceland Cemetery and the German Catholic Cemetery, when at a lonely spot five hundred yards from Sultzer Street he saw three men standing around a trunk which stood at the back of a bush, with one end thrust into the ditch which ran near the road.

Chapman reined in his horse and got out of his buggy. The cover of the trunk had been forced open. The interior was spattered with blood and partially filled with

**The bloody trunk
found in a ditch**

73

absorbent wadding, which in turn was saturated with gore. Chapman drove to Lakeview police station and reported his find, prompting Police Captain Francisco Villiers and a couple of his men to jump into a patrol wagon and head for the spot where the trunk lay. When they arrived they found a large crowd of gaping men and boys who had trampled down the grass in every direction. The trunk was taken back to the police station, where Captain Villiers placed his notebook alongside it and began to examine it.

There probably wasn't a more qualified man in all the state of Illinois to make that examination, for Captain Villiers had once practised as a doctor, although why this qualified doctor had become a police captain has never been passed down to us. It didn't take long for him to decide that a grown person had been murdered, thrust into the trunk, and then carted to the spot between the two cemeteries. The trunk was new and large, and a man six feet tall could be cramped into it. The captain summoned a trunk-dealer to the station to see if he could throw any light on its provenance. The trunk, the dealer decided, was made in either Racine or Milwaukee, both neighbouring townships. It was a cheap model, so cheap and so new it was probably bought for the purpose for which it had been used.

Subtly combining his medical knowledge and his talent as a sleuth, Captain Villiers decided that the trunk had been locked after the body had been placed in it, and the cotton wadding had been packed about the victim's wounds in order to staunch the flow of blood; this was doubtless to ensure greater safety while the trunk was being carried from place to place. Before the body was removed the lock of the trunk had been broken by two sharp blows with a blunt instrument. The marks of these blows were on both sides of the lock. In their haste to remove the body the murderers had thrown back the cover with such force that one of the sheet-iron hinges was broken.

Villiers picked out the cotton wadding and carefully examined it. Some of the absorbent material was still soft with blood, and there was a good deal of fresh blood in one corner of the trunk.

"My examination of the bloodstained wadding leads me to believe the murder must have been committed some time after midnight," he wrote in his notebook.

Embedded in a piece of wadding he found a lock of dark brown hair, which was almost as fine as a woman's, "but not so glossy," he noted. In those pre-forensic medicine days, this was the only tangible clue to the identity of the victim. The police captain put the lock of hair under a microscope and found it was filled with blood and particles of cotton. The hair had not been pulled out of the scalp, rather, it looked as though it had been chopped off with a blunt instrument. All the hairs were uneven in length and seemed as if they might have come off the cranium near the forehead.

The inside of the trunk lid was spattered with blood. Some of it had trickled down the exterior of the trunk, presumably when the body was dragged out on to the ground. There were no marks on the trunk, and apart from the lock of hair, absolutely no means of identifying the victim.

There was plenty of room for guesswork, though. And when a one-line report arrived that afternoon from East Chicago Avenue police station that Dr Patrick Cronin was reported missing from his home Captain Villiers put two and two together. The wadding in the trunk was just the sort of stuff a doctor would use, and Chicago was still a small enough town for Villiers to know Dr Cronin, and to know that the doctor had plenty of enemies in the Irish-American fraternity, where he was a zealous worker. The missing occupant of the trunk, the police chief decided, must be Dr Cronin, and he must have been murdered.

Captain Villiers ordered all his available officers to search the vicinity where the trunk had been found, confident that they would find the body nearby. All that Sunday evening police searched the empty houses, and the brush and prairie on the outskirts of Chicago for miles around. They discovered that so many people had trampled the grass at the place where the trunk was found that if any vehicle tracks had been left they were now entirely obliterated. Evanston Avenue was so well paved that a search for tracks along that much-travelled road was useless. The officers swarmed over the two nearby cemeteries. They studiously examined three boards of a fence which had come down in Argyle Street, but could find no evidence that they had been ripped out by murderers for the purpose of helping them to remove a body. When darkness fell they had failed to find a corpse; indeed, they had not found as much as a drop of blood or a particle of cotton.

When Captain Villiers demanded to know who had been first to discover the trunk, even that question couldn't be answered. One man whom he saw said the trunk was not along the Evanston road at six o'clock that morning. Alderman Chapman was the first person to report the discovery but he said there were others who told him they had been an hour at the spot before he came along in his buggy. So at eight o'clock that Sunday evening it was a fairly frustrated police captain who signed in Patrolmen Smith and Hayden as they came on duty for their night shift.

As soon as he entered the captain's office and saw the bloody trunk on the table Patrolman Smith exclaimed, "That's the trunk we saw last night!"

Villiers's jaw dropped. "You saw *what*?" he gasped. "Sit down, officer, and start talking."

Patrolman Hayden was equally convinced that the trunk was the same and as the two officers told their story of the encounter at the corner of Clark and Diversey streets Villiers now positively bubbled with excitement. He was already certain that the crime of the century was as good as solved. He might not yet have the

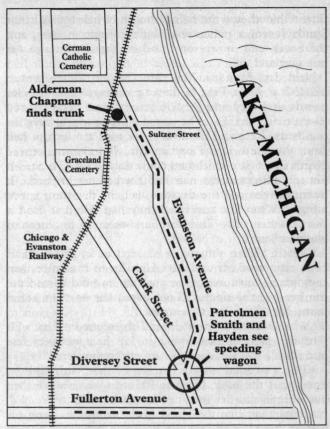

Route of speeding wagon ▬ ▬ ▬ ▬

corpse, but he would soon have that wagon. While the weary search-party was accordingly redirected to find the vehicle and its occupants the ex-doctor turned police chief looked again at the bloody cotton wadding and then came up with an amazing hypothesis – Dr Cronin, he said, must have received only one wound, inflicted at the base of the brain. He came to this conclusion because of the small amount of absorbent cotton used to stop the flow of blood, and the ragged bunch of hair found in the trunk. It was a remarkable finding, since at this point there was really no reason to believe that Dr Cronin was not alive and well.

Next day, Monday, May 6th, Captain Villiers was at his desk at dawn. First he drew up orders to have the clay ponds at Perry and Argyle streets and Wrightwood Avenue dragged. Later he issued more orders to drag the ponds in Graceland Cemetery. He took the lock of hair from the trunk to the barber, Mr. Hal Garsch, of 474 North Clark Street, who regularly shaved Dr Cronin. Mr Garsch examined the hair and then shook his head. It definitely was not the doctor's hair, he declared, it was altogether too fine and much too long. He had cut the doctor's hair only Thursday last week, so his memory was excellent.

Captain Villiers refused to be deterred by this setback. He summoned Mr and Mrs Conklin to his office, and they were almost as positive that the hair did come from the head of the doctor. Told about the barber's statement, Mrs Conklin was scornful.

"What does he know about it?" she scoffed. "That's Dr Cronin's hair, or exactly like it. His hair was very fine and silky. I tell you, captain – he's been murdered!"

Villiers needed no convincing of that, although he knew that the basic forensic facilities which were then available in murder investigations were able to establish no more than that the blood in the trunk was probably human blood, and that the hair was definitely human hair.

When Monday dawned the story of the disappearance of Dr Cronin and the discovery of the bloody trunk was front-page news in the Chicago press. Already Villiers at Lakeview and Schaack at East Chicago Avenue were caught in that unenviable trap that frequently looms early on in most big investigations – few clues and mounting media pressure to get something done. It must have seemed to them that half of Chicago had turned journalist or sleuth. Dr Cronin was immensely well known and popular in the burgeoning city; consequently Lakeview was swarming with the solicitous, the inquisitive and the gruesome searching sewers, mud-puddles and smelly ditches for his body. The methods used by the genuine policemen among the searchers were indistinguishable from those used by the amateurs; one observer noted two officers digging away at a mud-hole "that would not have offered a chance of concealment for the body of a small dog. It seemed to afford them satisfaction that they were doing something, whether it resulted in anything or not."

The muddle and indecision which prevailed among the police was undoubtedly aggravated by their being thrust suddenly into a big mystery for which they were singularly unprepared. At Lakeview Captain Villiers was on the point of retiring from the force and handing over the case, as well as all his other work, to his successor, Captain Wing, who was at once told to pass over the inquiry to Captain Schaack and his central Chicago men. Schaack, who was stuck with the basic mentality of a beat policeman, was bewildered by the speed of it all. One result of the confusion was that nothing was done, no decision was taken, without the whole town being instantly aware of it. When for instance Lakeview police turned over the trunk and its contents of crimson cotton wadding to the Chicago detectives the trunk was brought down from Lakeview police station in a patrol wagon followed by a flitting and whistling crowd described by a newspaper as "morbidly curious males and females of all ages and stations, all of whom feasted their eyes on the receptacle which is believed to have shielded one of the most mysterious crimes with which the Chicago police have grappled."

At East Chicago Avenue station the trunk was placed on a table. Schaack looked inside it, sniffed, and opined philosophically, "It might be blood or it might not. It might be human hair or it might not." His assistant,

Lieutenant Hermann Schuettler, another police officer of German ancestry but with a larger complement of brains than his boss, was more specific. "If it isn't blood," he said, "I'll drink it. If you ask me, that cotton wadding was put in there to absorb the blood and keep the trunk from leaking. I'll lay a bet there was a body in this trunk."

"Well, where is it then?" Schaack rejoined. He watched indifferently as Schuettler extracted a tuft of hair from the trunk and slid it into an envelope. But the captain was now having to admit that Dr Cronin was missing in peculiar circumstances. He was having to admit this because egged on by the Chicago press, who had descended on the Conklins, half Chicago had decided in common with Captain Villiers that the doctor had been murdered. When the story of the discovered trunk was juxtaposed with the report of an interview with the Conklins the result was clear beyond question to everyone except Captain Schaack – Cronin had been abducted, murdered, stuffed into the trunk and later the trunk, suddenly emptied, was abandoned. But why had the murderer gone to the bother of putting the body in a trunk and then carrying both trunk and body several miles out of town? Why had the trunk been left empty in a place where it was bound to be found in a very short time? Why had the body been taken away, if there ever was a body? With these questions still unanswered Captain Schaack took one of the several bizarre decisions in the Cronin affair for which he was later to be brought to strict account. He called off the entire investigation on the grounds that there was no evidence to follow up.

For the next few days officers who had been working on the case were transferred to other jobs and the Cronin case remained on the non-active file. Schaack remained indifferent as the clamour from press and public rose to a shrill crescendo. Then as dramatically as it had been stopped, the investigation was reopened when a man walked into Chicago's West Twelfth Street police station and said to the desk officer, "My name is Frank

Woodruff. I was the driver of the wagon everyone is talking about. Dr Cronin wasn't in that trunk."

The story Woodruff told was remarkable. He had hired the wagon and the horse from a man named Dean – not to be confused with Paddy Dinan – whose stables were on Webster Avenue, and on the instructions of a friend, Dick Fairburn, he had driven it to a barn at 528 State Street, where Fairburn asked him to load a trunk on to the wagon. There were two other men at the barn, one named William King [this was supposed to be the same King who rented the Carlson cottage before Frank Williams] and the other a brawny fellow referred to by his companion simply as "Doc." Woodruff remembered that as he loaded the trunk King said to him, "If we had let Tom alone, Doc, you'd be in the trunk as well as Allie." Woodruff had no idea who Tom or Allie were, or what the conversation meant. But it made him look twice at the trunk, which he said was partly opened and had enough of its contents revealed to show that it contained the body of a woman.

Woodruff drove the wagon with the trunk and Fairburn and King on board to Lincoln Park. There Fairburn and King got down from the wagon, took the woman's body from the trunk, walked along a path with it and threw it into one of the park's lakes. Back at the wagon they told Woodruff that they were returning to their homes on foot, but before they went they instructed him to drive off with the trunk and dump it somewhere on the Lakeview prairie. Woodruff drove northwards alone, and the place he chose to abandon the trunk was the place where it was found near Argyle Avenue early on Sunday morning.

Again, questions jostled to be answered. Who was this woman? Why should the three men leave the trunk where they must have known it would be found within a few hours? Why didn't they break it up and burn it? Woodruff was unable to help in any of these matters, claiming that he was simply acting under instructions. It seemed to the police officers who interrogated him that the men either did not have any sort of plan, or they intentionally left the trunk where it was found. The majority agreed that the second explanation was most likely, and that the trunk was some kind of a blind. That did not explain away the human blood, though.

Woodruff, Fairburn and King were all known to the police. Woodruff, who used the alias Frank Black, was born in Canada, educated in Michigan, and some years previously had murdered a man in Mexico. His last-known job was as a freight brakeman on the Hamilton and Ontario Railroad. Fairburn, who had been arrested in Chicago for vagrancy, had occasionally assumed the alias of Neil White after the original owner of that name had been sent for a long term to a Colorado penitentiary. Woodruff claimed to be very much afraid of Fairburn. William King had recently completed a short term of imprisonment for defrauding his employer – the catalyst which had obliged him to surrender the tenancy of the Carlson cottage. Woodruff told the police that in addition King was once a member of a gang headed by a man named Carr, who was then doing a long prison stretch in a western state.

Woodruff was shown three trunks, including the bloody one, and identified the right one without difficulty or hesitancy, and he also took the police to the exact spot where the trunk was found. During the course of that day Mr Dean, the owner of a livery stable from which Woodruff had taken the horse and wagon, laid a charge that Woodruff had stolen the rig. Apparently after his mission for his two confederates Woodruff had tried to sell the horse to one John Green "for a ridiculously low price." For this piece of horse-thieving Woodruff was taken before Justice Doyle, who after hearing the evidence of Mr Dean and Mr Green fixed bail at $1,000. Woodruff was kept in custody, and while he waited for his father and brother to come and bail him out he continued to be closely interrogated.

He was asked if he would be able to identify the man called 'Doc' from a photograph, and he claimed that he would. He was shown a bundle of about a dozen pictures, among which was a photograph of Dr Cronin. He looked at them carefully and said he didn't recognise any of them.

He was asked, "How do you know that Dr Cronin's body wasn't in the trunk?"

"Because the body was that of a woman," Woodruff replied.

"Did you see her face?"

"No."

"How do you know it was the body of a woman then?"

"I saw one of her hands. It was a plump and very white hand, considerably smaller than that of an average woman."

"How big was the woman?"

"I should think she weighed about 130 pounds. She certainly didn't weigh over 140 pounds. Dr Cronin wasn't in that trunk."

"Did you ever see Dr Cronin?"

"I never did."

"Is it not a fact that you know whose body was in that trunk?"

"I don't know whose body it was but I know Dr Cronin is still alive."

"How do you know that?"

"I know the body was that of a woman, and that Cronin was not connected with that trunk, and – and – well, that's why I'm sure he's alive."

With the whole city in the grip of trunk fever, the much-confused police were bound to be pushed into decisions and statements they might regret. Captain Schaack appointed Inspector Ebersold to lead inquiries on the ground, and the doughty inspector spent a whole day looking around the spot where the trunk was found. The inspector's day caused great excitement among loitering journalists, who were as desperate for something to happen as were the police. The extent of that desperation

on both sides can be read between the lines in the newspaper reports. Avid readers learned after Inspector
Ebersold's day in the country that his investigations
resulted in finding an important clue to the mystery. What
the nature of the clue was, however, the inspector wasn't
prepared to say. "It may amount to nothing," he said, "but
I think that it will in all probability substantiate the story
told by Woodruff and give us something definite in regard
to the contents of that trunk." Out of this sort of waffle
banner headlines and front-page scoops were created.

The *Chicago Herald* reported: "More testimony corroborative of the sensational confession of Woodruff was
gathered by Captain Schaack and his detectives yesterday, and they were of the opinion last night that they
were on the eve of discoveries that would lead to a
clearing up of the mystery of the trunk." All this was
essentially false rhetoric. The police hadn't even the
faintest lead on the contents of the trunk, and many officers were deeply suspicious of Woodruff. At East
Chicago Avenue station policemen were divided on those
who believed the new witness and those who thought he
was a hoaxer. One of those who didn't believe Woodruff
and who disliked him on sight was Lieutenant Schuettler.

Rummaging through the investigation file, Schuettler
found the statement made by Mr T. T. Conklin when he
reported Dr Cronin missing on Sunday May 5th. It was
full of assumptions and accusations, and the one name
that cropped up constantly was Alexander Sullivan, who,
Mr Conklin alleged, was dedicated to killing Dr Cronin.
There wasn't a jot of evidence in this statement against
Sullivan, but Schuettler was intrigued that the man Mr
Conklin was accusing had his office in the Opera House
block, the same building as one of Dr Cronin's two surgeries. The lieutenant also knew that if he questioned
Sullivan, who was a lawyer and knew all the angles, he
would be laughed at.

Schuettler decided that his best course of action was a
highly improper one. He would have to flout the law in

an attempt to get at the truth. Using a skeleton key, late at night and without a search warrant, he let himself into Sullivan's office. Pulling the blinds, he lit a lamp and went to work, opening filing cabinets and rifling through the lawyer's letters.

Schuettler's German background gave him neither any understanding nor much interest in the complexities of the Irish-American movement. What he read made no great sense to him, although he soon understood that Alexander Sullivan was the treasurer of an organisation called the Clan-na-Gael, and that Dr Cronin was an official of the society. Reading on, he discovered that Patrick O'Sullivan, the iceman whose call had brought Dr Cronin from his surgery in the evening of May 4th, was also a member, as was Detective Dan Coughlin, a member of Schuettler's own East Chicago Avenue police force. There was evidently big trouble in the organisation, and Alexander Sullivan and Dr Cronin were at the centre of it. Digging deeper, Schuettler found a list of the entire membership of the Chicago camp of the Clan-na-Gael, and among the names listed there was one Philip Finucane.

Here was a real stroke of luck for Schuettler, for he knew Finucane well. The Irishman was a petty crook whom Schuettler had arrested several times. Finucane would talk confidentially, because he knew Schuettler would make things tough if he didn't.

Closing the last filing cabinet and extinguishing the light, the lieutenant crept soundlessly out of the Opera House block. Next morning he went to see Finucane, who was working in a laundry and on sight of Schuettler instantly claimed to have adopted the straight and narrow path for ever.

"Philip," Schuettler said, brushing aside the Irishman's protests of innocence. "I want you to tell me everything you know about the Clan-na-Gael."

Slowly, hesitantly, Finucane went through the great quarrel, the charges of embezzlement and theft, the secret trials, accusations and counter-accusations. Finucane was certain Dr Cronin was a subversive element in the organisation, if not a British spy. He knew that a secret committee of clansmen had put Cronin on trial; more than that, as a mere rank-and-file member, he did not know. At the end of the interview Schuettler had learned enough to conclude that Dr Cronin had been murdered by the Clan-na-Gael, and that Frank Woodruff was a liar who for some reason not yet apparent had been put up to his story by the murderers.

Meanwhile, following a more orthodox line of investigation, Captain Schaack ordered his men to find Fairburn and King, Woodruff's nocturnal accomplices in the disposal of the trunk. From Woodruff himself they learned that William King had been keeping company with a Miss Maud Preston, living on Center Avenue. Miss Preston told officers who called on her that she had separated from King after a quarrel. She said she had not seen him for a long time, which was at odds with Woodruff's story that King had been with her very recently. Miss Preston then gave a description of King, which was so different from that given by Woodruff that they suspected she was trying to cover up her lover's tracks.

The day after Woodruff's arrest, Captain Schaack took the prisoner in a buggy, with two other officers following in a second buggy, over the entire route he claimed to have taken the previous Sunday morning. He guided the officers to Dean's stable on Webster Avenue to the barn at State Street, on to Lincoln Park, and thence to Argyle Avenue. The time taken by the expedition was carefully noted, and it agreed with all the statements previously made by Woodruff.

"He has been persistent in the most trivial details as to time, localities and persons," intoned the *Chicago Herald*, whose reporter accompanied Schaack, "and if, as some people believe, he has been hoodwinking the police, he has done it with a most ingenious romance."

All this began to look sad sack when the very next day

an enterprising Chicago detective named Rohan established beyond peradventure that Dick Fairburn, alias Neil White, was 500 miles away from Chicago and had been that far distant from the city for the past four weeks. It suddenly appeared after all that Woodruff had been hoodwinking the police, and not so much with romantic ingenuity as with crass naiveté.

But did some of what he said contain elements of truth? The question was asked because Detective Rohan's discovery was followed by a report from a Mr Anderson, living on Diversey Avenue. Mr Anderson had a business hiring out rowing-boats on Lake Michigan. Late on Saturday night, May 4th, he left Boat No. 12 securely fastened to the breakwater only a few hundred yards away from the spot where Woodruff said that Fairburn and King lifted the body of their victim from the trunk. Early on Sunday morning Mr Anderson found that his boat had been stolen, and he had had no tidings of it since.

That was enough for Chicago police to discontinue dragging the Lincoln Park lakes and convince themselves on the basis of Mr Anderson's testimony that the body of the woman alleged to have been inside the trunk in Lincoln Park must have been taken out and sunk to the bottom of Lake Michigan, and not one of the park's lakes. When Captain Schaack's leg-weary, muddied men heard the news they cheered with relief. Dragging the park lakes was filthy, exhausting work, and they had long since given up any hope of finding a body there.

Still bent on his one-man mission, Lieutenant Schuettler, now armed with his sample of hair he had taken from the trunk, called on the Conklins. When he showed it to Mrs Conklin she identified it at once. She had seen it before – she had no doubt that it was Dr Cronin's. As if to underline the veracity of her statement she then fainted in her husband's arms.

As he drove back to East Chicago Avenue police station Schuettler pondered the evidence so far. It intrigued the lieutenant that the white horse was seen only once, by Mrs Conklin and by Frank Scanlan, outside Dr Cronin's home – and that a different horse, a bay, was seen by Patrolmen Hayden and Smith cantering down Clark Street with the trunk in a wagon now thought to have been driven by Frank Woodruff. Reporting back to Schaack, Schuettler said, "It could be the two horses were used deliberately so as to leave as few clues as possible, and in that case the white horse might have been hired too. Shouldn't we get someone to check the livery stables?"

Schaack grunted. He didn't want to waste any more men on this line of inquiry, because he still implicitly believed Woodruff. But he knew that if he didn't get on with it the press would be on his back again. He couldn't ask Schuettler to check the stables, because the lieutenant now wanted to go off and interview the ice-dealer Patrick O'Sullivan. He ran his eye down the duty roster, and his eye fell on the name of a detective who had just booked in on duty.

"All right," he said."I'll put Detective Dan Coughlin on to it. I'll have him check out this hair again too."

Schuettler said nothing. He recalled that Coughlin was a member of the Clan-na-Gael, but he could scarcely tell his boss how he had found that out. He had no reason anyway to suspect Coughlin, who was a loyal and diligent cop.

The lieutenant found Patrick O'Sullivan in his office smoking a cigar, his feet on his desk. O'Sullivan guessed at once why the officer was calling. "The whole thing's a mystery to me," the iceman said, keeping his feet on the desk. "Sure I had a contract with Dr Cronin to handle all my accident cases, but I didn't call him on Saturday night because there was no accident."

Schuettler produced the card he had obtained from the Conklins.

"Anyone could have got that, lieutenant," O'Sullivan said. "I leave my cards at stores and saloons all over town. They're my customers."

Schuettler described the mysterious stranger who had summoned the doctor from his surgery, but O'Sullivan said he didn't know the man, nor did he understand how the man knew about his agreement with Dr Cronin. The lieutenant left the ice-dealer's office as puzzled as when he had arrived.

Detective Dan Coughlin arrived back at Captain Schaack's office at East Chicago Avenue station only minutes after Schuettler. The detective had had no success in locating the white horse. He had also taken the lock of hair back to Dr Cronin's barber, Hal Garsch. "He's positive it isn't Cronin's hair," he said. "He says Cronin's hair is darker and not so fine as this."

"But Mrs Conklin says it is Cronin's hair," Schuettler pointed out, aggrieved.

"Who'd be more likely to know," Coughlin asked, "his landlady or the man who's been cutting his hair for nine years?"

"The barber, of course!" laughed Schaack triumphantly. But Schuettler was not so sure.

Dan Coughlin said, "The whole thing's a big hoax, if you ask me. I don't think Cronin's dead at all. If he was murdered his killer would have to be crazy to dump the trunk on open ground next to a graveyard where anyone could find it. Take that together with the business of the hair, and it seems to me that Cronin wanted to disappear and cooked up all this nonsense himself."

"Why would he want to disappear?" Schuettler asked

"He could have had all sorts of reasons. Perhaps he got tangled up with a woman, perhaps he owes money. But I reckon he's alive and well right now."

"I think so too," Schaack nodded. The idea that he might have sufficient reason to call off the investigation a second time and get back to the easy life of routine work was crossing his mind. "We're all being taken for a ride."

Looking from one to the other in bafflement Schuettler began to think that perhaps he was the one being taken for a ride. Schaack he knew as slow-witted and indolent, but Dan Coughlin had a brain and was quick-thinking. He was also a member of the Clan-na-Gael – something Coughlin did not yet know that Schuettler knew. Yet here he was about to wash his hands on the whole affair. How much did Detective Coughlin really know, the lieutenant wondered. The captain and the detective got up and left the room, leaving Schuettler alone with the trunk. He picked it up, turned it over, turned it on its side, looked carefully at the bloodstained lining. Then he saw something which amazingly everyone had missed. Inside one of the fabric pockets was a label with the name Alexander R. Revell and Co., a furniture house on Fifth Avenue and Randolph Street, Chicago. Schuettler took out his notebook and scribbled down the address.

If the lieutenant felt he had found an important clue in the investigation he was soon to be disabused of that idea. For next day came a report that had most of Chicago rejoicing. Dr Cronin had been found. He was alive and well, and staying in Toronto.

What price the bloody trunk now?

7

OUR MAN IN CANADA

Ananias Long, the Canadian journalist who claimed to be the first man to find Dr Cronin a week after the doctor had disappeared, jubilantly filed his scoop to the *Toronto Empire*, where it was published on May 11th. In it Dr Cronin told Long that he walked out of his surgery and fled from Chicago on the evening of Saturday, May 4th, because for some time his health had been declining. "I thought it would do me good to take a trip," he said. When Long pressed him, pointing out that most of Chicago's leading citizens were in a pother over his sudden disappearance, he changed his story. He left the city, he said, because he was convinced that certain people were out to murder him. He travelled all that weekend, arriving on Monday evening in Montreal, where he took a room at the St. Lawrence Hall Hotel and got his meals at the house of a friend whose name he refused to divulge.

His intention was to book a sea passage to France, but there were no ships leaving the port for anywhere in Europe. He thought of going to New York and taking a ship from there, but decided not to risk it because he was too well known in New York, and might be seen.

Then, he said, he received word that it was known or at least suspected by those in Chicago who were out to kill him that he was in Montreal. Fearing for his life, he fled from the city and travelled to Ottawa, where he booked in at the Russell Hotel under an assumed name and giving a New York address.

He left Ottawa almost at once, he said, "because the town was so small that I was afraid someone might get to know me." He took the Canadian Pacific train for Toronto, arriving there on Friday morning, at about nine o'clock, almost a week after he had vanished from Chicago. He knew a lawyer in Toronto who he thought might be able to help him.

Dr Cronin, reported in the somewhat pretentious prose style of nineteenth-century journalism, told Long: "When I lived in St Louis I moved in the very upper crust of society and promptly identified myself in the Irish cause then disturbing the public mind. I worked in that city as a druggist, and soon got to the front rank. Meanwhile, I studied medicine and eventually passed my exams.

"I soon found that the great Irish field was to be entered either at Chicago or New York and after consulting my friends I decided to go to Chicago. I was armed with the very best letters of introduction a man ever had, and soon found myself prominent in Irish as well as other circles there."

He then went on to say that he soon discovered that large quantities of money being received by Alexander Sullivan, Dr O'Reilly of Detroit, John O'Brien of New York, and Patrick Egan, were not being handled properly, and that not more than three-quarters of it ever reached Ireland.

"I know," he said, "that at least $85,000 was gobbled up by certain persons in Chicago and when I began to 'call the turn' on them they tried to scare me off and, finding that a failure, they tried to bribe me. That wouldn't work, so their next move was to introduce me to a man who called himself Beach but who in fact was Le Caron, a British spy. He got nothing out of me, though, so that means failed.

"I had been warned several times to get out of the

country by friends, who told me my life was in danger, but up to last Saturday I thought I could hold my own. Last Saturday, however, I was put in possession of unquestionable proof that the Clan-na-Gael society had decided that my life should be taken. A man was appointed my executioner and preparations were in active progress to accomplish the deed. Enough to say, I made up my mind at once to fly."

Long asked him, "Did you plan for a man to call at your surgery in Chicago and ask you to go out to the ice house to attend a patient?"

"I won't answer that," the doctor replied.

What was his next move, now he was in Toronto? The doctor at first refused to answer that too, then said he intended to take ship for France as soon as possible.

"I left some very important documents behind in Chicago," he said. "I only hope that I can get to a country where I will be safe. Then I will make some disclosures that will open the eyes of the public generally and make the hair stand on the heads of several Chicago and New York gentlemen.

"The Conklins have made fools of themselves over the whole matter. According to the instructions I left with them, they should not have opened their mouths until I was safely out of the country. But it is the same old story. Tell a woman anything and you are sure to get the worst of it."

In answer to a question from Long, Dr Cronin agreed he had taken one trip out of Toronto since his arrival, to Hamilton. He agreed too that he was on the train in the company of a lady named Alice Brown but "she was quite unknown to me. She happened to be going to Buffalo on the same train I took out of Toronto and I left her at Hamilton." He was also asked about a man with whom he was seen in Yonge Street, Toronto. This, said Cronin, was a chance acquaintance; they had talked briefly, and the man had said he was on his way to Winnipeg.

Some of this was true, declared Long, and some was

false. It was true that the woman Alice Brown seen with the doctor was going to Buffalo. But Long himself had followed the male "chance acquaintance" to Collingwood, a small town 100 miles north of Toronto, and had questioned him. The man said he had no intention of going to Winnipeg, and refused to make any further comment.

The thrust of the report was tilted against Dr Cronin. It made him seem pompous in his speech, evasive in his conduct and captious with his complaints. The scornful attack on the Conklins, for instance, seemed like a vicious stab in the back for old friends. Clan-na-Gael members reading the story would have remembered that they had been told the doctor was a womaniser and would have smiled at the woman on the train, assuming perhaps that the nasty Cronin was up to his old tricks again. The "chance acquaintance" who was unidentified emerged in Long's report as a sinister figure, the type of man with whom Dr Cronin could be expected to keep company. "He [the chance acquaintance] is decidedly quiet and refuses to give an account of himself," the story hinted darkly. The complaint that not more than three-quarters of Clan-na-Gael funds reached Ireland would have appeared to be carping since it could be held that the other twenty-five per cent was a fair amount to cover administrative expenses. Altogether, *Toronto Empire* readers might have imagined when they had finished reading the story that an unpleasant man had come among them, a man who might even be a fugitive from American justice.

As for Dr Cronin's movements, readers were told in the blow-by-blow style of investigative reporting that he had left the Rossin House Hotel in King Street West, Toronto, where he was staying, shortly after midnight and walked down to the Yonge Street dock. "He did not take his bag with him, however, and returned to the hotel shortly after one o'clock."

Before the *Chicago Times* picked up this story from the *Toronto Empire* and published it they must have wondered how genuine was this Canadian journalist of whom they had never heard. So they hauled in Frank Scanlan, who was a friend of Ananias Long, to give an account in a separate story of the journalist's background, and his friendship with Dr Cronin. Frank Scanlan said he knew Long when they both worked some time previously in a Chicago wholesale grocery house. While they were there Long made an application for membership of an insurance society called the Columbia Council of the Royal League. Dr Cronin was the society's medical examiner and it was there that Long met Dr Cronin for the first time.

Scanlan's report went on: "Ananias Long finally left our firm, and worked for a time for some firm on Michigan Avenue. Subsequently he joined the staff of a morning paper, where he remained six or seven months. When he left the paper he went to the home of his parents in Canada.

"Long and Dr Cronin became friends through their secret society acquaintance. I belong to the same society myself. Every meeting night those of us who lived on Chicago's North Side walked home together. The boys would turn off at their respective streets, and Dr Cronin, Long and myself would be the last left. Long knows the doctor well. If he says he saw Dr Cronin in Toronto, he saw him there, you can rely on that. The only strange thing is that Long did not telegraph to some of us that he had seen Cronin."

The day after this report appeared, May 13th, the *Chicago Herald* trumped it with a banner heading, CRONIN MISSING AGAIN. The report, datelined Toronto, May 12th, again cast Dr Cronin in a very different light from the man so well known and respected in Chicago. Suddenly he is a man wanting to avoid surveillance, deliberately laying a false trail, running away from a possible murder charge. The report read:

"Dr Cronin is a fugitive. He has not been seen in Toronto since ten o'clock this morning, when Ananias

Long, his former Chicago friend, left him under the surveillance of an amateur detective, paid for the purpose.

"Cronin then was in a state bordering on terror, and begged frequently that detectives should not be put upon his track. When told his name was implicated in the trunk mystery in Chicago he denied that he knew anything.

"He stuck to that statement, even though he was told that detectives were waiting in the vestibule of the hotel and had a warrant for his arrest on a charge of malpractice.

"He was next asked if there was any truth in the story about his going to London to communicate with the British government. His manner and evasive replies tended to create this impression, rather than that he made his escape from Chicago over the trunk mystery. He said he intended in a day or two to return to Montreal, where he had been earlier, to get one of the Canadian-French line boats to Paris. Then, he said, he might go to England.

"Cronin said he did not intend to leave Toronto for a few days. He was not registered at the hotel where he was interviewed, and the scores of reporters who called were informed that he was not staying there, and had not been there. This was arranged by Cronin's occupying a room engaged by another party, so the hotel clerk had no idea that the doctor was in the house.

"The information contained in the interview was no doubt intended by Cronin to mislead, and the interviewer was well aware of the fact at the time. The interviewer put a friend at the end of the corridor and told him to keep his eyes open, and when Cronin was left alone in his apartment, to see that he did not leave it.

"Some few minutes after that Cronin made a dash from his room and went down the stairs. He had evidently seen the man who was watching him, and his action must have been taken after a great deal of deliberation. When the interviewer's friend saw him on the stairs he walked to the staircase leading to the ladies' entrance to intercept him there. Cronin, however, had only gone half-way down the staircase. Then he returned and took the elevator, descending to the ladies' entrance, where the detective, not finding him, thought he had been fooled, and again returned to the head of the stairs.

"Cronin has disappeared. There is no trace whatever of him since eleven o'clock. The people at the Rossin House Hotel know nothing of him getting out. The theory is that fearing arrest on a charge of murder, he has gone to Montreal again.

"The only trains leaving the city today were the morning and evening express and the noon train for Hamilton. Cronin was seen after the morning express had left. The evening express was watched, and few people went on the noon train, not one of them answering to Cronin's description. The livery stables did not hire out any rig that could have carried the man a great distance out of the city.

"His disappearance is a perfect mystery. Dispatches from St Catharines tonight say that Cronin is believed to be stopping there with friends. He could only have reached there by driving from Hamilton (St Catharines is 40 miles from the centre of Toronto). Several dispatches have been received at the Rossin House Hotel, making inquiries after Cronin."

As if all this was not sufficiently confusing for their readers, the *Herald* also published in the same issue another interview with the Conklins.

"They are as emphatically positive that Dr Cronin is a murdered man as they were a week ago," the newspaper report said. "The Toronto story and the alleged interview with Dr Cronin they unhesitatingly pronounce a base fabrication from beginning to end."

The *Herald* reporter asked Mr. Conklin, "Don't you believe this man Ananias Long knows Dr Cronin, and when he saw him in the street in Toronto he recognised him?"

"I have no doubt that Long knows the doctor," Mr

Conklin replied, "and that if he saw the doctor on the street, he would not be mistaken in the identity of the man. But he didn't see Dr Cronin. That interview is a tissue of falsehoods throughout.

"For instance, among other things it is alleged that the doctor said that he fled from Chicago to escape assassination at the hands of the Clan-na-Gael. Well, most of the Clan-na-Gael were his friends. That story is only a part of the big conspiracy I have always said existed."

The somewhat baffled interviewer asked Mr. Conklin who he thought Long was, then answered his own question rhetorically, "Long was a well-known Chicago man, a friend of Dr Cronin's, wasn't he?"

"Yes, the doctor had befriended him time and again; in fact, he gave him letters of recommendation when Long left the city. This is what he gets back for his friendship."

At this point in the interview Mrs Conklin just happened to come in and was immediately her usual defiant self. "Long is nothing but a British spy," she declared. "Yes, sir, that's what he is."

Three days later, on May 14th, after the Chicago newspapers had picked up Long's story from the *Empire* and published it, the *Chicago Times* came up with an "exclusive" that threw more dark shadows over Dr Cronin's career and character. It said:

"Dr Cronin was alive and well last Friday afternoon (May 10th). He was seen at the Rossin House Hotel in Toronto by an official of a Canadian railroad who arrived in Chicago yesterday. This official is in the city on a mission requiring some secrecy, and is unwilling to have his name used in connection with the case until his work is done. He is a prominent and trusted officer of a wealthy corporation, and a mis-statement by him would injure him greatly. His story is partly corroborative of Ananias Long's. He told a *Times* reporter of his seeing Cronin.

"'I am willing to tell all I knew about Dr Cronin,' he said, 'but I am here on a mission of such a nature that I do not want my presence known except by those I will meet during the transaction of my business.

"'I know Dr Cronin as well as anybody in the United States. I lived at St Catharines, Ontario, at the time Cronin was living there. He was then quite a young man.

"'He lived with his sisters. They all live at St Catharines now, and are all married to prominent businessmen in that town. They are Mrs Breen, Mrs Welch and Mrs Carroll. Mrs Breen's husband keeps the Breen Hotel, Mr Welch is a well-known grocer, and Mr Carroll is a tailor.

"'I was at the hotel kept by Mrs Breen two weeks ago. I naturally inquired about the doctor, and Mrs Breen replied that he was doing nicely in Chicago.

"'Some weeks ago one of the doctor's sisters told me that Cronin was possessed of a perfect craze for notoriety. She told me that when Alexander Sullivan and Patrick Egan caught a British spy the doctor was so crazed with jealousy that he came near losing his reason.'"

The "prominent railroad official" was then asked by the *Times* reporter to whom he was giving his story if he had actually spoken to Dr Cronin in Toronto the previous Friday. He didn't seem to be able to give a direct answer.

"'The circumstances were such that I was unable to have any protracted interview with him. There could be no mistake. I knew Dr Cronin when he was a boy. He came to St Catharines as a shoemaker. Relatives helped him to obtain a medical education. Having known him from boyhood, and knowing his relatives well, it was natural when I saw them to inquire about him.'

"'Why didn't you telegraph his friends here that you had seen him?'

"'I don't personally know any of his Chicago friends; besides, I did not care to be mixed up in the affair. Some of the people who insist that he is dead would probably say that I was hired to lie about it. I don't care for that kind of newspaper notoriety.'

"He was asked, 'Was Dr Cronin drunk, or under the influence of drugs?'

"'He used to get drunk. He was on a spree one time in Philadelphia, and became involved in a broil. I don't care to discuss his character. He was a strange contradiction, a mixture of rare moral rectitude, combined with morbid vanity and a love of notoriety.

"'His name was hardly dry on the records of any society he joined before he plunged to the front with disorganising assertions. Everything was always going wrong.'"

The prominent railroad man said that he assumed when he saw Cronin in Toronto that the doctor would be going on from there to visit his sisters in St Catharines. In any event, he did not see Cronin after Friday afternoon, although he called on him at the Rossin House Hotel.

No newspaper worthy of the name today would publish an anonymous interview of this kind, and it takes some believing that such a report could be published even in the newsroom panic for an exclusive about Dr Cronin – any exclusive. Although Ananias Long's report from Toronto made it clear that Dr Cronin was very much alive, the *Times's* outrageously hostile "exclusive" must have cast some doubts on that score in the minds of its more intelligent readers. They were entitled to ask who on earth was this "prominent railroad official," and if he knew the Cronin family so well, why this sustained character assassination of its most distinguished member? The whole thing might have suggested to them a fabrication made up to cast the doctor in an unfavourable light, although for what reason they may not have been able to imagine.

Meanwhile the *Chicago Herald* was updating its story with an interview with the Conklins. The newspaper reported that Mrs Conklin was complaining bitterly of the treatment she and her husband had received at the hands of the newspapers, claiming that they had been outrageously vilified, and all their statements distorted. Changing tack, the report concluded:

"A rumour to the effect that the Pinkertons had

dropped the Cronin case because they had traced the doctor to Ottawa, Canada, was denied yesterday afternoon by William A. Pinkerton.

"'It is not so,' he said. 'We dropped the case because we didn't think the Conklins could stand the expense. All the clues given to us by the Conklins were worked out by my men. I'll tell you candidly, I believe Dr Cronin will turn up again all right, for I don't think the man was murdered.'"

A few days later Dr Cronin did turn up again, and the manner of it stunned America.

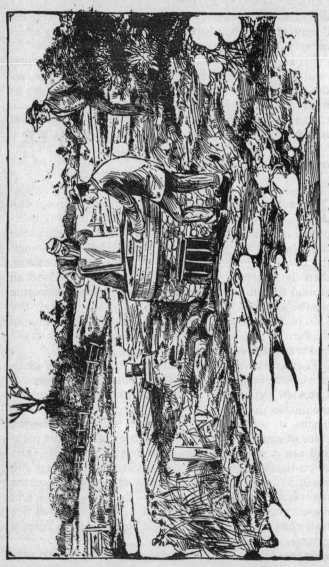

The catch-basin where a body was found

8
NASTY SMELL FROM A SEWER

Henry Rosch, a sewerman, was working on the prairie on the edge of Chicago on the day he was catapulted into the public gaze; Rosch remembered it was the day when he felt the summer arrive. Half-way through the morning the wind off the lake dropped to nothing; then the sun beat up, shrivelling the dry wasteland all around the rim of the metropolis. As the afternoon came on the spent heat from the city lapped out over the scorched prairie until it became oven-hot, awakening all the baneful smells of summer. It was the beginning of the bad season for sewermen.

That afternoon, May 22nd, Rosch and his two assistants, John Feningar and William Nichols, employees of Lakeview Department of Public Works, were digging out the ditches that ran across the open country to the catchbasins, or water-traps. The ditches were the gathering place of surface water that made little gullies in the paths and ran down a thousand channels in the roads. The catch-basins, which were like wells, six feet deep and about four feet across, were placed at intervals along the rainwater ditches to prevent the ditches flooding. Each of these structures, built substantially of masonry, had five iron rods on the lower part of their sides to form a grating, with the bottom of the rods being about even with the ditch. On the top of each basin was a wooden

frame about two feet square, covered with a wooden lid.
The job of the sewermen was to keep the ditches clean
and examine each catch-basin for blockages; if they
found any they must attempt to clear them by poking a
rod through the grating into the dirty, foul-smelling
water. If that failed, their next and much more
unpleasant task was to open the wooden cover, explore
the murky recesses of the clammy interior and remove
the obstruction.

At 3.30 p.m. Rosch, Feningar and Nichols began
working on the north side of Fifty-ninth Street on the
border of Lakeview. Half an hour later they had worked
their way up to the junction of Evanston Road and Fifty-
ninth Street. Despite the proximity of the city, this was a
desolate spot. Evanston Road was smoothly graded, but
the cross streets were in bad shape, sandy strips that were
just the skeletons of the roads to be built in the twentieth
century. The plots in the immediate vicinity were vacant
and covered with long grass and shrubbery. A portion of
the road at the north-east corner of the junction was cul-
tivated as a market garden; apart from that the place was
a wilderness.

Henry Rosch crossed over from the north to the south
side of Fifty-ninth and stood for a moment contemplating the ditch that ran between two catch-basins. The
ditch was narrow and shallow, and the water in it flowed
only sluggishly. Unless it rained hard, the water at this
point would never reach the catch-basins. For Rosch this
was a familiar sight; the city topsoil was sandy, and the
wind off the lake habitually blew sand into the ditches,
turning the water to the consistency of gruel, preventing
its flow. Rosch stepped down into the ditch and started
to shovel out the sand, moving at a brisk pace along its
length and ahead of his two assistants.

A few feet from the perimeter of the first catch-basin he
began to smell an odour which, heightened by the onset
of summer, was nauseatingly familiar. He called to his
two assistants, "Must be a dead dog down here," then

got down on his knees to peer into the catch-basin through the iron bars at the side of it. Inside it was dark, but the stink and the silhouette of the obtrusive bundle was clear enough. Rosch waited for his pupils to dilate. As the darkness became gloom, then grey, he felt the hairs on his neck rising and he stiffened in shock. This wasn't a dog – it was the body of a man. A corpse doubled up on itself remained on his mind's eye as he staggered back, a corpse partly obscured by a pile of cotton wadding thrown over it.

"Over here, quick!" Rosch called to Feningar and Nichols. "There's a man's body!"

The two men hurried forward to peer through the iron bars, then backed off, overcome by the noisome smell.

"Wait here and keep guard!' Rosch ordered. He was, he said later, very scared. He ran off in his swollen, sodden boots down the street to the Argyle police reporting point, nearly a mile away, from where he telephoned Lakeview police station. The call was logged there at 4.24 p.m.

Lakeview's new police chief, Captain Wing, was the first to jump into the patrol wagon. With two other officers on board, they made record time to Fifty-ninth Street. On the way Captain Wing did some swift mental calculations. Evanston and Fifth-ninth was nine-tenths of a mile north of the place where the bloody trunk was found, and two miles from Lakeview police station. As the wagon rumbled along towards the catch-basin which was its destination the police chief noted that the nearest house to it, owned by a Mr Bristle, was a hundred yards to the north. Argyle Park village was about a mile southeast of Evanston and Fifty-ninth.

The sewermen and the officers removed the catch-basin's wooden cover with some difficulty, for it had been damaged by whoever tipped the body inside. As soon as the lid came off the naked body of the man was revealed in the full light of the sun. It was floating, face downward, in about two feet of water, doubled up like a partly opened jack-knife. While the two policemen set about the delicate task of raising it Captain Wing examined the catch-basin, taking notes and muttering to himself as he went slowly round the structure. "Everything shows plainly that the lid was taken off the basin with some tool or pry," he wrote. "The body was then put in head first, and the cotton thrown in afterwards. The cotton was next to the grating and may have been crowded in from the outside after the body was tipped in."

The body, drawn up to the surface by a folded horse blanket placed under the arms and manoeuvred with a hoe handle, was wrapped in another blanket, and taken back to the small morgue attached to Lakeview police station where it was laid out on a zinc slab. As the blanket was removed, nearly all the moustache and a large part of the head hair were found to be sticking to it. This was unfortunate, because it made identification more difficult, though it did not prevent it from being made complete. In any case, Captain Wing had already decided that the body in the morgue was that of Dr Cronin, and confirmation of that decision was not long in forthcoming.

A sizeable gathering of morbid sightseers was soon surrounding the entrance to Lakeview police station, shoving and pushing its way through the door, so that soon the big policeman at the head of the stairs leading down to the morgue was having great difficulty in keeping the crowd from storming the place. The policeman had to heave them back to make way for Dr J. R. Brandt, of Chicago County Hospital, who was summoned to make an initial examination of the corpse. As the crowd surged down the stairs behind the doctor the big policeman gave up the unequal task and the crowd, like a coach party that has come to the high spot of its week-long tour, swarmed in and took up all the available space around the zinc slab, where they solemnly and mutely contemplated this evidence of violent mortality.

Dr Brandt, his shirt-sleeves rolled up, bent over a body that was entirely naked except for a blood-soaked towel that had been twisted around the throat. An Agnus Dei hung from the neck by a leather string. Decomposition had begun, but had not progressed to the stage where recognition was impossible. The body was badly bloated, and the outer skin had sloughed away, leaving the body quite white. The lower portion of the face was so swollen that the chin and the chest met, all evidence of a neck having vanished.

The most repulsive feature of the body was the head. Heavy bruises and great, gaping wounds bore horrific evidence of a ghastly killing. All of Dr Cronin's long, well-groomed moustache was gone, save for a tuft at the corner of the mouth. The bruised and broken forehead was hairless nearly to the crown of the head. The swollen cheeks made the nose seem oddly diminutive; they also exaggerated the size of the mouth to the point where it no longer looked like a human feature.

Overcome with curiosity, the grim-faced officials and the gaping gatecrashers peered forward and began silently shoving each other around the zinc slab in order to get a better view. Dr Brandt, examining the head wounds, did not seem to mind the audience, he seemed even to enjoy playing to it as he audibly described various aspects of the body. They in turn stood in silent awe, overpowered both by the presence of the corpse of the great man, grotesque and tumefied, and the stentorian recitation of medical vocabulary that flowed over it. For their benefit Dr Brandt, starting to revel in his newly discovered role of entertainer, noted out loud that there were seven head wounds, apparently inflicted with a hatchet, or some similar weapon, and listed them as follows:

"A wound on the left temple, at the corner of the left eye, one and one-half inches long. This wound crushed the skull; it may have been the last to be inflicted and may have caused instant death. A wound, one and one-half inches long, cut to the skull on the left parietal bone, and extending to the frontal bone. A wound, also cut to the skull, three inches in length, on the occipital bone, at its juncture with the parietal bone. A cut over the occipital bone four inches long. A cut over the right parietal bone two inches in length. A heavy contusion on the frontal bone, near the edge of the hair. A wound under the chin. There was, in addition, a large bruise on the right leg near the knee."

In plain language the skull was crushed at the outer corner of the left eye; there was a big dent in the forehead; a cut nearly two inches long on the top of the head; a cut over two inches long midway between the left ear and the top of the head; another cut joining this at the lower end and extending towards the left temple for two inches; a cut nearly four inches long on the back of the head, extending nearly from ear to ear, and a gash under the chin.

As Dr Brandt probed and measured the wounds a long perforated conduit extending the length of the slab sent tiny streams of water over the body and down on to the floor. The relentlessly dripping water was the only sound heard in the room. Soon the water on the floor was nearly an inch deep and the crowd was oblivious to the soaking their boots were getting.

Seeming to address his riveted audience, Dr Brandt said, "These cuts were made with a hatchet, I believe. They didn't break the skull, but cut to it. Any one of them might knock a man insensible and might result in death. The wound near the left eye would cause death almost at once, the temple is crushed in. None of these wounds, so far as I can now judge, was after death. The man must have put up a noble fight."

The crowd gasped and shuddered, and looked in disbelief from the shirt-sleeved physician to the grotesque blanched corpse as, in the mind's eye, they contemplated the visible scene, the cruel, frenzied assassins with their bloodied weapons, the screaming victim in the last moment of his agony, and all this wicked atmosphere of gore and blood enacted here, in their own fair city. Men's faces were white and set and muscles stood out on their jaws as they clenched their teeth with emotion.

"I want to say," continued Dr Brandt, like an expert giving in evidence the benefit of a lifetime's knowledge before a soundless jury, "I want to say that I have made an examination of the hair from this body. I am prepared to swear and to prove that it is identical with the hair found in the trunk." He did not of course have to say which hair or which trunk. Everyone in that theatre, with their universal look of assent and sympathy, already knew all the previous acts in the drama.

Captain Wing raised his arms to draw everyone's attention. "Right, folks," he said. "Let's clear the morgue. We've got identification business to go through." The curtain fell, and the audience, still absorbed with the performance, filed back up the stairs reverentially.

A friend of Dr Cronin, John Scanlon, was the first man sent for to arrive. He walked down the stairs to the morgue, and accompanied by Captain Wing and two or three police officers, stood looking for a full fifteen minutes at the body of his murdered friend laid out on the zinc slab. Evidently a very methodical man, Scanlon asked for the right hand to be moved. A policeman picked up the hand from its position at the side of the body and laid it across the water-swollen chest. The right hand was the only part of the body that still preserved a perfectly life-like appearance.

For a few more moments Scanlon continued to stare at the corpse. Then he said slowly, "It's Dr Cronin's body, I'll swear to that hand. The doctor was a very hairy man, especially about the wrists, as was this man. The goatee beard on the lower lip is exactly like Dr Cronin's. The long hair of this moustache is like his, so is the long hair left on the head. The size and shape of the body are his. The forehead is his, the teeth are his, the nose" – here Scanlon took a pencil from his breast pocket and gently

**John Scanlon and T.T. Conklin identifying
the body at the morgue**

lifted the nostrils – "is his. The body is Dr Cronin's. The Agnus Dei is the one he had around his neck. He must have been taken into a room, stable, or ice house and killed there."

He did not explain why he suggested an ice house, nor, curiously, was he asked. The irresistible inference must be that Dr Cronin's friends and the assembled policemen were already categorising their suspects, mentally sorting out who did what and where.

More witnesses streamed in. Dr F. S. Silber, of Lakeview, who knew Dr Cronin well, identified the body. F. O. Parker, a real estate agent, whose office adjoined Dr Cronin's surgery in the Opera House block, and F. Huxman, a dentist, also said the body was that of Dr Cronin, as did Henry J. O'Hara, of 54 Superior Street, and Mr. Fitzgerald, of Belmont House, Lakeview. Another doctor, Dr Parker of Lakeview, said the victim had been dead between two and three weeks.

A sizeable crowd was now gathering outside Lakeview police station. They surged into the lobby and seemed determined to get to the morgue. The big policeman at the head of the stairs took off his coat and fought them back. He was rescued by Captain Wing, who told the gathering he would make some rapid arrests among them unless they backed off out of the station. As the crowd sullenly withdrew Mr T. T. Conklin arrived, and had to plough a furrow through the human mass. He was a small, delicate-looking fellow. Entering the morgue, he seemed likely to faint. What seemed to register first on his disturbed and doleful mind was the Agnus Dei still hanging round the victim's neck on a leather thong.

"That is the one Dr Cronin wore, string and all," he said. "It was sent to him by his sister, who is in a convent. It's an unusual charm – she will be able to recognise it." His gaze wandered from the Agnus Dei. "The doctor had a tooth or two out, and wore a plate."

The blanched, swollen lips were raised and a couple of teeth were seen to be missing. The false ones and the plate were gone. Mr Conklin said he recognised the hands, wrists, hair, goatee beard, nose and other features as those of Dr Cronin. As he turned to the door he said, "There is no longer any doubt. That's Dr Cronin's body and he was murdered. My wife will be able to identify the teeth perhaps better than I can. Dr Lewis was his dentist – you'll find his offices at the corner of Clark and Division streets."

Still more witnesses arrived. Captain Wing was taking no chances – there had been too much speculation that Dr Cronin was very much alive and had fled the country for Wing to risk even the slightest doubt about the identity of the body. So Dr Rutherford, who was a colleague of Dr Cronin when they worked together at the County Hospital, Dr Patrick McGarry and Captain Thomas O'Connor, Clan-na-Gael friends whom we have met before, added to the positive identification. Frank Scanlan, the last friend of Dr Cronin's to see him alive as he got into the wagon outside the Windsor Theatre block at 7.30 p.m. on Saturday, May 4th, remembered the doctor's "peculiar teeth," and recalled that two of them were missing. "His heavy moustache came over his mouth and completely hid his teeth, but I've seen them. His upper teeth were large, nearly as wide as long, and had a space between them. The teeth on the under-jaw were small, crowded in tight, and stained black around the edges." This remarkable description – how many of us could recall a friend's teeth so expertly? – proved to be completely accurate.

Hal Garsch, of 472 North Clark Street, who was Dr Cronin's barber and who had held firm to his view that the hair in the bloody trunk was not the doctor's, now appeared to have no problems identifying the goatee, the hair, the body and the moustache. He must have thought that there was no place for vanity in death: "It is not generally known that Dr Cronin had his moustache dyed. I've shaved him every day for a long time, and I used to dye his moustache. The tuft of hair that's left of it still shows the dye." Captain Wing noted that Garsch's story seemed to be a remarkable change of mind. Since Dr Brandt had no difficulty in identifying the hair in the trunk as being the same as that on the body, why could not the barber have recognised the hair in the trunk when it was first shown to him? Surely, he thought, if Garsch could see the dye on this tuft of hair on the corpse, nothing would have been more obvious to him than the same dye on the hair in the trunk. Captain Wing was to discover the reason for the barber's *volte-face* later, but for the present he made no comment on it; he was content to have yet another positive identification of the corpse.

After the barber, the tailors. They were Messrs O'Keefe and Ahern, who solemnly measured the limbs of the corpse and then pronounced that the length of the legs and arms of the victim corresponded exactly with Dr Cronin's measurements in the files at their store.

At last Captain Wing closed his notebook. All those who had been summoned to identify the body were unanimous that it was Dr Cronin's.

Over at Evanston and Fifty-ninth, where reporters and newspaper artists were keeping vigil, bunches of cotton wadding which had been removed from the catch-basin with the body were being blown aimlessly by the wind across the wilderness of vacant plots. The few passers-by, already apprised of the discovery of Dr Cronin's body, stopped and studied these flimsy artefacts intently, as if the solution to the murder lay in them. Others ventured into the bush and fields, hoping to make other connected discoveries. A small group came hurrying back after half an hour brandishing a woman's severed finger found in a drainage ditch. Did this mean there was another body somewhere out there on the prairie? A couple of patrolmen took possession of the gruesome find, and while another excited crowd gathered around them the patrolmen tried to make sense of the contradictory babbling of its discoverers. Then an eager young man insisted that if they looked hard enough they must find Dr Cronin's case of surgical instruments, or at least a bloody smock or a stray lance. Watched by the knot of reporters, the young man led his search-party off through the stubble just as a three-seated carriage containing a party of ladies drew up.

"What's all the excitement about?" one of the ladies asked.

A reporter held out a handful of bloody wadding to her, and pointed to the opening of the catch-basin through which Dr Cronin's body was bundled to its murky resting-place. The lady gave a piercing scream and the horses were set forward at a fast gallop.

As dusk fell two wizened, wrinkle-skinned old women who were walking to their homes from the city also stopped and inquired what the roadside gathering was about. When they were told they turned on their heels in alarm and began to lumber back towards the city centre. They were overtaken and induced to return, several reporters promising to pilot them past the objectionable point. As soon as they and their volunteer escort had circumnavigated the place the two women set off at a lively trot and quickly disappeared from sight, no doubt not stopping until their front doors were locked and bolted safely behind them.

It was almost dark when the eager young man and his party called off their search. They had found nothing for their pains. Stretching away to where the sky appeared to meet the earth, as if there were no secrets between mankind and the stars in their firmament, there was only virgin country bisected by a line of drainage ditches slinking across the quilted landscape, no longer burdened by the oppressive influence of their terrible secret, with nothing more to yield up now beyond their promise of hope for the future.

9

ALICE IN WONDERLAND

They had their exits and their entrances in the Clan-na-Gael, and some played many parts. But for Mrs Alice Brown there was only one brief entrance, one exit, and one intriguing part.

Alice Brown was the mysterious woman going to Buffalo who was supposed to have met Dr Cronin on the Toronto-Hamilton train. She lived with her husband Kevin Brown, himself a Clan-na-Gael executive officer, in Division Street, Chicago.

Ananias Long, the reporter who claimed to have seen and interviewed Dr Cronin in Toronto after the doctor had been murdered, and whose exclusive story was now self-evidently a piece of fiction, had reported that Dr Cronin did not know the woman he met on the train – it was, the doctor was supposed to have said, a chance meeting. Dr Cronin never said that, nor was he on the Toronto – Hamilton train, because he was already dead. Whether Alice Brown was on the train is not known; what is known, however, was that she was in Toronto. To find out what she was doing there we have to return to the night of Saturday, May 4th.

Alice Brown's husband Kevin was part of the team whose job it was to get rid of Dr Cronin's body after he had been murdered, a plan which as it turned out went all wrong. It was proposed that the body should be brought to Brown's house by Frank Woodruff, in the wagon drawn by the bay horse hired from Dean's. There Brown would join Woodruff, and they would drive off on the prairie and bury the body. But because the organisation wanted no blame to attach to Alice Brown in the event of anything going wrong, they told Brown that he must ensure she was not in the house that night, and that he must arrange an alibi for her for the time of the murder.

Alexander Sullivan, or John Beggs, or whoever it was who made the detailed murder arrangements, guessed that it would not be difficult to get Alice out of the house because they knew what her husband only half suspected, that Alice was having an affair. She had already intended going out alone that evening, as she had been out alone every evening for the past two weeks. Brown had confided in some of his Clan-na-Gael confrères his concern over his wife's nocturnal absences, to which they merely smiled sagely. They knew all about what Alice was getting up to.

On May 4th Kevin Brown received a letter dated the previous day from a member of the organisation who did not sign his name. It said:

"The job is to be done tomorrow night, Saturday, between seven and nine. In order to throw off suspicion, I have arranged a plan, which I want you to carry out to the very letter. Call on [here a name was inserted, but it was later eradicated from the letter], the detective, and engage him to shadow your wife. You will assume the character of a jealous husband, which will not be very difficult for you to do, and be sure to have the detective at your house before seven o'clock. Start Alice out at about seven. He will follow her and she will keep him out until nine. It will be easy enough for her to prove an alibi in case anything should occur to associate suspicion with her. The detective himself will know she was not near. You know what to do then. Don't make any mistake."

Brown duly went at about 3 p.m. on Saturday May 4th to the office of the private detective. Afterwards the detective – in his subsequent account of what happened he refused to reveal his name, so we had best call him "Detective X" – wrote notes on the matrimonial case for which Brown hired him.

The first thing the detective had to do was to assure Brown that no one else was present in the office and no one was hiding behind the curtains.

"It's about my wife," Brown then confided. "We have been married for four years. I am pretty well fixed, and I think my money won her. I've found out that she had a fellow running after her before I married her, and I've pretty good reason to think he's still running after her. She goes out at night, and sometimes she doesn't get back until past midnight. When I ask her where she's been, she says she's been visiting friends. Now, I'd like to know who and where these friends are."

"Why don't you follow her and find out?" Detective X asked. If this appears to be an unhelpful way for a private detective to address a potential client, it should be said that Detective X had already decided he did not like Brown one bit. He wrote on his note-pad, "Treacherous, deceitful, mercenary – all in his shifting eyes."

"I've tried to several times, but she always manages to give me the slip," Brown replied apologetically.

Detective X hesitated before taking on the case. But he had lately been off work sick, and needed the money. He said, "It will cost you ten dollars a day, Mr. Brown. That's from 10 a.m. to 10 p.m."

Brown thought the price was pretty steep, but accepted, remarking that he only wanted his wife watched at night.

"What do you propose to do with your information, even if I succeed in furnishing you with any?" Detective X asked.

"I haven't made up my mind."

Detective X thought for a moment. Then he said, "I'll shadow your wife until I find out beyond doubt that she is playing you false. I'll want five dollars for each evening I work, providing that I'm not compelled to be out past midnight. For every hour past that time I will want an extra dollar, and when I've finished the job and furnished you with all the information it's possible to get, you will pay me a final sum of fifty dollars. Is that satisfactory?"

Brown nodded in assent. The detective smiled to himself. His client had agreed terms which were far more expensive than the first offer; it was likely to cost him considerably more than ten dollars a day in the end.

Brown said, "I want you to begin tonight. I know she is going out. You can start watching for her outside my house in Division Street."

Detective X noted the address and said he would be outside the house at 6.45 p.m. So far, Brown had carried out his Clan-na-Gael instructions, bizarre though they were, to the letter.

Devotees of Chicago's astonishing development in the last 100 years might be interested to learn that in order to reach his client's house by 5.45 p.m. the detective took a Madison Street horse-drawn car from near his home to Clark Street, and expressed his irritation that the West Side cable wasn't yet in working order, because that would have been much quicker. At the junction of Clark and Division streets he found Brown waiting for him. They hid in an alley off Division Street until Alice Brown left her house for her evening out, at which point Brown left the detective to get on with his work.

Alice Brown walked rapidly to Clark Street, where she turned left and headed in the direction of Lincoln Park. Then Detective X noted:

"As she passed the Windsor Theatre building I observed a horse attached to a light buggy, not remarkable for beauty or convenience, driven up in front of the building. I suppose it was the fact that the horse was white that attracted my attention."

He followed Alice Brown until she reached Center Street. She turned into Lincoln Avenue, where she knocked on the door of a house and disappeared inside. Detective X skulked around the grounds of the house and then, on the flimsiest basis imaginable, calculated that he had seen enough to conclude that Alice Brown was having an affair. He waited until she came out, some time after 10 o'clock, and followed her home.

Detective X set down his findings in a letter to Brown – which fortunately the client had no intention of using in a divorce court – and enclosed his invoice. When he read the report Brown called on the detective again, this time in a state of some agitation.

"You saw where my wife went on Saturday night?" Brown asked.

'Yes. I told you in my letter."

"Did you follow her when she left my house the second time?"

Detective X started. "The second time? I didn't know she went out again, after returning home."

"Well, she fooled you. When she came back to the house the first time she smiled when I asked her if she enjoyed her visit to the friend she had gone to see. 'I only had a little walk,' she said. 'There was a man following me, so I didn't go to my friend's.'

"But I saw her go into a house with a man she met in the street!" Detective X said, which was of course only half true.

"She probably did that to throw you off your guard. She went out again an hour after she had returned from the first trip. It was nearly two o'clock when she got home."

Where had Alice been the second time out? Some of the husband's friends in the Clan-na-Gael could have told him. They would have assumed that she left home that Saturday night at 7.30 p.m. to visit her lover, quickly saw that she was being tailed, guessed that her husband was having her followed, and called on an innocent friend. When she went out the second time she saw she was no longer being tailed, and went to the rendezvous with her lover, rather later perhaps than she had expected.

When his seemingly disgruntled client had left the office Detective X leaned back in his chair and thought about it. The morning newspapers, full of stories about the disappearance of Dr Cronin, were scattered across his desk. He had been out shadowing Alice Brown on the night of the murder, he remembered – although it now seemed he had made a bit of a botch of it. Outside the Windsor Theatre building he had actually walked past the horse and buggy that had taken the doctor for his last ride. It did not take the detective many minutes to figure out that Kevin Brown was probably connected with the murder, and most likely Alice Brown too.

Intrigued, Detective X began his own private investigation into the murder. He went to the spot where the bloody trunk was found, asked questions, watched the movements of Brown and his wife. He dug deeply, and was free and open with his questions. Very soon those with something to hide began to ask questions about him. Only a few days after Cronin's disappearance the Clan-na-Gael were aware that Detective X was on to them, and that their plan to use him to create an alibi to get Alice Brown out of her house that night had backfired on them. From the questions Detective X was asking, and the observations he was making, it was clear too that he was already better informed than the Chicago police. Urgent instructions were sent to Kevin Brown: Detective X was likely to find out too much, he must be removed from the city as fast as possible. The best place to send him was Toronto, where they had a reporter, Ananias Long, who was about to plant a story about having seen Cronin in that city.

How was Kevin Brown going to get the detective to Canada? The manner of it was not to prove all that difficult.

Alice Brown knew Dr Cronin – she was a patient of his – and she knew that he was a member of the Clan-na-Gael, an organisation to which her husband also belonged, and for whose aims she had considerable sympathy, although she would not have condoned murder. Like many people in Chicago, she was asking questions about the fate of Dr Cronin. She also remembered that she had walked past the fatal horse and buggy the previous Saturday night. She asked her husband if the organisation was in any way involved, as some people were suggesting.

"Cronin has fled to Toronto," Brown told her. "He will probably take the Hamilton train from there and then drive to St Catharines, where he was born. He has told people he is in fear of his life, which is nonsense of course. We urgently need to make contact with him, but he's hardly likely to talk to one of us. You know him – you would be serving a good cause if you went up to Toronto and gave him a peace message from us. We have a reporter up there named Ananias Long, who you can meet, and who will pass the message on to Cronin and arrange for you to see him. But you must tell no one what your errand is. When you get to Toronto book into a hotel. You can use your own name because it's common enough, but give a false address somewhere in Canada. The organisation will pay you well for it."

It so happened that Alice Brown had relations living in Toronto, and had been proposing for some time that she would go and visit them. She would not stay with them; she preferred to stay in a hotel and call on them daily. As she packed her bag she decided she would first go to spend the day with an aged aunt who lived in Milwaukee Avenue, near Robey Street, Chicago, and from there she would take the afternoon train to the Canadian city.

As soon as she was gone Brown went to the office of Detective X. "My wife is continuing to act suspiciously," he said. "You must stick on her tail. I'll pay you whatever it costs."

Detective X was much intrigued. He would be delighted to follow Alice Brown, he thought, because he was now convinced that she had something to do with Dr Cronin's disappearance. But again he was being hired to shadow her as a suspect adulterer. Masking his suspicions, he decided to take the bull by the horns.

"I think the best thing is that I should meet her," he said. "Where is she now?"

Brown bit his lip. The last thing he wanted was for his wife to meet the detective. But he knew Alice would have to leave her aunt's house at around 1.30 p.m. in order to catch the Toronto train. It was now 11.30 a.m., and Milwaukee

Avenue was 45 minutes away by horse and buggy.

"Sure you can meet her," Brown said. "But let's have a drink first. We're not in that much of a hurry."

Early that afternoon Brown and Detective X finally called at the house in Milwaukee Avenue. Their ring at the door-bell was answered by Alice Brown's aunt. "Alice has just left," the old lady said. "She's going out of the city for a few days, but she wouldn't say where to."

"Out of the city?" echoed Brown. "Well, that beats everything!"

The two men went back to the buggy and conferred. "You must have some idea where she's likely to have gone," Detective X said. "Think about it for a moment."

Brown thumped his forehead with his clenched fist. "The man she may be involved with may be a Canadian," he said. "She has mentioned Toronto once or twice recently – asked me what sort of a place it is, that sort of thing." He brought his right fist into the palm of his left hand with a dull thud. "That's where she's gone!" he cried. "I'll bet a thousand dollars that's where she's headed for!"

Perhaps because Brown was now behaving rather theatrically, the detective wasn't immediately impressed. He still had deep-rooted suspicions about his client, so he arranged another meeting for early the next morning and spent the rest of the day checking as best he could that Alice Brown had left Chicago. By next morning he was fairly certain that she had, and Brown was apparently able to confirm it. Brown had spoken to a friend in the ticket office at Chicago railroad station, he said, and the man had a distinct recollection that Alice, whom he also knew well, had bought a ticket.

"How fortunate you should have a friend in the ticket office," the detective mused out loud.

"I was formerly in the railroad business myself," Brown explained. "Most of the staff at the Chicago railroad station know Alice and me."

Detective X accepted that explanation. He had made up his mind that it did not matter if Alice Brown was chasing a man to Toronto; what mattered was that she must be involved in the Cronin affair, and by shadowing her he might pull off the sleuthing scoop of the decade. He wrote in his notes that he caught the 10.20 train to Toronto that morning and arrived early next day. He stayed at the home of a friend, Mr Hirsch, a Yorkshireman, at the corner of Jarvis and Adelaide streets.

Looking for someone in Toronto in 1889 would not have been the formidable needle-in-a-haystack task it might be today. In the last quarter of the nineteenth century the city was home to about 100,000 people, but by the standards of the time it was already widespread, stretching a distance of five or six miles, so that the downtown area, where the visitors congregated, was still comparatively undeveloped. It is plausible, therefore, that the detective soon saw, as he said he did, a man he had once known slightly in Chicago, whom he recognised as Ananias Long; that he followed him, and that as he turned a corner to enter King Street he saw Long stop outside the post office and talk to a woman whom he recognised as Alice Brown.

Long's part in the plot was not yet evident to the detective, for the reporter had not yet filed his story on the discovery of Dr Cronin in the city. That left Detective X with three alternatives: Long might be the man who was having an affair with Alice Brown; they both might be implicated in the disappearance of Dr Cronin and had arranged to meet outside the post office; or it might simply be a chance meeting of two Chicagoans. Still undecided, he followed Alice Brown to the Rossin House Hotel. By whatever methods detectives employ in these situations he managed to discover that she had registered there the previous day under her own name but had given a false address in Buffalo – so she did have something to hide.

Detective X left Alice in her hotel and returned an hour later with the intention of confronting her. He went to the reception desk, asked the clerk to call her, and was told that she had booked out ten minutes ago. She had mentioned that she was returning home to Buffalo.

"What time does the Buffalo train leave?" the detective asked frantically.

"At 1.40, sir."

It was then 1.35. Watched by the astonished hotel clerk, the detective sprang for the door and jumped into a hansom cab. The cabby put the whip to his horse which raced along the street; even so, the cab arrived at the station a minute after the train had left. The next one was at 6.10 p.m.

At the railway station the detective discovered that the next train to Chicago did not depart until the middle of the next morning. Disconsolate, he went back to the house of his friend Mr Hirsch, had a meal and fell asleep.

It was 8 a.m. when he woke next day to read Ananias Long's scoop in the *Toronto Empire* – a scoop picked up by the Chicago newspapers the following day – that the missing Dr Cronin was alive and well, if a little apprehensive, in the Canadian city, and that he had taken a train trip out of town to Hamilton in the company of a Mrs Alice Brown of Buffalo, who refused to be interviewed later.

When that report was republished in the Chicago newspapers it was natural enough for the Clan-na-Gael members in the know to nudge each other, hinting that for Mrs Brown of Buffalo just read Mrs Brown of Chicago, and everyone knows what kind of womaniser that Cronin is, and how liberal young Alice is with her favours ...

Detective X, unable now to follow Alice Brown, went off to look for Dr Cronin, and the way, he decided, was to find Ananias Long first. But that shadowy reporter and long-time member of the Clan-na-Gael, who by now the Chicago newspapers also wanted to meet, had wreaked his mischief and had gone to ground. When the following day's newspapers reported that Dr Cronin might have gone to Montreal, Detective X went off to Montreal too. Indeed, keeping the inquisitive private detective out of harm's way by having him chase the phantom Dr Cronin here, there and everywhere across eastern Canada was perhaps the one successful thing the Clan-na-Gael achieved after they murdered the doctor.

10
A CITY FULL OF THEORIES

Lieutenant Hermann Schuettler pulled his buggy up outside the furniture store of Alexander Revell and Co, on the corner of Fifth and Randolph. Inside, Mr Hatfield the salesman immediately remembered the well-heeled J. B. Simmons, and turned up the customer record to show Schuettler what he had bought. Simmons, the salesman recalled, was about 35 years old and had a long, sharp nose. He paid with bills from "a fat roll." The record showed that the trunk and furniture were delivered to 117 Clark Street.

Real-estateman James Marshall also remembered J. B. Simmons. "He decamped with all his bits of furniture without paying his second month's rent," Marshall complained to the lieutenant as they drove down Clark Street. At No. 117 Mr Marshall showed Schuettler rooms 12 and 15 on the top floor. Going to the window, the lieutenant noticed at once that it commanded an excellent view of the front door of one of Dr Cronin's surgeries across the road in the Opera House block. From office workers in the lower rooms at No. 117 Schuettler learned that J. B. Simmons's sick friend, for whom he was supposed to have leased the top floor rooms, never materialised, and that Simmons had only one regular caller, a lawyer who had an office in the Opera House block across the road. The only lawyer with an office in that block, Schuettler discovered, was Alexander Sullivan.

Reporting back to Captain Schaack, Schuettler said, "We need to get some men searching draymen's records to find out where Simmons's furniture was delivered after he moved out of the office."

"You'd do better to find out who Cronin was womanising with," Schaack replied testily.

"I've already checked him out," Schuettler said. He refused to let the captain needle him. "Cronin wasn't wealthy, but he was a good deal better off than solvent, and he had a healthy bank account. He was a confirmed bachelor, with no interest in women at all."

Schaack snorted. "All right," he muttered. "You'd better get someone checking the draymen then. But, lieutenant, I reckon that if I believed every last person who told me about their theory on this Dr Cronin case, I'd have hanged half of Chicago by now."

Pointing to the conflicting, polarised reports piled high on his desk, Schaack could be forgiven for his testiness. One report, dated May 10th, stated that Miss Anna Murphy, of Chicago, saw Dr Cronin on a streetcar on Saturday evening May 4th at 9 p.m. – about 90 minutes after the time that other reports suggested he was murdered. Another, from the St Catharines, Ontario, chief of police of all people, claimed that that worthy had himself seen Cronin in Sherwood, New York, on May 16th. Now here was Captain Wing's report from Lakeview dated May 22nd saying that the body found in a sewer had been identified as Dr Cronin's by almost everyone who knew him. If, as the post-mortem doctors said, the man had been dead two or three weeks, how could he have been seen by a reputable police chief only last week in New York?

Sometimes, Schaack went on, you could be forgiven for wondering who was in charge of this murder investigation – the police or the press. The press were everywhere, probing, declaiming, playing judge and jury, as ever exercising authority without responsibility. The *Chicago Times* had interviewed John Scanlon, who claimed that he had always believed his friend Dr Cronin was murdered; now that he was proved right, he wanted to say that the guilty ones were the doctor's enemies among the Irish nationalists.

"Why do you believe that?" the *Times* reporter asked Scanlon.

"It's several years since I belonged to any of these organisations, and I can't say much as to their workings of late," John Scanlon replied evasively. "But I believe Cronin had information that would have put some leading local lights in the Irish organisation in a bad position and it was in the interests of these parties to have his mouth closed forever."

Could he name any of them?

"It will come out too soon. It would have been out long ago, and these people would have been behind bars now if the police had done their duty." He and his friends had after all given the police plenty of clues about the likely killers.

What clues?

He wasn't saying. But the information he and his friends had would be placed in the hands of the coroner. After the inquest he predicted a number of arrests, "and the people of Chicago will be treated to an Irish hanging match."

A ferocious one, just because they were Irishmen?

"I don't care even if they are Irishmen, if they dabbled their hands in this man's blood, as I believe they have, I want to see them strung up, even though we have to break up every Irish organisation in the country to reach the guilty ones."

The press had got to Frank Woodruff too, in the County Jail where he was a prisoner. Captain Schaack drew the *Chicago Times* towards him and read again the newspaper's account of its interview with Woodruff, who had come from his cell in answer to a reporter's request, smoking a bad cigar and looking as if he hadn't a care in the world. The reporter told him that the body of Dr Cronin had been found.

"That so?" Woodruff replied. The surprise in his voice betrayed his assumed nonchalance. He sat down at a table and began to swing his long legs in a lazy sort of way.

"What do you think about it all now?" he was asked.

"I might tell you, but I've discovered that the police and newspapers think I'm a liar, so what's the use of telling you anything?"

"Now that the body has been identified as Dr Cronin's, could you explain your statement that the body in the trunk was that of a woman, and that Dr Cronin was among the people at that barn in State Street when you picked up the trunk?"

"I think Dr Cronin committed an abortion on the woman in the trunk, and that he was the most anxious person present that night to have the body disposed of as soon as possible."

"How do you know Cronin was at the barn? Did you know him?"

"No. But his being called Doc, and the description I afterwards learned of the doctor, convinces me that the man was Cronin."

"Then why should he be killed, and in all probability on the same night that you hauled the trunk away?"

"Don't you think that the dead woman in the trunk had friends or relatives who were anxious to avenge her death?" replied Woodruff.

"That would suggest that Dr Cronin must have followed you and the other two men out to Lincoln Park and been murdered there."

"That's one of my theories."

"Can you be certain that the body in the trunk was a woman's? Did you see the face and enough of the body to be accurate in this assertion?"

"I saw the hand and arm hanging over the edge of the

trunk, when the trunk was lifted out of the wagon at the park by King and Fairburn. The hand and the arm were slender and delicate. I did not see the face, because the mare became restive at the unusual proceedings and the sight of the white object, for the body was wrapped in cotton. I had to turn my attention to her.

"I heard the men say, 'Here's where we leave Allie.' That's a woman's name, ain't it? Another thing I heard was, 'If they had left Tom alone, he'd have had Cronin in the trunk in place of Allie.' That shows the doctor's connection with the case, and that the girl had friends, don't it? Well, that's why I say the body in the trunk was a woman's, and that Cronin had some connection with it. Easy to figure that out."

"Might King and Fairburn have been trying to throw you off by this kind of talk?"

"Don't think so."

"Can you say positively that the doctor's body was not in the trunk that you hauled that night?"

"Well, I didn't see the face in the trunk, but I know there was a man called Doc in the barn when the trunk was carted away. Of course I can't pretend to be positive that it was a woman's body in the trunk."

"The doctor's body was wrapped in cotton when it was found, the body in the trunk was wrapped in cotton, and you acknowledged that you scraped cotton from the bed of your wagon on the morning of your return from the park. Besides, the trunk was found within a stone's throw of where the doctor's body was found. How does that strike you as a refutation of your woman-in-the-trunk theory?"

Woodruff remained silent for some time, stroking his thin moustache and drawing on his cigar. Twice he started to say something, but only puffed. Then he said desperately, "Well, it looks odd, but I don't believe the body is that of Cronin."

"But it is the doctor's. It's been proved beyond doubt."

What the reporter did not understand, Woodruff said,

129

was that there was a connection between the trunk and the disappearance of Dr Cronin, but not the sort of connection that was now being claimed.

"William King doesn't live in Chicago, but he was in the city the Saturday Doc Cronin disappeared," Woodruff said. "Friends of mine who have come to visit me in prison told me this. I know much more about this whole business than I've so far said, but even if I do tell everything, and the police run it down, I'll still be held for horse-stealing."

The reporter suggested that if Woodruff were to cooperate and clear up the mystery, it was more than likely that Cronin's friends would "see him through this horse-stealing business."

Woodruff brightened at that suggestion. "I'll tell you what I'll do," he said. "If the police will send two men dressed in plain clothes to accompany me on my investigations, leaving me free to make inquiries, I'll agree to turn up enough evidence to clear up this mystery within forty-eight hours. I ask for no reward except my liberty. If Cronin's friends are anxious to run this thing down, they ought to put up my bail. I maintain that if the body found is Cronin's, he must have been killed later than the date on which I hauled the trunk. A close examination of the body will no doubt prove me right."

Reading the newspaper over Schaack's shoulder, Lieutenant Schuettler considered Woodruff. One of the strongest points in the prisoner's story was his description of Dr Cronin. It was in fact the only accurate description furnished of the doctor when last seen. When Woodruff said that the man he claimed was the doctor wore a goatee beard, most of the doctor's friends had scoffed at the idea. Only Mr Conklin, John Scanlon and Frank Scanlan, close friends, and Hal Garsch, his barber, knew about the goatee beard. The rest chorused, "Dr Cronin never wore a goatee."

But he did. When his crumpled body was drawn from the catch-basin he had a goatee beard. Many of his friends had not seen him with it because it was still only a few weeks old. Certainly Woodruff saw Cronin. He did not know him, but he saw him. In describing the doctor Woodruff was simply describing the corpse which was dragged from the trunk and thrown into the catch-basin. He told the truth when he described Cronin, Lieutenant Schuettler reasoned, and that could have been because he wanted Cronin's disappearance ascribed to the doctor's fear at finding the woman's body. There was of course no woman in the trunk, but if Woodruff could cause the belief that malpractice had happened and that Dr Cronin was connected with it, wouldn't the public believe his story when the doctor could not be found? Everyone would be asking, "Where is the doctor?" and the pundits would reply, "Why, he skipped off to avoid trouble about that woman in the trunk."

Lieutenant Schuettler flipped through the pages of Woodruff's record. There were frequent arrests, statements full of thieves' slang, a boast that he knew all the "hard men" in America, the murder in Mexico and a whole mélange of violence and thieving. Crime was an ineluctable condition of his inheritance, he must have become accustomed to it like a wart on his skin. It was the dossier of a crook with enough brutality and native cunning to bring him to the notice of the criminal fat cats, who had used him before and might have used him again on this occasion. If that were so, they might be behind the deliberate false trails which Schuettler was convinced Woodruff was laying. For instance, he had made a statement that when the body was taken from the trunk he drove alone northwards with his associates Fairburn and King and with the trunk and dumped it on the Lakeview prairie. This was a lie, for Fairburn was 500 miles away at the time and King, who had been found by the police, was out of town during the weekend of May 4th – 5th. Then Woodruff had changed his story, claiming that he had driven the wagon northwards alone and dumped the trunk himself. But Patrolmen Hayden

and Smith of Lakeview police saw the bay horse and
wagon twice on that fatal morning; on the first occasion,
when they also saw the trunk in the wagon, there were
three men in it. Woodruff's first story was therefore probably true except that the two men were not Fairburn and
King, but two of the murderers. Who was Woodruff
trying to protect, Schuettler wondered?

Then there was the statement of T. T. Conklin.
Captain Schaack had completely changed his contemp-
tuous view of Conklin since they first met at the police
station the day after Dr Cronin's disappearance. It was
now Schaack's opinion that Conklin was a nervous,
excitable little fellow, but an honest one. After identifying
Dr Cronin's body at the Lakeview morgue Conklin had
gone to visit another relative, then gone back to his home
at 470 North Clark Street. There he collected a bundle
of documents and took them to East Chicago Avenue
police station, where he spoke to Sergeant Koch. As a
result of their conversation Koch drove Conklin in a
police wagon to the home of Captain Schaack, who was
ill and in bed, in North State Street.

What Conklin told the sick police chief concerned the
Clan-na-Gael's first trial of Dr Cronin (he did not of
course know about the second one), and the subsequent
trial of Sullivan, Boland and Feeley by a trial committee
which included Dr Cronin.

"If Dr Cronin had an enemy it was Alexander
Sullivan," Conklin said. "He feared for his life, and told
me if he were to be killed I should look no farther than
the Triangle of the Clan-na-Gael." Conklin spread out
across the counterpane letters and notes written in Dr
Cronin's own hand. "Read this lot," he said. "It's all the
proof you'll need."

Schaack was sufficiently impressed to send out an
order for a round-the-clock watch on Sullivan. He did
not want to bring the lawyer in for routine questioning
for the moment, because Conklin had convinced him
that if Sullivan and the Triangle were behind the murder,

there might still be plenty of others involved. He also wanted to find out, if Sullivan, then why? Conklin's claim that it was a personal vendetta within the organisation was supported only by the notes written by Dr Cronin before his death. But in downtown Chicago the gossip was that Cronin was a British spy who had inveigled his way into the Clan-na-Gael, relayed all its secrets to the British government, and got a spy's just deserts when he was unmasked. His murder, it was being suggested, was nothing to do with the financial and administrative irregularities rumoured to exist within the organisation, it happened simply because he was a traitor.

Corroborative evidence for this view, it was held, was the fact that the religious charm around his neck, held sacred by his fellow-Catholics, was not removed when the body was stripped. The murderers must have seen the Agnus Dei, and could have pulled it over his head, or cut the leather thong holding it, in a trice. That they did not was held to be proof that even a traitor was entitled to his sacred emblem. It was of course equally corroborative of the killers being too scared to touch the emblem after they had washed their hands in the blood of its owner. Either way, they must have realised that it would be a valuable aid in identifying the body, but they did not touch it.

As soon as Captain Schaack had risen from his sickbed and got back to his office at East Chicago Avenue police station another intriguing report landed on his desk. As a result of information from a member of the public, a policeman had been sent to investigate a rented cottage a few yards from the home of the ice-dealer Patrick O'Sullivan. It seemed that the cottage's tenants had hardly ever been in occupancy, which had caused the owners' son, John Carlson, to investigate. Young Carlson thought he saw blood in the hallway, and confided his discovery to a milk dealer named Diekman, who in turn told his customers, one of whom had passed the information on to Captain Wing of Lakeview who had passed it to Captain Schaack in Chicago. The policeman's report lay on Schaack's desk, in a separate pile from the Cronin dossier. Schuettler picked it up in error, flipped through it and whistled softly.

"Has anyone looked into this cottage?" the lieutenant asked.

"Not yet," Schaack replied. "We haven't had time with all this Cronin activity."

Schuettler gazed at his senior in detached disbelief. "Perhaps the two are linked," he suggested gently. "The unknown man who called Dr Cronin from his surgery to his death was working for this iceman O'Sullivan. One of O'Sullivan's employees had his leg crushed in an accident, so it was said, and there was a deal between O'Sullivan and Cronin that the doctor would care for any of the iceman's employees who got hurt in an accident. Now we've got a summer rented-cottage with the possibility of blood in the hallway, and it happens to be only yards away from where O'Sullivan lives."

Schaack shrugged. "Maybe they're linked and maybe they aren't," he replied.

"I think I'll call on this fellow O'Sullivan and have another word with him," Schuettler said. "I'll take a look at this cottage too."

At Lakeview Schuettler found Patrick O'Sullivan taking nips of Irish whiskey from a hip flask while he supervised the loading of an ice wagon. The lieutenant asked him if he knew anything about the cottage across the way and its two occupants.

"Nothing at all," O'Sullivan replied. "I'm a busy man – didn't even know there was a cottage for rent over there." He took a nip from his bottle and offered it to the lieutenant. "Have a drink?"

Schuettler declined with thanks. "It could be that this was the cottage where Dr Cronin was murdered," he said. "If that's true, why do you suppose the killers picked a place so close to you?"

O'Sullivan shrugged. "Your guess is as good as mine. Come to think of it, though, I suppose if they aimed to murder the doc maybe they figured he wouldn't get wise so soon if they took him to a place near mine, where he thought he was going."

That sounded logical enough, but it still left too much unanswered, not least of which was the part played by the trunk and why it was abandoned empty where it would so obviously be quickly found. Schuettler left the ice-dealer with his whiskey flask and paid another call on Mrs Conklin, where she allowed him to visit the doctor's bedroom and examine a hairbrush on the dresser. From the bristles he pulled out a couple of dozen hairs, indubitably those of Dr Cronin, and compared them with those in the envelope which he had taken from the bloody trunk. Both samples were long, of fine texture and slightly wavy. Studied under daylight at the window, both samples were almost of identical hue, a brown so dark it was nearly black. Why had the barber Hal Garsch not recognised instantly what was so transparently obvious, Schuettler wondered, just as Captain Wing had wondered. Then he went to call on Jonas Carlson, to ask him to unlock the rented cottage.

Meanwhile, the Chicago press continued to take a leading role in the investigation. Reporters asked John Scanlon about the $5,000 reward that had been put up for the discovery of Dr Cronin. He told them, "The reward was offered for the discovery of his body and evidence that would lead to the arrest and conviction of his murderers." This was to disappoint sewerman Henry Rosch, for the inference was plain enough that the reward would not be paid for the discovery of the body alone.

Unfortunately, while Mr Conklin was hurrying to Lakeview police station to identify the corpse, then hurrying off to a relative, a *Chicago Times* reporter got to the Conklin home first and brought the news to Mrs Conklin of the discovery of Dr Cronin's body.

She swayed, then quickly got a grip on herself. Her voice was low and her eyes downcast when she spoke. "I'm not a bit surprised," she said. "I always said he had been murdered."

But by whom, she was asked. She picked up a little terrier dog playing around her feet and held him in her arms. "I can't say. I told the police a good many things that would have made it easy for them to find the body before this had they wanted to. I should think people would feel ashamed of themselves now for believing that he was insane or that he could be guilty of trying to get up a sensation."

The reporter continued to ply her with questions, but Mrs Conklin had had enough of the Chicago press. Grasping the terrier to her bosom, she slammed the door in the reporter's face.

11
PADDY DINAN DOES SOME THINKING

The mind of Paddy Dinan, livery-stable owner, had been racked and riven ever since the newspapers had started on about Dr Cronin's disappearance. No sooner did Dinan's eye alight on a journal than he seemed only to see the words "Dr Cronin," and then his tortured thoughts sailed back to that visit of Detective Dan Coughlin to the livery stable last Saturday morning. Paddy Dinan and Coughlin were the best of friends, Irish patriots above all else. Dan Coughlin linked with murderers? It didn't seem possible. Yet there it was, spread out across the front pages in dark hints that fuelled the suspicions of Paddy Dinan – that peculiar connection of a white horse and buggy with the mysterious disappearance of Dr Cronin. Paddy Dinan remembered only too well that the horse he hired out that night to Dan Couglin's friend Smith was a white one. And Dinan remembered too that the same horse and buggy were returned to the stable by the same friend Smith, if that was really his name, at 9.30 that evening – just two hours and twenty minutes after they were taken out.

Paddy Dinan might have been able to live with all this had it not been for his wife, who the day after Dr Cronin's disappearance was reported in the newspapers woke up in the middle of the night screaming and clutching the arm of her husband.

"I had a terrible dream," she wailed. "I saw Dr Cronin being driven in that rig towards a small house, and then he was being beaten to death! It was your rig, and the white horse was harnessed. I saw the doctor raise his eyes appealingly to me. He stretched out his hands as though crying for help."

As first light broke over the stable yard, while Paddy Dinan was still in bed and still thinking about the hired rig and his wife's disturbed night, a stable hand shouted up at his bedroom window, "Mr Dinan, there's an officer here, a policeman. He wants to know if any white horse went out on Saturday evening."

Dinan's mind raced. He was on the point of telling the man to wait, he would get dressed, come down, tell everything. Then caution took over. What would his pal Dan Coughlin say if he did that? He had been asked to keep quiet; suppose there was nothing in this business about Dr Cronin anyway? Calmly he called from the window, "Tell the policeman no such horse went out on Saturday."

But Paddy Dinan still had his wife to reckon with. As he drew back from the window she insisted that he should go at once and tell the proper authorities all he knew about the hiring of the white horse.

"Something wicked must have happened!" Mrs Dinan cried. "Something terrible! And you've got yourself all mixed up in it!"

Paddy Dinan was an impressionable man, and now he was also confused. One thing was for sure, though; if there had been a secret assassination he did not hold with that sort of thing. He drank a cup of coffee, then, his mind made up, he set out for East Chicago Avenue police station. He had read in the newspapers that the officer in charge of the investigation was Captain Schaack – if he told the captain about this curious coincidence maybe his white horse would be eliminated from the inquiries and he could breathe again. At the police station he was just about to ask the desk officer for Captain

Schaack when Detective Dan Coughlin came through a door at the side of the office.

"Paddy!" cried Coughlin. "You're just the man I want to see." He motioned the liveryman through a gate in the counter and towards a small office. "Come in here and have a quiet word with me, will you now?"

Closing the door, the detective told Dinan to sit down. "Listen, Paddy," Coughlin began, choosing a revolving chair for himself. "I don't want you to say anything to anyone about that affair of Saturday night. I've never been on good terms with that man Cronin, as you know. This thing may make talk and cause me trouble. Some people may think I had something to do with his disappearance."

"Well, did you, Dan?" Dinan asked directly.

Coughlin, his face like colourless rock, slumped back on to his shoulder-blades, as if in shock. "I did not, I'm telling you," he said, contemplating the other with assumed serenity. "I think you should go off home and forget all about this. Just keep quiet about it until I find out more. There's far too much speculation going on in this town about Cronin." He leaned forward and patted Paddy Dinan's knee confidentially. "That man was never any good, and if he's disappeared it's because he's fled this country. He's been up to no good with women, I can tell you that, and we'll be watching for him when he comes back to Chicago. Now be off with you. I know I can count on you."

So, faintly reassured, Paddy Dinan went off. But that night the more he thought about it the less sleep he had. Next morning he went back to the police station, asked for Captain Schaack, and this time he saw him. When he had told his story Paddy Dinan said, "I think a full report of this should be given to Mr. Hubbard, sir." Mr Hubbard was the Chicago Chief of Police.

"Thank you, Mr Dinan," replied Captain Schaack stiffly. "I've made a note of that suggestion. And I'll attend to the matter you've raised."

Off went Paddy Dinan again. That same evening, he happened to have a fortuitous meeting with Dan Coughlin. The detective told him, "I've had one hell of a job trying to find my friend Smith who came to you for that horse. Seems like he's left town. I reckon he's gone to New Mexico, like he said he might."

"No one's paid me for hiring the horse yet, Dan," Paddy Dinan observed.

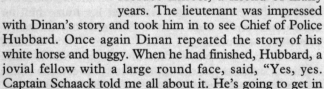

"Well, I got three dollars from Smith before he took off," Coughlin said. "But I guess I must've spent it. Don't worry, Paddy, I'll settle with you, though it'll have to be some other time." In fact Paddy Dinan was never paid for the hire of the white horse and buggy.

A couple more days went by, then, becoming suspicious that Captain Schaack had done no more than made a note of what he had said, Paddy Dinan went back to the police station a third time and met Lieutenant Horace Elliott, a friend of many years. The lieutenant was impressed with Dinan's story and took him in to see Chief of Police Hubbard. Once again Dinan repeated the story of his white horse and buggy. When he had finished, Hubbard, a jovial fellow with a large round face, said, "Yes, yes. Captain Schaack told me all about it. He's going to get in touch with you." He was slightly impatient, thoughtful, like a man with weighty work to do.

Chief of Police Hubbard

After that, Paddy Dinan was later to recall, he felt much easier. Sure enough, the next evening Captain Schaack called at the livery stable and asked to see the white horse and buggy which had been hired out on May 4th. Paddy Dinan took the horse out of the stable, harnessed it to the buggy, and the police captain led it away. An hour later he came back, still leading the animal.

"It's all right, Mr Dinan," Captain Schaack said. "This wasn't the horse that was driven to Dr Cronin's."

Paddy Dinan's eyes popped. He had convinced himself that his white horse must have been the one that drove Dr Cronin to his death; now, inexplicably, he was being assured by the police that it was not. Taking the horse from Schaack, he did not know whether to continue feeling uncomfortable or to start feeling relieved.

Captain Schaack's failure to get the white horse identified by the witnesses was another of his monumental blunders. What had happened, it later emerged, was that no sooner had he left Paddy Dinan's stable than rain began to fall in shilling-size drops; by the time he arrived at Mrs Conklin's it had turned to a deluge. Schaack tied up the horse and buggy some distance up the road beyond 470 Clark Street and invited Mrs Conklin to come and inspect it. She was to claim that she peered through the rainswept darkness and announced that she was quite unable to identify the horse in such atrocious conditions, whereupon Schaack drove the animal back to Dinan's.

Whether or not her story was accurate, it was eventually discovered nearly three weeks later by the investigative *Chicago Times*, which, deciding that here was another crass police error, revelled in it. The next day the newspaper sent a reporter, Charles Beck, to Paddy Dinan's stable to hire the same horse and buggy. Stable hand Napier Moreland put the white horse between the shafts and before Beck drove it away he asked Paddy Dinan, "Are you absolutely sure that this is the rig that Detective Coughlin's friend got?" Dinan had no doubt about it. He also had no doubt that it was the same rig taken out the previous evening by Captain Schaack. The reporter drove the buggy up Clark Street to the Conklins' apartment in the Windsor Theatre building. Brought out on to the street to be confronted with the rig, Mrs Conklin needed no second glance. She told reporter Beck, "That was the horse and buggy which carried away Dr Cronin the last time he was seen alive. I identify it." The rig was also shown to Frank Scanlan, who identified it. The *Times* published Beck's story with evident glee, and indignantly asked its readers if they thought they were getting from their police force what they were paying for it.

That story, highly critical of the Chicago police, was published on May 25th. When Chief of Police Hubbard read it he decided that enough was enough. He called Captain Schaack to his office. The two officers talked for twenty minutes, then they sent for Detective Dan Coughlin.

"I'm locking you up, Coughlin," Hubbard said. "You're not under arrest, though. Just for the moment I'm going to hold you at the Armory police station – more as an important witness to a serious crime than as a suspect."

Dan Coughlin's six foot one inch frame sagged slightly. He said nothing, and was led away.

One reason Hubbard had decided upon this unusual strategy was to keep Coughlin away from prying reporters while further police inquiries were made. He was not able to keep them away from Paddy Dinan, though, and when they learned that as a result of the *Times* story Coughlin had been called before the Chief of Police (they did not then know that he had been locked up) they decided that Paddy Dinan might be worth questioning. The reporters got the liveryman out of bed in the middle of the night. Mrs Dinan bade them all sit down in the front parlour, while Paddy Dinan, in a hastily pulled-on shirt, and with no prior warning of why he was suddenly so newsworthy, was subjected to a machine-gun barrage of questions. The first was, "Do you know Detective Dan Coughlin?"

Dinan, it was reported, "paused and turned a trifle pale." He seemed to the men with their notebooks pressed upon their knees that he was on the point of denying that he knew the detective. He checked himself, so it was said, and replied, hesitantly, "Yes, I know him."

"Did you know that Coughlin was called before Chief of Police Hubbard today?"

The question, it was suggested, made Dinan uneasy, but he answered readily, "No. I didn't know that."

"You have had some business dealings with Coughlin?"

"Oh, yes. I've been in business since 1871, and the officers often get rigs from me."

"Did Coughlin ever ask you to keep your mouth shut?"

"No."

"If an affidavit were sworn to the effect that he had said that to you, the affidavit would be false, then? Now, didn't he say something of that kind to you when he was inquiring about a white horse?"

"I believe something of that kind was said."

"Did he say there was any danger that he would get into trouble?"

"Listen, I'll tell you how it was. He did say he wanted me to keep quiet about it, because it might get him into trouble. He said Dr Cronin and himself were not good friends – there had been some trouble between them – and he might get into some trouble over the doctor's disappearance."

"Did you see Coughlin the Saturday that Dr Cronin was abducted?"

"Yes. On Saturday morning. He said to me, 'A party will come here tonight for a horse. Let him have one.' I asked him what kind of one to give the man and he said anything would do. That's why I thought the old white horse would answer the purpose."

"What time did this friend come?"

"About 7.10. I had been out; I came in when he was at the stable."

"What did this friend of Coughlin's look like?"

"Um-m. I didn't take his description, because the officers told me when they sent for a horse to keep quiet, ask no questions, and pay no attention to the man sent."

But later on during the interview, according to the

Times, Paddy Dinan seemed to forget his answer to that question and proceeded to give a detailed description of the stranger. He was asked who paid for the horse and buggy and replied, "Coughlin was to pay for it."

"Did the officers come to see you about the horse after Dr Cronin's disappearance attracted attention?"

Dinan recounted the visit of the uniformed policeman on Monday morning while he was still in bed, and when asked why he hadn't told the truth on that occasion he said, "The officers were always particular, you know, and so I didn't tell the policeman."

Reading the *Times* report, Police Chief Hubbard breathed a sigh of relief that Coughlin was under lock and key; if the press could do this to Dinan, who seemed to be just a bit-part player in the Cronin affair, what might they do to Coughlin, who had clearly played a major role, if they could get at him? Then he summoned Captain Schaack to his office. Hubbard was becoming increasingly concerned about Schaack; he was beginning to think the captain was being made a fool of by the press and by public opinion.

"I reckon the man who could tell you a great deal more about this Cronin case is Frank Woodruff," Hubbard told Schaack tersely. "Get over to the County Jail and grill him. If he won't talk, do a deal with him on this horse-thieving business. We've got a big murder on our hands, and we're not looking too smart in this city right now."

Schaack called a detective to drive him in a wagon to the County Jail, at the intersection of Indiana and Dearborn streets. At Schaack's request the prisoner was brought into the interview room by a jail guard.

"Hello again, Frank," Schaack said. "I reckon it's time you did some straight talking. Seems like telling the truth's at last becoming the fashion in this case. We're going for a ride, you and I, and you're going to show me exactly everything you did that night. This time it's all going to be true, and if it isn't, you're going to be spending the rest of your life inside a place like this." The captain gestured around the walls of the dingy jail while the prisoner rubbed his chin thoughtfully.

Outside Woodruff was helped into the police wagon. He sat alongside the detective who managed the reins, and Schaack sat behind him, his notebook on his knee. After giving directions to the driver, Woodruff leaned back to speak to Schaack.

"That Saturday afternoon they told me to get a horse and wagon from Dean's livery stable," he said. "They told me to drive it to the neighbourhood of the Carlson Cottage, on Ashland Avenue, and to wait there until a man came out of the cottage and gave a signal for me to drive up by stamping his foot on the wooden porch. They told me I would be picking up a dead body from the cottage."

As the police wagon rumbled along Woodruff described how he arrived at the cottage about twenty minutes before Dr Cronin was driven up, and placed his horse and wagon at a point near the cottage where he could keep an eye on the front steps. He saw the white-horse rig containing Dr Cronin and his driver, and three-quarters of an hour later a man he knew as Frank Williams (Martin Burke) came out and stamped his foot on the porch. Woodruff drove up to the cottage at once and helped by Williams and another man who emerged from the cottage (whose description placed him as Patrick Cooney, alias Williams's brother, alias J. B. Simmons) he loaded the trunk on to the wagon. Cooney then went back into the cottage. Burke jumped on to the wagon behind the trunk and directed Woodruff to drive eastwards to a point on the lake, where they picked up another man (Kevin Brown).

The intention was to dump the trunk and its contents into the lake, and that would have happened had they not seen the two Lakeview policemen Hayden and Smith step out of the shadows to observe them. Burke and Brown then decided on a rapid change of plan – in order to get as far away from the officers as they could they took a circuitous route through Edgewater near Lake Michigan. Then disaster struck. A rear wheel of the wagon got held fast in the lake ooze, and as the three men jumped off and started digging it out the watchman came along. Fortunately for them, he was a genial fellow, and when they had freed the wheel he cheerfully indicated the way they should take back to the Evanston road via the lake-shore drive. They had now been driving for nearly an hour with their ghastly load, and were getting desperate. They decided to give up the idea of the lake, and one of the men then suggested a sewer catch-basin. Woodruff was told to stop the wagon at the Fifty-ninth Street intersection of the Evanston road. Burke and Brown got down and forced the top off the man-hole on the south-east corner, then they lifted the trunk from the wagon.

Now an unexpected difficulty presented itself. While it might have been possible to drop the trunk with the body into the lake, it was a physical impossibility to dump the trunk in the catch-basin. The two men conferred and decided to take the body out of the trunk, drop it into the catch-basin, and return with the trunk to the Carlson cottage, where they would burn it. But – someone had forgotten the key of the trunk.

Cursing, Martin Burke kicked the lid off the trunk. "We can't waste any more time on this," he said. All three of them lifted the body out and threw it into the catch-basin. They put the trunk back on to the wagon. It was intended to go south for a distance, then drive north to the cottage and deposit the trunk.

"Right here," said Woodruff to Captain Schaack, pointing to the exact spot where the trunk was found, "we heard a noise of wagon wheels from the south, and the two men, one of whom had been sitting on the trunk, picked up the box and threw it out of the wagon and I was told to whip up the horse and drive west. When we reached Fullerton Avenue both men got down, said good-night to me and left me to drive home alone."

12

INSIDE THE CARLSON COTTAGE

As soon as Captain Schaack had deposited Frank Woodruff back in the County Jail he returned to East Chicago Avenue police station. Waiting for him on his desk were two brief, hurriedly written reports both apparently confirming Woodruff's latest account of the crime scene. One was from a detective officer confirming that two draymen had taken J. B. Simmons's furniture from Clark Street to the rented Carlson cottage at 1872 Ashland Avenue. The other was from Lieutenant Schuettler, who was waiting for Schaack at the cottage, and concerned an interview the lieutenant had had with John Carlson about the story of blood supposed to have been found there. Moments later Schaack was in a police patrol wagon heading down Clark Street towards Lakeview. He found Schuettler outside the Carlson cottage with John Carlson, and two detectives.

After a brief word with his lieutenant, Schaack signalled John Carlson to open the cottage door, and the police captain and his men filed in. They stood in the darkened hallway for a moment. When their eyes had adjusted to the darkness the detectives went forward and opened the blinds. As the dim light filtered through the rooms every far wall seemed to be a distant shadow, every corner like a cavern, loath to reveal any part of its dreadful secret. Despite the warmth of the late May afternoon, Schaack shuddered. The empty, wall-less house was like a body without life, held in time and steeped in mourning for its last visitor that terrible Saturday evening three and a half weeks ago.

With daylight penetrating the cottage, the officers were presented with an astonishing sight. All over the floors and walls were great splotches of thinly applied yellow paint, a surrealist nightmare of bright colour daubs on every visible surface. The phantom painter must have hopped about the rooms on one shoeless foot, for occasionally the impress of a bare right foot was visible, first in the hall, by the front door, and then several times in the two downstairs rooms. The bare-foot marks could be seen faintly through the yellow paint, clearly applied in an attempt to obliterate something, but in one instance the painter seemed to have missed his mark and his footprint was gruesomely incised in dried blood.

Guessing that the painter had been making a feeble effort to cover other bloodstains, Schaack sent out for some turpentine. When the spirit was applied the paint dissolved even while the iron-faced detectives watched, revealing huge areas of blood. There was indeed much more blood on the walls, floor and front stairway than there was turpentine to cope with it.

Helped by some reporters – who never seemed to be far away from an incident in the Cronin case – the police cut out sections of bloodstained wood from the flooring and stairway and sent them off for analysis. Lieutenant Schuettler found a paintbrush with dried yellow paint on it in the attic, and in one of the downstairs rooms another officer found the key of the trunk. Outside police began interviewing the Carlsons and their neighbours. They heard about the Williams brothers, and the fraudulent book-keeper William King, who rented the house before the Williams; they learned that for the whole of the first month the cottage was empty, and was relet again only on the basis of the story of the Williams' sick sister going there to convalesce. Inside they began to dig up the cellar and the ground under the main stairway in a search for Dr Cronin's missing clothes, but they found nothing.

Word came back from the police laboratory that Dr Brandt, who conducted the post-mortem on Dr Cronin, and Dr Hectoren, a pathologist at Cork County Hospital, had examined the bloodstained wood and concluded that the blood was human and from the same source as the blood found in the trunk – they decided this because "the corpuscles were similar and the pigmentation and the crystals were the same."

Somewhere towards the end of that day reporters who had got into the Carlson cottage and had earlier helped the police cut away the bloodstained woodwork noted that one Officer Jacobs, who was supposed to be guarding a downstairs room, was absent from his place of duty. Taking advantage of the situation, the reporters began cutting out some extra pieces of bloodstained woodwork for themselves, presumably with the object of taking it back to their offices to be photographed. During this unlawful operation Officer Jacobs arrived back at his duty station, and beside himself with fury at this wanton destruction of his patch, drew his revolver and drove the reporters out of the front door at gunpoint. Lieutenant Schuettler, who saw this happening, then suspended Jacobs for being absent from his place of duty.

For the reporters, for whom the unpredictable was normal, there were still plenty of stones to be upturned in the vicinity of the investigation. They flocked around the Carlsons' home behind the cottage and hammered on the door. Young John Carlson appeared and barred the doorway with his form; behind him the reporters glimpsed two detectives from East Chicago Avenue station.

"You've heard about these stories of the rented cottage?" a *Herald* reporter asked him.

"Yes, I know all about that, but I can't talk to you," John Carlson replied "The police have asked me to say nothing."

"It's a fact that the cottage was rented by two mysterious

people who paid the first month's rent and haven't been seen around here lately?"

"Yes, but I tell you I cannot talk about it. The *Herald* will get all there is as soon as anybody does."

"How about the blood you saw?"

"You can't get anything out of me and there's no use trying. I won't talk."

"Can we see your mother?"

"No, you can't. I can't let you in at all."

Ejected from the front steps of the Carlson home, the reporters moved like a stampede down the road to the home of Patrick O'Sullivan, the ice-dealer. Their knock on the door was answered by someone described by a newspaper as "a bright young woman." She may have been O'Sullivan's housekeeper, Mrs Tom Whelan, who was also the wife of the iceman's cousin and herself a fervent Clanna-Gael supporter. The iceman was out, she announced. She refused to give her name, but catching the brief scent of stardom she bubbled like a spring with tit-bits about the renting of the cottage. Leaning against the door-frame, the bright young woman stared into the middle distance vividly recalling everything she could, while the reporters, their notebooks held in space, scribbled frantically.

"Not quite two months ago I noticed that the 'For Rent' board in the window was taken down, and my milkman told me that the cottage had been rented," the bright young woman said. "I was glad of that, for the Carlsons had had so much trouble about their cottage.

"The man who was in it before embezzled some money from the Brunswick and Balke Company. He was sent to the penitentiary and the family had to leave, and the cottage was vacant for a while. About three weeks ago, one Sunday night, we saw a light in the house, but as far as I know no one has been there since. Mrs Carlson said she didn't know what to make of it, and if they didn't come to take possession today she was going to take it herself and rent it again. The tenants had the key, but she was going to get in anyway."

Leaving the bright young woman still searching back through her memory for anything else they might like to know, the reporters moved on to a grocer's shop a couple of blocks away, where they learned that the cottage had been the subject of much discussion. When the woman behind the counter recovered from the shock of so many frantic men crowding into her shop she said, "I understood the cottage was rented by two young Irishmen who gave it out that they were going to work for Mr O'Sullivan, the iceman, and that their sister was going to keep house for them. Mr O'Sullivan, though, says he hired no such men, and doesn't know anything about them.

"I should think it was about a month ago that they came to the house in the evening and put their carpets in, but I don't know as they have been there since. There's something very mysterious about the way they've acted. Mrs Carlson saw them only once, she says, and described them both as young and evidently Irish working men. The story of their going to work for O'Sullivan wasn't true, and they might have been concerned in Dr Cronin's murder."

At this point the *Chicago Times* decided that they definitely were concerned in Dr Cronin's murder. Distilling all its journalists' information from the investigation scene, the newspaper reported next day:

"The Carlson cottage, 1872 Ashland Avenue, in which unmistakable evidences of a terrible crime were discovered and where there is now little doubt Dr Cronin was foully murdered, was surrounded all day yesterday by a crowd of police officers and curiosity-seekers.

"Women with babies in arms and children hanging to their skirts lingered around the place until driven home by hunger or thirst. They saw nothing and heard only their own chattering as they spoke in low tones of the bloody floor, the trunk, and the desperation of the men who assassinated the doctor.

"The police have only one opinion. The house was

rented for the purpose of murdering Dr Cronin in it as guardedly as possible, and the cause of the cottage being rented in both March and April was for the reason that no favourable opportunity to make away with the physician had presented itself.

"Yesterday the police were busy with young John Carlson, who gave about the best description received of the two men who rented from his mother. He was spirited away from Lakeview.

"The police suspect two men known as the Williams brothers, and are trying to run them down. It is thought they are not in the city."

Perhaps the most bizarre commentary on that momentous day for police and press came when Captain Wing, of Lakeview police, told the Carlsons that the forensic examination of their cottage would take another three or four days, and he therefore proposed to pay them thirteen dollars to cover a full month's rent. Mrs Carlson seemed pleased enough with this. She had already decided she wanted no more truck with tenants like the Williams brothers, and had turned over all future lettings to a Lakeview real-estate agent named Lukens. But when Mr Lukens heard of her deal with the police he shook his head in disbelief. "Heavens above, Mrs Carlson!" he cried. "At this time I could have got you a hundred dollars a week for it from any newspaper in Chicago!"

13
BURIED WITH HONOURS

The idea that Dr Patrick Cronin knowingly laid down his life in defence of the purity of patriotism was sufficient motive to cause a frisson of excitement in every American breast; we are still, remember, in the same century as Abraham Lincoln and the Civil War. So it was that Chicago, burgeoning city in the land of the free, prepared to demonstrate on a presidential scale its abhorrence of secret political assassination and its fierce pride in patriotism. Chicagoans were determined that nothing was to become Dr Cronin so much in life as his death. All through the afternoon and evening of May 25th, the day before the funeral, it seemed that the whole city, filled with affectionate and touching sorrow, came to file by the body lying in state in the Cavalry Armory.

Sentries from the Hibernian Rifles, Dr Cronin's regiment, stood, arms at rest, at each corner of the raised platform holding the catafalque and coffin. A large crayon portrait of the doctor, draped in black, stood near the coffin. A huge cross of white pinks and marguerites, woven in with smilax, was placed at the head of the bier; a harp and a smaller cross stood at his feet. A candelabrum with seven tapers flickered in front of the cross; ropes of smilax and white roses were looped from the coffin and about the catafalque, and potted plants were grouped together at the corners of the platform. A canopy of Stars and Stripes hung above the bier, and festoons of black and white twined the bars above it.

The *Chicago Daily News* reported: "A crowd that filled Michigan Avenue stood before the Armory. The police kept a passageway open for those who wished to enter the funeral hall, and two uniformed riflemen leaning on bayoneted muskets lent the glamour of their accoutrements to the military air of the place.

"For three hours the procession marched in double file across the platform. Only the picture and the big silver plate on the coffin lid testified that all that was mortal of Dr P. H. Cronin was within the casket. The line of sightseers was turned out at the south door, and few people remained in the building."

At last the solemn file was halted; it was now Sunday, the day of the funeral. An estimated 40,000 people lined the streets to watch the 7,000-strong procession. Interestingly, quite a number of onlookers in that impressive gathering must have lived on for thirty-odd years into the 1920s to see their city become synonymous with the worst excesses of gangsterism, outraging public morality on a scale unequalled elsewhere in the Western world. But Chicagoans in 1889 were not yet ready for that. Their presence on the streets bore witness to their intolerance of the squalid nether world of corruption in their midst; it might also be seen as evidence that the culture of the next century, which was to make itself more and more miserable by desperately struggling to be happy, had still not been conceptualised.

Inside the Cavalry Armory the pall-bearers took up their positions. At their head was Luke Dillon; the others were Edward O'Meagher Condon and John Devoy of New York, and Thomas P. Tuite, of Detroit. The first three were prominent Irish nationalists, the last, also an Irishman, was a school friend of the doctor. Following them, representing the friends of the dead man and the societies to which he belonged, came Frank Scanlan, Patrick McGarry, Charles Barry, Michael Kelly, Daniel

Dr Cronin's mourners at the cemetery and below, his body is placed in the vault

Sullivan, Thomas McEnerny, Dudley Solon, John T. Golden, Maurice Morris, Dr John Guerin, ex-Alderman McCauley, John P. Ryan, W. P. Rend and John Scanlon.

Outside the Armory the casket was placed in a hearse drawn by four black horses. The procession lined up behind it with a platoon of police, Lieutenant Wilson in command, at its head. Marshal P. J. Cahill and his aides headed a posse pushing a way through the dense crowd in Michigan Avenue to let the procession pass. After the police detachment came a drum corps, then the Hibernian Rifles with arms reversed, then the cortege, with the hearse in a panoply of black, a guard of honour from the Rifles, and the pall-bearers. Next were the Clan-na-Gael Guards in grey uniform with tricoloured plumes; the uniformed ranks of the Royal Arcanum, in their olive-coloured suits, followed by hundreds of members of the Ancient Order of United Workmen, without uniforms. After them came 1,000 members of the Ancient Order of Hibernians, 1,200 men representing a number of courts of the Independent Order of Foresters, and 2,700 Catholic Foresters. Uniformed members of the Royal League, the Sheridan Rifles, the Catholic Benevolent Legion and fragments of a number of other orders swelled the line.

It was a line that reached from Indiana Street on Rush Street to Chicago Avenue and around to Superior Street at its intersection with State Street. It took thirty-five minutes to pass the corner of Indiana and Rush Streets, four abreast. Four bands and half a dozen drum corps played dirges or marked the slow time of the funeral march. Scores of standard-bearers carried furled flags draped in black and society banners edged with crepe. The regalia and badges with emblems of mourning, the green of Ireland, the Stars and Stripes of America, the slow tread of the marching hosts, the sable pall and plumes, the bands and drums with their solemn strains – all this drew silent tears from the mute thousands crowding pavements and windows, climbing on stools and boxes, sitting on roofs and the tops of unfinished buildings. Chicago, shouldering all the shame and guilt of its murderous underworld, was there to see Dr Cronin off in style, and was overcome by it.

The vast auditorium of the Cathedral of the Holy Name was filled two hours before the funeral service; there was another immense crowd outside. As the procession approached, the bell in the cathedral tower began to toll measured strokes for the dead. The organ pealed the opening bars of a funeral march as the pall-bearers moved up the centre aisle and lowered the casket on to a catafalque in ebony trimmings. Although nearly one-half of the cathedral was set aside for the marching societies, the space reserved turned out to be inadequate for the half of them – only an escort of the Hibernian Rifles and a hundred or so representatives of the different societies finally managed to get in.

There was a requiem high mass (according to custom, this was never celebrated in the cathedral on Sunday, so that Dr Cronin's funeral was accorded an unusual honour), some solemn music by Mozart, a bass solo, a benedictus by Gounod, a vocal quartet and the Agnus Dei by Reisinger.

Three trains had been laid on to take the crowds to Calvary Cemetery and they filled thirty-six carriages. Hundreds more drove out from the cathedral service, and more still poured in from neighbouring suburbs. It was reckoned that 3,000 people crowded into the cemetery and that many more would have had gone had it not been for heavy black clouds in the west – and a rumour that Dr Cronin's enemies intended to blow up the funeral train with dynamite.

And so Dr Cronin was laid to rest, but he was still to be apostrophised at a memorial meeting of citizens called by the Personal Rights League in the Central Music Hall a month later. His own newspaper, The *Celtic-American*, understandably waxed lyrical in its account of the meeting, "the large and beautiful hall was filled to overflowing with the very best class of people made up of all nationalities," it rather quaintly reported. United States Senator C. B. Farwell was there, so too was Bishop Cheney, Judge Richard Prendergast, and two members of the House of Representatives. There was a run of eulogistic speeches; one of them, by W. P. Rend, a long-time friend of Dr Cronin, painted a colourful if rather melodramatic picture of the doctor's last moments.

"In his love of liberty and zeal to advance the cause of Ireland," declared Mr Rend, "Dr Cronin connected himself with several patriotic associations intended for the promotion of this cause.

"Among others he joined the Clan-na-Gael, but he found this society dominated by a certain conspiracy of men posing as patriots. They were false patriots, however. They were only patriots for plunder [Applause]. He unmasked their schemes, he denounced their villainies. Here his trials and troubles began. Thenceforward his steps were dogged by spies and scoundrels. Efforts were made to attack and assassinate his character. His life was inquired into. Hired detectives were engaged in order to disgrace and ruin him. He felt that his enemies were plotting against his life, and that hired thugs, like sleuth hounds thirsting for blood, were following him bent upon his destruction.

"He protested to his friends against this danger and this persecution. But in this civilised community no one could think it credible that such a fearful crime could be even contemplated. His friends decided that these fears were only idle delusions.

"On May 4th, however, his unrelenting enemies found means to execute their fiendish plot. On this day we see Dr Cronin, in all the strength and vigour of perfect manhood, starting forth to a call for assistance. Unconscious of all danger, he leaves his office, believing that he was going to staunch the wounds, bind up the fractured limb and alleviate the pain of a suffering fellow-creature. He little dreamed of the deep, dark treachery that was luring him to the scene of his death in that lonely Carlson cottage, then occupied by cowardly assassins.

"On arrival at this cottage, he hastens up the fatal steps. The door quickly opens, and quickly closes upon him. He rushes unarmed, helpless and alone into the very arms of his murderers. The bludgeon soon does its tragic and deadly work. He falls prostrate upon the floor in the crimson pool formed by the blood gushing from his gaping wounds. The walls give forth his faint cry for assistance and mercy. His life is soon beat out. He dies a most tragic death.

"The sight of his mangled and lifeless body satiates the hellish hate of his brutal butchers. They gloat with savage joy over this prostrate, bleeding body. Denuded of his clothes, his corpse is next packed into a trunk, purchased seventy-two days before as the intended coffin for his clandestine burial.

"On that Sunday morning, so sacred to God's worship, while the pitying stars of heaven are looking down upon the cruel fate of this murdered man, these fiendish assassins convey his corpse through the streets of our city and throw it into the catch-basin of a public sewer. Here they believe the body will soon decay beyond any chance of recognition. Here, with this body, they imagine that this horrid crime will also be buried in eternal silence.

"Believing that evidences of the crime are hidden and that the concealed body will never be discovered, his murderers make light of his disappearance and calumniated his fair name by the most atrocious slander. False rumours are spread. The public are informed that he fled to escape the exposure of the consequences of some disgraceful crime, or that he was a British spy and had gone to join Le Caron. These and other infamies are heaped upon his memory. 'Murder will out,' however, proved true in this case, as in many other foul massacres. After a few days his body is found; it is identified, and its shattered skull gives startling evidence of the foul, murderous deed."

Another speaker, Judge Prendergast, said Dr Cronin was "an unselfish, public-spirited, honourable and honest man. And those who hated him and lured him to his death did so because of that character of his, which could neither be bent nor broken, swerved nor turned aside by threats against his life, by attacks against his life, by plots against his life."

And Senator Farwell, denouncing the murder as "un-American, un-Irish and un-Christian," called upon the citizens of Chicago "to leave nothing undone to bring to justice every man connected with that barbarous murder, no matter who it may be or what his heretofore position was. No guilty man must escape."

Fired up with this oratory, the memorial meeting passed a unanimous resolution that they "encourage all lawful efforts to bring to justice, which shall not discriminate, and to adequate punishment, the instigators and perpetrators of this murder."

Fine words, Police Chief Hubbard thought, listening to it all from his seat in the hall and alert to the ebb and flow of emotion in the damp-eyed congregation. But who exactly were the instigators and perpetrators of this murder? He had the statements of Frank Woodruff, the Conklins, Frank Scanlan, the Carlsons, Paddy Dinan and a number of the doctor's friends, the latter strong on innuendo and allegation but tellingly short on fact. How many people in the hornets' nests of the Irish-American societies were implicated, the police chief wondered.

Who should he arrest – and who should he leave out?

14
TWO ARE APPREHENDED

It was at this point in the Cronin affair that Alexander Sullivan earned himself the sobriquet of the most thoroughly watched man in Chicago. Wherever he went, day or night, a shadow followed him. His office was under constant surveillance, as was his Oak Street home. Detectives lounged at the corners of corridors in his office building or hung about around the Clark Street entrance. Men with the brims of their hats pulled low over their eyes tracked him through the streets, through the corridors of the Court House and in and about the downtown offices where he carried on business. Everywhere that Sullivan went he knew they were there; he would have had to walk with his eyes closed and a white stick to miss them.

All his friends knew they were there too. Those who came to his office noticed that when Sullivan went out the shadows disappeared and others appeared in the street; when he came back those in the street disappeared and those in the office building took up their positions again.

The press loved it. They asked Chief Hubbard who was responsible for this brazen show. The Chief admitted that the police were watching Sullivan closely but when asked why he thought it was necessary he declined to comment. Under pressure he admitted that of all the direct evidence that had poured into his office not one single thing pointed to Sullivan's culpability. But after that the Chief had nothing more to say to the reporters.

Hubbard's dilemma was transparently obvious. Everyone who knew anything about the case knew that Sullivan was the mastermind behind the murder. There were numerous testimonies and statements to the effect that he was Dr Cronin's avowed enemy, that Cronin had openly said that Sullivan made him fear for his life, that Sullivan was constantly trying to expose Cronin's defalcations and to destroy his reputation in the nationalistic societies.

But where, asked Sullivan and his friends, throwing their arms apart in tragic astonishment, was the evidence that he had murdered Dr Cronin? So far as they could tell, the onslaught against him appeared to be led by the cranky Conklins and the prejudiced Frank Scanlan. The police, Sullivan complained, had spent many hours listening to these informants viciously grinding their axes, and it all added up to a vindictive and malicious campaign against him. Casting himself in the role of the persecuted innocent, the lawyer declared that he knew so little about Dr Cronin's life and habits, and was so disinterested in the man's affairs, that neither he nor his friends could have the slightest interest in wishing the doctor dead.

Chief Hubbard shrugged. He was overtly putting the heat on Sullivan in the hope that the lawyer would crack in time for the grand jury hearing. If the grand jury indicted Sullivan on the facts before it the police would have the necessary time to examine the evidence piece by piece and build up a case against the lawyer. But that was more likely to happen if Sullivan was pushed and pressurised by police tactics, and it was these tactics which the Chicago police were now employing.

At the same time that Sullivan was under constant surveillance Captain Schaack decided to take a man named Peter McGeehan into custody. Those who knew the players in the case were mystified by this arrest. Who, they asked, was Peter McGeehan? It seemed that McGeehan had mysteriously disappeared from his home in Philadelphia three months before the Cronin murder, and this event, coupled with the facts that he had a thoroughly bad criminal record and was an Irishman, was apparently sufficient justification for his apprehension. McGeehan soon proved that he was in Pullman on the night of the murder and was released.

Iceman Patrick O'Sullivan was also arrested. He was taken to Lakeview police station and closeted with Captain Wing, Captain Schaack, Lieutenant Schuettler and the city's Mayor Boldenweck. The mayor, an old friend of the ice-dealer, was brought in by the police in an attempt to persuade O'Sullivan to talk.

"You'll have to spill the beans, Paddy," the Mayor said gruffly. "It's best to tell everything, because it's all going to be found out anyway."

O'Sullivan, who had hitherto told the police that he had known Detective Dan Coughlin only since the murder, and did not know anyone else in the Chicago police force, now confessed that he had been a friend of the detective for years. He admitted he was a member of the Clan-na-Gael and had met Dr Cronin – at Lincoln Hall, in Lincoln Avenue, on the night of March 22nd when the doctor took one of the official chairs at a meeting – before he made his contract with him.

"I was a streetcar conductor once, employed by the North Side Street Car Company," O'Sullivan reminisced. "I met Dan Coughlin there – he was a streetcar driver at the time. I guess I got to know a good few policemen and detectives on the North Side when Dan joined the detective force." He had also worked as a miner in the iron mines of Hancock County, Michigan. Hancock County was Coughlin's home base, and while O'Sullivan was there he got to know several of Coughlin's relatives. O'Sullivan had plenty to tell the mayor and the police that day, but there was also plenty he did not tell.

He had for instance no answer to the question of why only a few weeks before the murder he signed the contract with Dr Cronin to take care of any of his employees if they were involved in accidents at work, and how it came about that the very first occasion the contract was invoked was on the night of the murder.

"That wasn't one of my men who called for the doctor," O'Sullivan replied. "None of my men was hurt that day. That fellow who called on Cronin was a hoaxer."

"But, Paddy," argued Mayor Boldenweck, "why did you make the deal in the first place? After all, you've only got three employees. Firms with twenty times more men than you employ don't think it's necessary to make a deal like that with a doctor. And why Cronin, anyway? Dozens of doctors live closer to you than Cronin."

"Well, I believe in looking after my workers," replied O'Sullivan, beginning to twist and fidget anxiously. The granite-faced policemen stared back mutely at him. There was even less conviction in the iceman's voice when he protested that people who said they had seen him talking to the men who had rented the Carlson cottage must have been mistaken. Filled with anticipatory alarm about his fate, O'Sullivan whined, "They were all strangers to me. I've never seen any of them in my life before."

At lunch-time Captain Schaack pushed back his chair and closed the interview. "Don't leave town, Paddy," he said with calm determination. "We're going to need you again soon."

Back in Schaack's office the three police officers talked together, sifting through the depositions, for the rest of the day. That same night, May 27th, they arrested Patrick O'Sullivan and Detective Dan Coughlin on a warrant sworn by John Joseph Cronin, a brother of the murdered man. It read:

"State of Illinois, County of Cook, City of Chicago.

"The complaint and information of John Joseph Cronin, in the said county, made before George Kersten, Esq., one of the justices of the peace in and for said county, on the 27th of May, 1889.

"Said complainant, being duly sworn, upon his oath, says that Daniel Coughlin and Patrick O'Sullivan, on or about the 4th of May, 1889, in county and State aforesaid, feloniously, maliciously and wilfully did conspire and agree, together with a number of persons whose names are unknown to said affiant, to kill and murder one Patrick Henry Cronin, and in furtherance of said conspiracy, the said Daniel Coughlin and Patrick O'Sullivan, and a number of persons whose names are unknown to said affiant, did feloniously, maliciously, wilfully and unlawfully, and with malice aforethought, on the 4th day of May, 1889, and in said county and State, kill and murder the said Patrick Henry Cronin, contrary to the form of the statutes in such cases made and provided.

"That this complainant has just and reasonable grounds to believe that said Daniel Coughlin, Patrick O'Sullivan and a number of other persons whose names are unknown, committed said offence, and therefore prays that they may be arrested and dealt with according to law. (Signed) John Joseph Cronin."

Patrick O'Sullivan had just finished eating his supper at home when two detectives called to take him away. Under normal practice he would have appeared before a justice of the peace with his lawyer and been formally remanded in custody, but because there was no lawyer available he was simply clapped into a police cell for the time being.

Detective Dan Coughlin, who was still being held at the Armory police station pending inquiries, was formally received into custody by Police Captain Bartram and, followed by a train of reporters, taken from the police station across a few corridors to the main office of the jail, where he arrived at five minutes past midnight. Coughlin marched up to the reception desk alongside Captain Bartram as if he were out for a nocturnal walk. He was "perfectly unconcerned," it was reported, as he watched night jailer Thomas Turner making entries in the prison register.

"Well," said the ex-detective, pleasantly, "it's about bedtime, ain't it?"

Mr Turner assured him he would soon have an opportunity to go to bed, and stay as long as he liked.

"Search the prisoner," said the jailer roughly, making it clear that Coughlin was getting no preferential treatment for having been a law-enforcement officer. Coughlin, nonchalantly smoking a cigar, made no objection as Deputy George Reich and Detective Barney Flynn went methodically through his pockets. Turner meanwhile wrote Coughlin's particulars in the jail record book ... prisoner was 30 years old, described himself as a police officer, lived at No. 116 Jay Street. He had light-coloured hair, a sandy moustache, brown eyes and a mole on his right cheek. Charge was murder. When the deputy and the detective had finished the body search, and the necessary forms were filled in, Coughlin, as composed as ever, said, "Well, good-night, boys," and was led into the body of the prison by a warder. On his way to his cell, No. 25 on "Murderer's Row," he told a reporter, almost running at his elbow, "Nothing to say."

The inquest on Dr Cronin opened two days later on May 29th, a week after the discovery of the body. After the Carlsons and Mrs Conklin had given evidence – the Carlsons making it quite clear that iceman O'Sullivan knew the occupants of the Carlson cottage intimately, and Mrs Conklin identifying the white horse and buggy as the one Dr Cronin got into – a milkman named William Mertes was called to the stand to give an account of Dr Cronin's last moments before he died.

Mertes told the jury, "I was driving past the Carlson cottage on the night of the murder. I saw a buggy containing two men and a white horse drive up to the door. The man seated on the left (the horse was facing north) jumped hastily from his seat and ran up the steps. He carried two packages.

"Before he had time to knock at the door it was opened, it seeming to me that someone was waiting inside the hallway. At the instant the man stepped inside the door the man in the buggy whipped up and drove rapidly north to the first street, where he turned west and was lost to sight."

The milkman had some business to do at a grocery store not far away. That done he went back home the way he had come, passing the Carlson cottage about thirty-five minutes later. A single light burned from the house, magnified by the night. From within, the milkman remembered hearing "a hammering or smashing sound."

If anyone had any doubts about Alexander Sullivan being the mastermind behind the murder they must have been dispelled when Dr Cronin's friend, Patrick McGarry, took the stand. McGarry told the coroner that he had known Cronin for six years. On two different occasions Cronin had told him his life was in danger. The first time was on the night that Dr Cronin pressed for an investigation into Alexander Sullivan's methods of running the Clan-na-Gael. On that occasion he told McGarry he "took his life in his hands." McGarry remembered the exact words Cronin used, which were, "That may have been a fatal night, but I am determined to show up Alexander Sullivan's thievery and treachery to the Irish people, even if my life is taken for it." Later, after the trial of the Triangle in Buffalo in 1888, Cronin remarked on Alexander Sullivan's hostility to him and said to McGarry, "Mac, I believe that man will be the instigator of my murder. If I am murdered, there are papers relating to this trial, and an affidavit where his name is mentioned, in Mr Conklin's safe. I will depend upon you to see that the proper authorities get them."

McGarry was asked by Coroner Hertz, "Who were the people who preferred charges against Alexander Sullivan and the Triangle?"

"Dr Cronin was one, and there were also John Devoy and Luke Dillon."

Luke Dillon, a member of the executive committee of the Clan-na-Gael*, told the inquest he knew Cronin intimately. "He was intensely patriotic and very useful in the Irish movement."

*After the resignation of Sullivan and the Triangle the Clan-na-Gael was governed by a nine-member executive committee.

He was asked by the coroner, "Have you ever had any conversation with Dr Cronin touching on his being in any danger?"

"Yes, sir, we have spoken of it," replied Dillon. "He told me that Alexander Sullivan's personal ambition to rule both in Irish and American politics in this city would be the cause of his death, for he felt that the man had no more blood than a fish and would not hesitate to take his life. I thought at the time that he had Alexander Sullivan on the brain, and that there was not the slightest likelihood of any man hurting him."

Dillon had changed his mind about that at the trial of the Triangle. "Alexander Sullivan's language to Dr Cronin at that time was very abusive, and I felt that a man who could speak so disparagingly of another was capable of going to greater extremes. Another reason why I have changed my mind, and why I believe that Alexander Sullivan is responsible for this murder, if not indeed the principal in it, is that Dr Cronin's verdict against Sullivan and the two others was that they were guilty."

Luke Dillon said that after the trial of the Triangle he received, as a member of the new executive committee, a request that Alexander Sullivan should be permitted to send out a protest*, along with the trial report finding him not guilty, to the different Camps. He, Dillon, objected to that, because at that time Sullivan was no longer a member of the order, and because he objected to the remarks Sullivan was making in the protest about Dr Cronin. "But I was evidently overruled, for his document was eventually sent out, although the trial report was not."

Although the protest, which was effectively a considerable attack on Dr Cronin's integrity, was dated September 1888, it was only circulated in May or June, 1889, just after the murder of Dr Cronin. "The protest may be dated September," Dillon said, "but I don't believe it was written for another six months after that. It certainly never came before the executive of our organi-

*See Chapter 3.

sation until about the day Dr Cronin disappeared."

Asked about the tone of the protest, Dillon said, "I didn't believe the things he was saying about Dr Cronin. I knew Cronin to be a thorough gentleman, thoroughly patriotic, and his membership of the British militia company, about which Alexander Sullivan so much protested, came about because of his love for Ireland. Cronin himself told me that the reason he joined the militia was to learn his duty as a soldier in the event that he was called upon to fight for his country – it was not to swear any allegiance to Her Majesty. We have another member of the Clan-na-Gael, Tom Tuite, city treasurer of Detroit, who was also a member of that same militia company, and Tom is a patriotic, good man."

He was asked, "Why do you think Alexander Sullivan was such a passionate enemy of Dr Cronin?"

"It was for personal revenge," Dillon replied. "Because Cronin found him guilty of theft, and because he exposed Sullivan's treacherous conduct to members of the organisation."

"Do you believe that Dr Cronin's opinion of Sullivan was correct?"

"I don't know. I used to think he exaggerated Sullivan's importance. At the time I looked upon Sullivan then as only an ordinary villain. But Cronin looked upon him as a very dangerous man, and a very able one, too. Now I am inclined to agree with Cronin – Alexander Sullivan was a professional patriot, sucking the life-blood out of the Irish organisations."

Asked about the dynamiters who had been betrayed, Dillon said there was no direct evidence of treachery, because the names of dynamiters sent to England would be known only by the Executive of the time, and at that time the Triangle and the Executive were one and the same. All orders to the dynamiters were secret, were issued only by the Executive, and no one else had access to them. Dillon did not recall Dr Cronin ever charging Alexander Sullivan with betraying the dynamiters, but

"Cronin did tell me that he believed men had been betrayed through the intimacy of Alexander Sullivan with the British spy Le Caron during the time Le Caron was Senior Guardian of another Camp."

Dillon explained that the misappropriation of the organisation's funds had resulted in the under-funding, or non-funding, of the dynamiters. In June, 1882, it was John Devoy's guess that the Triangle commanded Clanna-Gael funds of more than $300,000 and of this $128,000 had been spent in violation of the constitution. After June another $100,000 was collected and paid into the funds. "This money was supposed to have been used in violent measures against England or in carrying on what was termed the active policy." A moment or two later Dillon mitigated that observation by adding, "The funds were supposed to be used in case of England becoming involved in difficulty in aiding Ireland to liberate herself." As a result of a resolution taken at the Boston convention the vouchers and papers in connection with the expenditure of the $128,000 were burned.

Dillon himself was not a member of the Boston convention – it was his charge that that convention was packed with proxies. There was only one delegate listed as having come from Chicago. This was the dynamiter Captain Mackay Lomasney. "He was not selected or elected by his camp, he was not present at the convention, in fact he was not even in the country at the time."

Dillon was emphatic that there was no mandate on the Executive to support the dependants of the dynamiters. "There is nothing in the constitution of this organisation that requires men to give up their lives in the cause, and there is nothing in the constitution directing the Executive to support the families of those who go out to conduct the active policy. But we believe that common decency and common Christianity would compel an Executive to do that. We have never had any answer to the question of whether the Executive – the Triangle – ever helped any of the dependent families. In fact, I know they didn't."

The reason why Alexander Sullivan had left the organisation was because he thought his crimes would find him out, and that Dr Cronin, John Devoy, Luke Dillon and others, "who were endeavouring to purify the organisation, would finally bring him to judgment before the rank and file."

But, Dillon added, "I believe that when he resigned he did not cease to rule. I have seen his handwriting on circulars issued to members of the United Brotherhood a year after his resignation was supposed to have taken place. I believe he is able to influence the men although he is not now in the order."

Dillon was asked a series of questions by the foreman of the inquest jury, a man named Critchell, about the character of Dr Cronin. In reply, Dillon said the doctor was not a quarrelsome man – "he was as mild and mannerly as any lady." Nor would he have done anything in his medical practice which would have brought discredit on him.

Critchell asked him, "Do you think the feelings of partisanship aroused by the quarrels in the organisation would have risen high enough to lead to the death of any of the members?"

His reply, "No," was in direct contradiction to his earlier evidence, when he said that he believed Alexander Sullivan was responsible for the murder. He added, "Irishmen, generally speaking, are violent perhaps during discussion, but afterwards they generally settle all their differences with a drink. In controversy or debate they are naturally hot-headed, so violent that they sometimes make threats, but they forget them in five minutes."

He said he did not know Dan Coughlin, Patrick O'Sullivan, John Beggs, or a man named Kevin Brown, but Dr Cronin had spoken of them when he was referring to the men who were opposing him in Chicago. "He believed they were local politicians whose words would carry no weight, but that they were inspired to do him an injury through their obligations to Alexander Sullivan. Dr Cronin told me, for instance, that Dan Coughlin owed his appointment on the police force to Alexander Sullivan. He also told me that Brown was just a stool pigeon of Sullivan's."

Dillon's answer to the next question, from Coroner Hertz, must have decided the jury that although his evidence was doubtless delivered in good faith, his partisan passion was perhaps overcoming his reason. The coroner asked him, "I want to ask if you know what amount was charged by the Executive as being paid to Dr Gallagher, who is now under a life sentence in England?"

"The Executive – the Triangle – inspired the belief within the organisation that they had supported Dr Gallagher with funds," Dillon answered. "But he was never sent by the Executive to do any active work for the order."

But Dillon was wrong. There is overwhelming evidence that Dr Gallagher was sent on a dynamite mission to England funded by Irish-Americans. When he arrived in London he teamed up with a technical expert named Alfred Whitehead and half a dozen other Irishmen trained in bomb-setting. Scotland Yard had been tipped off about Gallagher's arrival and about the activities of his accomplices, no doubt by their spy Le Caron. The police waited long enough for the dynamiters to manufacture a large quantity of nitro-glycerine, then arrested them all on April 5th, 1883. Gallagher, Whitehead and two others were sentenced to life imprisonment. The coroner's jury would have been aware of this, and they must have been disconcerted by Dillon's emphatic response that none of these things happened.

They must have been intrigued too when Dillon said that on Sunday, May 5th, when he learned of the disappearance of Dr Cronin the previous day, "I straightway felt sure that he was murdered." He went to a meeting of the Executive that same evening and tried to appropriate $3,000 from the organisation's funds to hunt for the murderers, but the other members of the Executive would not support him because they refused to believe Dr Cronin was dead. Small wonder. It surely must have been baffling to Dillon's fellow-members on the Executive to be asked for a mandate for $3,000 expenses to conduct a search for the murderers of a man who at that stage was not even known to be dead, let alone murdered.

Just as he had finished recounting this, Dillon began, "There is one thing I would like to say to the jury, as it is an animus we are looking for ..." when Foreman Critchell interrupted, "We are not looking for anything but facts."

"I will give you facts that may show animus," Dillon ploughed on. "Dr Cronin discovered that the friends of Alexander Sullivan in Chicago were in the habit of saying that the verdict at the trial at which Dr Cronin was one of the judges was in favour of Alexander Sullivan. The verdict was supposed to be kept secret, but it somehow leaked out unofficially through the organisation, and the two doctors (Dr Cronin and Dr McCahey) were pointed out as the only two people who found Sullivan guilty of any crime, and that Alexander Sullivan was not guilty. Dr Cronin, in order to prove that he was in possession of information which if they heard it, or if he was permitted to read it, would prove the guilt of Alexander Sullivan, stated that he had in his possession at least three hundred pages of testimony which would be produced at the coming convention to prove that these men were all that the charges had specified they were. The Executive ordered him to send that three hundred pages of testimony to their chairman, but he refused to hand them over."

The date of the coming convention, Dillon said, had not then been fixed. Both Dr Cronin and Dr McCahey – who was now at his home in Philadelphia "very sick with brain fever" – insisted they must keep their documents because they needed something at the coming convention to justify their verdict of guilty.

When the friends of Alexander Sullivan began to clamour that there was a majority report in favour of his acquittal, Luke Dillon wrote to Dr Cronin advising him to drop his crusade against Sullivan. "I thought it was unwise of him to be making an assertion of that kind,"

Dillon told the inquest. "It was dangerous; he had too many enemies here in Chicago."

More than anyone else, Luke Dillon was thus able to establish a motive for the murder, and to point to those people interested in having Dr Cronin killed. The coroner's jury returned a verdict of murder, and recommended that Alexander Sullivan, Patrick O'Sullivan, Coughlin and Woodruff be held to answer before a grand jury. The moment the verdict was announced Chief of Police Hubbard sent two detectives to Alexander Sullivan's office on the seventh floor of the Opera House building and placed him under arrest. Sullivan was brought to East Chicago Avenue police station and held for several hours before being allowed bail on a $25,000 bond, which he had no difficulty in raising.

But revealing though all the evidence so far was, as far as Alexander Sullivan was concerned much of it was of an inadmissible nature. The stories revealed at the inquest needed admissable evidence to sustain them, and there just wasn't enough of it. Accordingly, when Sullivan was brought before the grand jury on June 29th they refused to return an indictment against him, and he was discharged. He immediately asked for release from his bond, and Judge Baker, after listening to legal arguments, agreed. As Sullivan walked smiling from the court, a free man, Chief Hubbard, who had been watching the proceedings, had no doubt that one of the biggest fish had got away. Captain Schaack, sitting beside his chief, appeared to remain bewildered by the whole course of events.

15
BRIBING THE JURY

Even now, with the arrest of Frank Woodruff, O'Sullivan and Coughlin, Chief Hubbard was still not sure he had all the conspirators in the bag. With Schaack and Schuettler, he bent over the piles of evidence again in an attempt to decide who should be added to their trio of prisoners. More evidence was coming in to suggest that by arresting Dan Coughlin they had got the general manager of the plot. Milkman Mertes, who testified at the inquest, and who lived near the Carlson cottage, now claimed that he had seen Coughlin going into the cottage about eight o'clock on the evening of the murder, May 4th. Mertzes had also heard Coughlin make threats against the life of Dr Cronin on several occasions. Another witness was prepared to say that Coughlin had once offered him $100 to kill Dr Cronin. As the layers were peeled back on the life of Dan Coughlin, the three police officers must have wondered how a man like this ever got into their police force. Coughlin was evidently at the centre of a wide ring of Chicago crime; if they failed to get a conviction in the Cronin case they had already collected enough evidence while he was on remand to indict him for blowing up a Chicago distillery with dynamite.

Although circumstantial evidence pointed beyond all doubt to Coughlin being one of the killers at the Carlson cottage, throughout the conspiracy he had revealed the appetite of a mollusc for the limelight, preferring to play out his managerial role through dupes and stool-pigeons, except in the one instance where he held himself responsible for hiring the white horse and buggy. His decision to order the rig personally from Paddy Dinan's livery stable was something he must now have bitterly regretted.

The iceman Patrick O'Sullivan had been far less covert. It emerged that his friendship with Dr Cronin went much deeper than he had ever suggested; he was exposed as the veritable Judas Iscariot of the plot. On investigation, O'Sullivan's peculiar contract with Dr Cronin, made a few weeks before the murder, was revealed as a piece of shallow subterfuge. That O'Sullivan, doing a small business in retailing ice in an out-of-the-way locality at that time beyond the city limits, and employing only three men, should agree to pay a doctor an annual salary of $50 for no other purpose than to attend any of his men who might be hurt was stretching credibility, more especially because O'Sullivan was neither a practical nor a theoretical philanthropist but a hard-nosed businessman. As Mayor Boldenweck had indicated, men with twenty times more employees did not think it incumbent upon them to put a doctor on their payroll.

Even if the iceman had been a humanitarian, there were, as Lieutenant Schuettler had pointed out to him, plenty of doctors in the six-mile stretch between his Lakeview warehouse and Dr Cronin's surgery. O'Sullivan had also stood sponsor for Martin Burke when the elder Carlson asked about his reliability. O'Sullivan said to Carlson, referring to Burke, alias Frank Williams, "He's all right. I know him and his brother; he'll be responsible for the rent." Frank Williams made frequent trips between the Carlson cottage and the iceman's house. The two were seen regularly together; in fact O'Sullivan's house seemed to be the headquarters for the whole gang of murderers –

when they were not at the Carlson cottage, they could usually be found at O'Sullivan's. And Jonas Carlson was now prepared to testify that when Frank Williams rented the Carlson cottage he said, "I'm going to work for the iceman over there," indicating O'Sullivan's house. (This, it has to be pointed out, was slightly different from the testimony of his daughter-in-law Annie Carlson, who remembered that when Frank Williams was in the Carlson house signing the lease for the Carlson cottage he was asked his line of business and, appearing to be vexed at the question, merely said, "I am employed downtown.") The police expected to prove that O'Sullivan, like Coughlin, was one of the principals in the actual assassination of Dr Cronin; that he was in the Carlson cottage on the night of May 4th between seven and nine o'clock, and that the can of yellow paint used to cover up the bloodstains came from his house. O'Sullivan, it was noticed, seemed to have gone to greater lengths to cover up the blood than to cover his tracks, for a week or two after the murder a high fence on the north side of his house was freshened up with the same kind of paint as that used in the cottage. Curiously, all three of the iceman's employees seemed to have been aware of what was going on and were willing parties to the plot; at one point Hubbard considered having them all arrested and tried for complicity.

In jail O'Sullivan lost much of his bravado and talked dolefully to his lawyer of making a clean breast of it and throwing himself on the state for mercy. He was advised that this was not necessary, that he stood in no danger of conviction; the state, he was told, had no case against any of the prisoners as long as they kept their mouths shut. When the lawyers went away the iceman was visited by his housekeeper Mrs Tom Whelan, who came to see him regularly two or three times a day. Mrs Whelan, the jailers noticed, was an iron lady with a remarkably strong influence over the prisoner which she used to further the needs of the Triangle. If O'Sullivan intended at any time to squeal, Mrs Whelan equally intended that he should not do so.

The police, like the grand jury, could make out no further case against the lawyer Alexander Sullivan – this man who had undoubtedly plotted the murder seemed certain to avoid arrest. The police then turned to the Camp 20 secret committee that had "tried" Dr Cronin.

The third man they arrested was Senior Guardian John Beggs. They discovered the correspondence between Beggs and Edward Spellman, district officer of the Clan-na-Gael, concerning the Cronin trial committee, at his home and at Spellman's home, and there was plenty in it to incriminate the Senior Guardian. The only other members of the Cronin secret trial committee left then were Martin Burke (Frank Williams) and Patrick Cooney (J. B. Simmons).

A week after the murder, when the police were calling for witnesses to come forward, a young tinsmith named Gustav Klahre reported that on Monday May 6th a tall, well-built Irishman with a knife scar under his right eye arrived at his basement workshop with a metal box measuring about 14 inches by 26 inches. A piece of rope was tied around its middle. The Irishman, whose description fitted that of Frank Williams – not known at that moment by the police in his real name as Martin Burke – asked the tinsmith to solder up the box. When Klahre made to cut the rope in order to solder the galvanised strips without hindrance Burke pushed the tinsmith's arm aside roughly and told him not to touch the rope. Burke also prevented Klahre from opening the box. While he was working with his soldering iron Klahre talked about the disappearance of Dr Cronin. Burke without any hesitation declared that Cronin was a British spy and ought to have been killed. Klahre remembered that the Irishman spoke extremely coarsely about the missing doctor. The young tinsmith took over an hour to finish the job. When he had securely soldered the galvanised iron bands around the box Burke opened the door leading up the store stairway to the street and a man instantly came down the stairs and carried the box away. Klahre thought that his customer brought the box in one of Patrick O'Sullivan's wagons, and that one of the iceman's employees was with him.

What had Burke got in this box that he needed so zealously to guard from the rest of the world? The obvious conclusion for the police theorists was that it contained Dr Cronin's clothes – though why Burke did not choose a way to dispose of them with less hassle was not a question they asked themselves. In fact, the theory was wrong, as we shall see. The secret of the tin box remains a mystery to this day; no one ever discovered what it contained, or indeed what became of it. But reporters bent on garnishing their stories remembered the amputated finger of a woman found near Dr Cronin's body, and surmised that a woman must also have been murdered that night by the conspirators in the Carlson cottage and that her remains were in Burke's tin box. This it should be stressed was an unsubstantiated newspaper hypothesis with no basis in fact – no woman was reported missing that night. Like the tin box, the amputated finger remained one of the unsolved elements of the Cronin mystery.

Some time after his visit to the tinsmith, and probably after the discovery of the body of Dr Cronin on May 22nd, Martin Burke, travelling in the name of Frank Delaney, escaped over the frontier into Canada. He may or may not have had his tin box with him, but he almost certainly was accompanied by fellow-conspirator Patrick Cooney who, unlike Burke, got clean away and was never seen again.

Their ultimate destination was Ireland, and somewhere in Canada they decided to split up. Burke afterwards claimed that he worked his way to Winnipeg. When he was captured by Chief of Police McRae of Winnipeg on June 17th he had on him a railway ticket from Winnipeg to Montreal, an Allen Line steamship ticket from Montreal to Liverpool and $58.20 in cash. Inspector

John McKennon of Winnipeg police described the prisoner as "nervous and excited" when he was brought to the station house. While Burke was being held awaiting extradition proceedings the spirits of the other prisoners in custody back in Chicago sank to a new low. The one man they wanted most to escape was Martin Burke, for if anyone was going to squeal it would be this nervous, excitable fellow. Now the state had in its hands a man who might easily turn state's evidence and blow their defence to smithereens.

Chicago police sent Thomas Martensen, one of the two draymen who had been hired by Burke to carry the furniture from the Clark Street apartment to the Carlson cottage, to Winnipeg to identify Burke. This gave Martensen no difficulty; he may even have relished the job, for after he had finished hauling the furniture to the Carlson cottage Burke had refused to pay him his full due. The subsequent altercation gave Martensen plenty of chance to fix Burke in his memory and the identification procedure in Winnipeg gave him the opportunity he wanted to atone for his shortfall in pay.

Martin Burke arrived back in Chicago under police escort in the evening of August 5th. His triangular friends were dismayed at his altered appearance. To bolster his flagging courage they arranged for three good meals a day to be brought into the prison from a North Clark Street restaurant, and on frequent visits to his cell they pampered and petted him. More than anyone else, they feared that Martin Burke would break down.

Burke was the fifth man to be arrested – the sixth had Chicagoans shaking their heads in wonder. For 23-year-old John Kunze had never figured in any newspaper story, he was not a member of any Irish organisation, and he was not even an Irishman.

His role in the crime, as far as it was known when he was arrested, consisted in having driven Detective Dan Coughlin – with whom he was implicated in blowing up the distillery – to the Carlson cottage on the evening of the murder. That this should land him in court on a murder charge was baffling, the more so because Chicago police hinted, but refused to elaborate, that he had played an important part in the crime. Apart from the fact that he had a long record of petty crime, no one knew exactly who he was. Nevertheless, the Chicago press, as ever, tried their best to find out. Was he a close friend of Coughlin, as some people claimed? Well, said Kunze, he had been, but he wasn't any longer. He had recently started calling himself John Kogel for no other reason than to escape Coughlin's importunities. Was he born in Luxemburg, as he claimed? No, indignantly riposted the Luxemburgers living on Chicago's North Side, Kunze was a German, the illegitimate son of a woman whose husband was in an asylum for the insane in Germany.

Kunze was ably equipped for his bit-part as clown prince of the proceedings. On June 29th he made a brief appearance before a grand jury who returned an indictment against him. A newspaper reported that when he was in court "he smiled and nodded his head in the most foolish manner, and carried on generally as the ideal empty-pated dude is popularly supposed to deport himself." Kunze declared in an interview that a couple of years before his arrest he worked in the furniture factory of A. H. Revell (this was of course long before Patrick Cooney, alias J. B. Simmons, became a customer of Revell's), but he left after ten months because he had come into a large inheritance. The inheritance was Kunze's favourite story, used in a number of con-man swindles which were set out in his crime record. While in custody he wrote a letter to a Chicago newspaper admitting he had been very foolish but, borrowing freely from George Washington, he thanked heaven he had never told a lie.

Six arrests, but now only five prisoners, because as soon as Kunze was arrested Frank Woodruff was released. The reason given was that there was insufficient evidence to make a case against the horse-thief, a decision that was as bizarre at least as several others in the case, since Woodruff had actually admitted his part in the disposal of the body. With Woodruff thus eliminated from the proceedings Kunze was ideally suited to take over the one humorous, low-comedy part in the dark hideousness of the Cronin tragedy.

A light industry quickly sprang up to avoid bringing the prisoners to court – an industry managed by lawyers, Irishmen, false witnesses and crooked cops and funded by apparently inexhaustible supplies of money. Private investigators were employed by the defence to shadow detectives working on the case, reports were sent to newspapers vilifying the reputation of Dr Cronin, faked evidence was suddenly discovered, motions were put before the courts to have the case set aside. The biggest offensive mounted by the defence concerned the selection of the jury. The state was determined to have no juror who was friendly to the prisoners or in sympathy with the Triangle conspirators; the defence was equally determined that the jury would be composed of as many Irish-American patriots as it could muster.

The result was predictably incredibly laborious. From September 26th until October 22nd the main courtroom of Chicago's Criminal Court was the scene of that essentially American judicial investigation in which hundreds of potential jurors are questioned about their religious and political beliefs, their families, their actions and their instincts, and prosecution and defence then exercise a given number of rejections, all in a praiseworthy but sometimes desperate attempt to enlist twelve good men and true. By the twenty-sixth day 1,115 men had been auditioned in this overture before the grand opera, and just nine of them had been accepted. At that rate another nine days might suffice to get the number up to twelve.

Then, just as the afternoon session was about to begin on October 22nd, an usher whispered urgently in the ear of Judge McConnell. The judge, signalling counsel to follow him, left the court for his chambers. Waiting for him there were two Chicago detectives and a Mr E. V. Page, an oil merchant, of Erie Street, who was later to be described by the *Chicago Times* as "a prominent Chicago citizen."

"Your honour," began Mr Page. "I have to tell you of a conversation I have had this morning with my works foreman, George Tschappat. He is a potential juror in the case now before you, and he tells me he has been offered one thousand dollars by a bailiff of your court to stand out for the acquittal of the accused men or, if it were impossible to clear them of the charges, at least bring about a hung jury."

A bailiff of the court no less! Were there no limits to the reaches of the Clan-na-Gael's tentacles? The incorruptible Tschappat was brought in to name the bailiff; he was Alexander Hanks, of Gilpin Place, married with two children. Hanks, who had got his job through the "spoils system," had

Judge McConnell

never been in trouble, at least during his seven years as a bailiff. When he was searched he was found to have a list of corruptible jurors which a newspaper had said some weeks earlier were being made out by the prisoners' friends. At first Hanks denied the accusation, then broke down and named fellow-bailiff Mark Salomon, another family man, as being in on the plot.

Their paymaster, they both confessed, was Thomas Kavanagh, partner in the firm of Brown and Kavanagh, steam-fitters and plumbers of Franklin Street. The "Brown" of the business was that same Kevin Brown who was married to Alice of the wandering eye. Kavanagh, a member of the Clan-na-Gael's Camp 135, had succeeded in getting Kevin Brown on to the list of potential jurors, although Brown had yet to be scrutinised. One newspaper in search of a story – any story – suggested that Thomas Kavanagh was in reality the elusive J. B. Simmons, but that was another of the wilder theories which abounded around Dr Cronin, for that distinction belonged to the escapee Patrick Cooney.

No one believed of course that the funds for jury-bribing were being supplied by the modest plumbing firm of Brown and Kavanagh. When Kavanagh was asked about the source of the money he named John Graham, a clerk in the office of the law firm A. S. Trude. Graham, another small link in the long chain that went back into the heart of the Clan-na-Gael, was immediately arrested.

Three more men were revealed as being in the plot. They were Fred Smith, a manufacturer's agent, of LaSalle Avenue, Jeremiah O'Donnell, United States storekeeper for the First District of Illinois, of DeKoven Street; and Joseph Konen, a greengrocer of West Madison Street, who had accepted $1,000 to stand for the jury and having succeeded, had accepted another $5,000 to vote for an acquittal.

A grand jury was quickly summoned to bring indictments against the conspirators, all of whom were given prison sentences when the Cronin trial was over. The whole unsavoury episode, prosecution lawyer Luther Laflin Mills declared in a grandiloquent manner, was "a most damnable organisation against the law of the land, a conspiracy against the jurisprudence of this country, a conspiracy of ramifications, of audacity ... it is no exaggeration when I say to you that you cannot magnify the damnable outrage of this conspiracy ... it is an assault on the very integrity of our institutions." If his outrage was somewhat inflated, none the less there was behind it understandable contempt for the sinister, swaggering arrogance of those Irish-Americans who, in order to satisfy their murderous interests were prepared to take the law of America by its neck and strangle it.

No doubt sobered by the bribery scandal, defence and prosecution quickly found three more jurors for the Cronin trial – by October 23rd, the day after Bailiff Hanks was arrested, all twelve were named. In view of the difficulties posed by the selection process, which cost the State of Illinois $3,800, it is interesting to look at what kind of men they were. Their foreman was John Culver, 40, a real-estate dealer of Washington Street. He was a Methodist and a temperance man. He had lived in Chicago for 30 years and, it was noted, he was not a member of any secret society.

James Pierson, 55, farmer, living near Glenwood, was an American of Dutch parentage and belonged to no church and no secret society; John Hall, 29, office draughtsman, of Fernwood was American-born, Methodist and temperance and belonged to no secret society; Charles Dix, 30, Chicago-born, of North Carpenter Street, was an insurance office cashier, Episcopalian and member only of a beneficial association. Henry Walker, 58, of Cottage Grove Avenue, was an American-born Protestant described as being "in the upholstery business;" Frank Allison, 39, also American-born, was a machinist who lived in Jefferson Street; Charles Corke, 30, a clerk living at Evanston was a Methodist of English parentage; William North, a manufacturer of sewing machines in Michigan Avenue, was American and Presbyterian; Charles Marlor, clerk, of Washington

Luther Laflin Mills, one of the attorneys for the prosecution

Boulevard, was American and Episcopalian; Elijah Bontecou was a salesman born in New York whose "intelligence and candour" impressed the scrutineers; Edward Bryan, of Maywood, a native of New Jersey, was also a salesman and also a member of the Congregational Church; and Benjamin Clarke, of Evans Avenue, had been in the real-estate business for twenty years and was chosen for his "fairness and intelligence."

As soon as the twelve had taken their seats the state prosecutor, Judge Longenecker,* asked for a week's adjournment in view of the diversions caused by the jury selection. The defence at once objected, as they were to object to almost everything during the trial. Senior defence lawyer William Forrest began to argue that "with all the police force of the city of Chicago at their disposal, and four of the best criminal lawyers ..." when the prosecution interrupted him – they could shorten their requirement to two days.

"I am inclined to think two days too long," intervened Judge McConnell. "I will give you a full day, until the day after tomorrow at ten o'clock." Thus the opening of the trial was fixed for October 25th.

State prosecutor Longenecker

---

*Two judges acted as counsel in the trial, Judge Longenecker for the prosecution, and Judge Wing, who represented Detective Dan Coughlin.

16
THE CASE FOR
THE PROSECUTION

"**Y**ou are not called upon to try the Clan-na-Gael," Mr Longnecker told the jury. "We are not here to prosecute that organisation or to defend it. But it is essential that I should tell you something about it. It came into existence in 1869 for the purpose of protecting Ireland. Into the organisation went patriotic Irishmen, Irishmen for political effect, and Irishmen for the money that was in it. A great many patriotic Irishmen went into it believing that some day they would set Ireland free and give her a republican form of government the same as we have here."

Stroking his long beard as he began the case for the state, Longenecker's slow, calm, low-pitched voice was in striking contrast to his massive frame – and it was soon evident that for the audience, if not the jury, it lacked sufficient force. The mass of people wedged into the courtroom were fidgeting audibly; this was not the sort of opening they expected. For them, and for the rest of America, the Clan-na-Gael was not only on trial, it was guilty of a most un-American crime committed by a secret society against a patriot. They had stood outside the court for three hours before the doors were opened, they had scrambled for seats, been pushed and shoved by frantic court bailiffs, pressed into each other on the hard wooden benches in the public gallery and they had come for blood, not to hear this. They stirred restlessly within their narrow confines and glared at the five men, Burke, Coughlin, Beggs, O'Sullivan and Kunze, under indictment for the murder of Dr Patrick Cronin.

"They had districts called Camps all over the country, spreading from ocean to ocean," Mr Longenecker went on. "This organisation was in existence for a number of years without the general public even knowing that such an organisation existed. The organisation had national conventions, and few of its members even knew when the national conventions were held."

After describing the onset of the Triangle regime he went on, "You will see that the power of this organisation was all vested in this board. They were directors from year to year; they were in charge of existing funds and raising new funds and an oath was taken that the money was to be used only to benefit Ireland. They then began to pursue a new and different policy; instead of waging legitimate war for the freedom of Ireland a dynamite policy which they called active work was pursued abroad and a system of embezzlement practised at home. Both policies were against the law and were atrocious. The money in the treasury was squandered in mysterious ways; men were sent to England on desperate missions, and a score of them are now in British jails. The commands of the Triangle were fatal. A man who should shirk the responsibility thrust upon him by Sullivan, Feeley and Boland in this corrupt era of the Clan-na-Gael was branded a traitor to the cause.

"The members had no right to question, the Executive Board of three was supreme. In 1884, the year of their adoption of the policy they called active work, this so-called Triangle was the closest corporation that ever existed. If a member was sent to England he was ordered to report there for funds, and his identity was made known to the English police and he was thrust in prison. This was done to enable the Triangle to steal the organisation's funds that had been accumulating for legitimate

The jury

purposes. They made an excuse that they were using the funds to support active work, until at last, when they made their final report, making the members believe that English detectives were among them, they claimed that from the original funds of $250,000 the organisation was now in debt to the Triangle personally for $13,000."

Mr Longenecker went on to tell how Dr Cronin took

189

up the campaign against the Triangle and how he was
expelled and branded as a traitor "simply because he had
exposed the doings of these men who were robbing the
order of these funds." Then came the trial of the
Triangle in 1888, by six committeemen of the reformed
Clan-na-Gael, one of whom was Dr Cronin. "The committee of six took days and days to hear the evidence. Dr
Cronin took full minutes showing what the Triangle had
done in this country and across the water. When the
committee disbanded and got ready to make its report,
four were against publishing the evidence, but Dr Cronin
insisted on publishing the evidence to all the Camps, let-
ting the members know what the Triangle had done.
Publication of the report would have shown that these
men robbed the order of its funds and robbed men of
their liberty, but despite Dr Cronin's insistence, it was
not sent out.

"The men in the Clan-na-Gael who supported the
Triangle kept that report back until May 4th, the very
day on which Dr Cronin met his death. On that day the
Executive Board was called together, and on May 5th an
order was sent out to the Camps together with Alexander
Sullivan's protest against being tried by Dr Cronin in
1888 charging that Dr Cronin was a traitor to the Irish
cause, that he was a perjurer, and that he had sworn allegiance to Canada.

"There was a twofold purpose in ruining Cronin's
record as an Irishman and a citizen. The first purpose
was for building up this Triangle and making it a power.
If it was necessary to kill Cronin, he must be killed, but
they never intended that this community should understand that Dr Cronin was killed. The second purpose
was that the unseen hand that concocted this conspiracy
to take the life of Cronin was also at work making this
community believe that Dr Cronin was still alive and that
he would appear on the other side of the water as a
traitor to the cause in which he was enlisted.

"But you will ask, what was the motive for this? Dr

Cronin's report had been sent to all the officials of the Camps, convicting these men of embezzling the funds for years, but it had so far not been published to all the members. So Dan Coughlin went around telling people that Cronin was a traitor, and in Camp 20 on the night of February 8th he and the other conspirators began to educate the Camps to believe that Cronin, this patriotic Irishman, was a British spy – another Le Caron. They excited the members to agree to remove Cronin for one purpose, when they were actually removing him for another purpose."

The Triangle had already gone out of existence, he said, when John Beggs, Martin Burke, Patrick Cooney and Dan Coughlin, meeting at Camp 20 on the night of February 8th, formed a secret committee to investigate Dr Cronin. Then, on February 19th, "a man by the name of Simmons appears at a real estate office and rents rooms at 117 Clark Street, opposite the Opera House building, where Dr Cronin has an office.

"We will prove that Burke was out of employment at that time and that he was doing nothing where he could earn a dollar; that Jonas Carlson had a vacant cottage; that Burke paid thirteen dollars for a month's rent and gave his name as Frank Williams. He went directly from there to Patrick O'Sullivan and told him that he had rented it. He put his furniture into the Carlson cottage with the help of a delivery man. We will prove that he came back about April 20th and paid another month's rent, saying his sister was sick in hospital; that at the same time Jonas Carlson wanted to carry out a piece of furniture left there by another tenant and Burke helped him to move it, and that Carlson saw the carpet and the trunk there on April 20th.

"Something had to be done to induce Dr Cronin to go to this cottage, so we will show that Justice Mahoney introduced Patrick O'Sullivan to Dr Cronin for the purpose of making a contract to have O'Sullivan's employees treated by Cronin in the event of an accident. We will

JOHN KUNZE

show that up to the time this contract was made, O'Sullivan's men never had an accident and never had any occasion for a doctor; that there were any number of doctors between Cronin's and O'Sullivan's places; that Coughlin, who was a bitter enemy of Dr Cronin, was a close associate of O'Sullivan – so that there was no reason for O'Sullivan to go and employ Dr Cronin to treat his icemen.

"It will appear in evidence that Dan Coughlin was seen in a saloon with O'Sullivan. They were drinking together, and Coughlin declared that a North Side leading Catholic would soon bite the ground – that he would soon be out of the way. We will prove that in the afternoon of May 4th Coughlin was asked by O'Sullivan to go out to the Carlson cottage. We will prove that on May 4th Coughlin was in the neighbourhood of the Carlson cottage with a man who fits the description of the one who drove the doctor to his death. We will show that Coughlin was recognised a short distance from the cottage by a man with whom he had done business.

"Earlier that same day, between eleven and one o'clock, Coughlin had been over to Paddy Dinan's livery stable to order a horse and buggy for a friend. Dinan asked what sort of horse and buggy the man would want, and Coughlin replied, 'Almost any kind.'

"About 7.15 in the evening of May 4th a man goes to the livery stable and wants the horse that Coughlin had ordered for him. When it is hitched up he objects to the rig, but when he is told it is the only one he can have, he takes it and drives directly to the Conklin house, which is only a few blocks away. He is there five minutes after he leaves the stable. He rushes up to the doctor's room, presents O'Sullivan's card, says O'Sullivan is out of town, that a man has had his leg smashed and the doctor is wanted right away. Dr Cronin lays the iceman's card on the bureau, hurries into the buggy and drives out to the Carlson cottage. This is about 7.20 in the evening.

"We will prove that Coughlin was seen going into that

cottage; we will prove that the man drove Dr Cronin to that cottage and that the horse and buggy that took him there were hired at Dinan's livery stable for that purpose.

"On the night of May 3rd there was a meeting of Camp 20. Recollect that it was on May 4th that those other things occurred. We will prove that at the meeting on the night of the third someone inquired whether that committee, or a secret committee, had reported. John Beggs waved his hand and said, 'That committee is to report to me, the Camp has nothing to do with it.' That we will establish beyond doubt. On the night before Cronin was taken away to be murdered, Beggs said, 'That committee reports to me, the Senior Guardian, and not to the Camp.'

"We will prove that Coughlin told other parties that Dr Cronin was a spy. We will prove that a year before these events he tried to hire a man to slug Dr Cronin, showing that his mind was against the doctor prior to the murder. We will show that the trunk bought at Revell's and taken to the Carlson cottage was filled with the body of Dr Cronin, placed in the wagon, and we will show the points where it struck on its journey; that it landed in Edgewater near the lake, where the driver told the watchman that they were looking for the lake shore drive; that they drove back to the Evanston road, and that the trunk was found just three-quarters of a mile from the catch-basin where the doctor's body was deposited. The key that unlocked the trunk was found in the Carlson cottage, covered with some of the paint found on the floor.

"We expect to show that after it was discovered that a white horse drove the doctor away Paddy Dinan went to East Chicago Avenue police station to see Captain Schaack, and Coughlin met him and said, 'Don't mention anything about the horse and buggy, because Cronin and I were not on good terms.'

"We will show that Martin Burke, under the name of Williams, hired the Carlson cottage and that Patrick Cooney appeared there after the murder and wanted to pay another month's rent. The old lady would not take it because as the cottage was not to be occupied, she did not want to take any more rent. Burke did not return the keys to the cottage, and on May 18th Mr Carlson received a letter from Burke in Indiana in which he said, 'I am sorry we had to give up the building,' and explained about painting the floor.

"We will show that when the men failed to move in Mr Carlson asked O'Sullivan why. O'Sullivan says, 'Haven't you got the rent?' 'Yes,' says Mr Carlson. 'Then,' says O'Sullivan, 'what is the use of your worrying?' Mr Carlson says, 'Do you know him?' And O'Sullivan says, 'I know one of them.' O'Sullivan made statements that he was in his house that night, but we will prove that he was not in his house at the time of the murder.

"It will be shown that after the disappearance of Dr Cronin, Beggs said in conversation with two men who thought the doctor had been killed, 'I know better than that. He will turn up all right. You are not in the inner circle, you don't know what's going on.' Then, you will remember that on May 6th Martin Burke appears at a tinsmith's with a box, the contents of which he will not permit the tinner to see. Remember that Dr Cronin's clothes were not on his body when it was found. Where that box has gone no one knows, but it is a circumstance in the case.

"As for John Kunze, we will prove that he was seen in the rooms at 117 Clark Street at the time those rooms were occupied by the so-called Williams brothers. He was seen at the window, washing his feet. We will prove that a short time before the murder Kunze was seen in company with Dan Coughlin in Lincoln Avenue, and that Coughlin told someone they met that Kunze was a friend. We will show that on the night of the murder Kunze drove Coughlin from the cottage; that Kunze had disappeared from the North Side in April and that after that he was in employment on the South Side as a painter, using an assumed name. We will prove that

Kunze said to a man on the South Side, when the papers were stating it was doubtful as to whether Dr Cronin was murdered, that he (Kunze) knew the doctor was murdered, but he never would be found, or an expression of that kind."

The jury would hear how after killing Dr Cronin the conspirators went to extraordinary lengths to persuade Clan-na-Gael members that he was a traitor to their cause, that he was still very much alive and had fled from Chicago in the knowledge that he was about to be unmasked. To enhance this false trail they caused faked newspaper reports to be published in Toronto and afterwards in Chicago stating that the doctor had fled to the Canadian city and had been interviewed there. They even arranged for a woman, Alice Brown, to travel to Toronto so that it could be suggested that she was some sort of dark lady associating with Dr Cronin in order to blacken his character. The conspirators also arranged that one of their number, Frank Woodruff, should lay a false trail through statements made to the police suggesting that a woman's body, and not Dr Cronin's, was in the trunk; that he, Woodruff, had taken a leading part in the disposal of that body, that Dr Cronin had committed an abortion on the woman which resulted in her death, and that among those who helped Woodruff dispose of the body was Dr Cronin himself.

The jury would hear too that Dr Cronin's barber, Hal Garsch, was given twenty-five dollars by the prisoner Detective Dan Coughlin to say that hair from the trunk could not possibly be the doctor's, although fortunately this false evidence was overwhelmed by other witnesses who identified the body. Garsch and Woodruff had since retracted their lying statements.

Mr Longenecker had been speaking for more than two hours when at 11.45 he asked for a recess until two o'clock "because I am minded that I might shorten my speech." When the court came back after lunch both the judge and the defence allowed him to till the same ground again, to the point that after a while everyone must have been wondering why he did not get on with what he had in mind. He told the jury, "This morning I called your attention to the fact that on the morning of May 6th, two days after Cronin was killed, Martin Burke appeared at the tinner's establishment to have a box sealed up. The tinner tried to raise the lid to clean out some dirt but Burke told him not to open it, and in order to solder it up he put a band around it. Having read the papers on Sunday, which announced that Dr Cronin had disappeared, the tinner mentioned the fact to Burke, who said, 'Oh, the —— —— ——, he was a spy; he will turn up all right,' or words to that effect.

"I also want you to bear in mind that Coughlin was a bitter enemy of Cronin's and that Patrick O'Sullivan was an intimate friend of Coughlin; that they were together on the night when he spoke about the prominent Irishman being put out of the way; that they were seen together at different points; that they were members of the same Camp. Remember also that Cronin and Coughlin were enemies, and every chance he had to declare his hatred of Cronin, Coughlin took advantage of.

"On March 29th O'Sullivan hunted for Justice Mahoney to get him to introduce him to Dr Cronin. Mahoney could not be found at that time, but two weeks later he got Mahoney and they went down to the doctor's office together to make the contract to treat the icemen. After they had passed the compliments of the day, Cronin asked them their business, and they said they wanted to see him on a private matter, whereupon another gentleman who was present in the office stepped out of the room. At that time O'Sullivan gave the doctor some of his cards and said he would send one such card when the doctor's services were needed, so that Cronin would know where to go. The night the doctor was sent for, one of O'Sullivan's cards was presented with the message that one of the iceman's employees was dangerously hurt.

"On the evening of May 4th Martin Burke was seen on

the front steps of the Carlson cottage, and he bid the time of day to old man Carlson. Later that same evening – and remember, this is following the meeting of Camp 20 on the night of the third – other people were inside that cottage. After everything was removed so far as Cronin and the trunk were concerned, Mrs Carlson, who is proud in regard to keeping the yard and the walk in good order, went to sweep the walk running along the front of the cottage. She noticed on the steps something that she supposed to be preserves. She supposed the people had moved in and broken a jar, and then swept it off. She thought nothing more of it until after the discovery of what transpired in the cottage.

"The rent had been paid up to May 20th, and another party appeared to pay another month's rent, when Mrs Carlson declined to receive it, stating she wanted it occupied. Although she got that letter from Burke in Indiana on May 18th, she still supposed she had no right to enter the cottage until the time was up, so she did not enter the cottage until the 20th, that being the time the rent of the cottage expired. At that time the Carlson people entered the cottage and found the floor had been painted; they found blood on the walls, footprints in the hall, where a man had stepped on the threshold of the painted floor, they found the carpet, which young Carlson had seen on April 21st, had been taken up and they found a general disarrangement of every particle of furniture in the house. The Carlsons told a friend of theirs who reported these facts to the police. When the police arrived to investigate the cottage they found the key of the trunk under the bureau. The arm of the rocking chair was broken, and everything indicated that a violent struggle had taken place. Indeed, when Dr Cronin's body was found the head was cut in a dozen places – from behind and on the temple – showing that they had killed him by giving him lick after lick until his life was beaten out. All that will be described by the doctors, and they will tell you that the condition of the body indicates that the blows were dealt from behind.

"I omitted to state this morning in reference to Kunze that a short time before the murder he was in company with some parties in a saloon near Patrick O'Sullivan's, and he exhibited a note of O'Sullivan's, saying that he had sold him a horse, or something of that kind, which shows the intimate acquaintance of Kunze with O'Sullivan. Then Dan Coughlin, Martin Burke, Kunze, and other parties in this case – whether Patrick O'Sullivan was present or not – were seen together on May 5th in a certain saloon, in which the man who fits the description of the one who drove Dr Cronin away was seen talking to Coughlin. So we see the association of these men was intimate prior to the murder, and the next day some of them met and talked together.

"I believe I mentioned this morning that the wagon was driven out to Edgewater. There were three men on the wagon, two sitting on the trunk, and one driving. They were seen at three different points. Just half a mile from Edgewater is where the catch-basin is located in which the body was found, and about three-quarters of a mile south of that on the same road, coming towards the city, the trunk was found besmeared with blood. In the trunk was also some cotton wadding. When the doctor was called for he grabbed some instruments and some cotton wadding and was driven away in the buggy. Cotton wadding was found in the trunk; cotton wadding was found in the catch-basin. After the discovery of the body and its identification Martin Burke disappears; he travels under an assumed name and is arrested in Winnipeg, in Manitoba, on this charge of murder, and extradited. He had a ticket to Liverpool with him. All this is evidence against Burke; flight is always considered as serious in a case of murder or any other crime."

The evidence would show that the conspiracy was well planned and, Mr Longenecker emphasised, it was most certainly a conspiracy. The fact that all the parties had separate roles to play did not lessen the guilt of any of them; the accessory was the same as the principal – the conspiracy made them universally guilty.

"A conspiracy is made up of certain acts by individuals, either together or separate, and every act that was done by either of these parties necessary to carry out the object of the conspiracy binds the others who were in the conspiracy. For instance, if the conspiracy existed, then the act of Coughlin in hiring the horse was the act of Burke, the act of Sullivan, or the act of Beggs, or anyone else engaged in the conspiracy. The renting of the cottage by Burke, under the name of Williams, was the same as if they had all gone there and rented it. The going over to Patrick O'Sullivan's to tell him they had rented the cottage was the going over of all those interested in the conspiracy, and so too was the making of the contract with Dr Cronin. Every act that was done by any of the parties before the commission of the crime was the act of all, if you believe there was a conspiracy to kill Dr Cronin.

"When you take all the evidence into consideration, when you take the fact that this man Coughlin hired the horse, and after Dinan had gone to the police station Coughlin said, 'Don't say anything about me engaging the horse and buggy, you may get me into trouble because Cronin and I were not good friends;' when you consider the hiring of the rooms at 117 Clark Street, the buying of the furniture and the trunk and the strap, the renting of the cottage, the contract between the doctor and this man O'Sullivan; the statement that a sister was to be there to occupy the cottage; the driving of the doctor from his house under the supposition that he was going to minister to the wants of an injured man; the appointment of a secret committee to try Dr Cronin; the fact that the Senior Guardian said that the committee reported to him and not to the Camp; the statements that Dr Cronin was a spy; the grouping together of all these things makes all the conspirators as guilty as if the murder was the act of one man."

If the jury were satisfied at the end of the evidence that

the accused did not conspire to kill Dr Cronin, "then of course turn them loose." But if the evidence showed a deep-laid conspiracy, "its premeditation, the coolness with which they planned it, then your duty is claimed to inflict upon them the highest penalty of the law."

17

WAS THAT REALLY
DR CRONIN DOWN THERE?

Mr William Forrest, defending all the prisoners, had given notice he would claim that the body dragged from the catch-basin had not been satisfactorily identified as Dr Cronin, so the first job of the prosecution was to prove through its witnesses the *corpus delicti*. The first of these was ex-Captain Francisco Villiers, the Lakeview police chief who supervised the lifting of the body from the catch-basin. He was described in one report as "a nervous little Frenchman with sparkling eyes." He had known the doctor for three years, he said, and identified the body the instant he saw it.

James Boland, who met the doctor every day for a year and a half; Joseph O'Keefe, the tailor who made Dr Cronin's clothes, and reporter James Holland were also positive that the body was that of Dr Cronin. Stephen Conley knew the body by its front teeth, Maurice Morris by the Agnus Dei, and Joseph O'Byrne by the broken finger of the right hand.

Mr Forrest tried a line of approach in cross-examination which rebounded badly when he attempted to extract admissions from the witnesses that the body was so badly swollen and discoloured that it would be impossible to identify it. His questions became so detailed that all they succeeded in doing was to get agreement that although the body was indeed swollen, and the hair on the head and the moustache had nearly all gone, there were none the less sufficient peculiarities for it to be recognised at once. The defence lawyer soon gave up this tactic and instead made a valiant effort to prove that the wounds on the doctor's head were inflicted during the removal of the body from the catch-basin. Sewerman Henry Rosch would have none of it. He refused to accept that he allowed the head to bump against the bricks inside the sewer. Mr Forrest persisted. With the head under one side of the catch-basin and completely shut out from vision, surely it would be impossible to remove the body without a violent effort and consequent mutilation? No, said Rosch, and he drew a picture of the catch-basin to show that Mr Forrest misunderstood its construction; it was impossible for any part of the body to get snagged during removal.

W S Forrest, leading attorney for the defence

Rosch was the last witness on the second day and as he left the witness stand the audience swarmed out excitedly, like a crowd leaving a football stadium after their team has scored a handsome victory. Next day, though, a good number of them stayed away. A cold, rain-filled wind was blowing hard off the prairie; it picked up the loose loam soil and dropped it on to the city, filling the streets with mud. The travelling conditions were atrocious – at such times Chicagoans went outside only when they had to. Inside the half-filled courtroom, in striking contrast to the first day, the air was damp and cold. Bailiffs walked around in overcoats and the women cleaners wore thick scarves around their necks. As the morning wore on the rain began to beat harder on the courthouse and thick fog rolled down Dearborn Street. The courtroom became so dark that the electric lights were turned on at midday.

When the court opened Beggs led the procession of accused men into the prisoners' box and immediately began reading a morning newspaper. Dan Coughlin and Patrick O'Sullivan stared ahead of them, indifferent to the busy comings and goings in the well of the court. Burke and Kunze grinned at the women spectators who were banked in three public benches at one end of the room. Their attentions were reciprocated with smiles and giggles. Later in the day Burke and Kunze began a flirtation across the courtroom with one of these women,

Daniel Donohue, attorney for O'Sullivan and Kunze

laughing out loud with them until Mr Forrest turned round angrily and told them to stop. Indifference to the dignity of the court was not confined to the prisoners. In the privileged guests' area long-haired Senator Kennedy of Wisconsin sat facing the court with his feet spread out on the table in front of him. Defence lawyer John Foster, who was defending only Beggs, was reading a novel. Daniel Donohue, who held a brief for O'Sullivan and Kunze, and Judge Wing, representing Coughlin, were late as usual.

The prosecution continued with their case for the *corpus delicti* and with seeking to establish that the body received no wounds in its removal from the catch-basin. They also sought to prove that the wounds on Dr Cronin's head were sufficient to have caused death. Then Mr Forrest made another tactical mistake, coming back vigorously on the first point, clinging to the idea that the corpse in the catch-basin was that of a man who in life was never Dr Cronin, despite the testimony of nearly a score of the doctor's friends who had given identification evidence by the end of the second day. They included John Scanlon, who knew the body by the arms and shoulders and the little tuft of hair which grew beneath the doctor's lower lip; Frank Scanlan, who recognised the teeth, and Patrick McGarry, who identified the doctor's long, slender hands.

Most convincing of all was the doctor's dentist, Dr E. V. Lewis, who told the court that Dr Cronin had once had a rather disturbing habit of removing his dental plate and twirling it between his fingers when he was deep in thought. To help him overcome this social problem, Dr Lewis had made an experimental plate which could not be removed easily, with four small teeth for the four lower central incisors, which had been drawn. The extraction of these teeth had left an unnatural or uneven absorption, which Dr Lewis noticed when he was making the plate. When the body of Dr Cronin was in the morgue at Lakeview police station, Assistant County Physician Dr Egbert, the pathologist who conducted the post-mortem after Dr Brandt's preliminary examination, had removed an unusual type of dental plate from it. Dr Lewis had identified this plate as the one he had made for Dr Cronin, and now produced it in court, holding it aloft to show the jury. Later the dentist took the plaster cast he had made to the undertaker's rooms in Chicago Avenue, where the body was taken after the post-mortem, and compared it with the plate. The cast and the plate fitted perfectly.

He was asked by Mr Luther Mills, one of the three assistant prosecutors, "What else did you see in the mouth of the corpse?"

"The rest of my work," replied Dr Lewis. "I saw the right back bicuspid I had prepared for crowning and the lower second molar I had filled with red rubber filling. I also saw the absorption of the lower jaw, which was so noticeable in life."

Seeing in their mind's eye an image of the mortuary scene, an image heightened by the ghastly-looking relic held up by Dr Lewis, the audience held their breath. Even John Kunze, who despite Mr Forrest's admonition, had continued to laugh throughout the evidence, fell silent. The jurors leaned forward and looked at the four tell-tale teeth in their plate. The defence lawyers conferred quickly about cross-examination tactics, agreeing that Mr Forrest should lead. But Dr Lewis refused to be shaken; he knew that dental plate, and when he left the witness stand no one in the court could have had the slightest doubt whose was the corpse in the catch-basin.

Assistant County Physician Dr Egbert was called to testify that he had indeed removed the plate, now passed by the last witness to him, from the mouth of the corpse. Since the post-mortem, he said, the dental plate had been locked in his safe. But when it came to Dr Egbert's cross-examination the wily defence lawyer was to score a badly needed point. One of the four false teeth on the dental plate was broken. Concealing the plate behind his back, and walking quickly to the witness's chair, Mr Forrest asked Dr Egbert whether the broken tooth was at the right or left end of the plate. The witness hesitated for a moment, then said it was at the right end of the plate.

"Are you sure?" asked Mr Forrest, advancing towards the witness.

Dr Egbert nodded affirmatively. Then Mr Forrest presented the teeth for his inspection. The broken tooth was at the left end of the plate. The witness looked crestfallen, while the prisoners grinned at each other. With an arrogant sweep of his hand Mr Forrest dismissed the witness and turned back to his place on the bench with his colleague, savouring the moment of triumph in which he had made his first impression on the wall of identification built by the state. For all that it could be seen only as an isolated impression, neither very damaging nor very material, and when Dr Egbert swore on re-examination that the plate being shown to the court was the same one he had removed from the mouth of the corpse it needed no more witnesses to prove the *corpus delicti*.

Mr Forrest had similar limited success in his attempt to establish that the body was mutilated during its removal from the catch-basin. The only witness who caused him any encouragement at all was John Feneger, a ruddy-faced German and one of the sewermen who discovered the body. With an imperfect understanding of English, Feneger was an easy prey to the cross-examiner and he became so hopelessly entangled that the audience was able to revel in a rare period of laughter. The witness, thoroughly confused, said many things he did not intend to say. He maintained that the police first tried to drag the body out with their hands, but when this failed they used a fence board and a hoe. His colleagues, however, contradicted him, testifying that the body was removed by poking a folded horse blanket beneath the arms with a hoe handle, crossing the blanket at the back, and then drawing up from either side. Ex-Captain Wing, of Lakeview police, and Officer Malie, who was with him, agreed that that was what happened, and even Feneger said that the body was handled with such care that the skin was not broken.

In order to prove that the wounds on the doctor's head were sufficient to cause death, the state had to recall Dr Egbert. The ghastly relic of the dental plate was as nothing compared with what Dr Egbert produced next. As he walked to the witness stand he carried Dr Cronin's stomach in a jar of alcohol, and the vegetable matter which was found in it at the post-mortem, wrapped in a piece of flimsy red paper. The pathologist had not benefited from his previous day's unsatisfactory experience on the witness stand, and cross-examination soon had him in a state of acute embarrassment. He could not remember a number of essential incidents at the post-mortem, but in his opinion death was caused by the head wounds. The doctor had died within three hours after

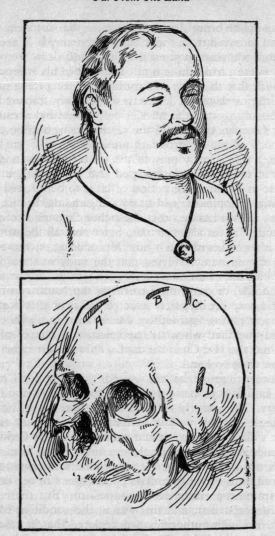

**The face and skull of Dr Cronin, showing the wounds which
were said to have caused his death**

eating his last meal, as some corn in the stomach, now produced in court, had not been digested. Mr Wing, for the defence, discussed each wound, and drew from the witness the admission that not one of the cuts was necessarily fatal in as much as they had not, according to Dr Egbert's investigation, severed a single artery, fractured the skull or dislocated the neck. Death might have resulted from concussion or contusion of the brain, but the postmortem failed to prove this because the brain had disintegrated. Dr Cronin might have bled to death if the flow of blood was not stopped and Dr Egbert, in the course of his rambling evidence, left it to be inferred that this was the opinion he held, notwithstanding the fact that there was blood in the heart – a scientific refutation of such a claim. He was also forced to agree that all the wounds could have been inflicted without producing unconsciousness or concussion. He thought, though, that the wound near the base of the brain would render a man insensible. He could not determine from the appearance of the wounds whether they were inflicted before or after death.

Any advantage gained by the defence in all this was quickly negated when the pathologist in charge of the post-mortem, Dr Charles Perkins, followed Dr Egbert on to the witness stand. Brisk and convincing, Dr Perkins declared without hesitation that in his view Dr Cronin had died of concussion produced by blows on the head from a sharp instrument. A sharp weapon, without a stroke, could not produce concussion. As a result of the brain's disintegration – it had liquefied, said Dr Perkins – one means of proving that the doctor had died from concussion had been destroyed, because a microscopical examination of the brain was sometimes necessary to determine the existence of concussion. But there was another proof left, and this was in the condition of the heart. Eminent authorities had declared that in cases of concussion the right side of the heart was invariably filled with blood, while the left side was drained of it. This was the case with Dr Cronin, and it convinced Dr Perkins that the victim had died from concussion of the brain. He also found that the incision on the jaw had severed the facial artery and that one of the wounds on the back of the head had cut the occipital artery. Neither of the arteries was any longer visible. The haemorrhage from these wounds must have been considerable, and would no doubt have produced death had not the injury to the brain proved fatal. There might have been contusion and compression of the brain as well as concussion, but this could not be determined at the post-mortem owing to the ravages of decomposition.

The weather on the fourth day of the trial was as bad as the previous day, but this time it failed to keep away the curious. A storm blowing off the lake drove rain against the windows of the court building and an hour before the court sat the day was so dark that the electric lights were switched on, much earlier than the day before. Braving rain and weather a large and noisy crowd besieged the Dearborn Street entrance to the court. "They howled for admission," declared one report, surely subverting truth to drama. "Men and women were flanked along the brick walk and received the pelting the rain gave them without any evidence of discomfort."

All the public benches were filled when the five prisoners, led by Beggs, tramped into the courtroom. Those on the Dearborn Street side of the room were filled with women, their bonnets and wraps disarranged by the storm. Among them was the woman who had been carrying on a long-distance flirtation with Kunze and Burke. She smiled at the prisoners as they marched to their chairs.

The prosecution did not offer any further evidence concerning the identity of the body, or any more evidence to strengthen their almost invulnerable proof that the corpse was not injured in its removal to the police station. But they did continue their inquiry into the cause of Dr Cronin's death, in order to substantiate the points made by Dr Perkins.

For this they called Dr D. G. Moore, who had assisted

The scene in court during the argument on the exclusion of Dr Moore's testimony

Dr Perkins in the dissection. His presence on the witness stand was clearly a surprise to the defence. Dr Moore did not testify at the coroner's inquest or before the grand jury, and he made no deposition for the hearing on the case for extraditing Martin Burke from Canada. Making these points, Mr Forrest objected to the doctor giving testimony and was promptly overruled by the judge.

Later, searching and probing in cross-examination, the defence lawyer was rewarded by drawing from the witness the admission that only a few hours before appearing in court he had read the newspaper reports of Dr Egbert's evidence of the previous day. Dramatically, Mr Forrest moved that because of that admission the whole of Dr Moore's entire testimony should be struck from the record. To the astonishment of everyone in the court, Judge McConnell agreed.

As the protesting prosecution lawyers leapt to their feet, Mr Forrest, beaming triumphantly, walked hurriedly past his associates and sipped a glass of water, beholding the onset of the pandemonium he had created. Assistant prosecutor W. J. Hynes rose and declaimed that with such a ruling as that delivered from the bench, the testimony of honourable men who would appear for the state, and who could not be influenced by newspaper reports, would be excluded, while the testimony of perjurers who would swear that they had not read the newspaper accounts of the trial would go on record. With much deliberation and a gratuitous encomium on the press for its enterprise and influence, Judge McConnell then reversed his decision and ruled that the testimony of witnesses who had read newspaper reports of the testimony of other witnesses was competent and that it could be admitted.

As the court recessed for lunch, the prosecutors went into a huddle. Their confidence had been badly shaken by this vacillating judge. Would he prove a bigger problem to them than their task of convincing the jury that the prisoners were guilty?

18

A PROCESSION OF WITNESSES

Making a sudden switch from the finding of the body and the sequel to the events of May 4th, the prosecution introduced Paddy Dinan, the liveryman. As Dinan began to recite his role in the story, Dan Coughlin shifted uneasily in his seat. Dinan had known Coughlin for five years. On May 4th the detective came to the stable and engaged a rig for a friend called Smith, who was to call for it at seven that evening. At that hour a young man who was closely muffled in a faded overcoat, and who wore a soft hat, the rim turned down so as to conceal his eyes, called and asked for the rig. Dinan noticed that the stranger's trousers were frayed at the bottom, his boots were muddy, and his moustache was dark at the roots but sandy at the edges. He also had about a week's growth of beard. The stranger found fault with the rig and suggested that he be given a bay horse which was in the stable. But Dinan refused to make the change. The stranger also objected to the buggy because it had no side curtains and Dinan overruled that objection too. Taking the reins, the stranger left the barn at about 7.10 p.m. and drove directly north in the direction of Dr Cronin's home.

Following Dr Cronin's disappearance, came the visit of the policeman to Dinan's stable and Dinan's subsequent visit to East Chicago Avenue police station to see

Captain Schaack. There he met Coughlin who, noticing the liveryman's excitement, asked him what kind of horse he had given his friend on Saturday evening. Dinan replied that the animal was white. Coughlin, becoming nervous, asked Dinan to keep quiet about the transaction as he and Dr Cornin were not good friends and exposure of the deal might cause him trouble.

After Captain Schaack had taken out the white horse and returned it saying that it was not the horse driven that night to Dr Cronin's house, Dinan met Coughlin again. The detective had heard of this incident and was exuberant. But Dinan was worried about the whole affair and said so. Coughlin then taunted the liveryman, "I'd hate to trust you with anything; you're a clear case of a weakener."

Mr Forrest made repeated efforts to have the conversation between Dinan and the stranger at the stable struck from the record, but the judge, as if to atone for his previous performance, overruled them all. The defence lawyer had no luck either in cross-examination. Paddy Dinan was blessed with a remarkable memory and could not be shaken.

Napier Moreland, the stable hand, remembered the stranger as vividly as did his boss. He also remembered the horse and buggy when it came back about half-past nine that night.

"I put the horse on the wash-rack in the stable," he said. "He seemed like he had been driven very fast for the length of time he was out. He was sweating all over and his nostrils were blowing. When I examined him next morning his front legs above the pastern joint were skinned considerably. There was still a little mud on his feet and a little sand mixed in with it."

Napier saw the buggy in daylight on Sunday morning, when he washed it. "It was covered with sand and boulevard mud. The sand was a kind of dirty yellow and the boulevard mud was very much like putty."

Mrs T. T. Conklin told the court that Dr Cronin made his home with her in St Louis before she came to Chicago and he had lived in her family in Chicago for about eight years. His apartments in the Windsor Theatre block were on the south side of the hall, fronting Clark Street. Originally they had been two separate flats – they were afterwards connected by a stairway dividing the north from the south portion. She saw Dr Cronin there about five o'clock on May 4th.

During her evidence Mrs Conklin indicated with a pointer a large plan of the apartments. Dr Cronin's rooms were a front room or reception room, with a bay window looking on to Clark Street, and a private room behind, with sliding doors connecting the two. His evening surgery hours were from 6 to 7.30. He also had another surgery down-town in the Opera House building.

The stranger who called to summon the doctor to Patrick O'Sullivan's employee arrived at 7.20 and acted "very nervously, sitting on the edge of the chair in a rather uncomfortable position while I went to fetch Dr Cronin." After the conversation between the doctor and the stranger, "the doctor sat down at the table and wrote a prescription for Miss McNearney, who was his patient at that moment, and gave it to her just as rapidly as he could do anything, and then he ran to his private room and gathered together some bandages and cotton wadding in his arms and brought them out, and also his surgical case, and a case of heavy splints, and drawing on his coat as quickly as possible he ran out, carrying these things in his arms.

"They went hurriedly out of the house just as fast as they could go. I could hear them running downstairs. They left the door standing open; the doctor did not even close the door."

In the meantime she had gone into the bay window and looked out at the horse and buggy.

"The horse had a very peculiar motion which I never will forget. It seemed to be from his knees down, something like that." Here, with a swaying motion, she described the manner of the horse.

"Giving it an uneasy appearance while standing?" asked Mr Longenecker.

"I object to that," said Mr Forrest. "That is leading. I ask that it may be struck out."

"It may be struck out," said the judge.

"I am not particular about it," said Mr Longenecker. "Is there any other description you can give?"

"Nothing, except the horse started on very well."

Then, in answer to the prosecutor's question, the sharp-eyed Mrs Conklin proceeded to give the best description yet of the man who called Dr Cronin away. Curious about the fellow, even slightly suspicious of him, she watched his every move in the surgery and from her position at the bay window looking down on Clark Street. Who was he? The court never asked, and was never told. But Mrs Conklin's recall of him will allow us to speculate, although with how much accuracy it is difficult to say.

"He was about five feet seven, as near as I could judge. He was a medium-sized man, with a small moustache, a dirty-looking face and straight hair. He had a slouch hat with a very low crown, and very faded-looking clothes. He had on an overcoat which looked too large for him; it had a greasy collar and was very much faded. He looked rusty and dirty-looking. His coat was buttoned at the neck, but the collar was not turned up at all. The rim of his hat appeared to be very soft – that is, bent and broken – and it fell down at the back. It was not a small hat that could be crushed up, but it had a very large crown."

"What do you mean when you say his face was dirty?"

"It was not clean-shaven. He had a small moustache; it was dark, not black. It was a long growth of beard, a stubbly and unshaven face."

"How about his build, as to whether he was heavy or light?"

"He was not a heavy man. He was well put together – I should say wiry, and quick in his movements. His eyes were very peculiar, very wicked. He had a most villainous countenance. I will say here, when he looked at you —"

"I object to that," said Mr Forrest.

"His eyes said, 'Don't look at me again.'"

"I object to that," repeated Mr Forrest.

"That may be struck out," said the judge, "both as to the villainous look and the other. The last two stanzas may be struck out."

Mrs Conklin was then asked, "Did you see Patrick O'Sullivan, one of these defendants, the next day?" Her lengthy reply to the question revealed her as arguably the conspirators' most formidable adversary – she was, it emerged, detective, investigator and cross-examining lawyer all rolled into one.

Mrs Conklin on the witness stand

She did see Patrick O'Sullivan the next day. First, as we know, her husband took her out to Lakeview to see O'Sullivan, but he was not at home. A little while after she got back home, O'Sullivan appeared at her door accompanied by Mr Murray, of the Pinkerton Detective Agency.

"Mr Murray, who had been briefed by my husband earlier that day about what happened on Saturday night, said, 'This is Mr O'Sullivan, Mrs Conklin.'" She ushered the visitors into Dr Cronin's reception room. Mr Murray told her he had already spoken to O'Sullivan about the events of the previous evening, and O'Sullivan was adamant that he did not send for Dr Cronin. Mrs Conklin began to question the iceman.

"I said, 'Mr O'Sullivan, you say you did not send for Dr

Mrs Conklin flanked by Longenecker and Forrest, exhibits a plan of her rooms

Cronin?' Mr O'Sullivan said, 'No, I did not send for Dr Cronin.' I said, 'Mr O'Sullivan, you made a contract with Dr Cronin a short time ago.' 'Yes,' he said, 'I made a contract with Dr Cronin.' 'Well,' I said, 'is it not very singular that your card should be used to summon Dr Cronin so quickly after having made that contract?' 'Well,' he said, 'it was about four weeks ago when we made that contract. 'No,' I said, 'it is not four weeks ago. 'Well,' he said, 'it is three weeks.' 'No,' I said, 'it is not three weeks since I knew of it.' 'Well, it must be about that long.' I said, 'Well, is it not very strange that you should make a contract with Dr Cronin to come six or seven miles to tend your men, when there are fifty or a hundred physicians near you, who are equally as skilful as he? Why did you do it?' 'Well,' he said, 'because Dr Cronin was so highly recommended.' I said, 'Who recommended Dr Cronin so highly?' 'Well,' he said, 'it was Justice Mahoney. He came with me down-town when I made this contract, and introduced me to Dr Cronin.' I said, 'You did not know Dr Cronin then, before that?' 'Well, not very well,' he said. I said, 'If you knew him at all, why was it necessary to be introduced?' 'Well, I did not know him very well,' he said. 'Well, Mr O'Sullivan, explain this thing,' I said. 'Well,' he said, 'I cannot explain it.' I said, 'You must make some explanation. You must admit this looks very bad for you if you cannot explain it.' 'Well,' he said, 'it does look awful bad, and I cannot help it.' In the meantime he would not look at me at all. He just sat this way all the time [here Mrs Conklin stared hard at the floor] and refused to look at me, twirling his hat, and crushing it, and turning it round.

"I said to him, 'Did you ever have an accident, Mr O'Sullivan?' 'No,' said he, 'I never had an accident.' I said, 'It is strange that you say you never had an accident,' and I asked how many men he employed. He said, 'At present I have three,' and I said it was very funny to make a contract with a physician when he had only three men in his employ. 'Well,' he said, 'I expect to have more men after a while.' He said he never had anyone injured, but he didn't know but what there might be."

The prosecution lawyer asked her, "Was anything said about the card the man presented?"

"He said he could not explain that at all. He said he hadn't sent for the doctor, that there was no one sick at his house, and he didn't know how that card came to be presented."

"Did you see that horse and buggy after May 4th?"

"I did."

"Where did you see it?"

"Just in the same place it was when it started to take Dr Cronin away – in front of our home in the Windsor Theatre block."

"Who was driving the horse then?"

"Charles Beck, a reporter." It was May 25th, she recalled, a very nice day, clear and bright, something like it was on May 4th. Mr Beck brought the horse to a standstill outside the block, and she stood in the same position in the north bay window, looking out of the farthest part of the window; "exactly the same position as I occupied when they drove the doctor away."

"Do you state to this jury that that was the horse and buggy in which Dr Cronin was driven away?"

"I do, most emphatically."

"When you looked at the horse for the first time that day, May 25th, did you observe anything?"

"Yes, sir. When Mr Beck came in I stepped to the window to look at something - I don't know what - and I said [here Mrs Conklin pressed her hand to her bosom in a startled manner], 'Where did you get that?' I was so startled."

"What caused you to make that remark?"

"Seeing the same peculiar motion of the knees of the horse. I said to my husband, 'See, it is doing the same thing.' It startled me."

"Do you know whether the card the stranger presented was removed from the mantelpiece after Dr Cronin put it there in the evening of May 4th?"

"Not until my husband took it from there the next morning."

"Did you then see the card?"

"I did, and read what was on it. My husband took it when we went out to look for Dr Cronin. That was between eight and nine o'clock on Sunday morning, May 5th."

"Did you know Patrick O'Sullivan before that?"

"I did not. I had never seen him before that day."

Beginning his cross-examination Mr Forrest was aware that if he could discredit Mrs Conklin's evidence he might have a chance of victory, for without the essential link between the white horse and Dan Coughlin the prosecution's case would begin to collapse. To do this the defence lawyer needed to satisfy the jury that Mrs Conklin's memory was faulty, and to establish that the horse she saw that evening of May 4th was not the same one hired from Paddy Dinan's stable. But, hammered with questions though she was, Mrs Conklin was unshakeable, refusing to contradict a single word of her evidence-in-chief. Then Mr Forrest asked her if she had seen the horse at any other time between the night before it drove Dr Cronin away and the day three weeks later when the reporter Beck brought it round to the Windsor Theatre block. She replied, "I saw a horse which was supposed to be the white horse. It was brought round by Captain Schaack, I think it was in the latter part of the week following the death of Dr Cronin. Captain Schaack said this particular horse was out on the night of May 4th."

"What else did Captain Schaack say to you?"

"He said, 'I have a horse here that I would like you to look at.' I told him to walk in, and he excused himself for coming in the rain by saying, 'Us fellows have to go out in all kinds of weather.' I said we were accustomed to that kind of thing too. He came in and asked me to look at the horse and buggy. We went to the bay window; the horse and buggy were to the north of that window."

"Do you say it rained all that time?"

"It rained all that time constantly."

"Don't you know that it didn't rain until the captain started to go away?"

"I beg your pardon, it was raining when he came in. He took his hat off and shook the raindrops from it, and he had his raincoat on."

"Did you tell Captain Schaack at that time that this was not the horse?"

"I did not."

"Did you tell him that it looked anything like the horse?"

"I told him I could not identify the horse in the rain."

Mr Forrest changed tack. If she did not say to Captain Schaack that the horse he brought did not in any way resemble the one which drove the doctor away, then had she not said at least that much to a newspaper reporter? Picking up a newspaper, he announced that he would read what she was alleged to have said. Before he could do so, the prosecution objected and the objection was upheld. "I will withdraw it," said the defence lawyer.

"Just as a man withdraws a knife after giving a stab," remarked assistant prosecutor Hynes. Mr Forrest either didn't hear this or didn't want to because he continued the cross-examination without responding.

"Do you remember meeting Patrick O'Sullivan, Lieutenant Schuettler, Captain Schaack, and Patrick O'Sullivan's workman, Mulcahey, in Captain Schaack's office?"

"Yes, sir."

"Did you not notice at that time that Mr Mulcahey had a very black moustache?"

"Yes, sir."

"Did you not say, 'The buggy driver had a moustache blacker than yours'?"

"No, sir, I never said such a thing."

"Do you remember meeting Patrick O'Sullivan, Mr Murray of Pinkertons and a reporter at your house?"

"I do."

"Did you not say at that time, in the hearing of those persons, that the driver was dark-complexioned?"

"I have said he was dark."

"Didn't you say, 'Even darker than you are, Mr. O'Sullivan'?"

"Yes, I might have said that."

Mr Forrest told O'Sullivan to stand by his side for a moment. "Now, Mrs Conklin," said the defence lawyer.

"Was he darker than O'Sullivan?"

"He was darker than O'Sullivan is now." [Laughter] His moustache was a little darker than that." Here she pointed to O'Sullivan's moustache. "It seemed to have a reddish colour in the centre, but the ends were darker than his. The man's eyes were dark and sharp."

The imperturbable Mrs Conklin was followed on to the witness stand by Charles Beck, the enterprising newspaper reporter who had hired the white horse and buggy on May 25th and driven it round to Mrs Conklin's home. Mr Forrest, who had evidently done some homework on Charles Beck, decided that his best way in through cross-examination was to attempt to throw a shadow across the reporter's character, one which, in the event, did not appear to have much substance to it.

Beck said he came to Chicago four years previously and had been a reporter for about fifteen years.

"How often have you figured as a witness in a criminal case?" Mr Forrest asked him.

"Well, I cannot remember; I have not been a witness in a courtroom since 1885. I was a witness on one murder case, and this case."

"You are the man that went to Jefferson insane asylum and pretended to be a detective, are you not?"

"Yes, sir, I am."

"You made the court and jury believe you were insane?"

"I did, yes, sir."

"You acted as a prosecution witness in the subsequent court case?"

"I did."

"The man on trial was acquitted?"

"He was."

"Did you ever live in Cheyenne?

"I did."

"What was your business there?"

The judge intervened, "I don't think I will allow this cross-examination to proceed. He is testifying to some inconsequential matters. I think it is utterly immaterial to this inquiry – anything except the bare fact that he drove a horse and buggy to a couple of places."

"That is satisfactory to us," said Mr Forrest quietly. "No more questions." His concession had nothing of the passionate emotion of his previous objections. Mrs Conklin was still very much on the defence lawyer's mind; he was aware that his failure to break her evidence was hanging like a black cloud over the defence case.

19

WHO WAS THAT STRANGER?

Who was the dark stranger who called at Paddy Dinan's for the horse Dan Coughlin ordered? That question was never answered beyond any doubt. The stranger was certainly not O'Sullivan or Martin Burke, both of whom were much taller than five feet seven. Nor could he have been Coughlin, who was also tall and would have been instantly recognised by Paddy Dinan; we also know that Coughlin was later driven up to the cottage some time after 7.30 by John Kunze. Frank Woodruff can be excluded; he had hired another rig, from Dean's and had another role to play in the killing. The stranger may have been Beggs, but it seems unlikely that the Senior Guardian would have thrust himself into such a key role. The little-known Kevin Brown was waiting outside his house with Detective X at about seven o'clock that night; whatever Brown got up to later, he could not have been the man who called for Dr Cronin. That leaves the elusive Patrick Cooney and John Kunze again, both of whom were exactly five feet seven – the height of the stranger as described by several witnesses.

If Cooney, Martin Burke, Patrick O'Sullivan and Dan Coughlin were the most likely people to have dealt the death blows inside the Carlson cottage, Cooney may already have been waiting at the cottage for the doctor's arrival. But it was possible that he could have been both the collector of Dr Cronin and one of the assassins, following Dr Cronin into the Carlson cottage and striking him down in the hall – which would make him a strong contender for the dark stranger. Apart from being the exact height, Cooney, in the guise of J. B. Simmons, was to be described later in the trial by Edward Throckmorton, cashier for the real estate agents Knight and Marshall, as having dark hair, a dark moustache, and dark eyes and, at the time he went to rent the offices at No. 117 Clark Street, he was wearing a heavy overcoat and a drab hat. Cooney too was known to his friends as The Fox, which, if it was an allusion to his physiognomy, suggests the sort of face remembered by Mrs Conklin and, as we shall see, by the McNearney sisters who were at Dr Cronin's surgery on the fatal evening.

Despite the striking out of that significant part of her graphic evidence, Mrs Conklin had given voice to her memory of the "villainous countenance" and it is noteworthy that John Kunze's looks had already been remarked upon at the time of his arrest by a newspaper reporter: "His face has rather a foolish expression, his cheekbones and his ears being its most prominent features."

George Ingham, one of the attorneys for the prosecution

Interestingly, Mrs Conklin never described the stranger as having an Irish accent; the only man within the conspiracy who was not Irish was Kunze. The young Luxemburger – or was he German? – was a close friend of Coughlin, who made all the arrangements for hiring the rig; Kunze must therefore also emerge as a possible candidate for the role of the dark stranger. The flaw in the argument centres on Mrs Conklin's apparent failure to recognise him as such in court. She had the best view of the stranger when he

called on Dr Cronin, and she was a long time facing the
defendants at the trial when she was in the witness box.
Even so, her inability to identify Kunze has to be seen
against the fact that the stranger was deliberately muffled
up; only his eyes, his week-old growth of beard (Kunze
was clean-shaven, apart from his moustache, at the trial)
and his moustache were visible. The stranger may of
course have been someone completely outside the conspiracy, but that would not have tallied with the habitual
working methods of Beggs and Alexander Sullivan, the
organisers of the murder.

But the fact that really suggests more than any other
that Patrick Cooney was the dark stranger is that he was
the only one of the conspirators who was not seen in his
own persona after the murder – because he had fled the
country. The lynx-eyed Mrs Conklin, the observant
McNearney sisters, the shipping clerk Frank Scanlan
with his eye for detail, none of them were able to identify
anyone they saw after May 4th as the dark stranger. Was
that simply because he was Cooney, and he was the only
conspirator who was no longer around to be recognised?

Sarah McNearney, who had accompanied her sister
Agnes, Dr Cronin's patient, to the doctor's surgery,
remembered the stranger well. She told the court that
five minutes after Dr Cronin had taken Agnes into the
consulting room the door bell rang.

"Mrs Conklin went to the door and I heard a man's
voice," she began to say, when Mr Forrest objected to
any evidence regarding what was done and said in the
presence of Sarah McNearney.

"It is the same old objection, I presume," said Mr Mills.

"Yes," said Mr Forrest, "the same old objection."

The judge overruled it and Sarah went on, "The man
asked if the doctor was at home and Mrs Conklin said,
'Yes.' He said there was an accident case and he wanted
the doctor right away; it was very urgent. She invited him
in and I suppose he hesitated in coming in."

The man sat down in the reception-room. To show the

court how he sat down, Sarah bent forward slightly on the edge of her chair, with her hands on her knees.

"He had a very uneasy look on his face," she said.

"I object to that!" cried Mr Forrest.

The judge thought the remark should be struck out, although the prosecuting lawyer Mr Ingham observed, "It is a matter of describing a man's appearance."

"But it is so misleading," said Judge McConnell.

"Suppose she were to say he had a restless eye?" asked Mr Ingham.

"You could say it was a restless eye," approved Mr Forrest. But Sarah came back with much more than that. "He had a stare that you would not see in many persons. It was a stare that was just piercing. He looked at me so sharp that I had to throw my eyes off his face. Every time I looked up he looked straight at me and would not take his eyes off."

"How tall was this man?"

"About five feet seven."

Sarah recalled everything the stranger was wearing as well as the entire conversation between the doctor and the stranger, and she remembered in punctilious detail every movement made by both men before the two sisters, accompanied by their mother, left the surgery at about 7.25p.m.

She was asked, "You say the man had a dark, piercing eye, a faded overcoat, and sat nervously on his chair?"

"Yes, sir."

"Do you know that Mrs Conklin testified to exactly the same thing and used the same language?"

"I object to the question as irrelevant and improper," interrupted Mr Mills, but the witness having already answered in the negative, the judge allowed it to stand.

Agnes McNearney corroborated her sister's evidence about the interview between Dr Cronin and the stranger. She said the man seemed to be quite excited and had a great stare in his eyes – so much so that she could not look at him. She was not a very good judge of such matters, but she thought the man was about five feet seven. Questioned about the look in the man's eye, she said, "It was a stare, but it was quite a bright eye. I looked at the gentleman just as I would look at you [Mr Forrest] and dropped my eyes again."

A swelling tide of irritation among the prosecutors at the bar could be detected when Mr Forrest asked her testily, "Do you know that your sister used exactly the same language in describing the same thing?"

The judge said, "I won't permit that."

"Have you and your sister talked about the way you would tell this?" Mr Forrest went on.

"No, sir, we have not," replied Agnes indignantly. "I know nothing of what she said."

"Can you tell how you hit upon identically the same language?"

"I object!" cried Mr Mills. "That is a misstatement."

The judge nodded. "It also involves too much of an argument," he observed.

"Counsel has no right to make such insinuations!" cried Mr Longenecker.

Mr Forrest replied, "If I have said anything improper I would like the court to tell me and I will withdraw it."

"I have ruled against it," said the judge.

Mr Hynes observed, "Your honour, it might be as well to act upon Mr Forrest's suggestion. He asked if he had said anything wrong. You should tell him because he won't know it himself."

The court erupted in laughter and the defence lawyer's anger was self-evident. "I would suggest that the prosecution are playing to the grandstand," he protested. Wisely the judge suggested they should move on. Agnes left the stand and after brief evidence of identification from John Cronin, an Arkansas farmer who was the murdered man's brother, Frank Scanlan arrived to tell his story of seeing Dr Cronin getting into the buggy outside the Windsor Theatre block, of his hurried conversation with the doctor, and the passing of the keys through the bows of the buggy. Could Scanlan help to identify the stranger whom he now saw taking up the reins of the white horse?

"His eyes appeared to be very dark," Scanlan said. "He had a rather fierce expression and I rather thought it was on my account."

"That won't do," interrupted Mr Forrest.

"His eyes were dark and his moustache was dark. It was a kind of moustache that clung to his lips – what you would call a 'moss moustache'. I could not see anything regular about his features. I do not think he had shaved for a week."

Like Mrs Conklin, his attention was attracted to the peculiar gait of the horse. "He tried to make two or three starts before he did go. You could not call it pacing; it was a kind of a rickety gait. I noticed it for half a block." How qualified was he to comment on a horse's gait, the defence wanted to know. Scanlan replied, "I am a shipping clerk and I have to watch the drivers of teams for our trucks. When a new man is put in, it is my business to see what kind of a teamster he is, and I generally watch the man to see how he handles the lines."

Then Scanlan said something which suggested that the stranger could have been someone on the periphery of the conspiracy. "When Dr Cronin said, 'I am going to attend to an accident at the ice house up north,' I supposed this was a large ice house and that this was the foreman connected with the barn, and that this was the rig used by the foreman to run errands of this kind. I noticed the buggy was not bright and new and the horse was not young. If an accident had happened to one of our men we would go out with that sort of rig." So was the dark stranger one of Patrick O'Sullivan's men? All three of the ice man's employees were regarded with deep suspicion by the police; it may be remembered that at one time Chief Hubbard, believing them to have been aware of everything their boss was involved in, wanted to clap them all in jail. The fault with this supposition, however, is that Scanlan's assumption about the rig was wrong - it did not belong to the ice house, it was hired.

Mr T. T. Conklin was not at home in the evening of May 4th, when the stranger called, so he never saw the man. But he told the court he was so concerned when Dr Cronin did not show up by Sunday morning that, convinced the doctor was at least in serious trouble, he went out and hired the Pinkerton Detective Agency to find him. Only after that did he go to East Chicago Avenue police station.

"Captain Schaack would not listen to any particulars," Mr Conklin recalled. "He said he would send out men on the matter at six o'clock (it was then mid-day), but he would not talk about it before that time.

"Later, in the afternoon, I went back to the police station and saw Captain Schaack again. I called his attention to the fact that he knew that Dr Cronin had enemies; that Dr Cronin had once sent him a circular in which he asked to be protected in regard to his troubles; that he knew the doctor was liable to be injured by someone, and that he ought to take action immediately in the matter in view of these things. Captain Schaack then instructed his sergeant, or someone in charge, to send out a description of the missing man. He referred to him all the time as the missing man."

"I also asked him to send two or three men up to O'Sullivan's house and investigate the matter, but he said he couldn't do it."

The fifth day of the trial brought the crowd back in force. Most of them were turned away, for by now the Sheriff was issuing passes, and only those with them were allowed in. The state began the day by calling five members of Camp 20 to describe the inner workings of their Camp. With one exception the witnesses resorted to every conceivable strategy to hamper the prosecution, but as they squirmed nervously and reddened with embarrassment it was clear that they were causing immense damage to the defence case. John O'Connor, recording secretary of the Camp, was confused and palpably evasive. He swore that he did not hear Andrew Foy ask any question or make any suggestion at the meeting of February 8th (this was the meeting which provoked Captain Thomas O'Connor, stung by Foy's plea that the organisation should be disbanded because of the traitors within it, to denounce the Triangle) and he could give no intelligent account of what Captain O'Connor had said. It was not until Mr Longenecker handed him the record book of the minutes of the meeting of February 8th that he could positively assert that a secret committee had been appointed to investigate the reading of the trial committee's report in another camp. When Mr Longenecker asked O'Connor if he had not discussed with three other members of the Camp the propriety of destroying the Camp's books the witness hesitated long enough for the defence to fire a broadside of objections. The judge ruled that the question was improper, and the crimson-faced witness visibly sighed with relief.

Andrew Foy himself was rambling and incoherent. He admitted he made "a few remarks at the meeting," but it was certainly no speech. He could not remember whether he was on his feet or sitting down when he spoke. He did not think there was any excitement when Captain O'Connor "made his remarks." He could, however, confirm the report that he had said that if there were any more spies in the Camp they ought to be expelled.

Junior Guardian Michael J. Kelly, although more concise than his predecessors, had an amazingly treacherous memory; he had seen almost nothing and heard hardly anything. Patrick Ford was more satisfactory to the state. Coughlin, O'Sullivan and Beggs stared at him unwaveringly all the time he was on the witness stand. Ford remembered that at one time during Senior Guardian Beggs's harangue on February 8th Beggs said he would have peace or open war, for he was getting tired of the bushwhacking tactics of the anti-Alexander Sullivan and anti-Dr Cronin factions in the organisation. There was much excitement at the meeting or, as Ford put it, "the members seemed to be very much heated."

Shortly after the February 8th meeting, Ford said, Patrick O'Sullivan told him that people he described as Irish traitors belonging to a rival patriot organisation called the United Order of Deputies, who wanted appeasement with England, were known to be infiltrating Dr Cronin's Camp and fraternising with its members. This in O'Sullivan's opinion was a sorry business for Ireland. The state's view of that conversation was that the iceman was attempting to spread the belief that Dr Cronin's Camp was a rendezvous for traitors undermining the work of patriotic Irishmen who were battling to establish a republic in Ireland, and that Dr Cronin himself was tainted by them.

The one lucid exception among the five Camp 20 witnesses was big Stephen Colleran, described by the *Chicago Herald* as "a lusty County Mayo lad," who was a close friend of Martin Burke before the assassination. There had been conflicting evidence from the first four witnesses about the presence of Coughlin, Burke, Cooney and O'Sullivan at the meeting of February 8th. Colleran not only knew the first three were there, he even described where they sat, and he was adamant that they were well acquainted with each other despite their assertions to the contrary. He had known all of them, except Kunze, for several years. He used to work with Burke in the city's water department and afterwards they kept each other company when both were unemployed. In January and February of that year they called three times at the office of John Beggs and asked him to use his influence as a lawyer to get them reinstated in the water department.

In March, at about the time the plot to murder Dr Cronin was reaching its maturity, Colleran had seen Coughlin and Burke walking together in the shadow of the Criminal Court building. He joined them on the pavement and all three walked to Clark Street. He had seen them with Patrick Cooney several times after that. The effect of Colleran's evidence was to show that John Beggs was acquainted with Martin Burke, that Coughlin, Cooney and Burke were close friends, and that all four were particularly interested in each other during the four months preceding the murder.

None of this, it should be said, was delivered willingly. Colleran frequently hesitated, but he lacked the subtlety of the first four witnesses. That the damaging admissions were wrung from him was due to the tough questioning of Luther Mills, whose steely gaze met Colleran's despairing eye every time the witness began to prevaricate. All the time Colleran fidgeted in his chair Dan Coughlin glared at him and Burke's face was alternately pale and flushed. O'Sullivan and Beggs seemed indifferent, while Kunze laughed and threw his legs over the arm of his chair as though none of this had anything to do with him. The hardest-worked of all, perhaps, was Mr Forrest, who kept up a constant fire of objections throughout Colleran's evidence.

Next day the court heard from Captain Thomas O'Connor what seemed a much more authentic account of the proceedings during the meeting of February 8th. He was followed by Patrick McGarry, Senior Guardian of Dr Cronin's Camp 95, and a good friend of the doctor. Closing his eyes while he spoke, as if to recall more vividly the scene, McGarry described a reunion meeting of Camps which took place on February 22nd. On that occasion he bluntly denounced the squabbles in the Camps, the foes of his native land, the Parnell Commission (which he referred to as the Forgery Commission), and "the cowards who would lay for a man in back alleys" – a reference that caused a perceptible wince among the prisoners.

Speaking in a rich, resonant voice, McGarry, a boilermaker by trade, gripped the side of the stand with black, hardened hands as he recalled the meeting, "I said it was all very well to talk of unity, and I wanted to see unity among the Irish people, but there could not be unity while members of this organisation would meet in back alleys and in dark corners and vilify and abuse the man who had the courage to stand out and take traitorism and robbery by the throat and strangle it. I said too that the man who gave Le Caron his credentials to go into our conventions was a greater scoundrel than Le Caron could pretend to be."

As McGarry paused a suppressed outburst of applause rippled through the courtroom. Then he went on, "John Beggs acknowledged that he knew who was referred to as 'a greater scoundrel then Le Caron.' Beggs said he knew it meant Alexander Sullivan, and that he 'was proud to proclaim himself as a friend of that individual.' Beggs then attacked McGarry for "coming among the friends of Alexander Sullivan to sow the seeds of dissension and discord," and called him a coward for excoriating a man who was not present to defend himself. McGarry again secured the floor and fiercely declared that he was prepared to express his opinion of Alexander Sullivan in any place and before anybody. At this more applause rippled through the courtroom.

McGarry also told how, when the murder was known, he went to iceman O'Sullivan's house to inquire about the mysterious contract. There were four or five men and a woman present when he arrived. The iceman admitted to McGarry, as he had admitted to Mrs Conklin, that things looked badly for him. Then one of the men present suggested that perhaps the United Order of Deputies had made away with the doctor. McGarry replied that the crime was much nearer home, and it would be found that one of Dr Cronin's own colleagues had killed him. When the man referred to the deputies, McGarry, suddenly turning his head, saw O'Sullivan make a grimace which might be construed as an admonition to say nothing more.

Enthralled, the court listened in silence as McGarry spoke. Then, lowering his voice, he carefully delivered his Parthian shot. "Before I left O'Sullivan's house I reminded O'Sullivan and his companions that once before Dr Cronin had been lured to a den to attend a fictitious sufferer. Desperately he plunged down stairs two at a time to escape death from the hands of conspirators who were hidden in the room, all the time shouting, 'My God! Did you bring me here to murder me?'"

Next day, Mr Donahoe, defending O'Sullivan, asked that this statement should be struck out and he was upheld. But by then it was too late – all Chicago was talking about it.

*   *   *

Although there were still many witnesses to be heard, many more days to go, Patrick McGarry was the turning-point in the Cronin trial. After McGarry, few cared much for the conspirators chances. The procession of witnesses who followed seemed like a ritual played out to satisfy the rules, a formality which could have no bearing on a decision already silently taken. George Reilly, a bar-keeper, of 238 East Chicago Avenue, remembered a night in March when Coughlin, in a harangue about the approaching municipal elections, declared that if a certain Catholic on the North Side did not stop talking so much, he would get the worst of it. His assistant, James Quin, corroborated this.

Every morning, starting a few days after the trial began, John Kunze was brought into court sick. He lay in an easy-chair, his head propped up on pillows and his face turned towards one wall of the courtroom. Nevertheless, he appeared to be the only one of the five on the prisoners bench to notice the bloody trunk as it was lugged into court by two bailiffs – the other four prisoners deliberately turned their heads away. The bailiffs set the trunk down a few feet from the front row of jurors. Its sides were splintered, its hinges shattered, its lock broken. There was a gaping hole in the lid through which a heap of dirty cotton wadding was clearly visible. Its purpose there was for it to be identified by Mr W. P. Hatfield, the salesman for A. H. Revell's who sold the trunk to J. B. Simmons, but its symbolism could not have been lost on the jury: here was the Clan-na-Gael, with its sides cracked open, a gaping hole in the top, and all its interior rottenness revealed.

Mr Hatfield recalled that of all the articles in the bill of goods selected by the mysterious Mr J. B. Simmons for 117 Clark Street, the trunk alone seemed to concern him. He had insisted upon a big trunk and a strong one, and to ensure its strength he bought a big strap to go around it. The first strap he bought was not strong enough and he returned next day to change it for a stronger one. Mr Hatfield recalled too that his customer laid stress on the fact that the goods were only for temporary use.

John Garrity told the court he had known Detective Dan Coughlin for four years and was well acquainted with him. About two years previously he had a conversation with Coughlin on the corner of Market and Ontario Streets.

"Coughlin asked me one afternoon if I thought John Sampson would do a job for him – a piece of work. I asked him what it was and he said he wanted to have a certain fellow slugged. I asked him who, but he didn't say. I said, 'What do you want done to him?' He said, 'Get a club and break his nose, or knock his teeth out or disfigure him for life, or something.' I said, 'You'd better find Sampson yourself and see if he will do it.' In the meantime I saw Sampson and told him Coughlin wanted to see him."

Giving evidence, John Sampson, commonly known as Major Sampson, said that about two years previously Detective Dan Coughlin approached him at the intersection of LaSalle Avenue and Erie Street, with a proposition to lay in wait for Dr Cronin as he returned to his home in the Windsor Theatre block one night and slug him. Sampson thought the undertaking too hazardous, but Coughlin persisted, and suggested he could get someone else to help him with the work. During their discussion William Linn, a friend of Sampson and a former Chicago policeman, stood at a corner on the other side of the street. Linn testified to the meeting of Coughlin and Sampson.

Cross-examined, Sampson admitted a long criminal career. He had been a shell-player,* had no visible means of support and had often been arrested by Coughlin on charges of robbery and vagrancy. But, he declared passionately, he had not been convicted on these charges, and Coughlin's pursuit of him amounted to persecution. Sampson provoked an outburst of applause when, taunted by Mr Forrest that shell-playing was a felony, he exclaimed, "Well, it isn't murder, anyhow."

Thus, by the end of the first week the case for the defence was looking distinctly worse than it looked at the beginning. When the case opened the five prisoners, confident to the point of arrogance, were relying upon four pillars which seemed to them to support an indestructible edifice. They were the question about the identity of the body found in the Evanston road catch-basin; the possibility of mutilation in removing the corpse from the sewer; the assumption that the blood in the Carlson cottage did not come from Dr Cronin's wounds; and the sweeping assertion that there was no conspiracy in the camps of the Clan-na-Gael to murder the enemy of the Triangle. Brick by brick the pillars had crumbled. The first fell at one push, the second soon after. The third was made of harder stuff. As the second week of the trial got under way only the fourth pillar was holding things up. But it was

---

*Shell is the U.S. name for thimblerig, a betting game in which the operator rapidly moves three upturned thimbles, often with sleight of hand, one of which conceals a token. The game is associated with cheating.

proving vital shelter for John Beggs, against whom very little was so far proved.

Next it was the turn of the Carlson family, those redoubtable Scandinavians, to tell their story, a story which chained Martin Burke, as Frank Williams, to the murder scene and which showed that O'Sullivan was deeply interested in the cottage and in the mysterious tenants who rented it. Jonas Carlson said that when Frank Williams left the cottage he walked over to O'Sullivan's buggy shed, a few feet away, and talked to the iceman. Old man Carlson followed his new tenant out of the house and heard him say as he greeted O'Sullivan, "Well, I have rented the cottage." About the middle of April, seeing no evidence of life in the cottage, Carlson asked O'Sullivan if he knew anything about the tenants. The iceman eventually agreed that he knew one of them, and that he was all right. He also gave the old man to understand that he would be responsible for the next month's rent in case Williams did not appear.

The next time Carlson saw Williams was at five o'clock on May 4th, the day of the murder. The young man was standing on the front steps of the house, but afterwards went indoors. Two hours later Carlson heard two men talking loudly in the front room of the cottage. He could not hear what they said, and the blinds were closed too tightly for him to see them. At eight o'clock all the members of the Carlson family were in bed. When morning came the old man, prowling about his property, saw strange stains on the front steps, which he thought were caused by someone breaking a jar of preserves. In the soft mud near the pavement in front of the cottage were the footprints of men who had worn heavy shoes, and near the kerb were fresh wagon tracks which seemed to lead south. He paid no attention at the time to these marks and stains until he received a letter from "F. B. W." in Hammond, Indiana, in which Williams wrote that he had lost the keys of the cottage; that he had painted the floors to save his sister the trouble of scrubbing them, and that if any damage had been done he would see it would be paid in full.

The letter aroused Carlson's suspicions, and he began an investigation which convinced him that all was not right. The doors were locked. One of the cottage's front wooden shutters had been cut, and through this aperture the old man passed his hand and sprung the catch. Then he raised the window and crawled into the room, followed by his son. Besides the daubs of yellow paint everywhere, there was a rocking-chair with its right arm broken, a chamber set of three pieces, a door rug, a bed without sheets or pillow-cases, and a wash-bowl and pitcher. The carpet was gone, and so was the big yellow trunk which the old man had seen when he peeped through the shutter several weeks before.

When he had finished his story Jonas Carlson was asked if he could see his tenant Frank Williams anywhere in court. He glanced nervously around him, keeping silent. The question was repeated, and for the second time Carlson scanned the audience without discovering the face. During the silence that prevailed Martin Burke sat with his gaze fastened upon the witness. Carlson was asked to leave his chair and walk among the people in the court. He took his black hat in his hand and strolled slowly past the jurors and lawyers. Then he looked at the prisoners, gazing at each of them in turn, until he reached the last one, Martin Burke. The two men were less than five feet apart when Carlson, with a grunt of satisfaction, shook his hat at the crimson-faced prisoner.

"Is he the Frank Williams you saw?" asked Mr Mills as the witness returned to the chair.

"Yes, sir," was the firm reply.

When Mr Forrest got up and began to cross-examine, old man Carlson scowled at him and refused to answer his questions. Only a few people in the court knew what this was about. Six or seven weeks previously Mr Forrest, in his zeal to defend his clients to the last breath, had hired a gang of roughs who went with the defence lawyer to take forcible possession of the Carlson cottage. Inside they tore from the floor and walls planks of wood containing some of the bloodstains claimed to have been made during the death-struggle between Dr Cronin and his murderers. They refused to take notice of Carlson's protests until the old man, departing abruptly, returned a few minutes later with a loaded revolver. Carlson pointed the gun at Forrest, and would undoubtedly have shot him had not someone standing nearby quickly disarmed him. Now the protagonists were facing each other again in open court and Carlson did not like the idea of his veracity being disputed by this man of all people in front of an audience. The judge told him it was his duty to answer; even so, the gruff old Swede was determined that Forrest would not get the better of him and some of his responses brought guffaws of laughter from the court. More importantly, the cross-examination failed to shake his evidence.

Carlson's daughter-in-law, Annie Carlson, corroborated his story. She had far less difficulty in recognising Frank Williams. Asked by Mr Mills, "Do you see the man?" Annie levelled the index finger of her gloved hand at Martin Burke. The prisoner chewed viciously at his tobacco, rolled his eyes wildly and wrinkled his face into a broad smile. Coughlin, Beggs and O'Sullivan looked away. Kunze, his head buried in a pillow, opened one eye as the gloved finger pointed at the man next to him.

Mr Forrest tried desperately to shake Annie Carlson on the point of identification. But she had made no mistake. She knew the man by his restless eyes, by his mouth, and by the contour of his face. Burke put his hand over his chin – the most striking feature of his face – as she began to describe him, but soon dropped his arm and grinned broadly, if somewhat helplessly, at the audience.

Then came a witness who reduced the court to silence with a sudden reminder of the reality of why they were there. She was Mrs Hoertel, a cleaner, and that night, and indeed the previous night, she had been deliberately locked out of her house by her husband as a result of some domestic tiff. Mr Hoertel had changed the lock, leaving his wife to spend the nights of May 3rd and 4th on the porch; the following night, apparently, she discovered a ladder and climbed through a second-floor window to get some much-needed rest. On the night of May 4th, furious at finding the door locked against her for a second time, and getting no reply from rapping the door, she went in search of her husband at Ertel's saloon, where he was well-known as a whiskey-supping customer. Mr Hoertel was not there. Disappointed, his wife left the saloon and made her way back to her house. As she drew near to the Carlson cottage she saw Dr Cronin alight from a buggy drawn by a white horse. He took a valise and a small case from the buggy and went inside. Immediately the door closed Mrs Hoertel, now level with the Carlson cottage, heard an agonised cry of "Oh, God!" Next she heard a noise which sounded like a blow, followed by a stifled cry, "Oh, Jesus!" and all was still. Uncertain of what it meant, and half afraid, she hurried back to another uncomfortable night on her porch.

20

FOUND: THE KEY
TO THE MYSTERY

Shortly after the afternoon session of the court opened on November 8th, two weeks into the trial, with still more witnesses filing in with their stories, three sewermen of Lakeview Department of Public Works were called to a briefing about a particular catch-basin at the corner of Evanston and Buena avenues. An inspector had reported that the catch-basin was totally obstructed and the back-up was causing flooding, reducing the surrounding unmade roads to mud. The three sewermen, Michael Gilbert, of Sedgwick Street, the foreman; and his assistants Mike Reese and W. W. McMillan, were to go along and clear the obstruction; if they failed, they were to call in a flushing gang to help them.

At that time obstructions to surface water drainage were common enough in the Chicago periphery, providing regular employment for half a hundred city council workmen, so it was perhaps understandable that no one thought to associate the blockage with the Cronin mystery. This was despite the fact that the place was not much more than a mile from where the body was found, and less than a quarter of a mile from the ditch where the trunk was picked up on the Sunday morning after the murder.

Wading through the flood-water at the site, the three men raised the cover of the catch-basin and Gilbert and McMillan lowered Reese into it. At the bottom Reese called up, "There's a box down here under the water."

The two men at the top, their voices magnified by the subterranean cylinder, shouted back, "What's in it?"

"Something that sounds like iron or tin."

Groping under the stagnant water, Reese put a rope around the box and called to his companions to haul up. It was a rectangular container, about a foot long, seven or eight inches deep and nearly as wide. There were small areas on its surface which bore evidence to it once having been highly varnished and polished. There was a brass handle in the centre of the lid which Gilbert used to carry the box beyond the flood water, where he forced it open. One glance was enough.

"This is Dr Cronin's box!" exclaimed McMillan. The "tin or iron" of which Reese had spoken was an assortment of extension splints the doctor had taken with him in anticipation of having to treat a fractured leg at Patrick O'Sullivan's ice-works.

Reese, still down in the catch-basin, called up that he had found a leather satchel and a bundle of clothes. He passed them up, then a moment later he found the broken frame of a second satchel whose cover had been reduced to slime by the sewer waters. The bundle of clothes was reeking with slimy, black refuse; the three men decided not to investigate it. Fifteen minutes later, in response to their call, the same Lakeview police wagon that drove Dr Cronin's naked body to the morgue was rolling up Evanston Avenue at a lively clip. The bundle of clothes, the half-consumed satchel, the instrument box and the leather satchel were loaded on to a stretcher and taken off to the police station in Sheffield Avenue. There Sergeant Koch telephoned Chief of Police Hubbard and was told to deliver the discoveries to headquarters at once.

By three o'clock the dirty packages were spread out on a rubber tarpaulin in Hubbard's office. The leather satchel was placed under a running hydrant before it was opened; inside the police chief found a book swollen to more than twice its natural size. He opened it cautiously, and through the veneer of dirt he read "Dr P. H.

Cronin." In another part of the satchel was a pack of the doctor's visiting cards in a fair state of preservation.

"We've got the whole thing!" exclaimed Hubbard, holding up one of the cards for his assembled police officers to see.

There was no question of that, but there were still plenty of questions. After the discovery of the trunk on Sunday, May 5th, the police had frequently boasted that they had searched every sewer in Evanston Avenue for the body or for artefacts such as these. When it became a settled fact that the murderers had driven north to Edgewater, and that during their return to the city they had dumped the trunk in the ditch above Sulzer Road, Captain Schaack claimed he had ordered a close inspection of all man-holes and sewers covered by that area. Until the body was found he had continued to assert that the inspection was thorough, and after the body was found he announced that that particular sewer at the corner of Evanston and Fifty-ninth Street had been overlooked. Now it seemed that the Buena Avenue sewer was also overlooked, and it did not take long for the Chicago press to observe that probably every other sewer in Lakeview was overlooked too. It was all too painfully obvious that the murderers had distributed evidence of their crime all along the road and the police had not found any of it.

The discovery of Dr Cronin's clothes and belongings also posed another question: what then was inside the mysterious tin box, covered with yellow dirt and sand, which Burke took to tinsmith Klahre for the lid to be soldered down? The prosecution had hypothesised that it contained Dr Cronin's clothes, although now it plainly did not. Once again the story of the woman's amputated finger surfaced, and now, it was whispered, that tin box must surely have contained the rest of her body.

The court, unaware of the find, was continuing to hear the prosecution's case. Their witness William Niemann, who had a saloon bar on the corner of School Street and Ashland Avenue, in Lakeview, gave an interesting account of how O'Sullivan, Coughlin and Kunze spent the hours immediately after the murder. Niemann said that on the morning of May 3rd, the day before the disappearance of Dr Cronin, O'Sullivan called on him to solicit a contract for ice. Niemann agreed to the deal, but O'Sullivan said he could not deliver any ice that day. Early in the evening O'Sullivan returned to the saloon, bought a cigar, and left. His men delivered ice to Niemann next morning, and the saloon-owner saw nothing more of O'Sullivan until 10.30 on the night of the murder, when he came into the saloon with two men Niemann now recognised as Coughlin and Kunze. O'Sullivan and Coughlin went to the bar and called for sherry, while Kunze stood near the door and asked for a beer.

"You need something better than that!" exclaimed O'Sullivan, turning to Kunze, who made no objection. The three men drank two rounds of sherry and each took a cigar. O'Sullivan paid the bill. O'Sullivan and Coughlin were in earnest conversation; their heads were so close together and they talked so softly that Niemann could not hear what they said. Coughlin did most of the talking, frequently emphasising points with gesticulations.

The court had just risen when news arrived that the victim's clothes and personal property had been found. Although there was nothing to see, a crowd gathered in the rain outside the Criminal Court building. Among them was a slim young man wearing a raincoat and light-coloured trousers. Others in the crowd noticed his face was sheet-white and he seemed in a state of agitation. He paced up and down for a few minutes, then walked into one of the corners of the Dearborn Street side of the building, put a revolver into his mouth and blew out his brains. He died instantly. A woman who saw the suicide fainted and the crowd, convinced that they had witnessed one of the murderers of Dr Cronin take his own life while overcome with remorse, buzzed with renewed excitement.

In the prosecutors' office Mr Longenecker and Lieutenant Schuettler left the bundle of clothing they were examining and hurried outside to the suicide. The body was taken to the detention hospital in the court building, where it was recognised as that of Edward Rehm, of Kansas City, who had once before tried to kill himself and had only recently been released from hospital. The young man was love-sick and disturbed about the conduct of his fickle girlfriend – so it seemed from a suicide note written in German and found in his coat pocket.

Next day, November 13th, the prosecution concluded its case and the court adjourned until Saturday November 16th for the opening of the defence. No one expected the prisoners to give evidence on their own behalf; none the less, when it was announced that they would not do so the decision had to be interpreted as an admission of weakness, as it frequently is today. What the five men were saying effectively was that it was up to the prosecution to make out a case against them; they did not have to defend themselves. Tactically that is perfectly acceptable when the prosecution's case is weak. By the end of the state's case in the Cronin trial it could not have been stronger.

A curious effort was made to discredit Mrs Hoertel's testimony by calling a man named Salzman, who lived in Hoertel's house and who testified regarding the date on which Hoertel put a new lock on the house in order to lock out his wife. Salzman claimed that he helped the husband, Hoertel, to change the lock and the lock was not put on until after May 8th. His evidence was almost at once discredited in turn by the woman who sold the lock. She remembered selling it to Hoertel because he told her that he wanted to lock out his wife, and she knew it was before May 4th. Her evidence was supported by Albert Kleincke, a builder who remembered seeing Mrs Hoertel climbing the ladder to get into her house on May 5th.

If this was scarcely material evidence the defence case was not improved by a procession of witnesses, led by a saloon bar keeper, William Coughlin, who, having established he was not related to the former detective, testified that Martin Burke was at Coughlin's saloon in East Chicago Avenue at the relevant time on May 4th, and another long line of witnesses who claimed that Patrick O'Sullivan did not leave his house after six o'clock that night and was in bed shortly after 7.30. In both cases the evidence of these alibi witnesses showed so many discrepancies in times and dates that by the time the last of them had given evidence few had any doubts about where Burke and O'Sullivan really were that night.

Then came another sensation. The state prosecutor rose to announce that new information had come to his knowledge that morning and he needed to introduce a new witness. Mr Forrest was furious, claiming that this was tantamount to reopening a trial that was all but finished. But Judge McConnell overruled him, and Mr Longenecker, turning dramatically to an usher, said with deliberate slowness, "Call Barney Flynn!"

One man in court reacted immediately to the name – he was Dan Coughlin. The big detective's face visibly paled; he shifted uneasily on his seat and his restless gaze wandered around the courtroom as if in search of a way of escape. In came Barney Flynn. He was a diminutive fellow with an air of self-assurance; he met Coughlin's agonised look with a chilly stare. He was sworn, and told the court that he was a detective currently serving at East Chicago Avenue police station.

"Acting on instructions from Chief of Police Hubbard I arrested Daniel Coughlin on May 27th and took him to the Armory police station," Flynn told the court. "There, in the presence of Captain Bartram, I searched him. I found two pocket-knives and a revolver on him. I took these to Chicago Central police station and locked them in my private box for safe-keeping. When I was subsequently transferred to East Chicago Avenue I removed them to my box in the vault of the Fidelity Bank. Yesterday morning I turned the knives over to Chief Hubbard, who showed them to Mr T. T. Conklin."

Recalled, Mr Conklin took the knives handed him by

Mr Longenecker, and identified one which was medium-sized and pearl-handled as a knife he gave to Dr Cronin about a year ago. "It was one I carried myself for nearly two years," he said. "So I know it well." The smaller knife was one he found about nine months previously. He took it home and laid it on a mantel, where Dr Cronin saw it and liked it, so Mr Conklin told him he could keep it.

Bemused, Mr Forrest merely asked Mr Conklin if the knives were not of a very ordinary pattern and then let him go. No one asked Detective Barney Flynn why he kept the incriminating contents of an arrested man's pockets locked up in his personal locker, or why Captain Bartram allowed him to do so.

Next day Mr Forrest paraded his rebuttal witnesses. A clothier, August Lowenstein, told the court that on April 27th Dan Coughlin came to his store and bought some trousers. As he tried them on he took some things from his pocket and laid them on a table. Among them were two knives, and Mr Lowenstein thought that the ones produced in court were the same. He recollected that the incident occurred on April 27th because there was an item on his books of a sale of a pair of trousers for $5.50 on that date.

"Was Coughlin's name attached to the entry?" asked Mr Longenecker.

"It was not," replied Lowenstein, "but I remember that Coughlin was the one to whom the sale was made."

Jack Lowenstein, brother of August and a discharged member of the police force, followed and swore that he had often seen Dan Coughlin's knives when they were travelling together. Shown the knives in court, he examined them carefully and then concluded that they were the ones he had always seen, basing his recollection on the peculiar manner in which the blades were ground.

The evidence had lasted for more than a month, and now it was over. None of the closing speeches was likely to be remembered for its oratory; the Chicago lawyers having seemingly picked up a thing or two on windiness from the city's legendary politicians.

Mr Longenecker's final submission spanned two days, and ended on a high emotional note: "Think of the fourth day of May; think of that man gathering his little valise and instruments; think of him bringing to his bosom the cotton to relieve suffering; think of the splints in the box; think of his rushing out to the buggy. See him enter as a gentleman into the cottage; hear the cries of God and Jesus when he was felled to the floor. Think of the wounds in his head; think of the grave in which he was placed; think of all these in making up your penalty, and may it be such a verdict as when his Honour pronounces judgment on it, that he, having an eye to God, may say, 'May the Lord have mercy on your souls.'"

Mr Wing, for Dan Coughlin, took the broad ground in arguing that proof of guilt was not established beyond a reasonable doubt.

Mr Ingham, for the state, scathingly reviewed the failure of the defence to offer the slightest explanation of the renting of the Carlson cottage by Martin Burke under an assumed name, his failure to furnish it as a man would who intended to live there, and the failure of the alleged sister to substantiate his story.

Mr Donahoe, for O'Sullivan and Kunze, was positively lyrical. There was no duty in the life of the lawyer, he affirmed, that afforded him more pleasure than defending the innocent; "therefore I plead for the life of my two clients with a heart as light as the newly-made bride as she goes forth with her husband after the bridal ceremony." When he had recovered from this he too argued that the prosecution had failed to establish any proof connecting O'Sullivan and Kunze either directly or indirectly with the murder.

Mr Hynes, for the prosecution, flayed the alibi evidence. O'Sullivan's own admissions, he said, showed that he was out of his house on the night of May 4th and only a few feet away from the Carlson cottage. As for Coughlin, it didn't matter whether or not he had an alibi, his connection as a principal in the crime was clearly proved by his employment of Dinan's white horse for his friend Smith.

Mr W.H. Foster, for John Beggs, told the jury that Beggs's position was that the "famous secret committee" was never appointed. One of the witnesses had said that to his best recollection the man who seconded the motion made by Dan Coughlin on February 8th for the appointment of the committee was Thomas Murphy, the treasurer of Camp 20. Why, Mr Foster wanted to know, was Murphy. who was originally marked down as a witness for the state, not called to the stand? "They did not want him to testify," the defence lawyer said solemnly, the inference presumably being that Murphy would say there was no secret committee appointed at that meeting. From the discovery of Dr Cronin's body to the present time the conduct of Beggs had been consistent with the theory of his innocence. Ignorant members of Camp 20, hesitating between their oath of secrecy to the Clan-na-Gael and their duty as witnesses, had appealed to him as Senior Guardian for direction. "'Tell everything,' was Beggs' instruction," said Mr Foster. "And by the statement of the public prosecutor himself, corroborated by the Chief of Police, it appeared that Beggs was the first to disclose the correspondence with Spellman, his senior."

Mr Forrest, representing all the defendants, talked at length about the unreliability of circumstantial evidence, citing as an instance of such unreliability the state's theory in the present case that Dr Cronin's clothes had been sent to Europe in the tin box which Burke had so carefully soldered up. If the clothes had not been discovered in the catch-basin, that theory would have been argued and upheld by the prosecution. He then argued that each of the state's witnesses had a personal interest in proving the defendants guilty. "It is worth for instance $100 a week to Pat Dinan to have it established that his horse is the horse that took the doctor away, because that is what he'll make from having that horse in the dime museum." The physicians had failed to show whether Dr

Cronin's wounds were ante-mortem or post-mortem, and the state had failed to prove that there was any human blood discharged in the Carlson cottage.

Finally it was the judge's turn. Judge McConnell instructed the jury on the law of conspiracy and murder. Under State of Illinois law, if the jury found the prisoners guilty they had also to recommend the sentence, and capital punishment was in force in the state. The length of their deliberations was in accordance with the importance of the trial. They retired at 4 p.m. on Friday December 13th. They spent the entire weekend reviewing the evidence in the jury room and did not emerge with a verdict until three days later, at 2.30 p.m. on December 16th. They found Daniel Coughlin, Martin Burke and Patrick O'Sullivan guilty of murder; John Kunze guilty of the lesser charge of manslaughter; and John Beggs not guilty. They fixed the sentence of Coughlin, Burke and O'Sullivan at life imprisonment, and that of Kunze at imprisonment for three years.

The prisoners did not flinch as the sentences were announced. But in the cells beneath the court Coughlin was furious and called the trial an outrage. O'Sullivan wept, Burke merely laughed. The three life prisoners were handcuffed and manacled together, with Burke in the centre, where he was literally bound hand and foot. They were dragged into a wagon and driven to a train which took them to the state prison at Joliet. Beggs, standing outside the court a free man, stayed to watch them leave by a back entrance, no doubt marvelling at his sheer good fortune – he had got off scot free from his part in the Phoenix Park murders and now four others were taking the rap for the Cronin murder he had helped to organise.

The trial, including the jury selection, had lasted 110 days – at that time the longest criminal trial in American history. In its efforts to secure a conviction the state spent a record $100,000. Still another record was set by the defendants, who spent even more than the state on their legal fees.

Captain Michael Schaack was not on trial, but he must

at times have felt extremely uncomfortable during some of the police evidence. His bungling of the investigation was so evident that when it was all over the police held their own inquiry and charged Schaack with incompetence. He was discharged from the force and his job went to Lieutenant Schuettler, who had distinguished himself despite the handicap of having to report to Schaack.

The marathon Cronin case left some unanswered questions. What was in Martin Burke's tin box, so painstakingly soldered up? Was a woman killed by the conspirators that same night of May 4th? Since Dr Cronin had once before been tricked into attending a sick man and had to flee for his life on that occasion, why did he not suspect the mysterious caller with the iceman's card and, even before that, the dubious contractual arrangement with O'Sullivan? What became of Patrick "The Fox" Cooney in Ireland, to where he undoubtedly escaped?

Martin Burke, who had been Cooney's close companion, and Patrick O'Sullivan both died in prison. Shortly after being sentenced, John Kunze was granted a new trial, which resulted in his acquittal. Dan Coughlin also pleaded for a new trial and by the time it was finally granted, on the ground that two of the jurors were prejudiced against him, so many of the witnesses had dispersed that the state had a much reduced case. Besides that, the ex-detective was said to have been provided with funds which this time he used successfully to bribe some of the jurors. And this time it worked – he was acquitted in what one Chicago newspaper called "a travesty of justice."

Coughlin seemed to regard the whole experience as a great joke. He opened a saloon on North Clark Street only three doors from where Dr Cronin had lived, and regaled his customers with stories of how he had beaten the rap. A year later he was indicted for jury-bribing in yet another criminal trial. When the Chicago police came to pick him up they found his saloon was closed. Ex-Detective Dan Coughlin had fled to Honduras, where he died in 1911.

THE CAST

Dr Patrick Henry Cronin
General practitioner, of Chicago.

The Triangle (Executive Committee) of the Clan-na-Gael
Alexander Sullivan, Dennis Feeley, Colonel Michael Boland

Police and detectives

Chief of Police Hubbard *(Chicago)*

Captain Michael Schaack *(East Chicago Avenue)*

Lieutenant Hermann Schuettler *(East Chicago Avenue)*

Captain Wing *(Lakeview)*

Captain Francisco Villiers *(Lakeview)*

Detective Rohan *(East Chicago Avenue)*

Inspector Ebersold *(East Chicago Avenue)*

Patrolman Hayden *(Lakeview)*

Patrolman Smith *(Lakeview)*

Chief Inspector Jerome Caminada *(Manchester)*

Lieutenant Horace Elliott *(East Chicago Avenue)*

Officer Jacobs *(East Chicago Avenue)*

Captain Bartram *(East Chicago Avenue)*

Deputy George Reich *(East Chicago Avenue)*

Detective Barney Flynn *(East Chicago Avenue)*

Chief of Police McRae *(Winnipeg)*

Inspector John McKennon *(Winnipeg)*

Sergeant Koch *(Lakeview)*

Officer Malie *(Lakeview)*

Mr Murray *(Pinkerton Detective Agency)*

Detective X of Chicago

The 1888 Triangle trial committee

J. D. McMahon, *chairman*

P. A. O'Boyle, *secretary*

Dr P. McCahey

C. F. Burns

J. J. Rogers

(and Dr Cronin)

Doctors	Friends of Dr Cronin		Enemies of Dr Cronin
Dr J. R. Brandt	Frank Scanlan, *a shipping clerk*	Henry O'Hara	Dan Coughlin, *a detective*
Dr Parker	John Scanlon	Mrs T. T. Conklin, *Dr Cronin's housekeeper & receptionist*	
Dr F. S. Silber	Luke Dillon	Mr T. T. Conklin, *her husband*	John Beggs, *Senior Guardian, Camp 20*
Dr Hectoren	Dr Patrick McGarry	Mr Fitzgerald	Martin Burke
Dr Egbert *Assistant County Physician*	John Devoy	James Boland	*(alias Frank Williams)*
Dr Charles Perkins	W.P. Rend	Stephen Conley	
Dr D. G. Moore		Maurice Morris	Andrew Foy
		Joseph O'Byrne	

The Cast

Patrick *(The Fox)* Cooney *(alias J. B. Simmons)*

Patrick O'Sullivan, *an ice dealer*

John Kunze *(alias John Kogel)*

Dynamiters

Captain Mackey Lomasney

Dr Gallagher

Cunningham

Newspaper reporters

Ananias Long

Charles Beck

James Holland

U. S. Senators

Senator C. B. Farwell of Illinois

Senator Kennedy of Wisconsin

Employees of Lakeview Department of Public Works

Henry Rosch

John Feneger

William Nichols

Michael Gilbert

Mike Reese

W. W. McMillan

Lawyers

Judge McConnell

Luther Laflin Mills

Judge Longenecker

W. J. Hynes

George Ingham

Henry Scanlan

William Forrest

Judge Wing

John Foster

Daniel Donohue

Judge Richard Prendergast

Justice Mahoney

Bribed jurors

Frederick Smith

Jeremiah O'Donnell

Joseph Konen

Court bailiffs

Alexander Hanks

Mark Salomon

Dentists

Dr E V. Lewis

F. Huxman

Tailors

Joseph O'Keefe

Martin Ahern

Other members of the Clan-na-Gael

Kevin Brown

Mrs Alice Brown

Patrick Egan

Edward Spellman, *District Officer*

Captain Thomas O'Connor

Major Henry Le Caron, *a spy*

Tom Tuite, *city treasurer of Detroit*

General Kerwin, *District Member for New York*

John Moroney

Mr Donovan

Thomas Murphy, *treasurer, Camp 20*

Michael J. Kelly, *Junior Guardian, Camp 20*

John O'Connor, *recording secretary, Camp 20*

Patrick Ford

Stephen Colleran

Criminals

Frank Woodruff *(alias Frank Black)*

Philip Finucane

Dick Fairburn

William King

Peter McGeehan

The Carlson family

Mr Jonas Carlson

Mrs Jonas Carlson, *his wife*

John Carlson, *their son*

Mrs Annie Carlson, *his wife*

Other players

Agnes McNearney

Sarah McNearney, *her sister*

Hal Garsch, *Dr Cronin's barber*

James Marshall, *real-estateman, of Knight and Marshall*

Edward Throckmorton, *cashier to Knight and Marshall*

William Hatfield, *salesman, Alexander Revell and Co.*

Patrick Dinan, *livery-stable owner*

Mrs Patrick Dinan

Napier Moreland, *hostler to Patrick Dinan*

Mrs Susan Lomasney, *widow of Captain Lomasney*

Mrs Tom Whelan, *housekeeper to Patrick O'Sullivan*

Alderman Chapman

William Mertes, *a milkman*

Gustav Khlare, *a tinsmith*

Thomas Martensen, *a delivery man*

E. V. Page, *an oil merchant*

George Tschappat, *an employee of E. V. Page*

Mrs Hoertel, *a cleaner*